Saint Praftu

by

Murray Anderson

Grosvenor House
Publishing Limited

This book is published by
Grosvenor House Publishing Ltd
28-30 High Street, Guildford, Surrey, GU1 3HY.
www.grosvenorhousepublishing.co.uk

A CIP record for this book
is available from the British Library

ISBN 978-1-907211-52-2

Introduction

The original manuscript of 'Saint Praftu' was written post-1967 after I returned to the UK from India, when my experiences during and after the War were still fresh in my mind.

'PRAFTU' was my personal mnemonic for the pre-take-off and landing drill which I used throughout my flying career (see chapter 4), in spite of the later introduction of written checklists. In time it became akin to a religious mantra.

Acknowledgements

To Sandy and Kelly Anderson for rescuing the original manuscript.

To Duncan Forbes for invaluable help with proof-reading and the Glossary.

To the friends who encouraged and helped me along the way, particularly Bob Large, fellow pilot in 161 Squadron Lysander pick-ups, the Koszarek families, Princess Emanuel Galitzine, and Mrs Dagny Hysing-Dahl.

To Helen MacEwan for practical assistance.

And finally to my wife Jean, for her work involving typesetting, proof-reading and editing.

Dedication

'Saint Praftu' is dedicated to those of my comrades who did not survive the War, and to the friends of my civil flying days in Burma, India and Nepal who also lost their lives prematurely.

Contents

PART 1

CHAPTER 1

Sepoy Sahib

IN 1920, when I was one year old, my parents took me to India. My father had been at the Royal Military Academy, Woolwich, before the First World War: he had served on the Western front. He was a Sapper, and after the war had been seconded to the Madras Sappers and Miners of the Indian Army, whose headquarters were at Bangalore. The atmosphere was predominantly military — large parade grounds of hard, red earth, roads lined with tall trees behind which stood the bungalows with their white verandas (ours was King Lodge), tennis courts, stables and hordes of servants. My mother went to parties at the Bangalore Club, and I was carted off by my ayah to birthday parties among the officers' children. My mother rode side-saddle and my father wore a large khaki topi, Sam Browne, and highly polished boots with spurs. In the evenings my mother played the piano and my father his flute in the drawing room, while I ate potato chips with Heinz tomato sauce. Those were the lotus days of the slowly dying British Raj, finally to be extinguished twenty-seven years later.

I was three years old, perhaps four, when I accepted the military life. I was going to be a soldier, not any soldier, but an officer in The Royal Engineers like my father. I was taken to Tattoos, held on the large, hot, dry earth maidan at South Parade, lined by tall trees and overlooked from one end by the C of E Cathedral. At these displays mounted officers, dressed like Gary Cooper in 'The Lives of a Bengal Lancer', charged with lances lowered and 'ran through' wooden pegs stuck in the ground. Then there was marching by pipes and drums of the Indian Regiments; and finally a battle took place. Khaki-clad sepoys attacked a wooden fort, mountain guns were assembled from the backs of mules and fired, with bangs and puffs of real smoke. The walls of the fort collapsed and black-turbaned Afridis and assorted wild men of the North West Frontier ran out screaming. There was more firing, tribesmen and sepoys fell dead. The last to fall was the Afridi Standard bearer: the black flag of Islam, with its crescent moon and Koranic hieroglyphics, sank to the baked earth beneath the afternoon sun. A bugle blew, the dead arose, rejoined the living and marched off amidst cheers and clapping from the onlook-ers. My ayah took me to our Ford — like those seen in Mac Sennet comedies — my mother and father sat in front and we drove back to King Lodge for tea, with cucumber sandwiches.

Occasionally, in the afternoons, the pipe band of my father's regiment came and played in the drive of our bungalow. When I was four years old I would fall in behind the drummers and march — a small boy in a large topi behind tall, dark, lean men wearing wide starched shorts, puttees and high cylindrical pugris. One day the pipe major brought a small pugree and diminutive puttees for my tiny legs. In this get-up I was addressed as 'Sepoy Sahib', a distinction which never, ever could be exceeded.

My brother Lindsay was born in Bangalore. I didn't like his ayah — she was small, but mine was big, maternal, and smelt of coconut oil. When I was five the family returned to England by boat and I remember seeing Mount Etna in eruption.

We lived with my maternal grandparents in Upper Norwood, near the Crystal Palace. Lindsay and I had a nanny, Mrs Bullen; we came to love her very much but during those early months I was miserable. My mother arranged for my Big Ayah to come to England. She arrived, but she was not the same. I was older, the sun colder, she was smaller and her smell of coconut oil lost its pungency in Upper Norwood. She returned to Bangalore. For the next twenty-five years my mother sent a card to all our servants at King Lodge. One by one they died. Big Ayah died at Bangalore in 1950.

When I was eight I was sent to Red House, a preparatory boarding school at Marston Moor. It was said to be haunted by the ghosts of Cavaliers killed at the famous battle, but it was the spirit of Dotheboys Hall that walked its draughty corridors. The headmaster was a retired sapper, Colonel Moseley, with a black moustache and a hook nose. On my very first day in class I was sent to the Colonel's study for drawing a small bi-plane in the margin of my atlas: I was bent over without ceremony and received three whacks of the cane. The place was cold and draughty, and we were underfed and unwashed. I went home with twelve weeks' grime on my knees, ankles, neck and behind my ears, and had to be rubbed with cold cream to loosen the dirt.

Sundays at Red House were purgatory. They started deceptively with two lovely fried sausages and half-a-slice of fried bread. We dressed in black bum-freezers and striped trousers with large starched white collars — like Tweedledum and Tweedledee — and walked over the frozen fields, then crossed the river Ouse by ferry to attend a long cold service in a small stone church. Occasionally we young boys were taken to York Minster to sing in the choir.

I hated the place. During my second year I was removed by my mother (my father was with his regiment in India), badly infected on my head with ringworm, caught from the Colonel's cows. After six months at home, recovering, I was sent away again, this time to a more kindly prep school, St. Ronans, in Worthing. The headmaster was W B Harris; his brother, who had started the school, had been killed in the First World War while serving with the Machine-gun Corps.

I still had no doubts about my future: I was going to be an officer in the Royal Engineers. I had only to pass the Common Entrance exam to Cheltenham College, and then four years later pass another exam into the Royal Military Academy.

One summer afternoon at St. Ronans, when I was twelve, a group of us were weeding the First XI cricket pitch. Mr Pool, the mathematics master who also acted as groundsman, was riding up and down on the motor mower, keeping an occasional eye on us. We were serving off our 'dots', given by prefects for mis-behaviour, ten minutes weeding for each dot. I'd done one dot with two to go, when a boy came up and spoke to Pooly; he waved me over and I was instructed to report to Mr. Harris' study. This was a large, cool room with flower-print curtains and matching colours for the sofa and armchairs. There was a large desk by the wide windows, a shiny black grand piano with flowers on it and hundreds of framed photos covering the walls. Harry, in his white flannels, light blue blazer, and white shirt with striped silk scarf, stood with his back to the mantelpiece. He told me to sit down. He continued calmly to explain that he'd had a letter from my mother to say that she and my father were divorced and that I was not to worry as I would continue to live at home, just as before. I was shocked and automatically burst into tears. Harry did his best to comfort me. I became composed under his assurance that all would be the same, school and home. He said I could stay in his study but that he was going off to the nets. I remained buried in a comfy armchair and hoping that if I stayed for half-an-hour I'd probably get off doing any more weeding.

The next term, my brother Lindsay joined me at St. Ronans. We were now Anderson 'Ma' and 'Mi', ('Major' and 'Minor') and a term later John Anderson arrived, no relation, and there was a 'Min'.

Towards the end of the summer term a few of the boys were always taken to see an evening performance of the Aldershot Tattoo, with its sights of grandeur, distant parades illuminated by searchlights, nostalgic even to a twelve-year-old. Massed pipes and drums played the music of sacrifices; then the drive back to Worthing, long past bedtime, through a tunnel of head-lit trees like the Flying Scotsman with twelve coaches, whistling through the dark night. Even more exciting for Lindsay and me, because we were nearer, were the afternoon Royal Tournaments at Olympia. The air perfumed by horses and cordite fumes, we bounced up and down with bladders full to the music of yet more pipes and drums and watched bewildered the confusion of the naval gun competition.

My next official visit to Harry's study came at the end of my last-but-one term. Boys leaving were made prefects for their last term. Harry informed me that I was to be a prefect next term and that he was sure I would be a good one. I was prepared for this, because the worm of opposition had been burrowing since the beginning of the term. I replied that I didn't want to be a prefect: so I wasn't. At the time I was quite certain what had prompted my rebellion. I liked Harry, as we all did. He was large, avuncular, with bushy red eyebrows, gregarious and kind. But I smelt hypocrisy. I was being made a prefect because it was my last term, not because I was really worthy. Secretly I cherished my reputation as a rebel; I did not want to have to behave and be an example.

There followed four-and-a-half years at Cheltenham College. I enjoyed shooting more than cricket, and I made the College Rifle Team. I played for the College Rugger XV, and I enjoyed military training in what was then known as the Officers' Training Corps. I also became a gymnast.

It was during my third year in the OTC that I fell in love. We were doing our fortnight's camping near Aldershot, eight to a bell tent, with rifles and equipment round the centre pole, palliasses and army blankets for beds and our kitbags on the periphery. One early morning, an hour before reveille, everyone was sleeping and the early dawn made light grey the tent's canvas. I stretched out my legs beneath the heap of blankets and my feet touched the legs of the boy next to me. They were beautifully soft and warm, he did not withdraw and so I stroked them with the soles of my feet. The next morning (it was always in the morning because by lights out we were dead tired and nothing could keep us awake), my legs found his again; he had removed his pyjama trousers so I caressed the soft

warm flesh from his thighs to his feet. We lay facing each other,
our eyes open, looking, but silent. There were five days to go
before we broke camp. An intense protective friendship developed during our marches and field exercises, which we hid
from others. The next term I had a rival, but we all got on very
well together. All three of us were gymnasts: the young boy was
becoming a good scrum half. I was playing in the College
rugger trials and the pressure was on me for my Woolwich
Entrance exam. During the term the boy began to shave the
down of his upper lip. He got pimples and that was that.

I learnt more about the feel of soldiering from my four years
in the OTC than I did at Woolwich. It was the OTC that helped
me to identify with the books, songs, plays and sculptures
which came out of the war. A boy of fifteen, during a 'field day'
exercise, in khaki serge and puttees, carrying full webbing
equipment, with his rifle topped by a long bayonet, wearing the
flat peak cap and standing in a steady rain, inadequately
protected by a cape ground sheet, was in the tradition of the
bronze gunners of the Hyde Park Corner Artillery memorial.
With the weapons of yesterday we played at soldiers.

'The Shop'

The Royal Military Academy at Woolwich was founded in
1741 to train Gunner and Sapper officers. It was known as the
'Shop': I went there as a young gentleman cadet from Cheltenham in September 1938. I did not expect to kill anyone as an
officer but rather to be killed. An officer would lead his men
'over the top', brandishing a black malacca cane surmounted by
a silver knob emblazoned with the Regimental Badge. He might
carry a Webley Scott revolver in a leather holster attached to his
Sam Browne, but he would be dead before he reached the wire.
This is what officers in the British Army had done since Marl-
borough. You stood in the forefront with your foot on a slight
mound, your sword raised, your head with its tall shako turned
towards your men, encouraging them, calling to them, until a
ball took you in the chest, or a round shot carried away your

leg. I had no desire to be a general, only an officer in the Royal Engineers; that was enough for the time being.

I was bored at the Shop, and so became disillusioned. The work was not hard nor the discipline severe. Our training as future officers concentrated on drill, PT and riding. The chief object was to instil in us the qualities of an officer and a gentleman. We were already the latter or we would not have got into the Shop. I had passed eightieth out of ninety, and I never did a stroke of work or felt the slightest interest in my studies. I did, however, learn the finer points of arms drill and square-bashing, also how to ride a horse and, most useful of all, how to drive a car.

The new boys, the first-termers, were known as Snookers, and we were divided into two companies. I shared a room with Aylmer. He had been at Wellington. Our room was regulation, with wooden floors and a large table on which we spent hours burnishing our bayonets, polishing with dark tan Kiwi the toe-caps of our boots, our belts and bayonet frogs. Black Kiwi gave our bayonet scabbards a finish like glass. We each had a shelf and a cupboard to take our few books and on which we laid out our clothes in regulation manner. There were two wooden chairs, two iron beds, a fireplace, and an old batman who had been at the Siege of Mafeking.

Every morning on waking, Aylmer's first words were "God! How I hate this place". For the first six weeks we were confined to the Academy grounds. We spent hours being drilled. Aylmer had difficulty co-ordinating his legs and arms when marching. He would start off on the wrong foot or suddenly start swinging the right arm forward with his right foot. This put our Drill Sergeant, Sergeant- Major Jock Miller of the Black Watch, into convulsions.

"Mister Aylmer - Saar.

"Fall OUT!"

This meant Aylmer had to quick-march to the officiating Captain (lurking in the background) and report himself.

Soon Aylmer was relegated to the rear rank and at the left end of the Company. In the early weeks of our drilling,

Sergeant-Major Jock Miller frequently bellowed from a hundred yards away, across the asphalt parade ground.

"Mis-tar Aylmer, Saar! Carry - ON! Ree-mainder, Cha-ange STEP!"

Sergeant-Major Jock Miller was a great man, moustached, red-faced, with a hoarse voice and a beery breath. He cut a fine figure in his kilt and white spats. He swung his kilt as to the manner born. We were proud of him; we came to love him. He dressed for ordinary parades in tartan trews, cutaway jacket, Glengarry, black boots with glass-like toecaps, and a red sash over his shoulder. Under his arm he carried his wooden pace stick — it opened like a large pair of dividers which he used to check the exact distance of our marching stride. He had a superb carrying voice.

"Layf - Layf - Layf - Rye - Layf. Companee — Abowt — wait for it Mistar Aylmer Saar. A-BOWT TARN! Arms still thar! Arms - up-up-up. Up to yer belt!"

"Layf - Layf - Layf - Rye - Layf. Companee — ABOWT — TARN! One - two-three-four. Arms back-back-back. Layeft TARN! Companee HALT! One - one -two. Standat EES!"

The last word of every command was unrecognisable; it came out as a loud, penetrating shriek. Every muscle from Sergeant-Major-Jock Miller's toes to the top of his close-cropped head, squeezed out that final extraordinary high-pitched screech.

At first with nothing, then with swagger-sticks and lastly with rifles we bashed up and down the parade ground in front of the old facade of the Shop. Occasionally a few cloth-capped onlookers, in old overcoats, old soldiers perhaps, peered at us through the surrounding tall iron railings.

It was during a parade for fixing and unfixing bayonets that we heard the only risqué remark ever attributed to Sergeant-Major Jock Miller.

"Companeeee will unfix bayonets — UnFIX! Wait-for-it. Unfix — you don't unfix Mistar Aylmer Saar!"

The left-hand marker took five paces forward, "BAYO-NETS", came the shriek. Aylmer was last and still fumbling to get his bayonet into its scabbard. There was a long delay.

"Mis-tar Aylmer Saar! Put some hair round it. Get it in - Saar!"

The Captain on parade had turned about and was looking vaguely at the old mortars by the clock tower. We continued with the unfix; the marker took five paces backwards. Sergeant-Major Jock Miller seemed to swell and get even more purple. His tunic tautened. He was wearing trews.

"Slow-ope Hyp!", came the explosion. "Officer on parade, Companeeee DISS-MISS!!"

We turned to the right, slapped our rifle butts in salute and marched off the parade ground. We won the drill competition. Aylmer was indistinguishable from the rest of us.

In the middle of our first term at the Shop, we snookers enacted the ritual of being made into men. This took place in the Gymnasium in front of the whole College on three consecutive nights. We put on a boxing tournament: everyone had to fight. Those who lacked expertise were expected to make up for it by a display of blood and guts. Aylmer cursed the ordeal as the night approached. We were both in the same weight and equally ignorant of what to do. The ring was lit in the classical style, and the cadets in overalls, patrols and Wellingtons, with instructors and Commandant in mess kit, sat around in darkness. A good show was all that was demanded. Luckily Aylmer and I were not drawn against each other, and both of us were defeated in our first fight. We were blooded. After it was over I returned to our barren room. Aylmer was flat on his bed, still in shorts and vest. Dried blood had coagulated round his nose and on his chest. He was swearing and cursing the Bloody Place. Aylmer was fair-skinned, rather red in the face, perhaps due to the daily shaving. He had pale blue eyes, fair hair, eyebrows and eyelashes. This gave him a slight albino look.

The next term we were no longer 'snookers' and moved out of the old rooms overlooking the parade ground and into ramshackle iron-sheeted hutments at the back. I saw less of Aylmer. We dug trenches in the small lawns surrounding our huts. This was during the Munich crisis. One night we were all awakened by a series of huge explosions. Everyone got up and milled around in each other's rooms.

"We're being bombed", someone said.

"I hope to God you're right, then they'll send us away from this bloody place," said Aylmer. (It later transpired that some compressed air cylinders had blown up in Woolwich Arsenal.)

Early in our second term the influence of a new Minister of Defence, Mr. Hore Belisha, was felt at the Shop. In the name of modernisation, 'forming fours' was replaced by parading in three ranks, and breeches and puttees were changed to long trousers. These innovations were not popular at any level.

During the Munich crisis we were lined up and asked our preference for regimental postings. It was rumoured that we would leave before completing our last term if war was declared. There already was a full-scale war in China, where the Japanese had massacred the inhabitants of Nankin and then captured Pekin and Canton. The College had a lecture in the Gymnasium on the situation; it was too far away for anyone to show much concern.

Woolwich catered for three regiments, the Engineers, the Artillery and the Signals. Aylmer chose the Gunners and I chose the Sappers. The crisis passed and term dragged on. My enthusiasm had gone. Military history was a desert of dry facts, of boredom. We had lectures on gunpowder, cordite and gun cotton; only the occasional bang, set off by the lecturer, awoke our interest. Aylmer and I took copious notes. Our minds had one thought, how to get down to our rooms at the end of the period, change into breeches and leggings and be on riding parade with our bicycles in fifteen minutes. We had interminable lessons on parliamentary government, the Army estimates, Britain's unwritten constitution (its advantages over all others) and the Statute of Westminster. We never saw a gun, fired a rifle, learned Morse or worked a radio.

From constitutional history we moved on to field works according to the Field Service Handbook. Aylmer and I were paired together for our out-of-classroom activities. We had to dig a field lavatory, lay some barbed wire and dig ourselves a small trench. After digging for three hours we were only able to protect ourselves up to our knees. Captain Hudson RA then ordered us to make the parapet thicker as in his opinion a bullet would go right through our effort. Before completing this improvement the period ended, we got on our cycles and returned to the Shop. We never saw our field works again.

The rigmarole of Plain Table drawing was even more futile. Dressed in jackets, breeches and puttees, wearing raincoats and then festooned with a wooden tripod, drawing table, magnetic compass and a haversack full of pencils, rulers and sandwiches, we bicycled to Woolwich Common. We had to map this dreary waste. With a strong wind blowing we set up our tables, took sights, bearings, drew lines, and rubbed them out. We moved to other points, dropping pencils, the wind tore the paper and drawing pins fell out. After four hours there was nothing but a smudgy mess to show for our efforts. Aylmer silently persevered. I cracked under the strain; nineteen years of unquestioned acceptance evaporated and I decided not to become a Sapper.

One evening, late in my last term, I heard a clanking outside my room. Some senior was pounding the boards of the ill-lit corridor. There was a knock at the door and Aylmer came in. He was in mess kit and wearing the spurs which he had just been given in the riding class. He was fascinated by their martial jingle. He looked just the same, perhaps a bit straighter, not quite so unco-ordinated, a bit redder but with the same albino look.

"Thank God, this is the end." he said. We had been thrown together by the alphabetic proximity of our names.

"What are you going into?" I asked.

"Oh! The Gunners, I suppose."

"Suppose? You don't sound very enthusiastic."

"It won't be so bad in a regiment. There's bound to be a war soon"

"Why the Gunners? You could be a Sapper."

"Oh no! My father and his father were all Gunners and I'm supposed to be one too. What about you?"

"Me? Well, I'm going into the Tanks!"

"Good God! The Tanks? Why? How did you fix that?"

"I saw Captain Wood, he fixed it for me. So now it's all settled."

"Well good luck to you. It doesn't matter what we do, we'll all be in it soon."

"Best wishes to you too, and thanks. You're right of course, there'll be a war. Things can't go on like they do here forever."

I had decided to break with Shop tradition. I could not stomach the Gunner mob. They were led by Cadet Madden, a harmless fellow but devilish horsey. He was small, perhaps five foot three, with thin legs. He had prematurely blue-red jowls and wore his cap well down over his eyes. This forced him to glare up at you. He was a good rider and got his spurs very early in the last term. From then on he was insufferable. Before falling-in for riding parades Madden and his clique stood with one leg forward and whacked themselves on their leather leggings with their canes, guffawing at some horsey joke.

I decided on something modern and mobile, which in spite of my ignorance I imagined would play a vital part in the coming war. Officers for the Royal Tank Regiment were taken from Sandhurst, so I had been in the wrong place for eighteen months.

The final examination provided a penultimate farce. I knew almost nothing, but had written copious notes, mostly verbatim, at every lecture. This gave an appearance of industry. I had learnt my first army lesson: Bullshit Baffles Brains. I wrote voluminously on every question, even if I had no idea of the answers. Our final marks included such indefinable factors as personality, leadership and general bearing. I passed out twenty-fifth, with Aylmer slightly higher.

The term ended, but the seniors had to spend seven days under canvas at Aldershot. It rained continuously. Our best boots, belts, jackets and breeches got soaked and lost their lustre, but now it no longer mattered. Going to the Regal Cinema in our officers' raincoats we were frequently saluted by the soldiery, much to our embarrassment. We broke camp and went to our homes. We were soon to be commissioned and then join our regiments.

I never saw anybody from the Shop again. Twelve years later, when wandering around the military cemetery at Kohima in Nagaland I came across the grave of Captain Langdon RE. He had been killed during the Japanese attack; we had been contemporaries at Cheltenham and at the Shop. I learnt early in the war of the death of another contemporary, PG Geary, a great cricketer and scholar. He had been killed when he walked out of the corridor of the last carriage of a troop train. Much later, I do not remember where or when, I heard of Aylmer's death. I never found out how he died.

CHAPTER 2

Mark One Infantry Tank

WHILE I was at Cheltenham my mother had married again. My stepfather, Major Cuthbert Sleigh, RE, MC, came from Leek in Staffordshire, where his family were minor landed gentry and owned spinning mills. He and my father were contemporaries in the Madras Sapper and Miners at Bangalore; because he was tall and paternal, he was known to his brother officers as 'Father'. I remembered him in Bangalore as my 'Uncle-Father'. He had been deeply fond of my mother for many years. Having been gassed in Flanders he suffered from persistent lung trouble, and shortly before his marriage was invalided out of the army. A modest, gentle man, he never spoke of himself. He bought a spacious, beautiful house in Camberley, Surrey, which was our home for twenty years.

I was twelve when my youngest brother, Sandy, was born in Aberdeen, just before my parents were divorced. Sandy, an uncomplicated, charming boy was to follow Lindsay and me to St. Ronans, from where he went on to Dartmouth and the Navy.

I was commissioned into the 8th Battalion Royal Tank Regiment, stationed at Perham Down on the Eastern edge of Salisbury Plain, and driven down by my mother and Uncle-Father. A large portmanteau trunk containing silk socks, black boots, white shirts and stiff collars, bow ties, and uniform jackets, tails and khaki shirts, had been sent on by rail. I was taken in to see the 'headmaster', Colonel Drake-Brockman, and handed over. After this initial meeting I remember seeing the Colonel only once, at a dining-in night. He was stocky, short, with an accompanying truculent mien. He disappeared soon after war was declared and his place taken by a more jovial and fatherly figure, Colonel Custance. A year later I read in the Daily Mirror of Colonel Drake-Brockman's disgrace. He had been cashiered for striking a captured German pilot. He went to Canada and enlisted as a private in an armoured unit. Later, he became a general in the Canadian Army.

I was totally unprepared for the shambles of peace-time life in the British Army. The Battalion owed its existence to the Army's reluctant drive towards. mechanisation: the junior officers had a theory that it was manned by enforced volunteers. The men, however, seemed decent enough and took their dreary life stoically. The tank strength consisted of one large medium tank and three light tanks of 1925 vintage, and the remaining forty 'tanks' were made up of a dozen Bren gun carriers, two-dozen 15 cwt lorries and a few Norton motor cycles.

The daily routine was short and dull. At seven there was flag hoisting by the Battalion Orderly Officer. Breakfast at eight. Then, from nine until twelve-thirty, troop training. There were games in the afternoon for the men. Tea at four-thirty. At six a bugle blew, the Orderly Officer lowered the flag by the guard room and the day was over. At mid-day on Fridays the weekend began. The officers changed into mufti and the mess was deserted until Tuesday morning. Company and Battalion Orderly Officers carried out their lonely duties throughout the long weekend. Officers on duty wore Sam Browne and swords. We made the rounds of the men's eating hall and asked, "Any complaints?" At other times we wore cloth belts with our barathea uniforms and carried ash walking sticks. We were all conscious of our social inferiority to the cavalry, sanctified by the possession of horses. We were despised as 'bloody mechanics'.

Two other junior officers joined with me. They had the advantage of coming from Sandhurst and having seen a

Vickers machine-gun and taken it to pieces — while I had only fired six rounds from a service revolver. A week after I arrived the first Mark One Infantry Tank appeared, and was passed round the Battalion for training.

Every unit has its characters; there seemed a lot of them in the 8th Battalion. Major Quin-Smith was elderly, moustached and wore a monocle. He had an MC which I assumed he won at Cambrai, but it turned out to have been on the North West Frontier. Captain Lindsay was short, dark haired, dapper and very good looking. He was friendly to the new boys. After the war was over I met Captain Lindsay in a brothel in Lal Bazaar, Calcutta; he was heavily decorated. The Battalion Reconnaissance Officer was Captain Howard-Jones, tall, with a small nose. His black beret sat on his head like a pancake. He was well in with the Battalion top brass, and I admired his familiarity with the Colonel and various Majors. He was also very knowledgeable about the strategic and tactical dispositions of the Brigade and even higher formations. During the 15 months with the Battalion I never knew where Brigade HQ was, and I never saw a tank of any other Tank Regiment.

I made friends with Lieutenant Booth. He was several years older than I, with large dark eyes, a black moustache and slouching unmilitary bearing. He scurried about like a bird. He smoked a lot, and was constantly tuning the engine of his black Citroen while a tiny cigarette stub hung from his lower lip. I admired this and tried to copy him in order to improve my image with the men, but the smoke got in my eyes. Booth was the Battalion messing officer, and his pockets were filled with bits of paper and small notebooks. These were lists of butter and egg stocks, jam and milk consumption, and other household matters. He was treated with humourous banter but took the jibes in good heart.

A month after joining the regiment there was a dining-in night. This entailed full mess kit and various traditional ceremonies during the course of the evening. My mess kit had still not arrived, so I was the only officer present in tails. Colonel Drake-Brockman conducted the ritual of passing the port and supervised the etiquette of smoking at the table. There was some esoteric dialogue between 'Mr President' and 'Mr Vice', and we all stood up and drank a toast to 'The King, God bless him'. This was followed by very small small-talk, smoking and port drinking. The other two new boys and myself sat at the far end of the table and maintained silence during dinner. Later we trooped by order of rank into the anteroom. The Colonel seemed to unbend a little, though it cost him considerable effort. Drinks were brought in by the mess orderlies, and the ante-room cleared for action. We new boys retired. I heard from Booth that Lindsay, Howard-Jones, Quin-Smith, Trotman and Scales were leading lights in a game of throwing billiard balls around the table. There followed some boyish romping in the ante-room and Booth had his trousers removed. The party came to an end at three o'clock.

A few days after the dining-in night, war was declared. The mess was stunned: everyone was very glum and for once Howard-Jones was speechless. I was terrified. This was not going to be the Aldershot Tattoo with massed pipe bands, but the real thing. I was Battalion orderly officer and had to sleep in the Orderly room. My batman, young Trooper Burnett, set up my camp bed and I retired at nine o'clock, fearing that the phone would ring and order the Battalion to France immediately,

At midnight the phone rang. Some major, whose name I did not get and was too nervous to ask him to repeat, was calling from Brigade. He demanded our strength and our state of readiness. I read out from a form the numbers of sick, on leave, AWOL and total present. He enquired about the officers; I replied that they were all present and that the Battalion was ready for anything. The caller asked me my name and rang off.

In October the Battalion received marching orders. We set off, to wander around Devon and Dorset for the next five months. Lorries and Bren-gun carriers transported the troops.

The baggage and our few slow-moving tanks followed by rail. I packed most of my uniform and finery into the portmanteau trunk and sent it home. All of us now reduced our baggage to one uniform, black overalls, an overcoat, a camp bed and a collapsible bath. We were billeted in village halls or dispersed among large country houses. The Battalion carried out TEWTs (Tactical Exercises Without Troops), over tracts of barren heather and along West Country lanes. We were still mainly armed with lorries and carriers, but a few more tanks had arrived. I now had one in my troop.

I had a wonderful Sergeant, Sergeant Paddy Doyle. He was like a father to me. He knew I knew nothing: I relied on him for everything. The men liked him and he knew exactly how to maintain the correct relationship between himself and his young, ignorant officer. The army had thousands of men like Paddy Doyle, who carried us young officers until we could stand and walk and hold our own. My tank driver was Trooper Crow, a long lanky East Londoner, who hated the I Tank for its slowness and took every opportunity to jump on a motorcycle or speed recklessly in a Bren-gun carrier. He was a first-rate mechanic.

The Mark One I tank was considered by all of us to be useless, and so it proved when the 'phoney war' hotted up in the early Spring of 1940. One of the other regular Tank Battalions went to France with Mark Ones and left them all behind. They were armed with only one Vickers machine-gun, so the Germans shot them to pieces; and as the tank could only do four miles an hour it couldn't run away. The Mark One was never used in action after France. It was powered with a Ford V8 car engine, with a standard four-speed gear box. It weighed eight tons, with armour four inches thick at the front end: the totally inadequate engine moved the tank at a fast walking pace. It was designed to accompany the infantry across 'no-mans-land', then crush the barbed wire and rake the German trenches and machine-gun nests with its single Vickers gun. It had a crew of two, a driver in front, and a Commander in the small turret acting also as gunner and radio operator. The turret was moved by turning a handle but the floor did not turn with it. The radio was on the floor. The tank climbed up any slope, slowly, engine shrieking, and then exposed its thin underbelly as it nosed over the brow of the hill. It would have made an ideal toy.

During an exercise the confusion inside the Mark One was chaotic. As we emerged from the hedgerow to advance across the battlefield, followed by imaginary infantry, an internal pandemonium began. I fired blank cartridges from the machine-gun, at the same time peering through the telescopic gun sight. I wound the turret round with my left hand, cleared gun stoppages with the right and shouted instructions to Trooper Crow. Steadily the empty webbing cartridge belt exuded from the gun and coiled onto the empty ammunition boxes on the floor. After a few turns of the turret the flex from the radio had wound round my neck, my boots had kicked the radio off-tune and had trodden flat my haversack lunch. With the turret hatch closed it was impossible to stand up; you sat in darkness on a canvas sling. When we reached the objective everybody opened his hatch for fresh air and watched the Company Commander's tank for the 'Rally Flag'. (He had long ago given up any attempt to contact his troops by radio.) We rallied round the Company Commander and awaited the post-mortem. The battle was over. Sergeant Doyle had very early on told me what to do on exercises. The troop was to keep formation, never get ahead of anybody else, keep quiet on the radio, and do as little firing as possible. Thus we would keep out of trouble and not be subject to comment at the post-mortem.

The troop spent hours dismantling its Vickers machine-guns, learning the name of every part, then reassembling them. Then we did it blindfolded. We learnt to clear stoppages, to hit, yank, and pull the gun to get it to fire again. Occasionally we drove a tank to the shooting range, the troop following in a lorry. Hours were spent in counting out ammunition before firing and then collecting all the empty cases afterwards. There was a terrific fuss at the armoury if we returned even one cartridge case too few. This, I was told, was a legacy of service on the North-West Frontier, when the tribesmen collected the empties to refill and use in their home-made rifles.

At Christmas 1939 when the Battalion was roaming around Devon, I got a week's leave. I went home to Camberley. The lakes in the grounds of the Staff College froze, and we went skating. I saw a young girl, small, plump and with very red lips. She was skating expertly. I followed her unsteadily until I managed to corner her on the bank. I did not know what to say, she was even more beautiful than I had at first realised. She looked over the lake, white puffs emerged from her cherry lips; she made no attempt to skate away. I took heart. I wobbled up on my skates and told her she was very beautiful and would she meet me that evening. She said she would, opposite the Thames Valley bus stop in Sandhurst village at 8 o'clock. She skated off with a smile on her red lips. That first evening we strolled down to the local lovers' lane in clear frosty moonlight. I met her off and on for the next six months. Often we lay in each others arms in the back of my mother's small Daimler, while German bombers passed overhead with their characteristic unsynchronised engine sound. Three hours later we would awake to hear them returning home. At other times we went on my 350 cc Velocette motorcycle to the cinema in Reading or Aldershot, and then back to Sandhurst to our favourite clump of trees. It was cold but healthy. I felt her cold, soft little nose pressed to my cheek.

After the New Year the Battalion stopped its wanderings and moved back to Salisbury Plain, this time into the Cavalry barracks at Tidworth. We kept our tanks in the stables, while the men slept in long dormitories above. The furniture was sparse but adequate — brown linoleum flooring, iron beds, iron lockers and chairs, and tall windows. They were regulation barracks built in 1885. They stood round the asphalt parade grounds. Everywhere there were red buckets filled with sand, and the roads were lined with grey nondescript trees which had struggled through small holes in the asphalt. The officers' mess was in a solid red-bricked building which stood on one side of the parade ground; more struggling grey trees protected the mess from the direct view of the soldiery.

I had only been with the Battalion six months but I was fed up. I envied the battalions that had gone to France, while we ambled round with half our equipment and did TEWTs. Our tanks were slowly being delivered, and then a new one appeared, the Mark Two I tank — 25 tons, slow, with a puny two-pounder gun. It was also useless but at least something new to play with.

A night exercise was announced. The whole Battalion was going on to Salisbury Plain for a night attack on prepared positions. We were to move off in daylight, assemble at dusk and attack during the night. Then we would regroup and move to another battlefield for another night attack; then regroup again and return to Tidworth. Sergeant Doyle advised me to take plenty of blankets and to bring a tin of cocoa. The Battalion moved off at midday, a motley collection of Infantry tanks, our old 1925 medium tank and light tanks, Bren-gun carriers and lorries. I was in the troop's only tank with Trooper Crow; Sgt. Doyle was in a Bren-gun carrier, Corporal Knowles in another. The carriers took the rest of my men. It was freezing. No one had any idea where we were going or to what purpose. The Battalion straggled into the bleak waste of Salisbury Plain at a snail's pace, each vehicle trying to keep the regulation distance from the one in front. This meant frequent stops, long waits and then a rush, flat out at four-miles-an-hour, to catch up. If you missed a gear change as you accelerated you could easily break a selector fork in the gear box. The engine and all its cogs were running flat out. The lorries overheated and the carriers champed at their bits. Various Reconnaissance Officers rode up and down the long line on their Nortons, exhorting us to close up, don't bunch, keep moving. Lt. Howard-Jones was in front leading the Battalion to the starting line. It got darker and colder. The sky was clear, the stars shone and we were indifferent to everything except the cold. The engine cooling fan of my tank drew the air through the turret and then over the engine, so Crow and I froze. Behind me came the two old soldiers, Paddy Doyle and Knowles, with the men. They were in Bren-gun carriers, sitting on each side of the engine with the doors open, bathed in smelly warm air and wrapped in great-coats and blankets.

At midnight we stopped. Leaving the engine running Crow and I crawled onto the back of our tank and lay on the hot engine plates. Char and wads were brought round. We waited for hours; by now everybody and the vehicles were freezing; we wandered off into the darkness until dawn. Somewhere there had been a battle, but our Company had been in reserve. The cold was terrible. The Company made camp, a tent went up in which the cooks brewed tea and fried eggs. Wearing double clothing, wrapped in a dozen blankets and lying on frozen ground, it was still impossible to sleep. I got a terrible stomach ache. It was impossible to shit in that cold, so I got up and stole Howard-Jones' Norton. I rode back to our Tidworth mess, only twenty miles away. There I had a shit in comfort, lay down on the sofa in the deserted anteroom in front of the fire and fell asleep. I was discovered by Booth. He had been left behind to prepare for our home-coming. We had lunch together and then I rode back to the Company. Neither I nor the Norton had been missed. Nothing was left of the warmth with which the Battalion had left Tidworth the previous afternoon. We were all frozen and remained frozen throughout the night. We traipsed around for hours going extra-slow so that the clop-clop of our tank tracks would not alert the imaginary enemy. It was our turn to attack. We lined up at 0200 hours. Engines were switched off and we waited for zero hour. Dawn came at last: we started up and advanced to the objective. We were victorious.

I began to wonder if there was some way out of the Royal Tank Regiment.

CHAPTER 3

Miss Dawes

THE 'Phoney War' hotted up in the early Spring of 1940, with the German attack through Holland and Belgium. The calm at Tidworth remained undisturbed, even by rumour. Nothing changed the daily routine of washing our obsolete tanks, tightening their tracks and passing the time in easy-going routine, with an occasional TEWT on Salisbury Plain.

In May the newspapers and wireless were full of the news of near-disaster at Dunkirk and the subsequent fall of France. We were not greatly perturbed by either event. Shortly afterwards our barracks were invaded by a few hundred tramps. Some wore French steel helmets, others the Kepi. They wandered around unshaven, unwashed, dressed in blue-grey greatcoats, bedraggled puttees and dirty boots. A miasma of Gaulloise and garlic enveloped their small disconsolate groups. They threw their moist stub-ends into the clean sand in our regimental fire buckets. They were the few of the French army who had escaped with the British from Dunkirk, with others who had sailed from western French ports on any boat they could find.

These Frenchmen were our first contact with the squalor of war: they heightened our sense of uselessness and further lowered our morale. Everybody had done something, even if it was to be defeated; but the 8th Battalion had been left in Tidworth, unnoticed and unwanted. This strengthened my determination to get away from the Battalion. But how?

One day Booth told me that several officers from other companies had already escaped by volunteering for secondment to the RAF. After the war they would be returned to the Army without loss of seniority. This apparently was the only way out: but did I really want to go to the RAF? I had been brought up in an Army family and trained for the Army. The RAF was a lower order, in fact the lowest. They were unmilitary, undisciplined 'Brylcream boys', flying machines I knew nothing about. I had thrilled to films like 'Hells Angels', and stories of air battles in 'Boys Own', but I had never wanted to emulate their heroic adventures. Two of my mother's brothers, Uncle Cecil and Uncle Fitzy, had been in the Naval Air Service during the First World War. Uncle Fitzy, closest to my mother and the joy of my grandmother's heart, had been shot down in November 1918. At home his large fur gloves, his naval cap and his maternity-jacket uniform were kept wrapped up in tissue paper, on top of my mother's wardrobe. The thought of flying terrified me. I imagined entering a boozy and boisterous mob. Yet I felt I had to act or lose face with Booth and the orderly room. I took the plunge, and submitted my application. I began to feel more at home with the Battalion.

About this time we got a new Company Commander, Major Runciman. He was small, with a skin like faded parchment. He talked very quietly but could be withering in his anger. He quivered with fury. The thought of going into battle with troops like us must have appalled him. Sometimes he managed a small tight-lipped smile; on very rare occasions there came a weak cackle which indicated laughter. Five years later, on VE day, amongst the thousands shouting and screaming in Lower Regent Street, I suddenly came face to face with Major Runciman. He was in the Tank uniform, a Colonel with DSO and MC, alone, just as I remembered him. He recognized me, and spoke to me quietly and pleasantly, with that same voice like the dry rustle of old paper. I saluted and we parted. I was moved by our meeting. I felt I had missed serving under a great man. I envied him his Tank uniform with its black beret and tank insignia on the left arm, the uniform I had deserted. I soon lost sight of his short figure in the crowd.

The Battalion set off on its wanderings again, this time towards the south coast, as part of the defence against an invasion. We had begun to receive more of the new Mark Two tank. Whenever we moved our tanks went by rail and the troops would follow in lorry and Bren gun carriers. Our first camp was at Aldershot: we went under canvas on the site of the events in the bell tent of four years before. Then we travelled by train to London and the whole Battalion was billeted in an evacuated Catholic seminary on the edge of Wandsworth (or was it Wanstead?) Common. Every day we would set off in our Mark One and Mark Two tanks and drive around the streets of London. In the evenings we painted different insignia on the tanks and drove around with them the next day. In this way we hoped to raise the morale of the population with our large tank force, and to bamboozle German spies about our true strength.

It was while we were at Aldershot that I fell in love. One weekend Lt Reeves asked me to run him down to Winchester on my Velocette motorcycle, to see his girl friend. She had two younger sisters and Reeves said that I could have one of them. We set off; Reeves brought his .38 revolver. We arrived before lunch at the usual suburban house, a drive, bushes in front and garden behind. The mother, Mrs Dawes, welcomed us at the front door, while the three daughters stood behind her.

At lunch Reeves sat between the mother and eldest daughter, and I sat between the other two. The atmosphere was gregarious and happy. The youngest may have been about fifteen. She laughed nicely. The badinage between Reeves and his girl friend seemed a little repetitive and conventional. I was also sure that the youngest felt the same. Reeves was two years older than me, he had a proper girl friend and I was just a hanger-on. Let him get on with it even if listening to them made me groan inwardly. My preoccupation with others was soon displaced by the realization that I was in love with the youngest daughter. I was enthralled by her unaffectedness, her good humour and her plump beauty. Lovely golden hair, dimples, a pastel-coloured cotton dress and her vivacity. Lunch passed in a flash. Reeves and his girl friend went out of the French windows into the garden, watched by the mother and other daughter. My new-found love and I cleared the table and did the washing up. We were groping for dirty plates when our hands met. We momentarily looked at each other, when there was an almighty bang!

"That's them in the garden," she said. "He's teaching her how to shoot."

"Good God! What for? I wouldn't do that if had a girl friend."

"What would you do?", she laughingly asked.

"I'd wash up the dishes with her after lunch."

"Oh, that! Well someone has to do it, and it's my turn today."

Reeves was standing with his arm round his girl helping her to point his revolver at an old tree: then Bang! It was highly dangerous and made a hell of a row.

We had tea and then said goodbye to the four of them. Reeves and I, wearing our officer raincoats, berets and battle-dress, set off, waving goodbye as we went down the drive. They stood clustered on the front doorstep. I longed to see her again. The Battalion moved and we never got a chance to return to Winchester. Perhaps it was just as well.

We moved on to Horley and the Company was billeted in the large, rambling house of Mr and Mrs Hicks who had three teenage children. The Hicks were poor, but very simpatico. Lt Squires fell in love with the eldest daughter.

One morning I was called to the Orderly room and told that I had to report to the RAF Medical Centre at the Aldwych at noon. It was a lovely hot day, with clear blue sky. I caught the train at Horley just as an air battle was taking place overhead. Only the noise of screaming engines and machine-gun fire could be heard; the planes were too high up and the sun too bright to see them. At the Aldwych I had my one and only medical exam of the whole war. The medical officer discovered I was slightly deaf in my left ear, a common complaint among tank personnel because the tank beret flopped over to the right; this meant that the right ear, with a radio headset on, was more protected from the clatter than the left. In the afternoon I went to Leicester Square and saw 'Gone with the Wind,' before going back to Horley. Perhaps, I thought hopefully, we would be sent overseas before I could be claimed by the RAF.

Before we moved again I was made Company Reconnaissance Officer and given a motor cycle. Trooper Crow rode my Velocette when we moved billets and somehow managed to get it filled with petrol from the Battalion fuel dump. Our next posting was to the Kentish coastal area, where we would form part of the anti-invasion force: the Battalion would be under canvas near Ashford, on the downs near Charing. I was speeding down the A20, to get to Ashford Station before our tanks were off-loaded; there was a large pantechnicon ahead and I pulled out to pass it, doing 60 mph. When I was abreast it suddenly swerved out and forced me off the road. I mounted the grass verge, rode over a drainage ditch and was catapulted twenty feet over the handlebars and landed on my back two feet from a telephone pole. I opened my eyes and saw blue sky and the tall hedge above me. I slowly raised myself; the bike was upside down with petrol pouring from the tank. Both of us, the bike and I, were undamaged.

I led the Company tanks to a lovely avenue of trees overlooking the Weald of Kent to the south and west: it was mid-September. We put up camouflage nets, erected our tents and then dug our own latrines. I was sharing with Lieutenant Pascoe, a new-found friend from another company. The next morning a furious air battle took place over Ashford and Maidstone and we had a grandstand view. It was another clear, sunny day, and sporadic battles went on until the afternoon. Sometimes we recognised Spitfires and Hurricanes by the half-white and half-black of their undersides. We heard the rat-tat-tat of RAF machine-guns and the deeper budda-budda of the German cannon. Engines whined louder and louder and with increasing pitch, until there was a distant thud, followed by a puff of smoke, as friend or foe buried himself deep in the Kent countryside. Parachutes floated down, while the fighters flew round them like angry insects. It was impossible to say who had won or lost; it was over as suddenly as it had begun, until the next attack in the afternoon. High up swarmed the small black dots of the Luftwaffe heading for London, and the screaming of engines began again as our fighters attacked them. I was very scared. I had not bargained for this. I prayed that my papers were well and truly lost. There was a rumour that the Battalion was going to Egypt and I hoped I would be well on my way before my posting to the RAF came through.

At night we heard the deep engine note of German bombers heading through the clear sky for London. Muffled thuds came from far away, and a red glow shimmered on the north-west horizon. They were dropping bombs. High in the sky we saw tiny flashes as the anti-aircraft shells burst. Later the bombers droned back on their way home, with the occasional rat-tat-tat of RAF night fighters having a go at them. Then the air battles stopped.

During the day I reconnoitred the roads to the coast. The company went in lorries and Bren-gun carriers to Dover, Folkestone and Romney Marsh, still doing TEWTs. I never saw any other troops or tanks. For those few weeks in Autumn of 1940 the invasion coast was defended by the 8th Battalion Tanks under the trees overlooking Charing. Much later I learnt how near we had been to invasion, but at the time none of us, at least none of the junior officers and men, had the faintest idea what was going on or how serious things were. A few signposts were pointed in the wrong direction and place-names were removed from roads and villages in order to baffle invading Germans. As a result of such subterfuge I led the whole company of tanks up a long narrow lane with high banks on each side, on the way to yet another TEWT. It was the wrong route, so fifteen Mark Two Matilda tanks had to reverse out of the lane. Major Runciman said nothing, but he looked like a pickled walnut.

At our camp, under the long avenue of large trees, whose leaves were beginning to fall, we were comfortable. Ammunition, radio sets, tools and all the equipment we had been without for so long began to arrive. We were definitely preparing for action: rumour was strong that we were moving to Egypt. I was having breakfast in the mess-tent one pleasant morning, when an orderly room clerk appeared, looking for Lt Anderson, 44673. I had to report to the adjutant. Captain Trotman apologised for mislaying the original signal — but I should have been at No. 8 Elementary Flying Training School, Woodley, the previous day.

I was to leave immediately. I found Major Runciman and said goodbye, gave Pascoe my camp bed, canvas bath and wash basin. I packed my kitbag and Sergeant Doyle got my Velocette fuel tank filled up. I said goodbye to the man who had been a father to me for the last year. I set off for Camberley to break the news of my defection to my mother and Uncle-Father, then to report to RAF Woodley the next morning.

CHAPTER 4

Saint Praftu

I ARRIVED home in time for tea. My sudden appearance, with my kit-bag strapped on the back of my Velocette, was a surprise; shock followed when I announced that I had left the Army for the duration of the war and was joining the RAF. Uncle-Father was philosophical, giving me undeserved credit for knowing what was best for me. My mother soon became reconciled to my defection when I explained that I was training at Woodley, near Reading, and could come home for weekends. The next morning I set off on my bike for Woodley, arriving at midday. I reported to the adjutant who informed me I was two days late and told me to get over to the Club house and find a bed.

Woodley aerodrome belonged to the Miles Aviation Company, and had been taken over by the RAF as the home of Number 8 Elementary Flying Training School. The Miles Company built light aircraft in hangers bordering the airfield: the Messenger, Mentor and training aircraft, the Magister and Master. On the far side of the airfield was the Club House, now a mess for the pupils. Woodley was used, at that time, for training officers seconded from the Army. The chief steward showed me to my room. I had a single room awaiting me, with clean bed-sheets, a basin and a bathroom nearby. Downstairs I found a sitting room and bar, attended by a white-coated barman. I ordered a beer and sat down in a deep leather armchair. I decided that after lunch was soon enough to join the course.

Suddenly there was a stamping of feet, and loud, excited talking. In came a dozen Army officers from assorted regiments; drinks were ordered and a loud animated chatter filled the mess. I felt very much a new boy, although the others had only been there two days longer than me. There was a lot of technical gossip about how to fly an aeroplane.

I hung around the outside of a group hoping to pick up some tips. I gathered that they had all been for their first flight that morning. The mess was full now with about eighteen officers. A good-looking, dapper officer came up and introduced himself. He was Lieutenant Keith Bailey of some line regiment; he took me over to be perfunctorily greeted by the group. The ones I remember best and was closest to for the next four months were Lt Higson, Royal Engineers, Lt Penman, Royal Scots, Lt Charles-Jones, Rifle Brigade, Lts Bowes, Rowbotham and Keith Bailey of county regiments.

Higson was the self-appointed leader, at the head of a varied crew of novices, ranging from acquiescing hangers-on to the independent and potentially bolshie.

Higson: "You've got to give throttle in a spin." (No one had as yet ever done a spin, but I didn't know this.)

Keith Bailey: "How do you know?"

Charles-Jones: "Yes! How do you know? You haven't done spinning yet."

Higson: "I read it in AP1234."

Bowes, taking his pipe from his mouth: "What the hell is that?"

Penman: "It's the Bible, mon. The Air Force Bible. The last book ye read before they carry you off, mon."

Higson: "The Magister is a rotten trainer, it's too vicious. We should be on Tiger Moths."

(We were being trained on the low-wing monoplane Miles Magister.)

Bailey: "Balls, Higson! You don't know one end of an aircraft from the other."

Bowes, taking his pipe out of his mouth: "We've got a long way to go."

Higson: "My instructor told me that we're the best Army course they've had so far."

Penman: "He must be nuttier than you, mon. We've ony been flying fa half-a-day!"

Higson: "Well you chaps can laugh, but this is a serious business. We'll be on 'ops' in six months."

This was a sobering thought for all of us.

During this exchange I had been standing behind Keith Bailey. Higson seemed so knowledgeable. How was I going to keep up with him and the rest? Where could I get hold of AP1234, obviously essential for a budding pilot? Did Higson really know anything or was he bullshitting?

After lunch I went with the course to the other side of the airfield. Half of us were on flying and the other half in the classroom. I was issued with a parachute and shown how to put it on, pull the ripcord, and take it off. The straps had to be just right, not loose or too tight; error could result in one's balls being squashed when the parachute opened. I was fitted with a leather flying helmet, goggles, leather gauntlets with silk linings, a Sidcup suit and Gosport tubes. These tubes were like a doctor's stethoscope, fitted to the helmet and plugged into a tube in the cockpit. The pupil and instructor could communicate after a fashion by shouting into a mouthpiece. The Sidcup suit, made of thin green wind-proof canvas with zip fasteners in strategic places, covered the body from head to foot. It had an artificial fur collar. There was a grisly joke about the Sidcup suit. In the event of a crash it made it easy to carry away your blood and guts by simply tying knots at the end of the sleeves and trouser legs. I put on my regalia and waddled round the stores. I was allocated a locker for my flying gear and was ready to start my new career. It was my turn to fly the next morning.

That evening, in the clubhouse mess, there was more talk about how to fly. Higson was making an authoritative pronouncement about footwear for flying. He recommended gym shoes so that you could feel the rudders better. Others preferred shoes, and a small group upheld army boots.

Higson: "Boots! We're not driving lorries! You can't feel anything in boots. Your feet must feel the delicate movements of the rudder."

Bailey: "Why not boots? Fighter pilots wear flying boots. They're big enough."

Higson: "They're not the same as army boots. They're made of special soft leather with lamb's-wool lining."

Charles-Jones: "In the first World War they wore riding boots!"

Higson: "This is not the first World War, my boy!"

Charles-Jones: "But the aeroplanes are nearly the same, at least the Magister and Tiger Moth are."

Bailey: "I don't see you wearing gym shoes. My instructor wears flying boots. If we get posted to fighters, your feet will freeze, so you'd better get used to flying boots."

Higson: "Balls, I'll stick to shoes."

Bowes, taking his pipe out of his mouth: "Pack it up you two for Christ's sake."

Higson: "Did you hear about the last course of Pongos?"

All: "No! What happened?"

Higson: "Three of them took fifteen hours to go solo! And three were thrown out for not having aptitude."

Anderson: "What's the usual time for going solo?"

Higson: "Between eight and twelve hours, my instructor told me. After that they begin to give up hope".

There was silence. Each of us pondered the fate of the unfortunates of the last army course. How long would I take to go solo?

After the first few days there was very little talk about flying. Most of us had retired into ourselves. The problems were the same for all but unique to each. Each of us battled with his own difficulties. No amount of talk could give you confidence or co-ordination. Theory out of sacred AP1234 was one thing; practice depended on yourself.

For my first flight I dressed myself in my Sidcup suit, helmet, Gosport tubes, gauntlets and goggles. I carried my parachute across my back, and plodded out to the aircraft. Flying Officer Cromelin was my instructor; he showed me round the small delicate-looking Miles Magister, and then instructed me how to climb into the cockpit: The first thing to master was how not to put your foot through the flimsy wing as you climbed up. He told me not to wear gloves so that I could feel the stick better. I was put in the front cockpit while the instructor sat behind. He strapped me into the seat with the Sutton harness and fixed in my Gosport tubes. His last words were to put the balls of my feet lightly on the rudder pedals, to hold the joystick with my thumb and first two fingers only, while the left hand rested on the throttles. He would fly the aircraft while I followed his movements on the controls. I was not to let him feel my hands and feet on the controls. He got in. There was a yell from the back, "Petrol ON!," "Throttle SET," "Switches OFF." An airman caught the propeller in his right hand and shouted "Contact." Cromelin bellowed "Contact." The airman gave a mighty yank on the propeller and the engine burst into life. I sat with my hands and feet lightly covering the controls. The controls moved, I followed them; perhaps he was testing me. The airman came in from the port side and removed the chocks from in front of the wheels. The engine note increased. There was a blast of air round my head, and we started to move.

I was encased in thin three-ply with pedals made of thin aluminium, the cockpit was small, my head stuck out with a tiny windshield in front. The Magister wobbled and lurched as we moved over the grass to the take-off point. The engine made a huge noise and the whole front of the aircraft rattled and vibrated. The rudders were jerked violently from side to side, the stick was pressed back into my stomach. Everything seemed haphazard and rough. Through some cracks in the floor I saw grass passing beneath us. The bottom of the cockpit had wires and tubes running fore and aft. We wobbled and rattled; with a burst of engine we turned across wind. An aircraft was coming in to land. We waited. I wondered how this small ramshackle thing was going to fly and if it could support two of us. I hoped that the engine was properly secured to the body.

"Are you ready?," bellowed Cromelin down the Gosports.

"Yes!"

He turned into the direction of take-off and bellowed down the Gosports, "Don't try to fly it, follow me."

"Yes."

The engine increased its noise; so did the wind past my head. We moved slowly forward gathering speed. We wobbled, bounced, rattled, the controls were jerking. Suddenly, I felt an easy, comfortable, smooth sensation. We were airborne. I looked forward. The controls were now moving very little and very gently, just one quarter of an inch this way, one eighth of an inch that way. The throttle came back, the engine reduced its noise and we were climbing. The feeling that I was sitting in a flimsy, rattling box, with coarse control movements, completely vanished. The aircraft was now a thing of precision and refinement. I enjoyed the sensation and felt quite at home. I waited for the next development. After we had climbed up a bit, Cromelin's shouts came at me indistinctly down the Gosport tubes:

"Right. Now look at your altimeter. Two thousand feet. Revs, twenty-one hundred."

"Yes, sir."

"Now follow me. Stick gently forward. Nose drops. Gently back, nose up. Forward. Level. Centralise stick."

"Yes, sir."

"Stick gently to port, banking. Centralise. Stick centre — level. Gently starboard, banking. Centralise, you've got to hold off bank!"

"Yes, sir."

"For Christ's sake stop saying yes sir! Right, now you try. Ready?"

"Yes."

"Stick a little forward. Gently — a little, damn you! Gently, I said! Centralise now! Back a little! Gently! Gently! Centralise.

Forward a little. Level and centralise. Bank to port, hold off! I told you to hold off bank ...

"Now a turn to starboard. Little starboard bank. Hold off, stick little back, gentle port rudder. A little rudder. A little! ! You're too rough! Centre stick, centre rudders. Now try to port. Port bank, hold off, stick back and top rudder. No, not port rudder! Top rudder! Okay hold it — hold it for Christ's sake! Gently! Gently, for God's sake! Do what I say, don't try any of your own tricks. Right! I've got her."

"You've got her," I answered.

We turned through one hundred and eighty degrees. I had no idea where we were. I looked around. The fact that I was airborne in a small, narrow wooden box, covered with cotton fabric and held together with glue and screws, did not worry me. I was engrossed in the view of the countryside below. Roads, railways, houses, green fields and woods, all appeared like a layout in a large toy shop. This was how I should have liked to lay out the nursery and into this scene to have put my farm animals, Dinky toys, motor cars, railways, and of course my armies of soldiers. Ahead I saw black specks in the sky. We were approaching Woodley. In the clear autumn sunlight, other aircraft were flying around the airfield doing take-offs and landings; we passed over the Reading-Wokingham road. I could see a red Thames Valley double-decker bus; it stopped to pick up some toy passengers.

"Wake up! Come on don't go to sleep. Follow me now, we're down-wind. Check the wind sock for landing direction. You see it?"

"Yes."

"Look out in front, below and to the sides. No one near us. Right, we'll land. We've passed the end of the field. It's just behind your port wing tip. Turn to port. Reduce speed, throttle back, engine-assisted glide. We're cross-wind. Follow me! Coming up to line up into wind. Turn to port. Flaps down, throttle-assisted. Watch the airspeed! Keep straight. You look ahead and to the port. Always ahead on the port side. We're over the hedge. Throttle back. Hold off. Hold it. Look to your left. Judge your height. Stick gently back. Hold it. Down!"

Bump, bang, wobble, rattle. We had made a perfect three-point landing. The rudder bar moved violently, we rolled straight ahead and stopped. The engine ticking over. The throttle went forward. The engine gave a loud farting noise. The stick came back into my stomach and we turned to starboard and wobbled and lurched over the grass to the instruction block and the time-keeper's office. The next pupil was waiting. The engine ticked over as we approached the parking area. A burst of engine, a violent movement of left rudder and the aircraft slewed round and faced the grass airfield. The engine stopped.

"Right. Out you get."

I undid the Sutton harness and gingerly levered myself out of the seat, careful not to put my foot through the cockpit floor. I climbed onto the wing root and jumped down on the grass. Cromelin still sat in the back seat waiting for his next pupil.

"That's all for today. We'll talk about it tomorrow. I've got you first thing in the morning."

"Thank-you," I said and tried to walk off, as the other pupil came over to the aircraft.

I couldn't move far without removing my parachute. I turned the central knob of the harness and gave it a bash. The straps fell away. I hoisted the parachute onto my shoulders. I was momentarily overcome by the greatness of my achievement. I had flown! Not myself, although I had been in charge for some minutes. To think only a few days back I had been at Ashford under canvas! As I walked towards the locker-room I caught a glimpse of myself reflected in the window of the time-keeper's office. I was reminded of the statue of Alcock and Brown after their Atlantic crossing. My artificial fur collar was down: it would improve the effect to have it up. Next time! I turned to enter the locker room, Higson and Bailey were coming out, dressed in their regalia. Bailey was very smart; his Sidcup suit, a little tight in the waist, looked as though it had been cut by a tailor. Higson's Sidcup was baggy and slightly too long in the crutch. The two of them could have been taken for neat and natty pupil and care-worn experienced instructor. I expect Higson thought so too. As we passed, Higson said to me: "How'd it go, okay? You're a fly-boy now!"

After I had packed away my stuff, I wandered back to the Club House for tea. I was now able to think about my flight. I was worried about my lack of co-ordination when putting the aircraft into a turn. Perhaps I had an inherent lack of co-ordination and I would be failed. I sat in an armchair drinking my tea, and making imperceptible movements with my right hand and feet as I put myself into imaginary turns to port and starboard. Most of the pupils were rather subdued, drinking tea, eating egg sandwiches and looking out of the window at the aircraft landing and taking off. They were all preoccupied with their own difficulties. I was not the only one who was worried.

"Well, if you don't do what he says, what do you expect?" I recognised Higson's voice.

"And I suppose you always do what he says," chirped Bailey.

"You bet your life I do".

"Then why did you do that colossal bounce, and have to go round again?" gloated Charles-Jones.

"What colossal bounce?"

"We landed before you and saw you, so come off it," said Bailey.

"Well everyone bounces when they're learning."

"Not if you do what the instructor says. Remember?" chorused Bailey and Charles-Jones.

My difficulties I kept to myself. Bailey came over to me.

"How did you get on, Andy?"

"Well enough I suppose. But my instructor's too impatient."

"They get like that. Mine's a nice fellow."

"How many hours have you done, Keith?" I asked.

"One hour and thirty minutes. Look, forget all that now. We'll all be out of here in a month. You've got that Velocette? Mine's a Triumph Twin."

"Yes, I saw it outside. It's a lovely bike."

"Well, what are we going to do about petrol? My units are nearly finished."

With the 8th Battalion RTR, which seemed a thousand miles and ten years away, Sergeant Doyle had kept the odd gallon for me in the section stores. During my forty-eight hours at Woodley, I had formed an idea of how to get a supply, but I did not want to be the first to suggest it.

"Have you got any ideas?" I said.

Bailey looked at me steadily: "Well not definitely, but there are sources of supply nearby."

"Well whatever the source, it's got to be tapped at night."

"What about tonight?" said Bailey.

"It wouldn't make any difference?"

"No, it's quite safe. We'll take one gallon from each tank."

After dinner Bailey and I slipped out of the Club House. We carried the necessary equipment of rubber tubing and a two-gallon petrol can. We got through the hedge into the airfield and there were the Magisters parked and tied down for the night. We picked an aircraft and siphoned off two gallons out of each of the wing tanks. In this way we kept ourselves supplied with petrol during our stay at Woodley.

The next morning, I went up again with F/O Cromelin. Everything was the same, we bumped, lurched and rattled to the take-off point. Once we were airborne, the aeroplane was in its element. I did more turns, which I found easier. Then we did steep turns, climbing turns and gliding turns.

"Have you flown before?" I heard over the Gosports.

"No."

I was surprised and then slightly elated. Perhaps I was not as bad as I thought.

F/O Cromelin was the Chief Flying Instructor, but I soon realised that I was not going to enjoy my instruction. He had a black moustache and a permanent seven o'clock shadow. He was impatient, gruff, shouted at you before a mistake had been made and he nagged. It seemed that the long line of pupes he had trained had brought him to the verge of paranoid exasperation. Fortunately I only did four flights with him and was then handed over to Pilot Officer List.

I took an immediate liking to List. He was tall, fair and quiet-spoken. I felt complete confidence in him and we got on well. I never had any trouble in adjusting myself to the unusual positions of the aircraft. When an aircraft banks over, a beginner may tend to lean away from the bank. This may be through a subconscious desire to try and right the aeroplane or keep oneself from falling out of the cockpit. Perhaps because I had done a lot of motor cycle riding, this banking of the aircraft did not worry me. I had been a gymnast at school; and as a result of back flips, hand-stands, parallel and horizontal bar work, I was always able to orientate myself to the ground.

After nine hours of dual instruction List got out of the aircraft at the end of a lesson and said: "Do two take-offs and landings." He jumped off. Today there are long lists of 'vital actions', which can be memorised for a small aircraft, or read out in the case of large multi-engined aircraft. These vital actions are checked before starting up, before taxiing out, before take-off, after take-off, turning down-wind, turning cross-wind, turning on to final approach and after landing. In those early days at Woodley, things were simpler. Each instructor had his own way of helping the pilot to remember the knobs. We had no lists, so P/O List gave me a simple mnemonic — PRAFTU. List's advice was "Say PRAFTU before you do anything and all will be well!"

'P' stands for anything to do with petrol or fuel: Fuel cocks on, contents of the tanks, including oil, petrol pressure gauges and mixture control.

'R' is for Radiator: position of radiator shutters and all temperatures.

'A' is for Airscrew selected for take-off, climbing, cruising and landing pitch.

'F' for Flaps as needed for take-off or landing.

'T' for Trim tabs as required, and lastly:

'U' for Undercarriage, select 'Down' or 'Up': check warning lights and undercarriage system pressures.

When List left me on my own I said "PRAFTU". This was easy, petrol on and plenty. 'R', no radiator to worry about on the Magister. 'A', no airscrew control on the Magister either. 'F', for flaps, no flap for take-off, only flap down for landing. I checked, my flap was up. 'T' for trim, there was only elevator trim on the Magister, so I set it slightly forward of neutral. Lastly 'U' for undercarriage, it was always down, so nothing to worry about there. All okay! So move! I opened up the engine and taxied forward slowly, moving my nose right and left so as to see in front of me. I taxied along the side of the field past the hangers and arrived at the cross-wind position. I looked around. Nothing coming in for landing, and all clear ahead. PRAFTU. Nothing to do but turn into wind and go. I lined up, and opened the throttle. The aircraft gathered speed. Full throttle, stick slightly forward, the tail came up, stick gently back and ... PRAFTU! I was airborne! The aircraft flew itself straight ahead and climbed. I throttled back to climbing revs and up I went. I had nothing to do except look around and keep an eye on the altimeter. One thousand feet. I turned gently to port and flew straight for a bit. As I passed the airfield on my left, I started another gentle turn to port. I was now flying down wind, heading for the down wind end of the airfield. PRAFTU! — it worked. I was airborne, alone, flying! Here, steady now 44673! Concentrate on the next stage, the landing. I looked around me, to starboard, in front, to port and below and behind. I looked ahead and down, one aircraft was landing. I was all clear to land. It was a grass field, so two or three aircraft could land together, spread out across the hedge. I remembered List teaching: "Let the aircraft fly itself". "PRAFTU. Thank you God." I watched the airfield pass behind my port wing tip. I did a gentle turn to port still at one thousand feet, then another port turn which brought me in line with the wind sock and the airfield. I throttled back. Petrol OK, Radiator, none. 'A' Airscrew, none. 'F' Flap, full down. 'T' trim back as I required.

Throttle-assisted approach, not too low, not too high. undercarriage, fixed down. Right, land! I looked over the port side
coming down nicely at the correct speed, correct height. Stick
steady, stick back gently, hold it. Bump, bang, wobble. I was
down, and a good enough landing. I held the stick back and
rolled straight ahead. "Thank you God. Thanks God! Thank
God!" The aircraft stopped rolling. PRAFTU! I turned to port
with a burst of engine and port rudder, looked to my left to see
if anyone else was. landing behind me. No. I taxied back for
take-off. There was another aircraft waiting at the take-off
point with a lone pilot in the front seat. Far away a Magister
was coming in on final. I gave my engine a burst of throttle to
keep the plugs from getting oiled up. The landing aircraft came
over the hedge. It held off too high: "Get it down, for Christ's
sake. Down!" No! It dropped from about ten feet up, bounced
and bumped down again. This time, it stayed down. I hoped I
would do better. The aircraft in front of me taxied into wind
and waited while the pilot said a prayer. I waited for him to go.
He opened up the throttle and moved off. I opened up, kept it
straight with bags of rudder. Tail up, I held it, the speed built
up to sixty, stick gently back and hold it. Once again I was
airborne and climbing. I had nothing to do except set climbing
revs and hold the correct airspeed. I got behind the aircraft in
front which would soon be turning to port. I looked at the
gauges and instruments, all okay! At one thousand feet I turned
to port and levelled off. It was easy. My God it was easy!

I crouched down in the cockpit and peered through the tiny
windshield. I was the demon fighter ace. Normally we did not
put down our goggles; I did so now. I was the ace, ready to blast
them from the skies. I peered to starboard, port, and looked
behind for enemy fighters. None! I sat upright in my seat, my
head above the cockpit in the slipstream, goggles down and
screamed to the winds: "PRAFTU! PRAFTU!" I forgot God
and List. My guardian spirit was Saint PRAFTU. He would be
with me always, and if I crashed it would be my fault. If I forgot
PRAFTU disaster would befall me. PRAFTU before me,

PRAFTU behind me, PRAFTU below me, PRAFTU inside me, PRAFTU to port, PRAFTU to starboard — by the sacred PRAFTU, I had gone way past the field on the down-wind leg. Don't panic! I turned to port and held one thousand feet. "Pull yourself together demon ace Anderson." I turned to port again and lined up with the distant field, a bit far away but otherwise okay, throttle back and lose height slowly. Speed steady. Full flap down. Lose more height. Engine-assisted approach. I came over the hedge, a bit high, I was looking ahead and down to the port. Down a bit. Throttle fully back, hold off. Stick back a little and hold it. Bump, wobble, rattle. I was down. PRAFTU. Flaps up, trim slightly forward of neutral. I rolled straight ahead and stopped. I turned to starboard and saw that all was clear behind me. I taxied back to the instructors' block.

List was talking to another pilot. I swung the aircraft round and switched off the engine, undid the Sutton harness, pulled out the Gosports and with the parachute banging my bum, climbed out of the cockpit and jumped to the ground. I walked over to the time-keeper's office window. Total time of solo flying had been twenty minutes. I felt like a compressed spring. Steady now!

List was standing by the time keeper's window.

"That's alright, Anderson. Sign the book. See you tomorrow."

"Thanks," I said, "see you tomorrow."

I walked around the edge of the airfield to the Club House. The grass was green and thick. No one was around. I walked, then PRAFTU! I leapt into the air, steady there! Steady boy! The sacred word is PRAFTU, said backwards UTFARP or, mixed, FUTARP or FARTUP or UPFART or PARFUT. PRAFTU. I leapt into the air. Stop! for Christ's sake, someone will see me. "I am a very gentle and PARFUT knight." Then behave like one. I walked on, hoping that my leaps had not been observed from the Club House.

By the time I reached the mess I had composed myself. My elation had subsided. Tea was in progress, and there was a general hubbub; I had not been the only one to go solo that day.

"No! that's no good", Higson was holding forth, "my instructor says FGMPTTU. It's easy, you can't go wrong — FGMP double TU. It covers everything."

"It's no good," said Bailey, "it doesn't spell a word. Mine's FUMFART. Fumfart. Fuel, undercarriage, mixture, flaps, airscrew, radiator, trim. Fumfart."

Knowles took his pipe from his mouth and said: "Fumfart. My word too."

"It sounds ridiculous, you can't go around saying 'Fumfart'. Mine's UMPART" said Charles- Jones.

"Fumfart or umpart all sounds balls to me," said Higson, "mine covers everything. FGMP double TU." I kept my sacred word to myself. They were groping after the truth. Indeed all the words had elements of the truth, even Higson with his FGMP etc. Only in my word did truth and reality coincide: I would not pronounce it. I would not subjugate its mysteries to the jibes of the ignorant. Could anyone for long repeat 'FUMFART' without realising it had no power? All power resided in PRAFTU.

That evening Bailey got hold of me, and we had a talk. We were now RAF pilot officers and were getting an extra twelve shillings a day. Our pay had gone up by thirty per cent. Bailey suggested that as we were now in the money, we should get rid of our motor cycles and buy cars. What car did I favour? During this discussion which was taking place in the anteroom after dinner, Higson joined us with a pint tankard in his hand.

"We'll be F/Os in another year, and Flight Lieutenants after two years," he said. "How do you know?" asked Bailey.

"I asked my instructor. It's all on time basis now. Enough casualties to make way for time promotions."

"When do we wear RAF uniform?" I asked.

"At the end of our training before going to the squadrons. Can do what we like then," said Higson.

"What do you mean?" asked Bailey.

"Why! You know damn well you can't disgrace an RAF uniform. We can stagger around the pubs and local dance halls, and whore around in general. No one cares, in fact it's rather expected of you. You know, youth! Operational types recuperating their shattered nerves!"

"Nonsense!" exclaimed Bailey, who was rather shocked.

"Is it hell! I have seen them and you know it's true. They're not called 'Brylcream boys' for nothing. In Army uniform we couldn't do half the things they get up to. The RAF's got no traditions to worry about!"

All this was enough for one day and I went to bed. I had been at Woodley seven days. That night before going to sleep I said my prayers:

"Gentle Jesus, meek and mild,
Look upon a little child,
Pity me in my simplicity,
And suffer me to come to thee. Amen.
God bless Mum and Dad, Uncle-Father,
Danty, Lindsay, Sandy, and help me to
be good. Amen, and oh yes! Thank
you God for P/O List and PRAFTU. Amen."

I then thought about my flight and decided to try and treat each flight as though it was my first. Never to become over-confident, always to do the same thing as much as possible, and to think about all emergencies and prepare myself well beforehand. I would listen to other people's experiences, make allowances, and store up their stories in the back of my mind, for one day a similar thing might happen to me. I decided never to talk about myself; somehow this tempted fate. If I ignored unpleasant events, they would not happen. If I kept to the routine myself, there would be no opportunity for untoward events to intrude.

Flying was not the only activity at Woodley. Half the time was devoted to classroom studies, and a few hours in the link trainer. We did elementary magnetism, navigation, theory of flight, engines and parachute packing. Nothing was difficult or beyond our capabilities. One morning there was low cloud and rain, and we were all in the classrooms. Suddenly, VROOSH - BANG - BANG! The whole building shook, and windows-rattled; some people dived below the desks. We had been bombed by a low-flying Messerschmidt. It was all over in seconds. Those in the know said it must have been a fighter flown in by one of the Germans trained at Woodley before the war. He had come back to show his gratitude. We all agreed it was a pretty good show, and that it was lucky the weather had not been better or he might have shot down some of us.

At the end of October I was passed out with 'above average' assessment, thanks to List's tuition and patience. The whole course was posted to No. 9 Flying Training School, RAF Hullavington.

Wings

My flying instructor at Hullavington was F/O McCarthy, small, fair, intense and humorous. He used to carry an eight-inch spanner in the breast pocket of his tunic under his Sidcup suit. This spanner, he explained, was for emergencies. If any pupil clung onto the stick in terror while the aircraft plunged earthwards, F/O McCarthy, from the rear cockpit, would bash the pupil on the head with his spanner, and take control of the aircraft.

We flew old biplanes — Hawker Harts and Audaxes. They had Rolls Royce Kestrel engines, and were fitted with large wooden propellers. They were bi-planes made of wood, covered with fabric, and held together by bracing wires. They looked very First World War. They rattled, wobbled and bumped over the grass airfield; however, their engines now gave a weak roar, more like real engines than the fut-fut of the Miles Magister. They had wheels with treadless tyres and wheel discs painted in different colours. You put your feet into toe-holes in the fuselage in order to climb up to the cockpit, which was small and airy, with leather padding sewn round the open-ing. Between and below your feet were wires, rods and cracks in the flooring. You were encased between metal tubes, wooden laths and doped fabric. I almost expected to see a Lewis gun fitted to the top wing above my head. After two hours dual, we were all going solo. At that time there was no radio control, and no flashing of lights from the control tower. We looked out for ourselves and used our common sense. We did more aerobatics with and without instructors, low-flying practice, formation flying and one or two short cross-country flights.

I enjoyed the formation flying. The instructor led the formation of three aircraft, and signalled his orders by hand. There we were, heads out of the cockpits in the wind, and goggles down. Some pupils sported coloured scarves. McCarthy in the middle of the 'V' formation would be signalling away like mad, the aircraft hopping around in response to his signals, now astern, now echelon to port, then back to 'V'. We were flying along approaching the Boche lines at 4,000 feet, somewhere near Arras. In and out of cloud and rain. The rain making hellish mud for the poor bastards in the trenches below. This was Baron von Richtofen country, so we kept a good lookout. All was quiet on the Western Front that afternoon, not even a shot at us or sign of an Albatross. Back we came to Bethune and landed.

There was a special field not far from Hullavington where we did our night flying. The instructors flew the aircraft over in the afternoon, and at dusk the pupils were motored out in a lorry with their parachutes. We sat for hours in a corrugated-iron Nissen hut, gathered round a coke stove waiting for our turn to fly. Sometimes there was fog or low cloud, and flying came to a stop. The runway was marked by gooseneck flares, which gave a dim, smoky-yellow light. The aircraft carried no landing lights; a floodlight was briefly switched on to illuminate the runway as we came in to land. In mist, this created the effect of landing in a blinding white cloud. Red, green and white Aldis lights were flashed at us from the controlling officer on the ground as we did our circuits. Having no radio, we requested permission to land by signalling a Morse letter on our identification light. On dark nights I kept my head inside the cockpit and concentrated on the artificial horizon and airspeed indicator. After the initial climb my eyes got accustomed to the gloom and I could fly visually. PRAFTU was with me.

During night flying we had our first fatality. A pupil was flying solo and crashed after take-off. It was pitch dark. The aircraft crashed a mile from the field and did not catch fire. It took some time for the control officer to realise that there was one less aircraft in the circuit. Then confusion started. Blackout precautions made the whole business more difficult for everyone. The ambulance and fire tender had restricted headlight beams. Since the aircraft had not caught fire, there was no way of locating it except by driving around. The ground was soft after rain. The makeshift blood wagon with its two medical orderlies drove around from field to field in the pitch blackness, with only the feeble rays of their blacked-out headlights. They were joined by the fire tender. All the other aircraft were grounded and the pupils sent back to Hullavington.

For two hours the vehicles floundered around in the muddy fields in the mist. At last they found the aircraft. They searched the wreckage by torchlight but could not find the pilot. Eventually they found the body some distance away; he had been thrown out of the cockpit when the aircraft hit the ground. Rumour had it that the wheel marks of one of the vehicles showed that it had run over the pilot while wandering around the field before locating the crash.

At the end of the course we got our wings. There was no ceremony; we were just told to put them up. We went to our rooms and sewed on the wings we had purchased in anticipation of the great day. Everybody appeared in the evening with their wings in place. It was just possible to see them on your left breast while looking down to read the lower columns of the newspaper, or while eating your food. By positioning yourself opposite the glass doors of the library shelves, you could casually observe your reflection.

The next day after lunch, Bailey and I decided to go into Bath, in order to show off our wings. I persuaded Bailey to accompany me to a chamber music concert starting at 14.30 hours. There would be a large number of people there. I received a rude shock to my ego before the concert. Bailey wanted to buy a toothbrush.

"Ah," I said. "Here is a chemist's shop. I believe we can make your purchase here. Come on Keith, let's go in."

We entered the shop. The place was deserted. I raised my voice, so as to announce our arrival to the shop assistant.

"What colour do you want for your toothbrush, Keith?"

"Oh, it doesn't matter."

"Soft, medium or hard?"

"Medium."

An elderly man had emerged from the door behind the counter. By his grey hair and starched collar, I took him to be the proprietor.

"We're looking for a toothbrush. Pink, and of medium texture. Do you stock such an article?"

I stood in front of him. He could not fail to see my wings.

"Firstly, this is a chemist's shop, so anyone with a modicum of intelligence would know that toothbrushes are to be found here. Secondly, if you lower your eyes you will see them on the counter in front of you," he replied.

I was struck dumb. Bailey stepped forward and bought the toothbrush. We left. I looked at the proprietor again, sideways. He caught my eye. He had a suspicion of a smirk, very slight, but it was there. My humiliation was complete.

The chamber music concert was a great success. Everyone saw our wings and seemed suitably deferential. There were no RAF there. It was rare for fighting men to care for chamber music. The whole audience was at our feet, gallant officers out for intellectual relaxation. I saw myself as a man of action and of culture. A complete man. I do not know what Bailey was thinking. He had not wanted to come to the concert. I had talked him into it.

CHAPTER 5

Initiation

I DO not remember that any of us were vitally affected by, or even interested in what we read in the papers or heard over the radio. Each of us was concerned with his own immediate future. Up until now our training had not engendered any team spirit. We were individuals preparing to get into a squadron.

As Army officers we were destined for Army co-operation squadrons, flying early models of the North American Mustang, Tomahawks, and perhaps Hurricanes. We would probably be posted to East Anglia, perhaps later to North Africa. None of us showed any enthusiasm to get to grips with the enemy. We knew that the 'usual channels' would direct us towards the foe soon enough. We were a much smaller and more subdued bunch than at our first coming together at Woodley.

We were posted to Old Sarum, an undulating grass airfield on the edge of Salisbury Plain overlooking the city. We flew the Lysander, which had last seen 'ops' during the phoney war. This was a marvellous aircraft. It had been specially designed for the short landings and take-offs needed for Army support, and for observation work. But it was slow, and with its inadequate armament it was at the mercy of the modern fighter. The Lysander was a lovely aircraft to fly. You sat high up with a regal view of everything around you, surrounded by sliding perspex windows. Behind you was the petrol tank, and behind that the observer-gunner under his glass-house canopy. When you were airborne there was a pleasant humming noise from the Bristol Mercury radial engine, and the fragrant smell of warm oil wafted back from the region in front of the rudder pedals. It was impossible to stall the Lysander. With the engine throttled back and the stick hard into your stomach, the airspeed could be held at forty-five miles an hour as the gentle creature sank slowly and sedately earthwards. If you dropped from a great height when landing, at the worst you might get a burst tyre. The sacred word PRAFTU held good as always.

Two events of importance occurred to me at Old Sarum. I learned to map read and I lost my virginity. Of these the most important was the first, for without this skill I would not have survived for long. All our exercises were carried out at low level. The aircraft were fitted with a primitive type of radio, which hardly ever worked; this was no loss since for the next two years I was to carry out operations on which we had no radio.

There was no dual flying instruction now; we had our wings, we were shown the knobs in the cockpit and then sent off to do circuits and bumps for the first day. There followed map-reading exercises all over Salisbury Plain. We would be given a dozen six-figure map references and fly off for forty-five minutes to find the object at each reference; a church, crossroads, dew pond, quarry or farmhouse. We did a few exercises at artillery spotting. White puffs of smoke were set off on the ground and we radioed back the distance of the shell burst from the target. The aircraft radio seldom worked, so artillery spotting was an excuse for flying around for forty-five minutes. We practised touching down on a 'T' laid out on the grass, dropping the Lizzy from fearful heights to crash down on the mark. Apart from shaking our backsides the Lizzy appeared unconcerned.

All this seemed unrelated to actuality, learning to handle an aircraft no longer used for Army co-operation. Like the Mark One I tank it had been designed for the First World War. However, by chance my training was invaluable, as operations were later to prove.

Among our Army instructors was a tall Captain in the Black Watch. He always wore his kilt with green ribbons, sporran, skean dhu, and thick, fawn-coloured woollen stockings. He cut a very fine figure. One day before lunch we were all in the ante-room drinking beer. The newspapers were full of the latest disaster, perhaps the fall of Singapore, or battleships sunk, or another retreat in the Western Desert. Keith Bailey and I were standing opposite the old leather settee, when the Black Watch captain, clutching a Daily Mirror, parked himself in its shabby depths. His kilt went up above his pale knees, and Keith and I had a full view of what looked like a timorous black rat with a pink nose cowering in the gloom. The Captain looked up and saw our astonished faces. He quickly lowered the Daily Mirror, opened at 'Jane', and scrambled out of the old settee. Keith and I were flabbergasted. Surely officers of the 42nd were trained at their depot in Perth to sit down, and perform other drawing-room antics without exposing themselves.

Charles-Jones, Higson and I used to take our cars into Salisbury on Saturday nights. Early in the course Bailey and I went one evening to a pub, where we ran into Charles-Jones boozing with a Canadian-Scottish officer. After a few beers — I did not like the taste and drank very little — we ended up at a dance above another pub overlooking the main square. The place was packed with Pongos and girls, hot and misty with smoke and beer fumes. Sweat gleamed on red faces. As I pushed my way to the bar I came across a girl holding a half-pint and wearing a black velvet blouse and a black hairband. I ordered drinks, the music started, I turned round. The black velvet blouse was still standing there. I took a step from the bar, leaving the drinks and asked her for a dance. She said yes. I took her drink and placed it on the bar next to ours, and off we went. Her arms were very white. We danced. I do not think we talked. The music stopped and we joined the others. Then more dancing. We all took turns, more beer was drunk and then more dancing. At these functions there was a strict social code. I had accosted her first so I had proprietary rights, although I only intended to exercise them by giving her a goodnight kiss and arranging a date for the cinema. She and I were dancing the last waltz, the inevitable 'Who's taking you home tonight?'. She grabbed my hand and pulled me out of the dancers.

"Walk home with me tonight. I live quite close," she said as she turned to collect her coat from the cloakroom.

"Yes, of course."

The others came up. We all left the place together. She held my hand tight and led the way. We were in front.

"Say goodnight to your friends. You can go later after we walk home," she said, or ordered. In a dream I did as she said. I turned to Keith.

"Goodnight Keith, I'm taking Betty home."

"Goodnight Betty."

"Goodnight Charles-Jones."

"Goodnight Andy." Etc etc.

What was I getting myself into? I was in an anticipatory funk. I was just twenty-one, and she could not have been much older. Perhaps she only wanted a goodnight kiss and a date for the cinema. I hoped so, and then I hoped .....

"Come on, it's quite close. It's cold and late," she said.

She lived over a shop. She got her key out and opened the door.

"Do you want me to come in?" I asked.

"Why? Aren't you going to say goodnight to me? You're not frightened of me are you?"

"Of course not," I lied.

"Then come on, it's cold."

We climbed some carpeted stairs. At the top she stopped and said:

"Quiet now, that's my little girl's room. Stay here while I have a look."

Little girl! My God! Where was the husband? Perhaps there was a mother or mother-in-law lurking around! She came back, took my hand and dragged me into the front room. A bedroom!

"Go on, sit on the bed."

I sat.

"But what about your husband?"

"He's dead."

"Oh! But your mother-in-law or somebody?"

She came over to me and put both hands on my shoulders and pushed me back onto the bed.

"My mother-in-law. I keep her under the bed in a trunk!"

I smiled weakly. There was to be no help. She lay on top of me. This was not the position I had been used to for a good-night kiss.

"How old are you?" she asked quietly.

"I'm twenty-one ... last December."

"What have you been doing?"

"What do you mean? Before the war I went to school, then I was an army cadet, and then as you see in the tank regiment, and now I'm learning to fly and will soon be joining my squadron."

"I thought so. Give me a kiss."

"What about your daughter?"

"She's sleeping like a little angel, and so is my mother-in-law. Kiss me, and tell me about the squadron."

I was very lucky. She was twenty-four, married before the war; her husband had been in the Army, killed at Dunkirk. I went to her home three or four times while I was at Old Sarum. She took complete command of the situation. The emotions and sensations she awoke in me were intense and violent. After our second meeting she made me promise not to indulge myself with other girls, although at the time the thought was far from my mind. She drummed into me that I must give all my energies and attention to my job as a pilot, or otherwise I would kill myself. In short, she thoroughly frightened me. Kiss them but don't screw them, was the gist of her advice. Perhaps she had qualms about the intensity of the emotions she had awakened in me. At that time I never gave the motivation for her advice a thought. I swore by the sacred PRAFTU that I loved her. I had told her about PRAFTU. She made me promise it would end after I left Old Sarum. I agreed with her. I loved her, but I loved life more, (though I did not want to admit it). My new life was to begin in my squadron. A new uniform in an arm that had been on active service since the first day of the war. I would be a new man, unattached, unencumbered, dedicated to my job of keeping alive. I was very frightened about the future. I was not longing to rush into battle for King and Country. I would go to battle but only 'through the official channels'.

The last time I saw her, Bailey and I met her in a pub. I took her home and kissed her goodbye. She opened the car door, got out and quickly entered her house. I sat in the car, my eyes wet with tears. I had to go back and pick up Keith. The thought of Keith Bailey, waiting for me in his smart khaki uniform with his wings up, pulled me out of my morbid and sentimental mood. This is the life, I thought. We've been trained. I can fly and now I hope we will go together to a Mustang squadron.

I returned to the pub and picked up Keith. Silently we headed back to Old Sarum. We left the main road and turned to the right down the lane leading to the mess and aerodrome buildings. It was a dark, clear night with shining stars. I was driving by the diffused light from my top-hatted headlights. There was a bump and a screeching. We had hit something. I stopped the car. Keith got out and walked back a few yards. The screeching went on in agonising, short pulsations. Keith came back.

"You've run over a cat. It's not dead. You'd better kill it. It's in agony."

"Kill it? How?"

"Hit it on the head with the jack or starter-handle. Put it out of its misery. You can't leave it there."

"You hit it Keith. I can't."

"You ran over it; you should go and kill it. Suppose I had not been here? You would have had to kill it. Go on! Finish it off, it's making a horrible noise."

"If I was by myself I wouldn't have stopped."

"Well, you have stopped."

"Yes, but you went back and found it."

"For Christ's sake Andy! Don't argue! It's making an agonising row. You must have broken its back. Go on! Get it over with!"

Four nights before, I had been with her. Her skin had been so palely white. That evening she had worn, once again, the black velvet blouse and black velvet ribbon in her hair. That night as she took me to her, she had said so seriously:

"Don't let this become your life, it will kill you. Promise."

"I promise."

"By the sacred PRAFTU," she whispered.

At that moment I loved her more than life, and she knew it. She was older than I was. I had been very lucky.

"Is the cat black Keith?" I asked.

"I don't know! All cats are black in the dark! What does it matter? Go on, kill it!"

"Right, I'll kill it!"

I took out the starter handle and went back to where Keith was standing.

"Alright, I'll do it. You go back. Go on, go back to the car."

Keith returned to the car.

I bashed its head again and again. The scene was dimly lit by a faint red glow from the car's tail light. The cat kept screeching. The bloody thing would not die. I bashed it again. Dull thuds sounded as I pounded its skull. At last it lay still and quiet. I could not touch it, so I picked up its limp body by draping it over the starter handle, and carried it to the ditch. I dumped it in the ditch and wiped the starter handle on the damp grass. We drove off towards the Mess.

A few days later we did our last flying exercises and the course was over. After breakfast we all assembled in one of the classrooms. This is it, men! We were going to hear our postings. At Woodley we had been about twenty strong; now, five months later, our numbers had already been reduced, by accidents and odd disappearances. At Hullavington we had a course photograph taken. I remember the frightened glee with which I drew haloes round those who had written themselves off, and inked in bowler hats for those who had been sent away.

On this final morning Higson sat at the extreme right-hand desk in the front row. On his left was Charles-Jones; behind them sat Bowes smoking his pipe, Bailey and I. The remaining seven members of the course sat behind us. In front was the wooden blackboard, and the instructor's desk and chair. We were all back at school, waiting for our exam results. Next term we would be joining the seniors and playing rougher games. Some smoked, others talked, and some sat silently. Higson was telling us the most likely squadrons we would go to. In walked the Sqn Ldr Chief Instructor.

"Good morning all! Ready to hear your fate? You lucky chaps, wish I was being ...."

"Hurray! Hear, hear! Bad luck Sir!"

We interrupted and commiserated with the poor Sqn Ldr, amidst general laughter.

"Right now, quieten down. You'll be going to Army Co-op Squadrons. I'm putting the list of postings up on the blackboard. You've got two weeks leave before you report to your squadrons. Don't forget, you're not Pongos now, you're RAF."

"Hurray! Hear hear! Up the RAF.

"Quiet! All right. Wait a bit. Now I want five volunteers for a Special Squadron of High Level Photographic Reconnaissance. It's in Coastal Command. You'll be going on ops almost immediately. This is a crack unit. You'll be flying Spitfires. Come on! Five of you."

He looked round. There was no movement. We were still Pongos, bred to the rule of 'Never Volunteer'. Then good old Higson put his hand up, followed by Charles-Jones on his left; then behind these two Bowes and Bailey put up their hands.

Higson and Charles-Jones had turned round and were watching. Bailey gave me a dig in the ribs. My hands were on the desk.

"Go on! Put your hand up!" he growled.

I slowly and sheepishly raised my hand. This performance was watched by the rest of the course.

"Right! That's five. The rest of you check your postings on the list. You can go off now or after lunch. Good luck to all of you!"

The rest of the course got up and gathered round the postings list. They wandered out of the classroom. Those who were going to a squadron together had already formed new groups.

"Now, you five! You're posted to RAF Station Benson. It's north of Henley-on-Thames on the Oxford Road. You report there after seven days. You'll be in RAF uniform from now on. P/Os all of you, and that stripe's damn thin. This is a special hush-hush unit, and you are the first batch of new boys straight from OTU. They usually only take experienced op types. Oh yes! Make a list of your names and numbers and give it in to my office. Best of luck you chaps!"

He turned round and walked out. We just sat there. My God! What had I let myself in for — ops, and so soon!

"What luck eh?" said Higson, turning round.

"It's better than Army Co-op," said Bailey.

"Coastal Command! We're in Coastal Command," Charles-Jones piped up.

"So what?" said Higson. "We're on ops, and a special hush-hush unit. You heard what he said."

Bailey turned and looked at me. I looked at him and said nothing. Bowes took his pipe out of his mouth and said:

"Well, come on, we can't sit here all morning. Let's make out the list and go."

"Alright now, men! Name, rank and number," said Higson. After the list had been made out Charles-Jones suggested we go off to pack, then meet in the mess for a drink before lunch. We entered the dining room; the instructors and the rest of the course were clustered at the end of the long mahogany table.

We sat down at the other end, already separated from the others. We joked and talked and felt a spirit of camaraderie spreading over us. We had volunteered for a crack secret operational unit, playing a vital part in the war! We would be on ops soon and the rest of the table knew it. We got up and left the dining room together. Bowes left in his old Morris. Higson and Charles-Jones drove off together. Bailey and myself left in my Singer. He was going to London, so I dropped him off at the railway station.

"What do you think, Keith?" I said.

"I think it's a good thing."

"Why?"

"Well, we've got to get down to it some day. This is a Special Unit. It'll be different, more interesting, don't you see?"

"Yes, you're right, absolutely right. If it hadn't been for you I wouldn't have put my hand up."

"I know. It's probably Higson who gets on your tits."

"Well, maybe. But I'm glad you made me do it."

"Okay Andy, see you at Benson. We'll be P/Os."

"Goodbye Keith. See you at Benson."

CHAPTER 6

Benson

WHEN our seven days leave was over, the five of us reported to RAF Benson at midday as instructed. Benson was a peacetime station. The officers' mess was brick-built, the first floor with bedrooms and bathroom, and the ground floor with anteroom, dining room, bar and billiard room. There were garages and two squash courts at the back. Benson was the home of the King's Flight, which flew Royalty and VIPs from A to B. It was a grass field with one narrow runway lying west to east. There were two large maintenance hangars, one for the Royal Aircraft and the other for inspection and modification of Photographic Reconnaissance Unit Spitfires.

PRU had recently moved from Heston airfield which after the War eventually became buried beneath the expansion of Heathrow. In 1940 it accommodated an embryonic PRU. The increase in Spitfires, maintenance hangars, photographic developing and printing laboratories, together with a growing photo interpretation and intelligence sections, necessitated the move to a larger field with on-site accommodation.

On that first morning, Keith Bailey and I arrived together. We got ourselves half-pints of beer and entered the large anteroom. In the middle of the room was a mass of 'operational types', some in RAF battledress, others in Service dress, yet others in a mixture of both; all had beer mugs, all talking and many smoking. We found the others, Higson, Knowles and Charles-Jones, sitting in wooden armchairs by the tall windows which looked out onto the car park and the road to Oxford. They were silent. Bailey and I joined them.

In front of the mantelled fireplace stood the dapper figure of Wing Commander Tuttle AFC, the Station Commander, beer in hand, surrounded by Flt Lts, F/Os and P/Os. The anteroom glass doors opened and a tall Flight Lieutenant entered, dressed in a shabby uniform with leather elbow patches and leather round the cuffs. His face was pinched, imperious. Wing Commander Tuttle turned to him and said:

"How was Hamburg, Alistair? Go alright?"

"Fine sir. Lovely weather. I'll be sending a Kiel flight this afternoon, sir."

Hamburg! Why, that was hundreds of miles away, inside Germany! In daylight — and there and back before lunch! Kiel! Even further — there and back before tea! My God! This was the real thing. On my left was an admin type reading the Daily Mirror.

"Excuse me please," I said. "Who is that Flight Lieutenant over there? The one with his back to us talking to the Wingco?"

"Oh him. That's God. 'E' Flight, Flight Lieutenant Alastair Taylor."

"God?" I enquired.

"Yes, God. G - O - D."

"Thank you," I said.

God now turned round and spoke to a scruffy-looking F/O who had a beer tankard in hand. Then we saw God's gongs. Below his wings was the DFC ribbon and with two rosettes. Three DFCs! At that time we were losing the war and gongs were very reluctantly distributed. Most of that jolly crowd were old hands, many had done fifty or sixty operational sorties. I never spoke to God. He was one of a different order, one of the greats of Photographic Reconnaissance.

We heard others talking; some had been to the Ruhr, Emden, Channel ports, and Cherbourg. All this was thrilling to Bailey and myself. We were in it! What we had only heard about was actually true, and we were part of it! This was war! We sat like bemused wallflowers at our first ball, watching the happy co-mingling of the habitués. Would anyone ask us to dance?

Wg Cdr Tuttle led the exodus to the dining room. We followed and sat together at the end of one of the tables, with its white tablecloth, silver-plated eating irons, and about to be waited on by white-coated WAAFs. After lunch, not knowing where to go, we returned to the empty anteroom and read the dishevelled newspapers. The others must be winging their ways to Dusseldorf, Mannheim, and the fighter airfields of northern France.

The tall doors opened, and in came Alistair Taylor, followed by Flt Lt Nebbie Wheeler DFC and F/O Sydney Dowse.

"Right, Anderson and Bailey," said Nebbie. "You're in 'B' Flight. Sydney will take you down to the hangars and get you airborne in the Fairey Battle."

Alistair Taylor had in the meantime left the anteroom with Higson, Knowles and Charles-Jones.

Nebbie continued, "After the Battle, Sydney will get you airborne on the Spitfire. 'B' Flight operates from Mount Farm. I want you both with the Flight as soon as possible."

So that afternoon Sydney showed us the 'knobs' of the Fairey Battle, and where everything was. We spent a couple of hours doing circuits and bumps. The Battle was large, heavy, placid and slow, and possibly the RAF equivalent of the Mark One Infantry tank.

The next morning Keith and I walked down to the hangars. Sydney arrived in the 'B' Flight transport, which proceeded to Mount Farm. There was a sky-blue Spitfire, X 4355, on the tarmac. Sydney got in while Keith and I stood on the wing roots, one on each side of the cockpit, and peered inside. It seemed very small. Sydney showed us the knobs.

"Fuel cocks on, main tank, wing tanks, rear tank. Oxygen, you've got five hours of the stuff. Flaps down. Flaps up. Trim wheel, neutral for take-off. Undercarriage up and down, check warning lights and check the little things poking up at wing roots when undercarriage locked down. Don't let engine overheat when taxiing, keep radiator flap open. Instruments are standard like the Battle. No radio, no camera fitted. You've got a long nose in front of you, so when taxiing, swing from side to side to look ahead. Don't taxi into the petrol bowser. Don't forget to sign Form 700 before each flight. This is one of our aircraft, just finished inspection. Just get the feel of it. And don't prang it!"

Keith and I succeeded in doing our first solos without mishap, while Sydney watched from the control tower. We did some more take-offs and landings. The WVS van arrived and we stopped for char and wads. Sydney told us to do some flights over Benson to height, to get the feel of it, and again not to prang it.

That afternoon, the sun shone, there was not a cloud in the sky. Sydney's last instructions were not to wear too much warm clothing so that we were free to move around in the cockpit, keeping a good lookout, and:

"It's what you don't see that shoots you down! Keep looking behind, each side, up and ahead all the time. It keeps you from going to sleep and alive."

Sydney announced he was leaving us to get on with it. He was playing squash that afternoon.

Keith and I tossed for it. I would take the first flight. Today everyone flies above 30,000 feet and higher, but sixty years ago only a fighter could get to that height, and then not pressurised but on a steady oxygen intake from take-off. If the supply of oxygen stopped while at height, you were unconscious in seconds, with the aircraft spiralling down out of control.

That summer afternoon I climbed to 30,000 feet in thirty minutes. Above was more blue sky; below, southern England lay like a map. I could see the mouth of the Thames, the North Sea, Southend, all London, Salisbury Plain, the Channel, Ashford. Were the tanks still there?

The engine note was melodious, steady and powerful. A tiny wing each side of me kept the Spitfire up. I was suspended in a capsule made from aluminium no thicker than a pan for boiling eggs! It was the ultimate miracle for which I had left the 8th Battalion RTR. I descended quickly, popping my ears on the way down. It was Keith's turn.

For the next two days we took turns, climbing to 30,000 feet and map-reading on flights to the south-west and Midlands. The sun shone; navigating in clear skies was a piece of cake.

Mount Farm

One evening in the Benson mess, after Keith and I had flown the Spitfire and had not pranged it, Nebbie told Keith and myself that the next morning at eight o'clock we would be joining the 'B' Flight Humber shooting brake to accompany the rest of the flight to Mount Farm. 'B' Flight was the only operator from what was the PRU satellite airfield. It was about five miles away on the road to Oxford. It had a triangle of runways, surrounded by a taxi track, with concrete dispersals around the field. It had its own Intelligence section for briefing and de-briefing pilots.

Keith and I were ready and waiting on the car park as ordered. The rest of the flight emerged, consisting of Nebbie, Sydney Dowse, F/O Jimmy Morgan and F/O Wysiekierski, the oldest and most decorated. He was a Polish Air Force Officer who, with many of his compatriots had escaped from Europe via Marseilles, from where they were shipped by a Royal Navy destroyer to Britain to continue their fight. His decorations were the Polish Vertuti Militari and a DFC.

The Humber brake arrived driven by little WAAF driver, Liza. Nebbie sat in front, the rest of us piled in. We drove to the Benson met office, always the first port of call before any oper-ation. It was a nice morning. Wg Cdr Tuttle was there with other Flight Commanders, accompanied by the pilots sched-uled for the day's flights. Smithy, the senior forecaster, standing in front of the hand-drawn synoptic charts, held forth on the weather over Europe. He put us in the met picture; high winds at 25,000 feet and above, cloud over various parts of Europe and the weather to be expected over the UK. It was always a wonder to me how the forecasters were able to give a fairly accurate picture when there was no synoptic information coming from anywhere in Europe, and none from the Atlantic shipping.

An Intelligence officer from the small village of Ewelm, on the periphery of Benson airfield, announced the targets to be covered. The Flight Commanders decided among themselves who would do what. Nebbie was going to Dortmund, Essen and Dusseldorf, and Sydney doing Cologne, Bonn and Koblenz.

As we entered Mount Farm we stopped at the Intelligence section to find out if F/Os Edward Hornby and Quentin Craig had any last-minute instructions for Nebbie and Sydney. They hadn't.

Our Nissen hut, a semi-circular tube of corrugated iron, was next to our dispersal, on which stood three sky-blue Spitfires. They bore the PRU identification letters LY on the fuselage.

The shooting brake drew up on the dispersal. Nebbie got out.

"Flight!" he bawled.

"Saar!" came the response from F/Sgt Hunn, standing in the entrance to our hut.

"Two aircraft! Full tanks for Sydney and myself."

This short exchange, with its concise familiarity, was pure RAF.

Erks emerged from the back of the hut, and started to prepare the two Spitfires. From somewhere, a dreaded petrol bowzer trundled down the taxi track towards our dispersal.

We entered the Flight hut. One third was ours, a table, two chairs and a filing-cabinet for Nebbie; a low table and three chairs in the middle for us, and two tall metal cabinets for flying boots, clothing and maps separated us from the ground crews. Two-thirds of the hut was for F/Sgt Hunn and his technicians together with their tool boxes, cameras, oxygen bottles, spare tyres, battery chargers, tea-brewing equipment, chairs, cupboards, and a secret apparatus which filtered green

100 octane aviation petrol, making it colourless, for F/Sgt Hunn's evening car journeys to London.

Nebbie and Sydney busied themselves marking out their routes on one-in-a million scale aviation maps, putting on sweaters, removing collars and ties. Erks came in and carried out their parachutes to put into the Spitfire seats. Maps were folded and tucked into their boots. They emptied their pockets and put everything into the Flight office desk. Neither wore a Mae West, deemed too bulky for complete freedom of movement in the cockpit, and unnecessary as they would only be over the English Channel for ten minutes, going and returning.

As Nebbie and Sydney left the hut, Nebbie turned and said, "Show them the ropes, Whisky."

We followed them out. They climbed into their cockpits. An erk followed each and stood on the wing root to help put the parachute straps over their shoulders, and last-minute advice given about camera exposures.

Nebbie started his engine first, closed the cockpit canopy and signalled for his run-up and magneto test.

Whisky pushed me in the back and said, "You go!" I ran out to the tail of Nebbie's Spit. The erk and I, one on each side of the rudder, lay on the tailplane with our bums into wind. Nebbie opened up to 3000 revs, tested his magnetos and throttled back. We jumped off. Nebbie signalled chocks away, and taxied out.

Whisky prodded Keith to do the same for Sydney's run-up. Bums once more into wind. Sydney opened up, mags tested. They jumped off. Sydney taxied out minutes behind Nebbie. We waited on the dispersal until they were airborne.

"Right, we play pontoon, I teach you," announced Whisky.

"But Whisky," I said, "What about showing us the ropes?"

"The ropes are for monkeys! First pontoon."

So we played. Keith and I lost.

"Right! Now monkey business," announced Whisky. "First, don't eat peas before you fly! They give you stomach-ache at 28,000 feet and make you fart. Always have a pee before you

start. You can't pee at 28,000 feet. Very difficult to undo everything and get little man out. Don't pee in cockpit ... it
condenses on the canopy, freezes, and you can't see out. Then
rata-tat-tat, '109' shoot you down.

"Next very important. Don't wear collar and tie. Wear silk
scarf. You look around all the time like this."

He sat on a chair and started to look on his left, then ahead,
then above, then to the right, then twisting his head right round
to look backwards. Then he started all over again.

"You do this all the time. Looking, looking, right, left, up,
down, behind, all the time! If you don't, '109' rata-tat-tat, and
you finished. Collar and tie make neck very sore; use scarf.
Watch for your condensation trail. If you make trail come down
lower. Don't eat peas, have a good piss, then like me you have
medals. Looking keeps you warm and gives exercise. That's
monkey business. Now we go to see Edward and Quentin."

So the four of us set off down the taxi track to visit Mount
Farm's Intelligence Section. The hospitality was lavish, and
amidst walls covered in maps, and aerial photos sprouting
multi-coloured pins and little flags we had tea, biscuits and
cigarettes.

On the 28th May, 1941 Nebbie sent me off on my first operational flight. I had to photograph four fighter airfields in the
vicinity of Antwerp, then Eindehoven, Rotterdam and the
Hook of Holland. The weather was clear and navigation
consisted of reading my map from 27,000 feet, with everything
visible for miles around. It was not difficult to cover the towns,
switch on the cameras and do a few runs up and down. I found
it difficult from five miles up to be sure I had flown over an
airfield. I flew over each airfield three times with my cameras
well on before and after, rather than run the risk of missing one.
The result was that I covered each airfield three times!

The PRU Spitfires of early 1941 were modified Mark
V fighters. Guns and radio were removed, and an odd assort-
ment of fuel tanks fitted. The standard main tank of the fighter

carried 87 gallons, behind the engine and in front of the cockpit. PRU fitted two smaller tanks within a faired blister under each wing. Some had a camera in one wing and fuel in the other. There was also a rear tank fitted behind the cockpit. Each fuel pipe at the bottom of the cockpit had perched upon it a metal tap, resembling a butterfly. These had to be slightly moved during flight, in case any condensation froze and prevented them being turned. It was inadvisable to allow a tank to run dry, which might cause air being sucked into the system.

Extra fuel capacity was necessary because of the increased distances we flew over Occupied Europe, in order to cover the results of Bomber Command attacks, and for Intelligence purposes. The original Fighter Spitfire had endurance for one-and-a-half hours. The later PRU Spitfires could fly for six hours, enabling them to reach Berlin.

On 18th June, 1941, I did my sixth operation in Spitfire X 4497. I flew to Flensburg and Schleswig at 28,000 feet, to photograph the battleship Leipzig. It was there. The flight took 4 hours 50 minutes.

Then on 25th July I did my eighteenth sortie at 28,000 feet in X 4944 to Hamburg, Lubeck and Travemunde, covering Emden while returning. This took five hours.

By flying high we could not be seen or heard, the Merlin engine was most efficient for power and fuel consumption, and we could see where we were. The cameras, of course, photographed a larger area from height.

St Eval

On 1st August 1941, 'B' Flight took its turn on the three-month detachment to the Coastal Command airfield at St Eval, a few miles to the east of Newquay. From St Eval, Wellingtons, Whitleys and Hudsons operated by day and night, in all kinds of weather, over the Atlantic and Bay of Biscay. They attacked with guns and depth charges any U-boat found on the surface. The PRU flights covered regularly the U-boat bases at Brest, St Nazaire, La Rochelle and south to Bordeaux. Besides the ports, our main chore was photographing the port of Brest, where the battleships Scharnhorst, Gneisenau and Prince Eugene were in dock undergoing refitting. They were photographed three times a day, morning, midday and afternoon, weather permitting. Besides these targets, we covered railway marshalling yards and German airfields.

A sortie to Brest took around one hour forty minutes: a sortie to Bordeaux, in the south of our area, four-and-a-half hours. If the photographic interpreters noticed smoke coming from a battleship's funnel, or camouflage net moved, a minor flap ensued at the Admiralty. If the next morning's sortie showed all was as usual, the flap subsided. Besides the anti-aircraft guns guarding Brest, there was a fighter base at Guipavas, eight miles east of Brest. However, the main obstacle to a successful sortie was the weather. St Eval was much at the mercy of weather coming in from the Atlantic. Cold fronts, warm fronts, occluded fronts, with high winds, low cloud and rain, affected south-west England and swept over the Brest peninsula.

Before we left Benson, Whisky got himself posted to a Polish squadron. Keith Bailey had been hijacked by Alistair Taylor and was now in a Benson Flight. We were joined by F/O Ron Acott and P/O Bennet as replacements.

In a house overlooking Watergate Bay and close to the airfield were the Intelligence, photographic developing and printing, and first stage interpretation sections, presided over by F/Lt Brown and P/O Boggis.

On 18th August 1941 it was my turn to do the midday sortie to Brest. It had been a foul morning at St Eval. An occluded front with low cloud, high winds and rain kept us playing dominoes in the flight hut. At eleven o'clock we all piled into the flight transport and headed for the met office. Their advice was that Brest was clear but would not be so for long. The front now over Cornwall was moving south-east. Brest would be clear for a few hours before the front reached the French coast. Nebbie decided the flight should go at once, as there probably would be no afternoon flight. Conditions on return would be better as the front would have passed through St Eval.

I took off in Spitfire N 3111, 'the Brest Express'. This aircraft had a wooden Rotol three-bladed prop, and a tank in the port wing; it was mainly used for Brest due to its limited range.

I took off in rain, and found myself in cloud at 300 feet. This was a first-time situation for me. I was out of Woodley less than a year ago. My four hours of instrument flying had been done in a plywood Link Trainer in comfort, and only a few feet above the floor. Now I was being buffeted about in solid rain, in turbulent cloud, water dripping from the cockpit canopy, climbing at a wildly fluctuating airspeed, shooting up in an updraught at 5,000 feet a minute, then violently down again. I was in a dark grey cumulo-nimbus, watching for dear life my jerking, bobbing, tilting, artificial horizon. My engine temperature was dropping — close the radiator shutter! The airspeed fluctuated between 100 mph at one moment to 150 mph the next. I was gaining height, climbing erratically. I prayed "Jesus Christ, get me out of this!" Miraculously things got better! At 20,000 feet I was climbing in less turbulence. The surrounding cloud got brighter. At 25,000 feet I was cold, and in calm cirrus cloud. At 28,000 feet I was out in bright blue sky, the sun shining, the blue sea below, and the Brest peninsula bathed in sunlight ahead.

I crossed over at Lannilis, a small port west of Morlaix. I was well ahead of the front, with green fields below. I headed for the fighter airfield, Guipavas. I flew over at 28,000 feet and turned starboard, switched on the cameras, and headed west for the docks. Up came the black, red and white puffs of bursting flak; some below, some above, but behind me mostly. I put my nose down, lost 1,000 feet and gained extra speed. The flak burst behind me. I turned south to cover the Seaplane base. Would they be shooting at me if there was a fighter up? Cameras still running I turned north to cross the docks and fly up the river with its concrete U-boat pens. There was a loud bang, as though I was in an iron bath-tub hit by a sledge hammer. A near miss, I hoped. I might have been peppered by shrapnel. The engine and oil temperatures were steady. If I had got a direct hit my worries would have been over. Press on! I was over the U-boat pens. All instruments steady. The flak was behind me. Camera off! I lost height to 25,000 feet, gaining speed. Watching my tail in my rear view mirror. Head in the canopy blister looking behind à la Whisky. Heading now, straight for Dodman Point. I was closing with the high cirrus. Once inside I would be invisible. Over the Brittany coast, still at 25,000 feet. The front had moved further over the Channel. I put my nose down. Speed 250 mph and losing height. It got bumpy. I was in rain, at 18,000 feet. I didn't care, I was invisible and doing 300 mph on the clock.

Because I had no radio there was no way I could be assisted in making a descent through cloud, over the land. I had to get below the cloud over the sea and well before the Cornish coast. I was in cloud at 10,000 feet. At 5,000 feet I saw in a break in the low cloud, the dark blue-grey sea. I pushed the nose down and lost height descending in the gap below the low cloud and heading for the Cornish coast. Visibility about four miles in the rain. I was down to 500 feet below cloud. To my port I saw a dim outline of land. It was either Dodman or Nare Point. It didn't matter which. Straight ahead, hit the coast and keep going north. I was now at 600 feet in rain, and heading for St Eval. I was flying over the excavation mounds of tin mines. St Austel to my right. Still raining but visibility three to four miles. I beat up the Intelligence Section, to let Brown and Boggis know I was back, and to get the chemical stews bubbling for my film. I was in the St Eval circuit, raining but no one around, cloud base 900 feet. PRAFTU! Wheels down and locked, flaps down, landed.

Nebbie and Sydney came out of the Flight hut under umbrellas. The two 'Bs' arrived in their car. A successful sortie of one hour thirty-five minutes. It was Ron Acott's turn next, probably in the early morning. I grew quite fond of N 3111.

It was early in our detachment that Sydney went missing. He was doing an early morning Brest and failed to return. The St Eval radar had tracked him almost to Brest but there was no radar contact thereafter. It was not until some months later that news came through via the Red Cross that Sydney was a prisoner in Stalag Luft III at Sagan, about 100 miles south-east of Berlin. Apparently he had been shot down. His involvement in the escape of 75 prisoners, through a deep-dug tunnel, the shooting by order of Hitler of some 50 escapees after being captured, and Sydney's subsequent adventures, are fully described by Alan Burgess in his book **The Longest Tunnel** (Bloomsbury). Another PRU Spitfire pilot, F/O Gunn of 'E' Flight went missing in July 1942, and was imprisoned at Sagan. He escaped via the tunnel, but was among the 50 that were subsequently recaptured and shot on Hitler's orders.

It was very rarely when someone failed to return from an operation that we knew why. It was usually months later that news might come through via the Red Cross or from a prison camp. To be shot down at 25,000 feet, and crash into the ground left little to identify. An engine failure, or loss of control in bad weather over the sea would leave no trace. The same over land might result in a forced landing and being taken prisoner. Whatever happened would be recorded as 'missing', and written in chalk on the ops room board.

CHAPTER 7

Return to Benson

AT the beginning of November 1941, 'B' Flight returned to Mount Farm. After dinner, while I sat in the Benson anteroom, Keith Bailey walked in. He filled me in with the news; Higson, Charles-Jones and Bowles had gone missing. As with Sydney there was no news of any of them.

Keith enthused over the latest PR Spitfire. The old multi-tank Spitfires had now been replaced by the latest, which carried fuel in both integral wing tanks. Because we carried no guns, the area between the main spars and the wing leading edges were 'empty', so each became a fuel tank with its filler cap at the wing tip. I cannot remember the new fuel capacity; it was possibly 90-gallons in each wing, plus the standard 87-gallon main fuselage tank. The aircraft was cleaner and without the jungle of pipes and metal butterflies. A VHF radio was now installed behind the cockpit, together with the oxygen bottles and two 36" focal length vertical cameras. These innovations caused the aircraft's centre of gravity to be moved further aft. This made the Spitfire unstable in tight turns, an inconvenience on the rare occasions when there was a 109 on your tail.

It was about this time that Nebbie was posted as the CO of a Coastal Command Beaufighter Squadron. They operated over the Dutch coastal waters, shooting up German shipping and their escorting 'E'-boats. 'B' Flight was taken over by Flt Lt Freddie Ball DFC, another ex-Cranwell cadet. I was lucky that my first two years in PRU were under two such officers. They were always cheerful, good natured, and expected the best from their pilots. We were friends. They both influenced me throughout my flying career over the next thirty-eight years. It was not what they did, because we all did the same operations. The nature of PR operations was that you were always alone. It was their attitude of 'press on regardless', while at the same time being aware of their pilots' limitations.

We were not the only flight operating from Mount Farm. Sqn Ldr Tony Hill, DSO, DFC had his flight on the opposite side of the field. We all met in 'briefing' On murky days when no ops were done, or when waiting for a sortie to return, Edward and Quentin plied us with tea, Huntley and Palmer ginger nuts and cigarettes.

Tony carried out a successful low-level sortie photographing a new type of radar installation, situated at Bruneval on the coast south of Fecamp. It had a large black dish, much like the TV dishes fixed to many of today's houses. The 'boffins' were very pleased with the photos, but not satisfied. They wanted the whole box of tricks with the dish. A seaborne commando raid succeeded in capturing the equipment, returning with it in the landing craft.

Tony did another low-level sortie to a tank repair depot at Creusot, south of Paris, shortly after it had been bombed in daylight by Lancasters. He was shot down by flak and died on his way to hospital. It seemed to us at the time that a day or two delay in sending the low-level sortie would have yielded the same information with less risk.

The few months I had been with PRU were during the summer. The weather had been mostly fine. My two long sorties to Flensberg and Travemunde had been in clear sunny weather. Navigation was not a problem. At St Eval, while there were the usual eastward-moving fronts from the Atlantic, they gave plenty of cloud, turbulence and heavy rain, but were predictable in their movement and passed over St Eval and western France rapidly.

On 9th November 1941 I was despatched from Mount Farm to photograph Chemnitz, 600 miles from Benson. The met office forecast the route would be covered by an occluded frontal system, which meant low, medium and high cirrus cloud in large quantities. The high wind at 26,000 feet was estimated as 50 mph from the south-west most of the way. The frontal system would reach Chemnitz within the next three hours. The navigation system to get me to Chemnitz, when it was most unlikely I would see the ground for three-quarters of the flight, was called 'dead reckoning', The only navigation aids carried in a PRU Spitfire were a magnetic compass, a wrist watch, a map and your own 'nous'. The RAF had a primitive navigation 'computer'. You marked on a panel your airspeed and track, also wind speed and direction, turned a knob, and you obtained a heading to steer which compensated for the wind speed, and also obtained a ground speed. These simple calculations were written on a piece of card; on the reverse was the information for getting back home. You drew a line on a one-in-a-million-scaled map between Benson and the target, and marked it off in 100-mile portions. You stuffed the map and the piece of card in your flying boot, or put the map under a thigh and the card behind your Sutton harness straps and set off. One comfortable thought was that getting back to England was easier than finding an aerodrome, factory or marshalling yard somewhere in Germany.

I climbed to 26,000 feet, passing over partially clouded north London, then getting a sight of Southend pier, then in solid cloud which broke up over a large estuary, which put me nearly on track over the Scheldt. No more ground seen for the next hour, flying at 26,000 feet in the occluded front, and holding my calculated heading. I came out of cirrus cloud with the earth clear below, and ahead of me a sprawling city. The met forecasters had been right. I turned on my cameras to do a few runs. I checked my map. The place was too big, the railway lines came at different angles, it was not Chemnitz but Leipzig! Fifty miles off-track! I turned south and after 15 minutes was over Chemnitz. Getting back was easier. I was in cloud for an hour. I recognised through a lucky break in the clouds the Rhine near Dusseldorf. The front had moved east during the last two-and-a-half hours. I next saw Antwerp below and the Dutch coast. England was too big to miss. Nose down, 300 mph on the clock. Then over Margate at 5,000 feet, west along the Thames and 2,500 feet at the Staines gasometer, Windsor Castle, Henley, and landed at Mount Farm after five-and-a-half hours.

On 29th December 1941 I was sent in AB 812 to photograph Salzburg and Berchtesgarten, which lay ten miles south. Perhaps 'intelligence' were hoping to get a photo from 27,000 feet of Hitler in his garden. Once again Dead Reckoning got me there and back, through much the same weather as 9th November. The duration of this sortie was six hours. Why did they want photos of Salzburg?

Tony and I

On 9th January 1942, F/O Tony Barber and myself flew our Spitfires to Perranporth airfield, refuelled and took off for Gibraltar. Our route was west of the Brest peninsula, then direct to Corunna, down the Portuguese coast, over Cadiz and then Gibraltar. We flew separately at 27,000 feet, in clear skies, and landed 20 minutes apart, after a flight of 1,100 miles in 3 hours 30 minutes.

We stayed in a hotel on the main drag. The day after our arrival we started our photographic sorties. The intelligence were looking for evidence in harbours and inlets that revealed they were being used to revictual U-boats operating in the Med.

From our hotel room overlooking the shops, came a perpetual cacophony of drivers banging on their car doors. They were not allowed to use their horns in case spies might honk out coded signals to other spies. I had brought an Everyman edition of Spinoza's propositions of the proof that God exists. This occupied our attention in the early evenings before we set off to have *omelette aux fines herbes* in a nearby restaurant. The omelettes made with seagulls' eggs were fishy, and the *fines herbes* seaweedy.

We finished our reconnaissance flights over the Spanish and Algerian coasts in fourteen days. For our return flight to the UK on 25th January, the met forecast 'heavy cloud over Spain, with strong westerly winds at height. The weather would improve further north'. The Gib met office suffered the same paucity of information as those in the UK. We were flying the new integral wing tank Spitfires.

Tony took off first at 0900 hours, and I followed fifteen minutes later. Our route was direct to Corunna, climbing to 25,000 feet, then across the Bay of Biscay to pass west of the Brest peninsula, and then Perranporth. We would refuel and get to Benson in time for lunch.

After take-off I was immediately in cloud and climbed in solid cloud to 25,000 feet. I was still in cloud so I climbed to 27,000 feet. I was surrounded by the whiteness of cloud without a trace of sunlight filtering through. Then after flying for two-and-a-half hours, through a break in the cloud I saw a coastline and a small port, before entering more cloud. I could have been over Bilbao or Santander. Either of these gave me a ground speed of about 210 mph, but what was much worse I was 300 miles east of Corunna. I decided to 'press on regardless'. Things must get better. I was really worried. If I kept my current heading I could end up over Cherbourg or even Le Havre. I would have been tracked by German radar and an easy, slow-moving target for fighters. If I tried to regain my correct track I would be flying more into the strong wind from my port side, reducing my ground speed even further. I kept going. Then after 10 minutes I was suddenly out of the cloud, flying beneath a sheet of grey cirro stratus at 25,000 feet with the west coast of France 50 miles away on my right. The thing that frightened me was there were no shadows. Everything was dim, in a haze of ochre. Was I in a high-level sand storm? The sea, the land were as if at early evening. I was cocooned in my thin aluminium cockpit, five miles above the earth, the Merlin engine giving a steady, powerful note. I could only 'press on'. Was the unusual condition of shadowless ochre-tinged twilight the prelude to 'The Second Coming'?

I became occupied with the problem of 'did I have enough fuel?' I was crawling along at 200 mph some 300 miles east of my track for 'Blighty', and in danger of flying over St Nazaire and then Cherbourg. There was no cloud below. I passed over the Ile de Re, and decided to avoid being blown further east and holding my track to pass over St Nazaire, then St Malo.

I held my course, and passed between St Nazaire and Angers; Rennes ahead on my right. Then I saw a thin light-blue streak of sky from west to east. The pall of cirrus was ending. I was 90 miles from St Malo. Ahead I could now see a bright blue sky; then the bright blue sea and St Malo. I knew now that I would run out of fuel. My ground speed was too slow, battling against a strong wind from my port side. I was over St Malo at 25,000 feet, blue sea and blue sky, but my fuel gauges getting lower and lower. 'Jersey, Guernsey, Alderney and Sark' of my school days, lay in a dark blue sea, wreathed by the white foam of breaking waves. The sun shone in a blue sky. To my right was Cherbourg. The engine stopped.

I had 90 miles to glide to reach Portland Bill. I put the propellor into coarse pitch, reduced speed to 90 mph, and descended in silence. I did not have a radio fitted, and I had little hope that anybody had me on their radar. I kept slowly descending in complete silence and hoping that I could make the coast. I could ditch near a beach. On my map was marked an airfield west of Weybridge. I was fairly sure it was unused and would be obstructed by stakes to stop gliders landing. I crept slowly closer to the Dorset coast, one hundred miles east of my destination! I came over the coast west of Portland Bill at 3,000 feet. I glided over the small airfield. It was staked. I was now at 2,500 feet and had only a few seconds to find a place to land. I turned back to the coast. As I crossed it I saw an empty stone-walled field rising very steeply to a lane with an overlooking farm house. No time to do anything but land.

PRAFTU! No fuel, no engine, propellor useless. Flaps down with the last of the air pressure. Trimmed. Undercarriage fell down, two little indicators popped up. Over the stone wall, stick back and landed, rolling 100 yards up a steep incline and coming to stop in mud opposite a five-bar gate. I jumped out of the cockpit and pissed under the port wing, then got two stones from the dry wall and placed them behind the undercarriage wheels. The amazed farmer's wife let me use the telephone. A policeman eventually arrived in a van from Weymouth, and kindly drove me all the way to RAF Warmwell, a fighter station. The Wing Commander said he would fly my Spitfire out of the field. I said "Yes sir". He set off in a 15 cwt truck with two erks, a hand pump and two drums of fuel. In the meantime I phoned Benson ops, informed them of my arrival and asked if there was any news of Tony. There wasn't. Years later I recognised a photo of Tony, looking older and wiser. He was Chancellor of the Exchequer in the Heath government!

Nothing to report

At midnight on 11th February 1942, the three battleships, the Scharnhorst, Gneisenau and Prinz Eugen escaped from Brest. No 1 PRU had been photographing them three times a day, weather always permitting, for over a year. The German met office had accurately forecast foul weather over the area Brest, English Channel and the North Sea. The battleships sailed at full speed and were not discovered until they reached the vicinity of Boulogne, protected by a pall of low cloud and rain, and a swarm of 109s and 190s.

They were attacked with torpedoes by Fairey Swordfish biplanes. Mines were laid ahead of them off the Belgian coast; they were damaged, but managed to limp into north German ports. PRU was unable to get any photographs due to the bad weather along the German coast.

On 18th February I was detailed to fly at low level along the German coast to Brunsbuttel, then up the Schleswig coast, past Husum to the Sylt on the Danish border 35 miles west of

Flensburg, looking for battleships. I took off, flying AA 794. The weather was not foul but impossible. Mount Farm to Clacton had broken cloud at 4,000 feet, but past Clacton I was in thick cloud and gingerly descended to get below. I came out of low stratus at 300 feet. The sea was dark blue-grey and calm. I hit the Dutch coast near Texel and then followed the Frisian Islands eastward. I pulled up into the cloud once or twice to find myself below a layer of medium cloud at 4,000 feet, so back down to 300 feet. One Frisian island looked much like another. After 1 hour 40 minutes I was over a large expanse of water, which I took to be the Elbe estuary. Then I suddenly found myself over a coastline running north. I was north of Brunsbutel, or so I hoped.

I turned north to fly up the Schleswig coast. The low cloud broke up, the visibility rose to ten miles, with medium cloud at 5,000 feet. No sun shone. I climbed to 3,000 feet to get a better view. Flat islands, like pancakes, dotted the coast. I saw a few houses, a church, but no cars and no battleships. I passed a grey, wet Hussum on my right. No 109s or 190s; perhaps all were fog-bound at their airfields. At the causeway between the mainland and Sylt, I turned back. I was fed up. I had done the whole trip with low engine revs and low boost. There was no hurry. I had plenty of fuel. I headed south over the same dull, flat wet pancakes. I decided to enter the bay which had Wilhelmshaven on the west side and Bremerhaven on the east. I was now down to 300 feet with visibility about half-a-mile. I slowed down to 140 mph, in order to give myself more time peering ahead. I was over snow-covered land. The black skeletons of trees stood in the snow. I passed a small group of black farm buildings. Where was I? Either near Cuxhaven or Wilhelmshaven. There were acres of flat virgin snow over what might be the sea. A dark grey shape loomed to my left, and then another dimly ahead at my level. Balloons! I immediately did an about-turn at 300 feet and headed north. I turned for home and followed the Frisians to Texel, still at 300 feet. I turned for Clacton, the cloud base rose over the North Sea. I flew over

Clacton at 500 feet and headed for Mount Farm and landed after a flight of 5 hours 15 minutes.

Two days later, in cloudless blue skies and from 27,000 feet, the Scharnhorst was photographed in Wilhelmshaven by Flt Lt Gordon Hughes, DFC.

'F' Flight to St Eval

On 26th March 1942, Freddie Ball took 'F' Flight to St Eval. We had several recently joined pilots who came to us from our OTU (Operational Training Unit) at Dyce.

I give here a list of 'F' Flight pilots from my log book, to show a typical complement of pilots. They were not in the Flight all together, at any one time.

'F' Flight during March 1942 to September 1942.

Flt Lt A H W Ball	Posted to 4 PRU as CO 9/'42
F/O M Anderson	Posted to 4 PRU 9/'42
F/O Vandam	Posted to L Flight 7/'42
F/O Ayres	Missing 4/'42 (St Bruic)
F/O Furniss	Posted Sqn Ldr 5/'43
P/O Devreux	Missing (Bremerhaven) 8/'42. Prisoner
F/O Stewart	Posted PR Mosquitos 5/'42. DFC 7/'42. Killed 1/'45
P/O Vant Sant	Posted Thornaby 3/'43
P/O Donaghill	Posted Gibraltar 10/'42
Sgt Miller	Missing (Bordeaux) 5/'42
Sgt Henry	Missing (St Bruic) 4/'42
Sgt Dixon	Posted 8 OTU Dyce 7/'42, then Gib Met Flight 5/'43
Sgt O'Connell	Missing (NW Germany) 8/'42
Sgt Wright	Missing (Cuxhaven) 8/'42
Sgt Snowdon	Posted Malta 8/'42
Sgt Lewis	Posted Malta PRU. Killed 8/'43
Sgt MacGregor	Transferred to USAAF

Now that the three battleships had left Brest we were rid of a considerable chore. We still covered all the ports on the west coast of France, watching the comings and goings of U-boats. There were airfields and railway junctions to be covered as well as the minor ports on the north Brittany coast.

On 10th April 1942 I was despatched by Freddie for another stint at Gibraltar. I flew R 7055, one of the remaining multi-tank Spitfires without a radio, permanently kept at St Eval. The day after I arrived at Gib, the Met office predicted low stratus over the Moroccan coast as far south as Mogador.

I was sent off to take low level photos of the French naval base at Casablanca. I took off and followed the coast from Rabat, flying at about 200 feet; came to Casablanca, photographed the destroyers along the outer wall, turned over the port and got a good photo of the battleship Jean Bart, which was undergoing refit. The next few days I spent photographing the Spanish coast up to Barcelona, over the Balaeric Islands and along the Algerian coast to Oran and Mostaganem, soon to be the scene of the 'Torch' invasion of North Africa.

On my last flight I was peacefully flying along the Spanish Moroccan coast taking snaps from 15,000 feet in the lovely sunshine, when opposite Mellila I saw a tiny black worm emerging from a join in the long engine cowling between me and the propellor. It slowly crept towards the cockpit. It was a trickle of black engine oil. I was lucky, if the oil leak had been lower down the engine block, I would have been unaware of it until it was too late. I turned immediately for Gib, 100 miles away. The engine sounded sweet, but for how long? I reduced power in the hope of lessening the rate of oil loss. I slowly descended. The oil by now covered the cockpit canopy with a thin dark film. I had no radio in R 7055, and no confidence that Gib radar had me or anyone else on their screen. Most of the chaps would be on the beaches; others, after beer, a good lunch, and more beer, would be snoozing in cool caverns.

I jettisoned my cockpit canopy. Should I turn upside down and bale out? No! Even if I did so, I was 30 miles from the Rock and 4,000 feet up. I did not think anyone would see me. I would float in my seat-pack dinghy until Kingdom Come. The engine sounded rough, but still gave a little power. I pushed the throttle fully open, with little effect. I was 2,500 feet on the east side of the Rock with the engine sounding like stones being shaken in a metal bucket. I was abeam the end of the runway at 800 feet. I turned to line up. PRAFTU! The undercarriage dropped down and locked. A red Very light shot up from the runway. "DON'T LAND!" I turned sharply to my left at 200 feet. Behind me was a Wellington on final approach. I had no power, no height, so I ditched about 75 yards off the beach. The nose sank like a stone. I undid my Sutton harness and parachute straps, inflated my Mae West, pushed with my legs and shot to the surface. I was immediately grabbed by half-a-dozen swimmers, pushed into my inflated seat-type dinghy, and towed amidst much laughter and cheers to the beach.

That afternoon R 7055 was dragged out tail first. The magazines were watertight, and the film satisfactorily printed. A few nights later I was flown back to Plymouth in a Sunderland Flying Boat and I arrived back at St Eval's mess in time for lunch.

CHAPTER 8

A Sortie to Hamburg

IN August 1942 'F' Flight returned to Mount Farm. Bomber Command had increased its raids on industrial and strategic targets in north Germany. Our routes to this area were over the Fresians to the Elbe estuary, or inland from the coast via Emden, Wilhelmshaven, Bremen, and Hamburg. It was no use sending a photo Spitfire just after a raid. Fires would still be burning, with black smoke rising to 10,000 feet above the area. Two or three days later the fires would subside and reveal the bomb damage. The increase in bombing led to an increase in PRU sorties, which also resulted in an increase of Spitfires being intercepted and some shot down. There was talk, and it remained just talk, of a fighter escort for a PRU Spit. This suggestion was quite impracticable. Any mêlée with 109s before reaching the target would put paid to the sortie. You needed peace and quiet and not a circus. Bombed areas required flying a pattern to obtain a photographic mosaic, which could take up to 20 minutes. The interpreters needed an overlap between one exposure and the next. This was obtained by the pilot setting the interval between exposures when he switched on his cameras. The interpreters peered through a stereoscope, a twin-lensed magnifying 'gizmo' placed over two adjacent photos. They then got a 3D image of the area.

While flying up and down over a target you were shot at by anti-aircraft guns. If you had not been intercepted before the target you could be afterwards. I comforted myself that if flak came up it was unlikely that a 109 was up dodging its own flak. If no flak then there might be a 109 around.

On 18th August in Spitfire AB 307, I did a sortie to Hamburg, bombed three nights before. Blue sky, blue sea, blue Spitfire all the way. I flew at 28,000 feet straight from Mount Farm to the Elbe estuary. For once the hot air, ducted from the under-wing radiator, kept me just above freezing point. The outside temperature was −30 degrees centigrade. I was wearing battledress, a sweater, silk scarf, flying boots to tuck my maps into, leather gloves and a Mae West from which I had removed the kapok stuffing. This last modification allowed me to do the 'Whisky' easily. At the Elbe estuary I turned south-east for the last 50 miles leg to Hamburg, keeping a continuous lookout for an interception. I had decided to do two runs over the east of the river, and three runs over the west side, covering an area of roughly 25 by 20 miles. I switched on my cameras, (setting the appropriate time interval) for the first run. Looking around all the time. Near the end of the run flak exploded behind me, a bunch of white, red and black carnations suddenly appeared and slowly defused and blew away in the wind. Another bunch slightly closer appeared. I turned to fly back parallel to my first run. I lost 1,000 feet, so going faster. The next bunch exploded where I had been, and above me. In this way I completed five runs. I climbed to gain height and lose speed, and lost height to gain speed. Thus I hoped to make it difficult for the gunners to set the bursting time for the shells. At the very end of my last run, over the south-west part of Hamburg, and at 28,000 feet, there was a God-Almighty 'BANG', like those over Brest. Two jagged holes appeared, each the size of a golf ball, in my starboard wing, halfway between me and the wing tip. I immediately turned west for Den Helder, 220 miles away.

I would soon know if I had any hope of getting anywhere but down. The engine sounded sweet. My oil pressure remained steady. Engine temperature was constant. I was not on fire. It seemed I was lucky. Shrapnel through an empty part of the wing.

I just had to head west for the Dutch coast. Then across 180 miles of the North Sea to Clacton, then Mount Farm. From 28,000 feet I could see 100 miles all round. I knew the route well enough. A spread of high cirrus would give me a hiding place, but the sun shone in a blue cloudless sky. I carried out the 'Whisky' drill by habit. Alone, and sitting in a small cockpit six miles up, I was kept busy looking, always looking. I mentally worked out a ground speed. I was heading to pass south of Bremerhaven on track to Groningen and Den Helder. I noticed in the little rear view mirror of my starboard canopy blister, a tiny black dot. Funny! I did not remember seeing a blemish in my perspex canopy before. I looked again: it was now two little black dots. I pushed forward the small over-ride lever on my quadrant, to allow me to open up to emergency boost. I was coming up to the south of Bremerhaven. The dots were bigger, but still dots. Abeam Wilhelmshaven there were two tiny little aeroplanes. Then they became two yellow-nosed Messerschmit 109s. No 2 was on the starboard side of his No 1, and, I thought, too close. No 1 was slightly to my right, not directly behind me. I kept going straight and level and gave no indication that I had seen them. I was a sitting duck. I did not put my head in the blister to look at them. No 1 would see my head and know I had seen him. I just kept heading west, straight and level. They got closer. I could see the bulge of their super-charger air intake on the port side of the nose cowlings. When would No 1 open fire? No 2 was still too close to No 1 who was still not directly behind me. They got closer. I yanked my stick back, with starboard aileron and top rudder. I turned through 360 degrees, heading west. They were nowhere to be seen! Then I saw below me on my port side a 109 spiralling down. Was he in a spin? I did not see him again That left only one.

I was now abeam Emden. He got closer. I turned sharply to port and headed for him. He shot past. I immediately headed west and lost height to 20,000 feet, going fast downhill. At a lower altitude I felt I would have more control in tight turns.

Then below and around me I noticed small puffs. They were exploding shells from medium flak, 'having a go'.

At 20,000 feet heading west coming up to Groningen, No 1 was getting on my tail. I turned towards him, continued the turn to head west. We repeated this dance: as he came in I turned into him, and continued west. We were over the Zuider Zee. We were going round and round at 20,000 feet. He was firing at me. Flashes came from his cannon which fired through his spinner. I held the Spit in a tight turn to port, with full throttle and the whole airframe juddering on the point of stall. He could not turn tight enough to give him sufficient deflection to shoot me down. At one stage I was on one side of the turn and he on the opposite side. I was out-turning him! He had stopped firing, perhaps out of ammunition. I looked at him and he looked at me! He suddenly flipped out of the turn and headed for the Fatherland.

I headed for Clacton going fast downhill. I crossed Clacton at 500 feet. I came down over lanes and fields and a Green Line bus, at 200 feet. To hell with 'Flying restrictions over built-up areas'. I rattled the windows at Chelmsford, South Mimms and High Wycombe, and landed after a sortie of 4 hours 15 minutes.

No 4 PRU

In September 1942 'F' Flight became No 4 PRU, and set up in a Nissen hut on the periphery of Benson. Freddie was our CO, and a batch of new pilots arrived to make up our establishment. Flt Lt Wally Walton was to be in charge of the photographic section, and F/Sgt McNiece was in charge of maintenance and our ground crew. We were destined for Algeria, once the Allied Torch Operation had been successful.

Our pilots were F/Os Ted Cowan DFC, Buchanan DFC, RNZAF, Raines, Clarke RAAF, MacKenzie RCAF, Clyne, F/Sgts Sammy Sampson, Iredale, O'Connell, and Taylor RAAF. We collected our maps of the area, flew practice sorties, went to Henley together for drinks, and awaited the outcome of

'Torch'. Freddie got married in Henley parish church, and I was his best man!

On 6th November we flew our six Spitfires to Gibraltar and waited. Our other pilots, the photo section, and our ground crews were going by boat, and we would meet up with them in Maison Blanche, the airfield for Algiers, which was our base. According to my log book we landed at Maison Blanche on 16th November. I had flown in two days before and found the place occupied by American commandoes. I spent the night in an airfield hut, during which I was woken by a crowd of American soldiers looking for somewhere to sleep. I instantly recognised one of them. It was A R Evill ... we had been at Cheltenham together five years before. He was not an American soldier, neither were his companions. They were a British regiment dressed up as Americans, in order not to ruffle French feathers.

The next day our Spitfires flew in from Gib. Freddie disappeared into the hinterland and came back after an hour. He had commandeered the mansion of a nearby vineyard. We moved in and the place became the home of 4 PRU. That same afternoon Wally, his photographers with their developing and printing caravan, and F/Sgt McNiece and his ground crews, arrived. They had been waiting on board ship in the harbour. We were operating the next day.

Tunis and Bizerta, 400 miles east of Algiers, were photographed daily. They were entry ports and airfield for German reinforcements. A fleet of Ju 52s arrived every evening from Sicily, and returned during the night. We covered regularly the area west of the Libyan border through which the 8th Army was advancing. The 1st Army was to meet up with the 8th Army and push the enemy out of Tunisia.

One night shortly after settling in our mansion, the airfield was bombed. A bomb fell near the hangar in which Wally had set up his photo laboratory. One of our men was killed and another wounded. A week later the airfield was again bombed at night. Two of our Spitfires were hit by incendiaries and burnt to ashes. The next morning Ted Cowan and I flew to Gib in a

Dakota. That evening we got a lift in a Sunderland flying boat to Plymouth. We took a train to Reading, and arrived at Benson in the afternoon. The next morning we flew two Spitfires to Gibraltar and arrived at Maison Blanche in time for tea at our mansion.

No 4 PRU was combined with the USAAF flying PR Lightnings, the whole operation being under the command of Col Eliot Roosevelt. The Lightnings had some technical troubles, which necessitated Freddie and Col Roosevelt working in close co-operation. It was some time in early 1942 that F/O Larsen joined us at Benson. He was an American who had come over on his own initiative to Britain after Pearl Harbour. He volunteered for the RAF, and after his pilot training was duly posted to No 1 PRU on Spitfires. We were pleasurably surprised to meet him again in Algiers. He had transferred to the USAAF PR Lightnings for the first US operation in Europe. Larsen was decorated by Col Roosevelt. He was killed during the fierce fighting in southern Tunisia, while carrying out a photographic mission near Maknassy.

We lost three pilots in December. F/O Clark went missing on a Tunis sortie (later believed to be a prisoner), and F/Sgt Iredale went missing on a sortie to Medjez el Bab. On 31st December F/Sgt Taylor failed to return from a sortie to Foum Tatahoum in southern Tunisia, through which the 8th Army was advancing. Then one afternoon in early January a most tragic accident occurred. Ted Cowan, returning from Tunis and Bizerta, was on final approach at Maison Blanche, when just as he touched down on the runway threshold a Hurricane fighter landed on top of him. He was killed instantly. No inquiry or investigations could alter the fact of his death. He was buried with full military honours. We had lost a most popular and experienced pilot as a result of carelessness.

On 21st January I was doing the late afternoon Tunis, Bizerta sortie. Flying at 30,000 in a clear blue sky. I had completed covering the port and airfield at Bizerta, and had set course for 'home' (Maison Blanche). About 2,000 feet below me, coming in my direction, were two pairs of FW190s. I immediately called up the Spitfire wing stationed at Bone on the Algerian Tunisian border. I got no answer. I did this so that Freddie would know what had happened if I did not return. I kept going west, we were closing at 700 mph, when quite unexpectedly one pair broke away and dived down into the dusk below. Had they seen me? The other pair flew below and passed me. Then as if suddenly aware of me they swooped up to get behind me. I kept going west, all levers fully forward. They just as suddenly turned to port and dived away. Panic over! Perhaps they had been on patrol and were short of fuel, or wanted to get down before light faded.

Sometime in January 1943 there was a battle in the Eastern Dorsal area, when the British 1st Army and Americans were pushing into southern Tunisia to join up with the 8th Army. The American sector met strong opposition from a German counter-attack. It was decided by Col Eliot to send three Spitfires to take oblique photos of the battle at low level. F/Os Raines, Mackenzie and myself would go. However Freddie wanted to 'earn his keep', as he put it, and went in my place. So the next morning they took off at 0700 hours and headed east. The result of their sortie was that owing to broken low cloud, and medium cloud above, unfamiliarity with the rocky terrain and dried wadis, unable to distinguish between an American puff and a German puff of gun smoke, harrassed by a swarm of FW190s beating up the allied positions, F/O Raines was shot down, Freddie was chased by a FW190 who put a cannon shell through his starboard canopy blister (fortunately his head was not in it at the time), and F/O Mackenzie took refuge in medium cloud.

In early February I was posted to the OTU at Dyce. I left Algiers by troopship and arrived in the Clyde. I reported to Benson. It was booming, Spitfires and Mosquitos were parked around the periphery of the airfield, and in two large hangars. I was fortunate that there was a Spitfire to be ferried to Dyce; this saved me a train journey.

Dyce and Benson

Embryo PRU pilots were trained at 8 OTU. There was a Harvard and a Miles Master for their dual flying before going off in the Spit. Practice photograpic flights were made to the Western Isles. Flt Lt Merrifield DFC was in charge of the Mosquito conversion flight. He suggested that I converted on to Mosquitos. I preferred to remain on the Spitfire, although it already was being superceded by the Mosquito. Further, as a 'pongo' I was destined to be returned to the RTR at the end of the war.

After my stint at Dyce, both John Merrifield and myself were posted back to Benson, John to a Mosquito Squadron and myself to a Spitfire flight in 542 Sqn. One afternoon an FW190 flew into Benson dressed in RAF garb. It was there for evaluation tests and was flown by Sqn Ldr Steventon DFC. I was happy to have in the flight newly commisioned P/O Sammy Sampson DFM, American Air Medal. He told me that F/O Mackenzie had failed to return from a sortie to Cagliari shortly after I left 4 PRU. Later, towards the end of the war, I met Sammy in a pub in Shepherds Market. He was now a F/O with DFC, and as ebullient as always. A real 'press-on' type.

I also had in my flight Flt Lt Leslie Whitaker DFC. We had been friends in 1942. I was much in awe of Leslie. He had been a reporter for the local Keighley newspaper, his home town. He knew about local and national politics. He drank quantities of beer without apparent effect. He smoked cigarettes which stained his luxurious moustache and his fingers. He obtained a brief notoriety in early 1942 by landing his Spitfire downwind at Benson. The hedge bordering the road to Oxford was approaching fast. He applied his brakes too hard, the following wind got under his tail and the Spitfire flipped over onto its back. Leslie hung upside down from his Sutton harness. Remembering reports of similar situations he did nothing and awaited rescue. Others less wise had pulled the pin from their harness and fallen on their heads with the additional weight of parachute and seat-type dinghy, and broken their necks. He bruised his upper lip when his head hit the cockpit combing, so for several weeks he wore white sticking plaster instead of his luxurious 'moosh'. Later, while operating from Wick, flying over Norwegian fiords, photographing German battleships, he was shot down and landed by parachute on a snow-covered mountain. He was rescued by the Norwegian underground. A few months later he was among a small group of RAF aircrew whom the Norwegians shepherded across the frontier into Sweden, from where he was flown back to the UK and Benson.

We were flying the Mark X1 PR Spitfire: it had a two-stage supercharger which took you up to 20,000 feet, then with a 'bang' the second stage supercharger came in automatically, and took the Spitfire to 40,000 feet, and higher if you felt like it.

One morning Leslie, Sammy and myself were driven to the Experimental Establishment at Farnborough. We were to be guinea pigs in the testing of a new type of Mae West-cum-pressure jacket. I believe it was a Canadian invention. We were put into a decompression chamber, wearing the new invention. The air was sucked out, finally reaching a simulated height of 40,000 feet.

The boffins peered at us through little thick glass portholes, to check that we were still alive. Oxygen under pressure was being fed into our masks to help fill our lungs as we breathed in. When we breathed out, a system of valves diverted the pressurised oxygen into the Mae West, which filled and exerted pressure on the abdomen and chest, thus helping to evacuate the lungs. I did a sortie to Berlin at 30,000 feet and came back at 40,000 feet. The Mae West worked beautifully. From 300 miles east I saw the afternoon declining sun reflected off the English Channel, behind me dusk came creeping up over Germany. Only the latest rocket fighter could have got at me. I still did the 'Whisky' drill.

Leslie had done a couple of sorties to the Ruhr, during which he got mixed up, but ignored, with droves of Flying Fortresses, Mustangs, 109s and 190s. He felt PRU was getting dangerous, not what it had been in 'the good old days'. He suggested we get a posting to another operational unit. So in October 1943 we both applied for a posting.

On two or three occasions I had taken high-level photos of open French countryside. These seemingly uninteresting areas were required by 161 Special Duty Squadron at RAF Tempsford, when verifying an area as suitable for a landing field for its Lysander and Hudson operations, which involved both landing and picking up French agents. One of our Intelligence officers at Benson told me that Sqn Ldr Hugh Verity was in charge of the Lysander Flight operating from Tangmere at night during the moon period. I had been at Cheltenham with Hugh Verity. I telephoned Hugh, who invited me to come to Tangmere. Leslie and I flew our Spitfires, parking behind the hedge overlooked by Tangmere Cottage. We were met by Hugh Verity and Robin Hooper, McCairns and Hanky, and deemed suitable. Our postings came through in mid-November 1943.

CHAPTER 9

Tangmere Cottage

I DID my 131st and last PRU operational flight on 27th October 1943. Nine days later, Leslie and I were posted to the Lysander Flight of 161 Squadron Bomber Command, stationed at RAF Tempsford.

We were useless to anyone until we had mastered the art of flying cross-country at night without getting lost. We were determined to complete our training in a month and be operational by the end of December. We practised circuits and bumps in a small field at Somersham, near Cambridge. Twice we had one Lysander between the two of us, and on the other nights we had one each. We were training a group of French 'Joes' (French Resistance) as well as ourselves. They had been brought back to England and lived in a large country house nearby, where they had been learning how to select a pick-up field, how to send an accurate description of it to London, and how to organise the Lysander reception. They were all potential Masters of Ceremonies, in charge of laying out the three torches that served as a landing guide, and receiving and despatching the agents.

For eight nights we flew around in pitch darkness, landing and taking-off, while the Joes practised their drill. After the course they would be landed, shipped or dropped back into France.

The flare path at Somersham was laid out exactly as it would be in France. Three torches were tied to sticks, and stuck into the ground in the pattern of an 'L'. When you were land-ing, you kept the first torch, which marked the limit of the touch-down area, on the left-hand side of the aircraft. Here would gather the Master of Ceremonies and the embarking Joes with their luggage. A hundred-and-fifty yards ahead was a second light, marking the direction of the landing run; from this light there was another four hundred yards of field over which the Lysander could roll. You landed to the right of these two lights. At right-angles to the second torch and about fifty yards away was a third torch. This marked the width of the landing run.

These dark period practices were excellent training - it was darker than it was likely to be on an op. You did not use the aircraft's landing lights. You dragged your Lysander in with all flaps out and down, plenty of engine, as slow as 60 mph, stick well back. As you came abreast the first light, keeping it on your left, you chopped the throttle and the Lysander thumped on the ground and rolled between the two lights ahead. Intermittent braking, with the stick held back, brought you to rest in two hundred yards. Taxi back to the first light, keeping the engine running. Now the Joes went into their act. The back canopy was opened, luggage passed out to the reception committee. The incoming Joes scrambled down the ladder fixed to the side of the fuselage. Embarking Joes climbed in, luggage was passed up and the canopy slammed shut. The Master of Ceremonies yelled "OK", and the Lysander rolled forward. Full throttle, straight ahead between two torches, stick gently back and you were airborne after less than five minutes on the ground.

After training at Somersham, Leslie and I were sent to the school for Joes, in its large country house. Here French, Belgian and Dutch Joes were being instructed in Lysander and Hudson pick-up techniques and in the procedure for receiving arms and Joes parachuted in from Stirlings and Halifaxes. Instruction was given in French, so at first Leslie and I sat marooned in a fog of incomprehension. However, we soon picked up enough franglais to enable us to understand and even communicate. -

'*Formidable*', '*Absolument*', '*Fantastique*', and '*Impossible*'. By using these in various combinations, with suitable vocal inflections, we soon became a couple to be reckoned with. Many of the Joes spoke English, so after classes we became the recipients of fantastique tales of escape, murder and intrigue which may or may not have been true. Either way, the telling of such tales provided some kind of release from the enormous tension under which the Joes had lived before getting to England. They were all destined to return to the continent.

During our five days stay at the country house I thought I fell in love with one of the drivers, Intelligence Corps, staff car (female). I hardly spoke more than a dozen words to her. I was attracted to her in spite of her buttons, collar and tie, and powerful-looking dark brown shoes. I hid my bashfulness behind a studied indifference, bordering on dumb insolence.

One evening after dinner, Leslie and I were in a large lounge among the Joes. It was like a psychiatric ward. Everybody, including Leslie and myself, was wrapped in an impenetrable cloud of egotism, an egotism created from sheer funk and determination to survive. In order to escape from yet more stories from the Joes, we decided to play 'L'Attaque' - a favourite among the games provided for the inmates. I had always liked 'L'Attaque', with its long thin cards and soldiers on their little tin stands. We set up the board and began to play. A tall khaki figure came and stood over us. It was she. I could see the brown shoes out of which grew her long legs covered in khaki cotton stockings. I was unnerved, my eyes rigidly kept to the board. Somehow, unconsciously, I beat Leslie. She stepped closer and said, "Right — give me a game."

"Yes, alright," I said.

I looked at her. She was determined, belligerent, and had me beaten already.

"What pieces do you want?" she asked.

"French."

"Set 'em up. Audace, toujours audace — remember!"

I said nothing.

She proceeded to demolish my forces. I got annoyed and flustered. My approaching defeat was galling. She must think me a fool. Perhaps she was putting me in my place, paying me out for my rude indifference. My final humiliation came when she captured my flag, capped her piece with it and withdrew in a series of masterly moves to her own territory. She got up and walked away, leaving me to cover my embarrassment as best I could by putting the pieces back into the box. I was more in love then ever, but impotent in every sense. I wanted her to take the initiative because I was incapable. She was made inaccessible by her uniform and shoes. Two days later Leslie and I returned to Tempsford and then flew two Lysanders to Tangmere for the start of the December moon period.

The pilots of 'A' Flight lived in Tangmere Cottage, a small picturesque house with ivy on the walls and roses round the door, opposite the entrance gate and guard room of Tangmere airfield. It was the home of a Spitfire and Tempest wing; we were there on sufferance. Across two hedges and a lane from the cottage stood our four Lysanders. Wing Commander Hodges and F/O Bathgate had brought down two others.

Flight Lieutenant Robin Hooper had taken over 'A' Flight after Verity had been posted to the Air Ministry. Unfortunately Hooper's Lysander had got bogged down in mud on his pick-up field in France. Wg Cdr Hodges, the CO of 161 Squadron had come down to bring him back before Christmas. There were two other very experienced pilots from the Verity era, Flight Lieutenant Stephen Hankey and F/O MacBride. Leslie and I felt very small beer amongst these old hands. We were there for training, to watch how things were done and to keep out of the way.

Sergeant Thomas, a very young and boyish-looking airgunner, with sandy hair and a pale, freckled skin, had come down in Hodges' Lysander. Thomas was the mentor who initiated us into the mystique of 'A' Flight.

On special occasions Thomas flew on Lysander and Hudson operations, as a change from being an airgunner in parachute-dropping Halifaxes. The Hudson operated from Tempsford, landing its Joes deep into Vichy France. Much to our amazement, we learned that it landed on a well-lit grass strip at least 1,000 yards long, guarded by cohorts of armed Joes. On one occasion a Hudson got bogged in mud and had to spend the day in France, returning the next night. Similarly in the early days of 'A' Flight there had been an epic exploit by Wing Commander Pickard, whose Lysander got stuck in mud on a French landing ground and had to be dragged out by horses and hidden in a wood until nightfall. We listened to Thomas' stories in fearful fascination. However, our innate optimism made us concerned chiefly for our own futures, and the night when we would be sent on our first operation.

The Lysander Hodges brought from Tempsford was fitted with a large hook beneath its tail, something like the retractable hook used by deck landing aircraft. The idea was that the French underground should suspend a mailbag between two poles and the Lysander would use its hook to pick it up. This of course was a night operation. There were various difficulties to be overcome, apart from the mechanics of raising and lowering the hook by an operator in the rear cockpit. The bag had to be hauled aboard. It was difficult to judge the height of the aircraft between two poles. Also there was the jerk on the aircraft when the stationary bag was caught. Why not land and be done with it?

When all was well with the weather and the Joes standing by in London, a cryptic message would be broadcast at the end of the BBC six o'clock News, which was picked up by the listening Joes in France. A phrase like 'The wild geese fly high tonight', would indicate that field 'Othello' was being used that night. A following phrase 'Mary's lost her little lamb' would be the signal that another Lysander was operating to field 'Juliette'.

On nights when operations were cancelled, Hodges would send Leslie and me on practice cross-country flights. My first route was Reading, Luton and back to Tangmere. I took off at about 8 o'clock. There was plenty of cloud and rain and the night was absolutely pitch black with no moon. Soon after getting airborne and climbing to 3,000 feet I was in a state of panic. It was like flying through Guinness — black and claustrophobic. There was no sense of movement, no indication of where I was, only a steady dull hum from my Mercury engine, and a tiny dim red light attached to my Sutton harness, with which I could see my map and flying instruments. I concentrated on my altitude and speed. It was a frightening change after two-and-a-half years flying Spitfires in daylight. I kept my attention glued on the instruments, my only hope of salvation. Through a gap in the clouds I saw a single, small flickering light, the only sign that there was someone alive below me. My time for Reading was up — but where was the town? I flew around, then another flickering light — it was moving eastward. I assumed it was the light from an engine firebox, so I was over a railway line, perhaps near Reading. I flew five minutes to the east, and then ten minutes to the west, but I saw no lights I could recognise as a station. The blackout of the houses and motor cars was excellent.

It was raining. I was lost, and thoroughly frightened. How could I set course for Luton if I didn't know where I was? More cloud; more velvet blackness. I turned about and set a reciprocal course for the south coast and Tangmere. After the correct time, and flying at 2,000 feet, I suddenly saw the red flashing beacon on Tangmere airfield. I was less than five miles off track! I felt very foolish, and ashamed of my panic. The black void had unnerved me. I had been lost because I thought I was lost. I had in fact been over Reading all the time. I was apprehensive that I might get the boot from 'A' Flight after this debacle. Hodges was unconcerned and said I could have another go the first night he had a free Lysander.

A few nights later I took off again for the same route. The night was as black as before. I steered a steady course. I looked around outside, my eyes became accustomed to the dark. I trimmed the aircraft and let it fly itself. I relaxed. I began to see the dark patches of woods and lighter patches of fields. I saw three or four lights following each other, curving left and right, cars on a winding road. I recognised small rivers, jet black unless they suddenly reflected a pale flash from the moon. Trains were easy to recognise, travelling steadily in one direction. I found no difficulty in convincing myself I had reached Reading, and set course for Luton. I was beginning to enjoy myself. I found Luton easily; lights from the town, a main rail line and main road. The cloud was breaking up and the moon lighting up the fields and shining on lakes and rivers. A few stars were visible. It was easy! From now on flying at night held no terrors. You saw less, but everything you did was significant. Leslie and I did three more cross-countries each, and rapidly got the hang of it.

While Leslie and I were groping around southern England in the unfamiliar dark, pick-up operations were being done by Bathgate, Hankey, MacBride and of course Hodges. Early in the period Bathgate and MacBride went on a double Lysander operation. (One aircraft landing and taking-off followed by the other.) MacBride got lost in rain and cloud and wisely came back, but Bathgate failed to return. We supposed he was either trudging to the Spanish border and then to Gibraltar, or being looked after by Joes, and would be picked up next month. I never heard any more of Bathgate.* He has the distinction of having signed my flying log book for November 1943.

Flt Lt Stephen Hankey was of middle height with fair hair thinning on top. He seemed the sort who enjoys tooling around in an open sports car, with his dog and his wife. He lived 'out' with his family, which set him apart from the rest of us. MacBride may have been an Australian; he was tall, well-built, with the face of a boxer. Leslie and I were in considerable awe of both of them. However, by mid-period Hodges had become my hero. He was unflappable, completely in charge, and absolutely approachable. He became another Nebbie, for whom I would do anything.

On ops the pilots dressed in a strange *mélange* of civilian and RAF battle dress. If the Lysander got stuck on a landing ground

---

*See **We landed by moonlight**, by Hugh Verity, pub 1978 Ian Allan Ltd then the pilot would be looked after by the undergound. In this case it was better not to be dressed in full RAF uniform. On the other hand if the pilot was captured in civilian clothes the Germans could claim he was a spy. So we aimed to look all things to all men; a civilian for escaping, but RAF if caught. We wore non-regulation shirts, dark polo-neck sweaters, battle-dress blouse and trousers, with non-regulation shoes or boots. Most took a small bag containing a raincoat, scarf and beret. Our pockets were emptied and we carried packets of French francs, the usual escape maps printed on handkerchiefs and the inevitable small compass hidden in a button or collar stud.

The resident intelligence officers were Major Bertram, who lived nearby at Petworth, and Lieutenant John Hunt, a pianist. These two liased with London, shepherded the Joes on their arrival at Tangmere, and despatched the incoming Joes back to London.

Leslie and I met a few of the Joes during the operational nights at Tangmere Cottage. Many had lived for years on the Continent, respectable citizens with families and businesses. Others were sent to do a specific job, either on their own or in collaboration with the underground. They blew things up and killed people. In appearance they were slightly sinister, vaguely dashing, and talkative — or so they would seem during those few minutes in the drawing room at the cottage before we flew off to France.

One night Leslie came into the ops room in great excitement. He had met some Joes going out that night. One was flashing a pistol about, others opened up suitcases and displayed radio transmitters, guns and explosives. Great care was taken to ensure that the SOE (Special Operation Executive) Joes were kept separate from SIS (Special Intelligence Service). The former attacked German targets, while the latter kept a low profile as intelligence gatherers.

Towards the end of the moon period a radio message was received by London from the French underground telling us that Robin Hooper was at a field waiting to be picked up along with some Joes. Hodges was going to do this operation. On the same night Hankey and MacBride were going to another field to do a double pick-up. Hodges was taking off first, at eight o'clock, and was due back around midnight. The other two would follow at ten o'clock and get back five hours later.

At six o'clock the red scrambler telephone rang and confirmed the operations. Hodges had checked the met; a clear, starry night was forecast over southern England and most of France, with a possible risk of fog at dawn, long after the Lysanders were back. The confirmation messages were broadcast after the BBC six o'clock News.

At seven o'clock Hodges came into the ops room with his hold-all, containing his escape clothes, money, maps and first-aid kit. We persuaded him to put on his black beret. In his beret and dark blue polo neck, and a scruffy, grey mackintosh he looked a small-town Frenchman about to play boule and expecting rain. He had already cut out and marked the strip map to his field. He completed his navigation log on a piece of white card and sat down to study his route. Sergeant Booker came in with bacon and eggs and toast for Hodges, with cups of tea for all of us.

No matter how many times a pilot had flown a route, he always studied the track and checked again the flak positions and salient landmarks. The flight was half done while sitting in the ops room and quietly going over the map.

There was a noise of doors banging, French voices and scuffling from the passage outside; Hodges' Joes had arrived and were being assembled by Major Bertram and John Hunt in the drawing room. I got Hodges' parachute, and Leslie and I walked from the cottage through the main gates and behind the guard room to the waiting Lysanders. I climbed up to the cockpit and arranged the parachute in the bucket seat. We stayed outside talking to the ground crew beneath the clear star-filled sky. The moon had risen. A Humber shooting brake arrived, and out got the Joes, Bertram, Hunt and Hodges. I climbed up the undercarriage after Hodges and passed the straps of his parachute and Sutton harness over his shoulders.

Only a small red glow came from the cockpit; the Joes were in the back with their suitcases. Hodges started the engine, the Lysander purred; nothing raucous ever came from a 'Lizzie'. He taxied as we stood in silence. The Lysander had no lights. Hodges lined up with the goose-neck flares and took off.

Sergeant Thomas was alone in the ops room when we got back. Hankey and Mac were upstairs having a snooze. Thomas wound up the gramophone, and now that Hodges was away, we dared to put on a record. We only had three records: *'Venez donc chez moi je vous invite'* was the favourite, followed by *'Antilles'* and *'Rhumba Negra'*.

At nine o'clock Hankey and Mac were in the ops room going over their maps and eating baked beans on toast, while *'Venez donc chez moi'* played for the thousandth time. Hankey liked this record, while Mac seemed indifferent to all of them. I don't think he could tell one from the other.

There was more banging and more French voices from outside; half-a-dozen Joes had arrived. There seemed to be quite a party in progress. The SOE Joes were a rowdy lot and carried the usual suitcases packed with radios and dynamite.

We took the pilots' parachutes out, and waited by the Lysanders. The night was still clear with the moon rising to the south. Two Humber brakes arrived, and a gaggle of people got out. Hankey and Mac separated and climbed into their cockpits. It didn't matter which Joes got into which Lysanders as they were both going to the same field. Hankey took off first with Mac about five minutes later.

We returned to the ops room for more of *'Venez donc chez moi ...'* and cocoa. At around half-past-eleven the control tower rang to say that they had a radar blip half-way across the Channel. This was Hodges coming back. We went out to meet him and welcome Robin Hooper. There was a pall of low cloud over the area, with the moon shining hazily through; underneath the visibilty was quite good. Hodges landed, taxied in and out got two figures. We learnt later that one agent and Robin had been brought back. They were whipped off by car to London, and we settled down again in the ops room for the three-hour wait for Hankey and Mac. Hodges had changed into battledress and drank coffee at the ops table. The gramophone was silent. Hodges finished his coffee and went to lie down on the drawing room sofa, keeping Major Bertram company.

Around half-past-one the telephone rang. I answered. It was the controller in the tower. He told me that the cloud base was a hundred feet and that fog was forming with visibility down to 500 yards. I thanked him and went to tell Hodges. He was asleep. I woke him up. Both of us went outside the front door and immediately felt a dampness in the air. We could not see the tops of the dark grey trees, in the enveloping eerie phosphorescence lit by the moon above. Hodges went back to the ops room without a word. The three of us sat in silence. The phone rang. Hodges made no attempt to answer, he sat with his eyes closed and looked pale. I picked up the phone; it was the controller again. Visibility was now nil, the moon totally obscured, he estimated the fog to be about four hundred feet thick. Hodges stretched out his hand; I gave him the phone.

"Where's the nearest diversion aerodrome?" Hodges asked. There was a long answer from the controller, while Hodges quietly listened. Then he lowered the receiver to his knees and sat staring. After a long delay he spoke to the controller.

"Right, put the first aircraft into the Ford Circuit and bring the other over Tangmere. Let's hope we can talk them down." (Ford was a Fleet Air Arm station between Tangmere and Littlehampton.)

I knew Hodges was blaming himself for sending the two Lysanders. It was not his fault, but all the same he was blaming himself, praying for things to turn out alright. Only his paleness belied his semblance of composure. If Hankey and Mac were being brought home it meant that the fog covered the whole of England south of the Humber. They did not have enough fuel for a long diversion. Our two Lysanders with half-a-dozen Joes on board were among the mass of four-engined bombers coming back from Germany, only to find their East Anglia and Midland aerodromes fogged-in.

We expected Hankey and Mac at any moment. They would find the aerodrome by their red beacons, which would illuminate the top of the fog blanket with a red, flashing, hazy glow. Leslie and I went outside and found ourselves enveloped in damp fog, surrounded by a deadened echo-less silence. We went back to the ops room. We avoided each other's eyes. I was nervous and frightened. There was nothing any of us could do — except pray. I prayed — "Oh God, get them out of this mess!"

The black telephone rang again. The controller told me that the visibility was nil at Tangmere and Ford and that radar had picked up two low and slow-moving objects about 40 miles off the south coast. I told Hodges. He sat with his feet on the ops table. He had his forage cap on — it had not been on before. He must have put it on when Leslie and I went outside. His hands were buried in the pockets of his too-large battle dress. I thought of Hankey and MacBride, and put myself in their place. They had no radio beacon equipment, only the control tower to give them bearings to steer for the airfield. They were sitting in their cockpits, dimly lit, tired after five hours of flying over France at 2,000 feet. They must by now realise their predicament; the moon would be shining on the sheet of silvery-grey fog which covered the whole south of England, and as far as the Midlands. There was only one course open to them. Press on and get down. They had no alternative and they knew it.

The telephone rang. MacBride was in the Tangmere circuit and going round and round on top of the fog. The controller was going to give him a succession of VHF bearings for the field. I told Hodges. My voice had become a deep bass, my vocal chords had packed up through nervousness. I tried to talk naturally, but I could only utter the words in a deep croaking voice. The telephone rang again. Hankey was in the Ford circuit. The controllers were talking to both aircraft. Occasionally we heard the deep fog-muffled drone of MacBride's Lysander as he flew a few hundred feet above us. The telephone rang again: Hankey had made two unsuccessful approaches to Ford. Both Tangmere and Ford had put out goose-neck flares and had their flare path searchlights on. But this only resulted in a bright, milky glow, marking the general area of the landing run and of no help whatever. Again the telephone rang. The Tangmere controller announced that Hankey had crashed in the Ford circuit and was on fire. The fire tenders were finding it difficult to locate the crash in the fog. I told all this to Hodges in a hoarse whisper. He sat motionless and made no indication of having heard me. It was half-past-three.

The telephone rang again. MacBride had crashed on his approach to Tangmere. The controller could see a red glow in the south-west and expected the worst. I couldn't make a sound. I took a deep breath and another, but still only managed to croak out the news in a hoarse whisper. My vocal chords were paralysed. I put my head on the telephone table. All three of us remained still. There was nothing to do. It was over. Hodges went out. Leslie and I sat and looked at each other. The others were asleep upstairs. We heard the Humber start up — it was Hodges heading for the control tower. Leslie got up and wound up the gramophone and put on 'Venez donc chez moi ...' A song to remember always. I never heard it again after I left 'A' Flight.

At about half-past four Hodges and Major Bertram came back. Hankey and his Joes had been killed. He had stalled into the ground in the Ford circuit. MacBride had been heading for Tangmere on VHF bearings, had come in too low and hit the ground before the airfield boundary. He might have got away with it, but the Lysander nosed over. Mac was trapped in the cockpit, and the whole lot went up in a mighty bonfire. His Joes were safe but shaken; they had been miraculously thrown clear.

Hodges turned to Leslie and myself.

"Right! It's you two next."

"Yes, sir," we managed to croak.

CHAPTER 10

Success and the Sack

BACK at Tempsford for the January dark period we were joined by a group of pilots: Flt.Lts Bob Large DFC, and Per Hysing-Dahl,* DFC, and F/Os 'Dinger' Bell, MacDonald, Tony Bruce, George Turner, Milstead, and Alexander. Turner had been a policeman in civvy street; his speciality was to press his curled-up fist to his lips and blow. In this way he would give us an excellent rendering of Purcell's 'Trumpet Voluntary', and then to lighter pieces such as 'The Constables' March'.

Milstead had a one-track mind, which he demonstrated from morning till night. Tony Bruce was a tall, lanky, horsey type, who stood at the bar with one hand in his pocket, the other holding a tankard of beer — the hunting squire at The Bruce Arms, amidst his lackeys.

Per Hysing-Dahl had escaped from Norway in 1940 with two school friends, sailing in a fishing boat from Bergen to the Shetlands. After training as aircrew in Canada, he had joined 161 Special Duty Squadron of Bomber Command at Tempsford. He had completed a first tour of Halifax operations and so was due for a rest period on non-operational duties. However, he

---

*After the war, Per Hysing-Dahl wrote about his experiences in the RAF. These included often hair-raising descriptions of dropping supplies to patriots in the Norwegian mountains. His book, *Vinger over Europe*, was published in Norway, and later translated into English, but not published in the UK. He entered politics, and eventually became President of the Storting, the Norwegian Parliament. Per died in 1989.

managed to wangle a posting to the 161 Squadron Lysanders Flight, and was now the most senior and experienced Captain on Special Duties. We, the rest of the Lysander crews, had not yet done an operation, so we were in considerable awe of Per.

One afternoon we were all squashed into my Singer, and marauding around the locality. We stopped at the village shop in Sandy. Tony discovered that the old couple in the shop had a full carton of small bottles of Bovril, which was hard to come by in wartime. He bought the lot, and proceeded to consume the contents. As we drove along, he inserted a large middle finger into each small bottle, winkled out a dollop of Bovril, and then sucked. We, the onlookers, were allowed to lick the lids, and clean out the bottles.

Bob Large was an ex-Fighter boy, irrepressibly ebulliant. He had been shot down, landed in the Channel near Dover, and rescued from his dinghy by an RAF launch, while one of his Squadron's Spitfires kept an FW-190 at bay.

The 1944 January moon period began by us all piling into three Lysanders, and flying down to Tangmere. The weather was foul, and no operations were done. Leslie fell in love with a WAAF in the Tangmere operations room, who lived with her parents at Bosham. We both went to tea there on a couple of afternoons. The Flight went twice to The Unicorn and Dolphin in Chichester for a booze.

Right from the beginning of the February moon period, the weather was fine. Leslie and I were allocated a field to the south of the Loire and west of Orleans for our first operation together. We made mental notes of all the likely pinpoints on our track; roads, railways, woods and rivers. We decided to cross the French coast north of Caen at 6,000 feet, and then lose height to 2,000 feet down to the Loire, which was considered the best height for navigation, high enough to see well ahead, and low enough not to wake up the Germans. The Lysander was very quiet, as well as being small, black and alone in the large night sky. I was going first, with Leslie following twenty minutes later.

We dressed in our assorted clothing, parachutes had already been taken to the aircraft. We settled down to relax, listen to the gramophone, and wait for the red scrambler telephone to ring and confirm the operation. Bob Large, Tony Bruce, Turner and Milstead were playing cards at the ops room table. We heard the Joes arrive. A message had been sent by the BBC after the six o'clock news, - 'The goose has laid a golden egg.' The agents in France heard the broadcast and radioed back that they were ready to receive the aircraft. My aircraft was 'D for Donald'.

John Hunt put his head round the door.

"All set Andy?"

"Right, I'm coming."

"Good luck," said Bob.

"See you soon Andy," interjected Tony, eyes on his cards.

I left Leslie sitting at the table studying his map. Hodges came out with me. It was just as I had seen Hankey and Mac, but this time it was I who was climbing up the starboard under-carriage leg into the cockpit. My mind was only on what I had to do, and how I was going to carry it out successfully. The Joes were in the back — I did not know how many; it was not my business. Sgt Booker climbed up and handed me a parcel about the size of a shoe box. It contained coffee, chocolate and sugar for the Joes in France.

On that first crossing I flew at 6,000 feet, in contrast to my previous flights to France. Then I had been flying twice as fast in clear blue skies, at 30,000 feet. There was no point now in looking around for fighters, my view behind was non-existent, to the sides a little better. A fighter could position himself behind me, and then let go with his guns. My Joes were probably asleep, and had no way of communicating with me, even if they saw anything.

Half-an-hour later I saw a faint, yellow flashing glow among the clouds, slightly to my left and below. I was mystified. It kept a regular, flashing sequence. This was one thing I had not been told about. I deduced it was the lighthouse at Le Havre, still flashing every night, after four years of war. I saw a white ribbon of foam, running east and west. I was coming up to the French coast, where the breaking surf separated the dark grey sea from the changing pattern of the land. I expected someone would fire at me as I crossed over. Nothing happened. I kept height until I was past Caen, and then descended slowly to 2,000 feet.

The moon and the stars were out, and I was on track. I could see ten miles ahead of me, and recognise pinpoints along my route. Villages showed no lights, only rivers and lakes reflected the moon's pale light. Large woods appeared as dark pieces of a jigsaw puzzle, which I easily recognised from my map. I was so busy navigating, determined to stay on track, that time passed without notice. Ahead I could see the sparkle of moonlit water, then a black ribbon running left to right. It was the river Loire. Over the Loire I turned on track for the field, twenty miles away, about ten minutes to go. A large, irregular forest appeared. To the east lay the field. I came down to 1,000 feet, then I suddenly saw a small, clear light flashing the letter 'D'. It worked! They were there! I flashed my answer, 'R B'. Suddenly three small, weak lights came on in the shape of an inverted 'L', my landing run. "Steady Anderson! PRAFTU!" The moonlight showed up the hedgerow round the field. "You're not finished yet." I lined up with the two lights. I lost height, trimmed the aircraft tail heavy, pushed in the fine pitch selector, and gave throttle. I dragged the Lysander in at 60 mph over the hedge. On the right of the first light I chopped the throttle, the Lysander touched the ground with a gentle bumpy-bumpy-bump. Perfect! I applied intermittent brakes and came to a halt. Gills open — trim set for take-off — turn round, and taxi back to the first light — turn again to face up the strip ready to go home.

I throttled back and heard faint shouts above the idling engine; the rear canopy opened. I imagined the drill. Suitcases out, Joes out, Joes in, followed by suitcases, canopy shut. I was in France! Surrounded by sleeping Germans. I peered to my left and behind, under the wing, shadows moved. Then one shadow climbed up the port undercarriage leg, a parcel containing the traditional gift of a bottle of scent was pushed through my window. I passed out Sgt Booker's shoebox. I heard the Shout of Shouts, "OCK-KAY". I opened the throttle, released the brakes, the Lizzy shot forward. Airborne. I'd been on French soil for ten minutes.

Leslie would soon be landing. I was dead on track, retracing my route home. Now the moon was behind me, water appeared black, the blackest patches of the night. Nearing Caen I started to climb to 5,000 feet. At this height the home radar could pick me up earlier. My bladder was filling up; I loosened my harness and bounced up and down. I rocked too and fro, urging the Lysander on, to Blighty and safety. I sang out, "Praise be to PRAFTU!" I was going round the bend. If the Joes in the back heard me, they would have thought they had a raving lunatic as a pilot. On the other hand, they might be singing too, as they got near to Angleterre.

I saw the tiny, red flashing Tangmere beacon. I switched on my VHF and called the tower. The goosenecks were alight. I landed and taxied back to our corner of the airfield behind the Tangmere guard room. D for Donald was back. I heard the rear canopy open, then babbling, excited and happy French voices. I sat in my seat ten feet up, with a wonderful feeling of relief and satisfaction. I had brought people, if only for a short while, back to friends and safety. I climbed down to the ground. Major Bertram and John Hunt were being hugged by three Joes. One rushed up to me and shook my hand, showing white teeth in a moonlit grin. Their luggage was piled into the shooting brake, and they were driven off to London. Hodges, Bob Large, and Dinger walked back with me to the cottage. Leslie was due back in half-an-hour.

In the ops room I had time for a cup of tea, accompanied by '*Venez donc chez moi je vous invite,*' before we all trooped out to meet Leslie. He had brought back two Joes and a bottle of scent. The jubilant scene was re-enacted, before they too were shipped off to London.

Shortly before the moon period ended, Dinger Bell and MacDonald took off to do a double operation. They both arrived within minutes of each other, and Mac went in to land. He overshot the lights twice, apparently coming in too fast. The next time he landed, watched by Dinger circling overhead. To Dinger's horror he saw Mac's Lysander belch a huge plume of flame from its exhaust; a bumpy landing could easily flood the carburettor, with the risk of engine fire. Suddenly the whole engine nacelle burst into flames, and the wind blew the fire along the fuselage. The black Lysander, with its long slender wings was silhouetted like a moth burning in a candle's flame. At first, Dinger thought that the Lysander had been shot at by waiting Gestapo. There was no possibility of his landing at the field, so he set course for Tangmere. Two days later we heard that Mac was dead, but his Joes had got clear.

Through all these vicissitudes it was the character of Hodges that held us together. He was the connecting link with the great Lysander pilots of the past. He was utterly unflappable. By the end of the moon period I had four bottles of scent. I visited London with Leslie, who introduced me to the Brevet Club off Berkeley Square, a gathering place for Air Force types, which was started by Clive Revitt, who had been a stores officer at Benson. I sold two bottles of scent to Clive, and kept two.

When we returned to Tangmere for the March moon period, a Wing Commander Boxer had taken over from Hodges. Boxer was the CO of 161 Squadron, to which A Flight belonged. Boxer was taller than Hodges, good looking, clean-shaven, blue-eyed, fair-haired, with a DSO and DFC. He wore a pressed battledress, a new peaked cap, which sat squarely on his handsome head. His collar was starched, and with a neatly knotted tie. He seemed cold, aloof, and superior, without an ounce of humour in him. I loathed him after exchanging less than a dozen words. My attitude was unfair. He was inferior to Hodges, and any successor had also to compete with the memory of Nebbie Wheeler and Freddie Ball.

The Second Front was imminent, and the south coast had to be cleared for action. 'A' Flight would have to vacate Tangmere, which would be operating Spitfires and Tempests, and might be bombed to hell by the infuriated Luftwaffe. The Lysanders would operate from Tempsford, landing at Tangmere at night for refuelling, and a last minute check on the weather, before crossing to France. This would give us two extra hours flying, with the added difficulty of deciding to carry on or not after consultations with the local met.

Dinger did the first op of the March period to the Loire. He was approaching Caen, heading south at 6,000 feet. There was a lot of cloud about, the night was dark, when his engine suddenly stopped. His heart stopped too. After a few seconds he returned to life and carried out the drill. Check magneto switches, check fuel contents and fuel cocks. Everything was on. The propellor windmilled silently. He pulled the stick back into his stomach, out came the leading and trailing edge flaps. He sank earthwards slowly. He switched off the fuel and ignition, prayed that he wouldn't land on top of some Germans, or catch fire when he hit the ground. Both possibilities were highly likely, the former especially, with troops thick on the ground in anticipation of the invasion. He kept the nose up and continued to sink silently. Four thousand feet, two thousand feet, one thousand feet. He hit the ground with a terrific wallop, which jarred his backside. That was all!

After a few seconds he realised he was unhurt. He opened the cockpit window, and stepped out onto the ground. The three Joes were already out with their suitcases. No one was hurt, the aircraft was squashed flat like a swatted insect, the undercarriage had collapsed, the wings and tail plane had fallen off, and the engine buried in the soft earth. In spite of the huge belly tank being split open, and the place reeking of petrol, there was no fire. They had landed in the middle of a ploughed field, surrounded by Germans. Their forced landing apparently, had not been seen or heard by anyone.

They started to walk into Caen, with the idea of getting rooms for the night. It was pitch black and they met no one. At about midnight, the four of them walked into a hotel in Caen, and asked the Reception for two double rooms. The place was stiff with German officers, boozing and dancing with the local girls. No one looked less like a Frenchman than Dinger. He was tall, blond, blue-eyed, he could not speak a word of French, and he blushed easily. He had the air of an over-grown schoolboy, which in fact he was. He was wearing his RAF raincoat without a belt. Under this he was wearing his battledress with a dark blue polo-neck sweater. His trousers were outside his flying boots. He was terrified by the proximity of the Wehrmacht, but no one paid any attention to them. They retired for the night, and the next morning took a train to Paris! Absolument fantastique!

Dinger was locked away for the next ten days. Two days after their landing, London got a radio message from Paris to say that he and his Joes were safe, and that Dinger would be taken to Angers, so that he could be picked up before the moon period ended. A few days before we were due to leave for Tempsford, the message came through to say that Dinger and a few Joes were waiting to be picked up. It was my turn for the op, and the last of the moon period. I had to get Dinger out on this flight, or leave him for another two weeks.

The weather was not good; I was in cloud over the French coast and turned onto track for Angers. Two hours after leaving Tangmere, I was still in rain clouds, and had not seen the ground once. The moon was not due to rise until about thirty minutes before I arrived at the field. It was like my first unnerving cross-country flight, but now I was relaxed, concentrating on holding height and compass course. Then suddenly I broke out into clear sky, filled with stars, and to the south peeped the yellow rim of the rising moon. I lost height to 2,000 feet, and made a pinpoint which put me ten miles off track, a real piece of luck. Ahead I saw an irregular sprawl of grey mist over the rain-sodden valley of the Loire. My met forecast had been accurate. I recognised my position at the Loire, but mist covered the whole area. I turned on track for the landing ground. After a few minutes I saw a weak light flashing at me through the mist. I flashed my letter. The lights came on. I could see them from above, but horizontally there was no visibility at all. I lined up with the two lights and made a low run in the direction of the landing, flying about fifty feet above the ground, with my Lysander partly in and partly out of the layer of fog. I swooped up and looked behind me as I turned. My slipstream had blown away the mist, leaving a clear swathe along my landing run. I did a low-level circuit, lined up with the clearly visible lights, and landed. Once again I passed out Sgt Booker's parcel, and got my bottle of scent in exchange. I waited. Saw nothing, heard the shout, "OCK-KAY!" and opened up for home.

Back at Tangmere, Dinger got out with the three Joes. We spent the few hours before dawn listening to Dinger's adventures. After eight days hiding in Paris, he had been put on a train escorted by a female Joe, and taken to Angers. They had been inspected by German police at the Paris railway station, again on the train, and yet again at Angers station. He had spent two days waiting at the pick-up field. Only the incredible sang-froid of the French underground had made it possible to carry a large, blond, speechless RAF officer, part-uniformed, and in every way un-Gallic, from Caen to Paris, then to Angers, and deliver him back to England within a fortnight.

I was enjoying myself on pick-up operations. It was all that Leslie and I had hoped for when we left PRU. The terrible events of December, and MacDonald's death were sad memories. A new era of successful pick-ups seemed to be starting. However, my pathological aversion to Wing Commander Boxer only grew. I found it difficult to be precise about my reasons for disliking him. I may have been under a nervous strain which my outward cheerfulness and equanimity hid, but did not alleviate. I needed a father-figure; Nebbie and Hodges had these qualities, but Boxer did not.

A week before the end of the April moon period, a really challenging pick-up was laid on to Macon. The field was in the maquis area in the field north of Lyons, a round trip of 800 miles. It had been done by the Hudson, and attempted by the Lysander in Verity's day, a year ago. Ideally, Macon should be done early in the moon period. If the operation was done later, the flight out would be done in darkness, with a small late-rising moon for the landing. Coming back would present another problem, because nearing the French coast it would be dawn. I became obsessed by the Macon operation. I imagined that Boxer was getting back at me by not laying on the flight. The moon got too small, and rose too late, so the period ended and we all returned to Tempsford.

Two days later I was called to the ops room, just before lunch. Boxer was on the dais, enthroned behind a large desk, surrounded by WAAF clerks. This was the first time I had seen him in his official habitat. Authority personified. I saluted, and approached the dais. I was wearing battle-dress, a forage cap and a non-regulation Viyella shirt, rather frayed at the collar. I was within the norm of borderline scruffiness.

"Right, Anderson. There is some news at last. Macon flight is on for tonight. You will ferry a Lysander to Tangmere, pick up the Joes and continue to Macon."

I stood still, my pent-up loathing mounted within me. The smarmy bastard. I went cold, and my breath came in short, restricted gasps. The WAAFs went about their business inno-cently. Boxer looked at me in his humourless, authoritarian way, faintly apprehensive.

"Not by me, sir. We've been back at Tempsford for two days, and there's no moon."

"What! Why?"

"It's too late. It's a seven-hour trip. The moon is rising too late and it's too small. I will be going in complete darkness, and returning in daylight. Do it yourself!"

"You refuse? You refuse an order?" Boxer gasped out.

"Yes, I refuse. I know damn well you could have laid on the flight a week ago. Now you've been given a raspberry for not sending the flight, and you want to put the responsibility on me!"

By now the WAAFs were moving like sleep walkers, listening in silent excitement.

"You talk to me like that in the ops room?!"

"Yes, and anywhere else you like. I refuse to repair your blunder. Have you checked the met? Am I to fly one hour to Tangmere, then seven hours to Macon and back? You have no right to order anyone to do this, when the moon period is over."

"I'll see the Group Captain. Get out of here."

"Sir — Macon is an important field, and you are on the carpet. Good!"

I saluted, and left the ops room. Of course my behaviour was very bad, and I should have been shot on the spot by the orderly WAAF. I could not help the antipathy to Boxer getting the better of me. I heard that the Macon Joes had been on the field for fourteen days. Next morning I got a summons to report to Group Captain Fielden's office.

My interview with Fielden was short and sharp. He threatened me with deportation to the RAF salt mines, a disciplinary squadron where the inmates were subject to continuous drill at the double, and kit inspections in the intervals!

I pointed out I was a regular Army officer, seconded to the RAF, and that I needed no instruction in discipline. I was prepared to defend my stance before any authority. Neither Fielden nor Boxer wanted 'trouble'. I suggested I should find myself a posting, and leave the Squadron as soon as possible. To my amazement, Fielden agreed. I saluted and left.

Leslie agreed with my attitude to the Macon flight, and said he wanted to leave the Flight too. I persuaded him to stay on. Only he and Dingle were operational for the next moon period. I was now a pariah, out in the cold and jobless. The Second Front was coming in a month or two, and I ran the risk of being out of it. Bob Large suggested that I should go down to the headquarters of Fighter Command at Stanmore, and see some of his cronies, who would get me a posting.

That evening Leslie and Bob persuaded me to go to a party in the WAAF Sergeant's Mess. I did not feel like a party, especially with uniformed WAAFs. The Mess was in a Nissen hut, brown linoleum on the floor, benches round the walls, with tables, chairs, and a bar at one end, the place lit by naked bulbs, beneath white enamel shades. Two WAAFs were behind the bar dishing out beer. We joined a party of WAAFs. Somehow I collected a small blonde WAAF, with down on her cheeks, and little beads of sweat mingled with a rim of beer around her lips. I thought how nice it would be to lick them. One of the WAAFs said she was in the ops room that morning during my tiff with Boxer. Some laughed. A gramophone started up, and we danced on the brown linoleum. The little blonde and I clasped each other with sweaty hands. Ties were loosened. I took off my battledress blouse. The blonde and I returned to the bench by the wall, where our glasses were on a table. Suddenly, the lights went out. My WAAF was kissing me, sucking my ear, and guiding my hand to her thighs. I was amazed, but entered into the spirit. I gasped out in whispers, "The lights! They'll go on!"

She reassured me urgently, "Don't stop! Don't worry — I know. It's all right. Don't stop! Go on!"

I went on. I had one hand on her thigh beneath her knickers, WAAF. She clasped me in heavy spasms. It was quite fantastic. Then after I don't know how long, but long enough for her, the lights went on. I did not dare look around, but slowly disengaged myself. We drank some beer.

The next morning, feeling like death, I slowly dressed, and on an empty stomach took a train from Sandy station for London. Feeling slightly better, I arrived at Fighter Command HQ. I wandered around its gravel paths, between yew hedges and well-trodden lawns, circling the large country house. I knew no one, and had no idea where to go. Then I came face to face with the squat, broad-shouldered figure of Group Captain Stratton, who had been Station Commander at Benson after Wing Commander Tuttle. I saluted, and introduced myself. He remembered me, and took me to his office marked 'Postings'. We entered by a diamond-paned glass door from the lawn, and I sat before his desk beneath a low-beamed ceiling. I explained what had happened with Group Captain Fielden, and how I was threatened with deportation. I asked him if he could get me a posting to Fighter Command. Yes, he could.

He took my name, number and home address, and said I would soon be posted to a Fighter OTU for a month's training, and would be assigned to a squadron.

"How's that?" he asked.

"Thanks sir, thanks awfully." I saluted, and left.

I was back in the swim again. That night at Tempsford I met the blonde Sgt WAAF again, and gave her my last bottle of scent.

The next morning I left Tempsford for home, to await my posting. It arrived after four days. I was ordered to report at RAF Kirton Lindsey near Scunthorpe, a Spitfire OTU.

CHAPTER 11

Mustang

ALL through my time at the Fighter Operational Training Unit the weather was sunny; we flew intensively. I was back in Spitfires again, but this was a new kind of flying, completely different from the lone operations I had been used to. At twenty-four, older than the others, I was an old 'new boy', a Flight Lieutenant with some three years of operations, and with gongs. Now I was to be part of a team. There was a great camaraderie in the mess; everyone knew that from this course we would be posted to squadrons. For most of the pilots this would be their first operational posting. After a month of formation flying and shooting at drogues, I was sent to a holding unit at Redhill. The Second Front had started a month earlier.

At Redhill I had a choice of flying the Spitfire or a Mustang. I chose the latter. The Mustang was a lovely aeroplane, but very different from the Spitfire. It was larger, heavier and stronger. The cockpit was roomier, with floorboards, side panels, and a control column that no longer had a spade grip like the Spitfire and Lysander, but a straight stick with the firing button on top. It had the same Griffith engine, only made in the States and mounted into the aircraft on rubber engine mountings. This made it quieter than the Spitfire and gave less vibration. It carried two point-five-inch machine guns in each wing. The main difference for me was that the Mustang was an aircraft I rode in and drove around the sky, while the Spitfire was something I flew as if its wings were my own. The Mustang went downhill very fast, but after the initial climb from the dive it could not climb as steeply as a Spitfire. I liked it very much.

At Redhill we were all waiting for vacancies in the squadrons. The local pubs and dance halls of Redhill were our haunts. 'Marezydotes and Dozydotes and Little Lamzy Tivey' ('Mares eat oats and does eat oats and little lambs eat ivy') was the current song, and we went to the dances after the pubs were closed and ground ourselves into our girls, and then back to the airfield and our tents. It was on a night early in my stay at Redhill that the first of the V1 buzz-bombs flew overhead on its way to London. From then on a continuing succession of bombs came over by day and night.

At the end of June 1944 I was flown to France in an Anson, and joined 65 East India Squadron 83 Group 2nd TAF, commanded by Sqn Ldr Lamb, stationed at B 2, a hastily made airstrip near Bayeux. We landed at an airstrip in the Beachhead and were told to make our way to our respective squadrons. I hitch-hiked a lift to B 2 in an ambulance. I arrived during lunch, which was being eaten in a large tent. The squadron was billeted in tents in an orchard. The other two squadrons of the Wing were also dispersed around the airstrip.

From now on I knew next to nothing of what was going on. I cannot remember the numbers of the other squadrons in the Wing, and I do not think I ever bothered to find out. My world consisted of 65 East India Squadron, flying and living in our tents on various airstrips. What was happening in the battle or the Beachhead, or what Wing was where, or which army was doing what, did not concern me. I was just a pilot flying the aeroplane to bomb and strafe where I was led, and returning to the domesticity of the mess and my tent. All the time I was with the Squadron the weather was sunny and hot, clouding a bit when we reached Belgium.

I did my first operation in a Mustang in the afternoon, the day after I arrived. The squadron was ordered to bomb a bridge. I was to fly No 2 to a sergeant section leader. At about fifteen hundred hours a jeep came round driven by Sqn Ldr

Lamb. Twelve of us piled into it and on it, and we drove out to the dispersed aircraft, where each pilot jumped off opposite his Mustang. The runway had been made only a week before by bulldozing the cornfields. The aircraft were kept in the adjoining fields with paths bulldozed for them to the wire net-covered runway. I took off on the left of my No 1 and slightly behind him. We rushed down the earth-and-netting runway and got airborne, each with two very large five-hundred-pound bombs hanging from our wings. We were the last section airborne; above us, making a large circle around the airstrip was the Squadron, waiting for each pair to come up and take its position.

It could not have been more than three minutes from the time the Squadron Commander took off with his No 2 before he was joined by us, his last section. We set course in squadron formation, climbing hard and making for the bridge. I do not know what height we climbed to or where we went. It was not far. The Squadron formed echelon to starboard, and the aircraft began to peel off for the dive. I was watching my No 1 and his tail. After each Mustang dived down and released its bombs, it climbed up and rejoined the others, acting as top cover for the tail-end of the Squadron.

At last it was the turn of our Flight to dive down one after the other. I still had my eyes glued on my No 1; I had not yet seen the target. He peeled off and started to dive. I kept a respectful distance behind and followed him down. Now I saw what we were supposed to be bombing. Below me as I headed almost vertically down was a small river winding through a wood, and there was the small white bridge with a white dusty road leading to it on both sides of the stream. I was supposed to blast this rural ornament to hell. My No. 1 was pulling up into a climb. I did not see his bombs exploding. I continued down, pointing my nose at the bridge and determined to hit it. I did what I had been told to do. I looked at the airspeed indicator: "By Christ!" In a matter of seconds I was doing 400 mph. I pressed the bombs' release button and started to pull out

of the dive at 1,000 feet and into a shallow climb. I pulled
harder on the stick and gave full throttle and shot up to 8,000
feet to join the rest of the Squadron. I glanced at the bridge
below me. It was intact. We had dropped twelve thousand
pounds of bombs and missed the target.

I found the Mustang very deceptive in the dive: the engine
did not make the increasing roar of the Spitfire. It dropped out
of the sky with no indication of its increasing speed or altitude.
We re-formed and headed for B 2. The Squadron flew in close
formation. As we got near the strip we adopted 'line to star-
bord', and one by one peeled off by Flights to come in for landing, while the remaining Flights gave top cover over the
airstrip. I was the last to land, and so I saw the wonderful
rapidity with which the Squadron landed. No 1 would be at the
far end of the strip with his No 2 rolling half-way up the
runway behind him, with yet another No 1 touching down at
the beginning of the strip and his No 2 on short final. Three
aircraft on the runway all the time and all moving. Within three
to four minutes the Squadron was down.

My flying now became completely automatic. I was always
following someone. I never looked where I was going, but kept
my eyes exclusively on my No 1, to my right or left and behind
him. During the next seventy sorties in 65 Squadron I never
once knew where I was, except the time when we bombed the
Seine barges. After depending completely on a map for three
years, I now gave up even carrying one. It was hard to get used
to not knowing where I was. For three years I had been dependent on myself alone for navigating to my target and back. Now
I simply followed; I could have been over Siberia and none the
wiser. I hardly ever saw the ground except when bombing and
strafing. I spent the whole time flying around looking sideways.
We either flew in close formation within a few feet of each
other, or in extended formation with up to 400 yards between
aircraft. We held formation and flew steadily through heavy
flak. On take-off there was no chance to check my boost setting
and gauges. I took off with my wing tucked in behind No 1 and

with my eyes fixed on him. All I had to do was to keep up with him and use what throttle setting was necessary to keep my position.

Later on we did Wing sweeps; thirty-six aircraft would take off, section after section. For me there was an endless fascination in this take-off, forming up in formation, and in landing after the sortie. It gave me a wonderful feeling of belonging to the group. I realised that the very essence of the Fighter Squadron was in the camaraderie or the formation; you started off in formation and hoped to come back in formation. Each had his place. The beautiful shape of the aircraft, its power, your own image in the next aircraft (for he looked to you as you looked to him), were unfailingly moving. I was an individual, with a place reserved for me in the formation. I was one of the group. It was wonderful to watch it all from the air, awaiting your turn to land in your Squadron, in your Flight, and in your section. The huge roar of the aircraft as they formed up over the airfield; the return, as they formed squadron echelon to starboard, each squadron landing in quick succession, while the others circled the field to give protection from enemy fighters — these were sights and sounds that brought a lump to my throat. I longed to be part of the formation on the next sortie.

A week after my arrival at B 2, the Wing moved to B 12, further into the Beachhead and towards Caen. I never got to know where we were in relation to the enemy. We could hear the guns pounding away all day and night, so we could not have been very far from the Front. As at B 2, the airstrip and dispersals had been bulldozed out of the fields and woods. Our trouble was dust. It had not rained for weeks, the soil was dry, and whenever our aircraft moved they blew clouds of dust into the sky, over everything and everyone near them. We lived in tents about a hundred yards away from our aircraft. When we arrived at B 12, four large guns were ranged along the east side of the runway. During our first night, the four guns fired continuously. The noise was awful, made more horrible by the huge spurts of red and yellow flame which came from the guns and lit up the night sky. We all prayed that the Germans would not counter-fire, and that the charges of our guns were good, or else one of the shells might trickle out of a barrel and land on us. The next morning, after we returned from an early sortie, we discovered the guns had been hauled away, much to our relief.

We were doing three sorties a day and in between we were supposed to dig pits large enough to sleep in and put our tents over the top; these were known as 'wanking pits'. I made friends with an equally bewildered fellow, Allison, a Canadian. We decided to share a tent together, but since we didn't relish the idea of digging pits three foot wide by four foot deep and six foot long, we erected our tent over a ditch which ran along the hedgerow under some trees. We dug a little bit to level the floor and settled ourselves into the ditch. The others put up their tents, some dug 'wanking pits', others just slept on camp beds on the ground. Three sorties a day by each squadron meant one-hundred-and-forty take-offs and landings every day. The surrounding trees and grass fields were covered in a fine, dry powder of earth dust. The aircraft were dusty and so were our tents and ourselves.

One night we all went to bed early as usual. The moon was not up, but the sky was clear and the stars shone. At B 12 all was rural calm, except for the not-so-distant rumble of the guns. To the south we could see the flashes of the guns illuminating the horizon. At midnight there was a terrific CRASH, and everybody woke up; all were apprehensive. More crashes followed. Everybody kept still except those foolish virgins above ground. We were being shelled. Our sandstorms of the previous days had given our position away and the Germans were doing something about it. The shells were coming over steadily at thirty-second intervals, and were bursting on impact so as to scatter their fragments and do most damage to the aircraft.

Not a sound came from the squadron tents, although everyone was wide awake. Allison and I were lying terrified in our ditch, consoled only by its depth and the thought of the trees above us. We heard the patter of large, bare feet and three others dashed into our tent, and dived into the ditch. The three had brought their steel helmets. One of them was Flying Officer Rivers who was very proud of the colony of crabs he had collected from one of his partners during his last London leave, and which he cultivated in his bush. It was Rivers who instructed us how to protect ourselves with our steel helmets. Under his guidance we lay full-length on our stomachs with our steel helmets perched on our bums. Rivers' reasoning, which seemed very sound, was that if we were hit in the balls we might as well be dead, so we should put as much between our balls and the sky as possible. While we were getting into this safe position, the shells were coming over regularly. Most were going over us and landing amidst the other two squadrons. After two hours the shelling stopped and Rivers and his two companions returned to their tents.

The next morning saw the results of the night's bombardment. The ground around our tents and aircraft was pitted by shallow depressions where the shells had hit and exploded. About a third of our aircraft had been slightly damaged by shell splinters, but miraculously none had a direct hit. The other two squadrons were not so lucky. None of their pilots had dug wanking pits, so that when the shelling started everybody was in his tent and above ground. There was an immediate rush for the mess tent, tables and chairs were upturned to give cover; others made for ditches or burrowed like rabbits into the mounds of earth left by the bulldozers. The aircraft got a good peppering. Within two days all of them were serviceable. The foolish virgins now dug their wanking pits.

It was decided that our Mustangs should carry two one-thousand-pound bombs in place of the five-hundred-pounders, increasing our bomb load by one-hundred-per-cent. The explosion of the one-thousand-pounders created a terrific shock wave which made it necessary not to fly too close behind the aircraft in front. They were fitted with delayed-action fuses, so the shock waves of the bombs dropped by an aircraft in front, hit the aircraft that followed behind. In the early morning we could see the shock wave like a large balloon of ever-increasing waves of mist, pulsating from the point of impact.

A day or two after we had been fitted out with out two thousand-pounders, we were sent to dive-bomb the Seine bridges. My No 1 peeled off at the start of his dive. I followed a few hundred yards behind. Suddenly, right in front of me, appeared a large black cloud, and before I knew what had happened my No 1 had disappeared. I started my dive, dropped my bombs, missed the target again, then pulled up into a climb to rejoin the Squadron. We set course for B 12 and landed. Not many of us had seen the No 1 blow up; some assumed he had been hit by flak. If his bombs had gone off I would have felt the concussion and would probably have been blown up with him. Similar incidents occurred in the other two squadrons, yet no one saw any flak. Two days later in a very quiet area the same thing happened again. The armament officer was most insistent that a bomb could not blow up unless it had been released. Others thought that if the aircraft was put into a rough wing-over and allowed to side-slip violently, before diving, the extra weight on the wings would set up an excessive strain on the structure and might cause the aircraft to break up. The wing had lost four or five aircraft in this way, when it was decided that no more thousand-pounders would be carried. Sometimes a bomb got hung up under a wing and could not be released; but the Mustang did not seem to mind landing with an extra five hundred pounds under one wing. We had no accidents from hang-ups, even when a bomb fell off on landing and proceeded to roll up the runway.

On a bombing sortie somewhere north-east of Le Havre, I had a piece of good luck. The target was a wood which was supposed to contain a large German petrol and ammunition dump. We had to drop our bombs within the wood, which was certainly easier than trying to hit a bridge. The sortie was made in the afternoon in a clear sky. The Squadron arrived over the target, formed echelon to starboard and proceeded to peel off for the dive bombing. There was an immediate response from flak, so we knew we were over the target. Puffs of white smoke were bursting at all heights as, one by one, we dropped from eight thousand feet towards the target. My Mustang gave a sudden shudder. I continued to dive, released my bombs and pulled out of the dive. I looked to my right to find the Squadron, then I noticed a shell had gone through the leading edge of my starboard wing. We formed up and headed for home.

After landing I looked at the damage; a flak shell had gone straight through the wing, but luckily the shell fuse had failed, leaving a hole about the size of a grapefruit. The ground crews got the hole patched up and the aircraft was ready to fly the next morning.

Apart from flying, none of us did much. We stayed mostly at the airstrip, drinking beer, sleeping or walking around talking and hob-nobbing with the locals. We bought eggs, milk and cheese from the nearby farms. Sometimes we went to Bayeux for hot baths, or just for the ride. We looked like no Air Force anywhere. Many of us had discarded RAF uniform and wore Army battledress, or American khaki trousers we had managed to scrounge, with T-shirts and wind jackets, without wings or badges of rank. By now, if I had stayed on in PRU I would have been a Squadron Leader, flying occasionally and sleeping in comfort at Benson. I had no regrets.

The Wing was commanded by Wing Commander Johnson, who had been senior to me at Cheltenham. There was Squadron Leader Westenra who had done over five-hundred sorties on fighters and fighter bombers in the Western Desert. I never came across anyone who 'shot a line' or had a belligerent, tough attitude. I never heard anyone 'pull rank'. Sergeant pilots, most of whom were very experienced and had a goodly sprinkling of gongs between them, joked and fooled around with officers, from the Wing Commander downwards. We all lived together, ate together, and flew together. In the air the leader of the formation was the boss, regardless of his rank. I flew No 2 mostly to sergeants or Flying Officers.

Jimmy Muir was a Canadian and spoke French. His theme song was 'Amour, Amour, Amour,' which he used to burst into at appropriate moments, and especially if a shell landed near our tents. Jimmy, from the depths of his wanking pit would bellow forth, "Amour! Amour! Amour!"

During these summer days the weather was perfect. We made sorties to the Seine and tried to drop bombs on hundreds of barges which were assembled to ferry Germans across the river. All the Seine bridges had been destroyed, so these barges were the only way to get troops, ammunition and food across. The Germans were eventually trapped in the vicinity of Falaise. For three days running we did four sorties a day to the area.

We would take off by squadrons, fly to the area, and drop our bombs on any target the Squadron Commander chose. Then we flew around at tree-top height, pouring point-five-inch machine-gun bullets into hedgerows, vehicles jammed in the country lanes, woods and any shade that might be giving cover. The whole area was crammed with German troops, tanks, guns, vehicles, motor cycles and ambulances. There was not a road or a wood or a shaded tree line that did not have troops and equipment in hiding. It was impossible not to find a target. We attacked a line of ambulances; they stopped, troops jumped out and ran for the ditches. The Germans were using any vehicle to bring up reinforcements and would use any vehicle to get themselves away. The confusion on the roads was terrible and added to the carnage.

From far off, as we approached the area, we could see green fields and the darker green of the leafy trees. The sun shone, but from the ground arose a black wispy mist of smoke, which climbed slowly in the hot, still air and hung over the burning tanks, vehicles, and men jamming the lanes and trying to hide in the shade. No enemy fighter came to molest our attacks and nobody left alive on the ground would shoot at us for fear of giving away their hiding place. As we made passes over the entrapped enemy, we had only to watch out in case we flew head-on into a Mustang attacking from the opposite direction.

A few days later, some of us were taken by the Army Intelligence Officer to see how the other half of the world was living and dying. A familiar landscape of bombed villages, burnt-out tanks, shattered vehicles and swollen carcasses of horses, cows and men was displayed before our innocent eyes. The result of our handy-work. We drove in our jeep through the carnage, knowing we could return to the comfort of our base while the soldiers remained day and night in the stench and destruction.

As we rode forward in our jeep, we first noticed with increasing intensity the sickly-sweet stench of putrifying flesh. This smell got less intense as we neared the Front Line; death was more recent there. The weather was hot and sticky, the trees were lushly green, flowers grew everywhere and there was cool blue shade below the trees that lined the country lanes and borders of the fields. The air was heavy with the odour of gas from the bloated stomachs of the dead farm animals. Their cadavers lay on their backs with their short legs protruding toards the sky, in a world truly turned upside-down. Everywhere were flies, some a beautiful brilliant green, emitting in their millions a steady, busy buzzing, darting from one delectable corpse to another. For me it was the sunshine and shade which was unreal. Man had made the scene of desolation and I had helped; even if my bombs never hit any bridges, they fell in the fields and killed.

Our first view of the Front was a tall hedgerow where trees cast a shadow over resting soldiers. We stood by our jeep and looked at the scene. It reminded me of my school Training Corps during a 'Field Day', with everybody lying around hot and worn-out, not knowing or caring what was going on, drinking orange juice from our World War One water bottles, and starting to eat the haversack rations of jam sandwiches and hard-boiled eggs. The scene before us was not very different. The soldiers lying beneath the hedges were older than schoolboys, though not much. Some were eating. I half expected to see Major Holland commanding Cheltenham College OTU, with his white umpire's arm-band, announcing that the soldiers could all consider themselves wiped out as the Blue Army had won, and they could return to the rallying point.

The four of us stood by the jeep in the shade. We asked our Intelligence Officer what was going on. He explained that we were at the Front Line during a quiet moment. The Germans were two-hundred yards ahead of us, dug into a small wood. We looked through the hedge in the direction he indicated, but we could see nothing. I noticed a few cows peacefully grazing on the intervening fields. They were alive, which in itself suggested danger.

The resting troops were due to attack in twenty minutes, and we would be taken out of harm's way before the fighting started. Their unconcern was the most disconcerting thing. No one shouted orders, looked grim or rattled sabres; they all rested and ate, indifferent to everything, because nothing mattered except the possibility of death which faced them in a few minutes. They knew what to do and trusted their training to carry them through. We turned away, got back into our jeep and drove away before things got dangerous.

We drove two or three miles, and came to a small village. In the main street were two large German tanks, one with a hideous hole blasted into its turret by a rocket from a Hawker Tempest. The other tank seemed undamaged, with its gun pointing menacingly down the street. It also was dead. We stopped, and the Intelligence Officer showed us the tiny hole made by the armour-piercing shell, which on entering the turret had whistled round at high speed cutting the occupants into mincemeat.

Opposite the two dead tanks was a small church set among trees. It was here that we decided to have our lunch. We had each brought an American 'K' ration, filled with all sorts of lovely things, like compressed ham-and-eggs, biscuits, chocolates, a small packet of Camel cigarettes and a French letter. We wandered over into shade; through the trees we saw a small, sunlit lawn beside the church. We opened our rations and started to eat. We were not alone, for there were four soldiers in one corner of the lawn. Two soldiers were lying down on their backs, sleeping. One soldier was standing in an oblong hole up to his knees, shovelling earth, the other soldier stood watching him, with his hands resting upon the handle of his spade. None of us spoke; we just ate. All the soldiers were tall, the two digging were blond and sunburned. They must have been Guardsmen. The diggers had their battledress blouses off, showing open-necked shirts with sleeves rolled up and braces. They looked like angels, Stanley Spencer's angels. Two Gabriels digging, their wings laid aside. The two sleeping soldiers were fully dressed and lay with their arms by their sides. The stench of the battlefield was fainter now because we had got used to it. How peacefully they slept, and how unhurriedly and rhythmically the Gabriels dug. They finished one hole, marked out another and started to dig together. It was then that I realised that they were digging graves. There was no blood, no mutilation; the sleepers lay relaxed upon the grass, their skin white and clean. The four of them, the living and the dead, were detached from everything and completely indifferent to us sitting a few yards away. They must have been friends. We finished and walked back to our jeep.

We drove on through a landscape of trees splintered by mortar bombs, until we came to a slight plateau of fields of clover and grass. Ahead of us was a crossroads with a broken signpost. We stopped a few yards from the crossroads. Over to our right were the enemy lines, about half-a-mile away. All was quiet. Then we saw coming along the road opposite us a line of British soldiers, a section of eight or ten marching in single file. They looked like dwarfs. Their steel helmets seemed too large. They marched along indifferently, rifles slung over their shoulders, their battledress jackets open, their webbing equipment too big for them, with its two large ammunition pouches on either side of their chests.

Then the leading soldier got something from beneath his left arm, and I saw the three drones of his pipes settle on his left shoulder. He blew up and from the distance I heard the notes of *'The Haughs of Cromdale'*, the first tune I had been taught on the chanter by a fellow-cadet at the 'Shop'. It was extraordinarily moving to hear the tune played under these conditions. I wondered what *'The Haughs of Cromdale'* meant to them, a tune played during wars long past, played today, and to be played again in wars to come. When they reached the crossroads, the piper stood at the corner and played as the section turned to the left and trudged down the road towards the enemy.

Indifference and quietness hung around them; no shouts, no orders, no bravado of weapons. They were so small, perhaps Highland Light Infantry. I wondered where Sergeant-Major Jock Miller was; perhaps at some training depot or dead on a desert battlefield. The piper fell in behind the last man and they trudged off. Their coming battle and their familiarity with action and death set them apart. We drove back to B 12. I felt guilty that I was returning to our dusty tents and not trudging along with those I had left behind.

After the slaughter at Falaise the Germans retreated fast towards the Rhine. The Wing moved to the abandoned German fighter aerodrome at Beauvais/Tille for a few days. From Beauvais the Squadron moved to an airfield outside Brussels. Flying Officer Molesworth and I decided to have a night out. We went to a night club called *'Sous les Toits de Paris'*, which had an opaque glass dance floor lit from beneath. There was a singer, a lovely slender negress. Molesworth and I sat drinking brandy and looking innocent. Across the dance floor was a homely-looking girl with an elderly man. The man got up, seeing me eye his companion, and invited us to have a drink at his table, as a gesture of friendship we supposed. Brandy was ordered and we drank a toast to the *'Libération'*. Soon afterwards he excused himself and ordered us more brandy as he went out. He even paid for it. We felt obligated and overwhelmed at his generosity.

The girl spoke a little English. I asked her name, where she lived, how old she was, was she married? (no), who was the man? (her friend), what were the Germans like? (sale Boche), did she come here often? And then we lapsed into silence. I asked her to dance, which we did. I asked her for *"une autre fille pour mon ami"*. *"Mais oui, certainment, mais pas ici."*

We returned to the table and ordered champagne, Molesworth had a dance. We drank up the champagne and left.

We went to a restaurant stiff with men, women and military. The hubbub was continuous and loud. I ordered more brandy. The girl excused herself and left. She returned with her friend who sat next to Molesworth. She took Molesworth's hand and kissed it. Molesworth blushed furiously, which amused the girls. More brandy was ordered. My girl asked me if I had any cocoa, coffee, butter, sugar, chocolate and cigarettes. I explained that I had none of these groceries with me except a packet of cigarettes which we were smoking, but that I would be glad to bring her some of each the next evening. She made me write down her address. The two girls looked at each other and giggled. They bent towards each other and conversed rapidly and happily, As they talked and giggled, they each grasped Molesworth and myself by our free hands. They clasped us unconsciously, as though we were large, filled shopping baskets deposited on the chairs next to them.

Suddenly, my girl jumped up and waved to some people in the crowd; a man and a woman pushed themselves to our table and sat down between the two girls. Molesworth and I were pushed round the table and sat close together, our hands still clammily clasped. Now and then the four would cast a surreptitious glance at us and then all burst into shrieks of laughter.

Jimmy Muir was in the crowd, talking French to some men and women. He was holding forth and a very animated conversation was going on. I imagined it was about politics, freedom, the future and what sacrifices and sufferings Belgium had gone through. (I asked Jimmy the next day what they had been talking about. It turned out that the conversation was on the subject of cocoa, coffee, butter, sugar, chocolate and cigarettes.)

The man and the woman at our table got up to go. Still clasping our hands the girls dragged us out onto the pavement and everybody said goodnight. But there was no release for Molesworth and me. "*Ah chéri, venez!*" said my girl, and we were led off. These were the first words spoken to us since our promise of the groceries. We approached a large hotel at one end of the open square. It was near midnight, and quite obviously we were expected to sleep with our companions. I knew that Molesworth was petrified and so was I. Our two companions may have been healthy all over, but under the circumstances we both felt an element of doubt.

We arrived at the hotel. My girl told me to go up to the desk and ask for two double rooms. I paid, got the keys and off we went to the first floor. Our rooms were next to each other. Molesworth was led in looking white and resigned. My girl explained that I would have to leave by five-thirty a m in order to catch the working-men's tram to the aerodrome. She proceeded to undress down to her petticoat and then jumped into bed. I undressed down to my blue Viyella shirt and followed her. Being totally unprepared I was petrified at the possible consequences of copulation. This was quickly resolved by my companion. "Not tonight, chéri. Like brother and sister. Come to sleep." She clasped me to her breast, and I was so relieved and grateful that I felt like a brother to her. Up till now I had experienced no physical symptoms of being capable of consummating our short relationship. Also, I didn't like her smell.

I woke up at five o'clock, feeling less like a brother. The terrors of the night before had faded. She awoke, fully practical, and took charge of the situation. I was given no opportunity to demonstrate the change I felt in our relationship. I had to get up and wash and then check that I had her address. She made me promise to come to her house the following evening with the groceries. She explained how to get to the tram stop. She made me thump on the wall adjoining Molesworth's room and ours. There was an immediate answering thump. She held out her plump arms which were an invitation to seal my promise with a kiss. I left the room and tapped on Molesworth's door. He came out and we left for the tram stop. Apparently Molesworth had a similar experience to my own, and for the same reason. He had, however, spent the night chivalrously on the floor. The following evening we took the girls their box of groceries.

The situation was static now, and we resumed our regular two or three sorties a day; but we still saw no enemy fighters! The flak became more intense and more accurate. We operated over Holland and into Germany, strafing and bombing, attacking any train we saw, shooting up columns of German transport, all now heading east.

Lamb, who had been our Squadron Leader since B 2, went missing. I heard he was shot down by flak while strafing a column of motor transport. He was too low to bale out, so he force-landed his Mustang in the flat fields bordering the long, straight road. He was shot in the cockpit by the troops, who had had to endure his strafing. After landing from a sortie there was no time for a detailed post-mortem, or to gather reports of witnesses. The aircraft were refuelled, guns reloaded, bombs attached, and the Squadron was airborne again. Someone went missing on the first sortie of the day; he was forgotten by evening.

The columns were travelling down the long, straight roads with open country in each side and a few trees lining the road-side. We beat up the transport. The lorries stopped and the troops ran into fields. Many lorries were soon on fire. There was withering light flak from tanks, transports and dispersed troops. We flew down the roads pouring point-five-inch machine gun bullets into the transport. We attacked at ground level. No zooming up after a run, but turning low, and then in again for another run. We had to watch out for each other as the Squadron had broken up into sections and was busy hunting out the batches of hiding soldiers. The lorries stood starkly on the long, open roads and burned, pouring out black smoke which blew away in the wind in horizontal plumes. Before our ammunition was exhausted we re-formed and headed back to base.

On one of these sorties Jimmy Muir was shot down by flak, but managed to parachute out of his aircraft and land near a farmhouse. Some of his Flight had seen soldiers run out of the buildings and shoot him in his parachute as he landed. None of us expected to be welcomed with open arms.

One morning I was called to the Wing Adjutant's office and told to bring my flying log-book. The next day I was informed that I was being posted to rest duties; I should report to the Air Ministry in London in a few days' time. In the middle of September 1944 I left Brussels by Anson and was flown back to England. I never saw any of 65 Squadron again. Later, I heard that shortly after I left, the Wing was sent back to England for a rest. I believe they occupied their time by trying to shoot down doodlebugs (V-1s).

CHAPTER 12

Emanuel

WHILE 'on rest' in London, I used to visit the Brevet Club. After hostilities ended, as a regular army officer on secondment only for the duration of the War, to the RAF, I would be back in the Royal Tank Regiment. The flying I had done convinced me that I wanted to continue as a pilot, being the only thing I could do to earn a living.

One evening in the Brevet Club I met a chap who gave me some good advice which I acted upon. He advised me to apply immediately for a twin-engine conversion course. He explained that at the end of the course I would have to pass an exam on navigation, instruments, the law, and meteorology. I would then receive an RAF certificate, which could be exchanged for a civilian captain's 'B' licence. I would get my instruction free from the RAF, which otherwise I would have to pay for, and which would take longer. I was posted to RAF Coleby Grange, near Lincoln, to start training on the docile Airspeed Oxford.

Shortly before I left London, I met Bob Large and Alexander at the Brevet Club; they told me about Leslie Whitaker's death, which occurred on 4th May, three weeks after my row with Boxer. Leslie had been on an operation carrying a suitcase of money for the underground in the Paris area. During the War, Paris was never 'blacked-out'; on clear nights it shone with a yellow glow visible for miles. He was to land at a field to the west of Paris, but was shot down and crashed near Etaples, possibly by ground fire or a night fighter. The crash site was strewn with bank notes. Leslie was buried at Etaples, south-west of Paris, by the French authorities.

I arrived at King's Cross Station to catch the evening train to Lincoln. It was packed full of soldiery and I could not get a place even to stand. I went to the guard's van and pulled rank as one of the 'boys in blue'. The guard allowed me to sit on the mail bags. I found another RAF chap comfortably settled on his suitcase amidst surrounding mail bags. We introduced ourselves. He was Flt Lt Emanuel Galitzine, who had been on fighters and was going to Coleby Grange for the same reason as myself. Emanuel, like me, was returning to flying after a 'rest period'. He had been operating pressurised Spitfire IX fighters, and on one occasion had intercepted a photographic JU 88 at 43,000 feet over Southampton. When he fired, one of his cannons jammed, which caused a wing to stall, and Emanuel to lose control of his Spitfire at that rarefied height. I had never been above 37,000 feet, except when Sammy Sampson, Leslie and myself had been guinea pigs in the decompression chamber at Farnborough.

Emanuel and I shared a room at Coleby Grange in the spacious married quarters now used for an influx of pupils. Our ultimate destination was Burma, to drop troops and supplies for their attack on the Japanese. Emanuel, I soon learned, was a Russian prince! His family had escaped the Russian Revolution from the Crimea, sailed to France and finally settled in England. He was married to Gwen, (née Rhodes) from a landed family in Ulster. His father opened a small antique shop in Berkeley Square. Emanuel, who was a year older than I was, and his elder brother, George, had gone to Lancing.

After four weeks flying the Oxford, we went to RAF Nuneaton to finish our training on Wellingtons as Dakotas were in short supply. We passed our exams and got our certificates. We were flown to Karachi in the same Dakota and there awaited our Squadron postings to arrive from the headquarters in New Delhi. We were stuck in Karachi transit camp in sweltering heat. One afternoon while we were attempting to cool ourselves beneath lukewarm showers, someone burst into the ablution hut and bellowed "The War's over!! They've dropped an atom bomb on the Japs and they've surrendered!" We continued showering.

The next day both of us were posted to No. 52 Dakota Squadron at RAF Dum Dum Calcutta. We were given a lift in one of the Squadron's Dakotas flying back to Dum Dum via New Delhi, flown by Sqn Ldr Horsfall, who told us what to do and promptly went to sleep in the cabin for most of the long flight back.

I was billeted in the old Dum Dum munitions factory over-looking the road from Calcutta to the airport. Opposite my first storey window and on the other side of the road was the NAAFI for the troops, run by Mr Abdul Gharni, which had been Lord Kitchener's bungalow.

The Squadron flew VIPs between Burma, India and Ceylon. We wore white cotton-drill uniforms as befitted carrying important persons. All the crews were concerned to boost their flying hours, which would help them to get civil flying jobs on return to Blighty. Now that the War was over, it was first in first out. I had to wait six months for repatriation and came back by boat from Bombay.

Stuck out at Dum Dum, forty-five minutes by taxi from Chowringhee, my social life was confined to Lord Kitchener's old bungalow. Emanuel however had an enviable ability to find congenial company. One evening he invited me to the '300 Club' in Theatre Road. I said I would make my own way there. It was dark when a rickshaw wallah dropped me at the Club. There was the aroma most noticeable in the cool-ness of Indian evenings which I came to think of as Brahma Gas, a mixture of beedee and charcoal smoke, jasmin and cow dung.

I entered the gates of the 300 Club which was guarded by a small stocky Gurkha chowkidar, armed with a large sheathed kukri. He saluted me vigorously. Inside the compound was a tennis court lit by a bright electric light bulb hanging from a tall lamp post. In the shadows was a single-storey bungalow. I was surprised by a sight common to the old hands. Thousands of flying insects of all sizes dashed themselves to death in their frenzy to reach the glaring light. The dead bodies fell on me and littered the ground as I approached the entrance to the Club. I was welcomed by a chap in a white dinner jacket, and the sound of someone singing a sad Russian song accompanied by infrequent chords plucked on a guitar. The singer was Emanuel, who introduced me to Boris Lissanevich and to Keera, his wife. She was petite, with the look and figure of a ballet dancer. As a young boy cadet Boris had escaped from a military school at the outbreak of the Revolution, then by the trans-Siberian railway to Vladivostock. Then with other Russians he had followed the trail through China to Hong Kong, Siam and Burma, always one step ahead of the horrors until he and Keera reached India. Soon after I met them, Boris and Keera were divorced. Boris remained in India and Keera went to America. (See *Tiger for Breakfast*, by Michel Peissel, Hodder & Staughton, 1966.)

I returned to the UK by boat in mid-1946, and soon afterwards I got a letter from Emanuel. He was flying Dakotas for Air Service of India from Juhu Airport Bombay. Gwen had joined him as well as his friend Michael Graham, a fellow fighter pilot, also flying for Air Services. This little group was joined by Vaska Stubbs and his wife 'Baby', an exiled Russian princess. Vaska was also flying for Air Services. The airline manager of Air Services was Wg Cdr Bill Burberry DFC, who had been in the RAF in Mesopotamia before the War, flying Westland Wapitis. Emanuel had extolled my virtues to Bill Burberry, who agreed to give me a job, and furthermore if I went to the Scindia Steamship Company's office in the city of London a contract awaited my signature. Air Services of India was a small pre-war subsidiary airline of the Scindia Steamship Company of Bombay. I got on my bike immediately and signed my contract. I was then told that I would be flying a De Haviland Rapide to India which had been purchased for short-haul routes. It was being overhauled in Derby. The winter of '46-'47 was snowy, wet and cold. While waiting for the Rapide to be ready I took the Dakota technical exam and got my certificate. I took off from Croydon on 19th April 1947.

I had a large trunk of Emanuel and Gwen's domestic paraphernalia on board the Rapide. It took me nine days to get to Bombay stopping every 350 miles to refuel. I moved into Emanuel and Gwen's spacious top-floor flat in Pedder Road. Michael Graham also boarded there. Gwen had a baby. The whole ménage was under Gwen's control, ably assisted by Rancho, an absolute jewel of a head bearer.

The chief pilot of Air Services was Capt Moore, one of four Australians. I did my circuits and bumps in the Dakota and was issued with Indian B licence No. 514 by Mr Subramanium, Director General of Civil Aviation, Talkatora Rd., New Delhi. Air Services operated routes on the west side of India. Indore, Bhopal, south to Bangalore and Cochin, north to Cawnpore, Delhi and Srinagar and north-west to airfields en route to Karachi. The four Australians left Air Services, two going to Cathay Pacific in Hong Kong and two to Garuda Airlines of Indonesia. Their places were taken by Captains Peter Brumby, Bartelson, a Norwegian, and Jimmy Grace from America.

After Independence Day, India was divided into three parts, West Pakistan, India, and East Pakistan. All hell broke loose. Trainloads of Hindus and Sikhs moved from West Pakistan to India, mainly Delhi. From India Muslims moved to West and East Pakistan, Hindus moved westward to Bengal. Trains were attacked and passengers murdered by those of the other community. It was murder and mayhem by each community on the other.

Wingco Burberry sent a Dakota flown by me, First Officer Bunny Cariappa and Radio Officer S.A. Kirtikar to Delhi, followed a week later by a second Dakota captained by Capt Peter Brumby. Engineers and crew stayed in The Marina, a boarding house in Connaught Circus, New Delhi.

Our office in Delhi took bookings from a Muslim family to fly them to Pakistan; the parties had to arrange for a Hindu family to fly back to Delhi. Somehow it worked. There was always a family waiting to be brought back. We mostly landed at out-of-the-way uncontrolled airstrips, built during the war. The Hindus leaving Pakistan from an out-of-the-way airstrip always had their baggage searched by the police for gold ornaments, money and jewellery before we were allowed to take off.

At the end of August we did a refugee flight to Chaklala, the airfield at Rawalpindi, and picked up a Hindu family. As we taxied out for the return flight to Delhi, we had a fine view of half a dozen buses speeding eastwards along the dusty road south of the airfield. Inside and on the roofs were a crowd of turbaned tribesmen, cheering and waving rifles as the buses sped north, leaving plumes of dust behind them. Bunny, who had been at Miramsha on the north-west frontier during the war, recognised them as Pathan tribesmen.

A few days later Kashmir was invaded from Pakistan, and the significance of what we had seen came home to us. An invading force of tribesmen, with promises of plunder and rape, had been transported by bus to invade Kashmir. By the time the burning and pillaging and gunfire could be heard in Srinagar, all the airline companies had sent every aircraft they could spare to Delhi, leaving only a skeleton staff to carry on the much reduced schedule routes. We carried troops as fast as we could from Ambala, Ferozepur, Delhi and Amritsar to Srinagar. The troops just piled into the aircraft, with no nonsense about load sheets, manifests or weight schedules. The aerodromes at Srinagar and Jammu were grass fields. After the first wave of troops, we were switched to flying in ammunition and army rum in gallon glass flagons. The refugees, Kashmiri Hindus who had been burnt out of their villages, were pouring into Srinagar airfield.

After off-loading troops and ammunition we taxied to another part of the airfield to the waiting refugees; immediately the aircraft was surrounded by a screeching, pushing and struggling mob. Bunny, Kirti and myself retired to the edge of the airfield to eat samozas and drink tea, served by bearers from Nedou's Hotel, while the people scrambled into the Dakota and then started to scream for their luggage to be passed up by friends and relatives. Gradually the refugees realised that there was no violent hurry and quietened down, and as a result became more manageable. We flew them to Jammu on the south side of the Bannihal Pass.

On several occasions we carried over sixty souls in the Dakota together with their miserable belongings. No manifest or other papers were asked for or needed. The passengers were thin and emaciated women, children and old men.

On 7 September 1947 we did a refugee flight from Delhi to Quetta via Karachi. We took off early in the morning from Delhi with a Muslim family accompanied by large battered tin trunks, each locked with two or three huge padlocks. We off-loaded the family at Karachi, refuelled and pressed on. When we landed at Quetta, the control tower appeared to be deserted. Then from a cubby hole at the bottom of the tower a policeman in khaki shorts emerged, carrying the usual .303 service rifle. He knew nothing, so we sat in the shade under the wing of the aircraft and waited. The sun got hotter and hotter. The concrete runway, parking area, and macadam taxiways gave off a shimmering vapour of hot air. Around us were the rocky hills, silent and desert. The policeman returned to his hideout, and we were left in solitude. We were used to such a reception. Bunny took off his jodhpur boots, Kirti opened his Film India magazine, and I lay down under the fuselage to sleep. After an hour or so, a car drove up with more police on board. We explained why we had come. The police seemed to know all about it, and told us to wait as the family was coming.

The police retired to the control tower and were as anxious as ourselves for the family to arrive, but for a different reason. Another hour passed. At last an old Buick arrived packed with tin trunks. A man in sherwani and pyjama begged us to wait as his whole family was on the way. We told him to relax and that we would wait for another hour, but time was getting short. We had to get back to Delhi that night in order to carry out the following day's refugee flight. We were also apprehensive about getting stuck in Quetta. There was always a possibility that some petty bureaucrat might ask us for permits and other non-existent papers. After another hour there was still no sign of the family. The town was about twelve miles from the aerodrome. We got up from under the wing and the man started to dance around us doing a jig of terror and pleading. We could not wait any longer. We got into the aircraft. The man beat his hands on the cabin door, rushed to the front of the aircraft and started hopping around. We felt awful. The police came out of their cover and stood around laughing at the miserable panic-stricken man. We started the starboard engine. The poor man was wringing his hands in supplication. Without looking at each other, we taxied down the burning hot taxi track, lined up on the runway, and took off. After we got airborne I flew down the long black ribbon of road leading to Quetta. We had a good view of the road as it wound its way across the hills. Three cars were speeding towards the airfield. I turned downwind, put the undercarriage down and landed. The man was where we had left him, sitting and crying. He looked up at us and put his head back on his arms. We got out and told him to get up and get ready as we had seen his cars coming down the road.

Bunny, Kirti and I would take charge of the situation, by making the refugees load their luggage under our orders. In this way, if the police wanted to interfere they would have to come to me as commander of the aircraft, and in charge of the loading. The cars arrived. The three of us waved our arms and shouted at them to draw up near the aircraft. The dilapidated old Buicks were filled with wives, grandmothers, daughters, sons, cousin-brothers, brothers, babies, sons-in-law, daughters-in-law and every other possible degree of relation. More tin trunks, some painted with garish roses, or pictures of the Taj Mahal by moonlight, all with two or three large padlocks, were lugged out by the males. Kirti supervised the loading of the aircraft, which meant just packing the stuff into the gangway, while Bunny and I shouted at the family. We quickly got the women and children into the aircraft. After the tin trunks came the bed rolls in canvas covers tied with leather straps or pieces of rope, then smaller tin boxes and lastly the brass pots. We had forty souls on board. I simply could not fathom where all the luggage came from. It was packed into the old Buicks in every conceivable place, except under the bonnets.

By now the police, about six of them, had moved from their shelter, and stood about a dozen paces from the cars. They watched and wondered what to do as they saw the luggage, with its imagined contents of gold and treasure, being loaded aboard. We were putting up a great show of ordering people about, and the passengers were terrified of us. Everybody was sweating. Just before the last piece of luggage was loaded, I got all the passengers on board and told Bunny to go to the cockpit and that when I banged the fuselage with my hand he was to start the starboard engine. I had a suspicion that the police might jump into the aircraft before we left, so a quick getaway was essential. I took out the undercarriage pins and made a show of swinging them nonchalantly about by their tapes. I went up to what appeared to be the senior policeman and shook him by the hand with a great show of affability. All were aboard. I banged the fuselage, got into the aircraft, pulled in the passenger steps and shut the door. By the time I had scrambled over the luggage which blocked the gangway, and got into my seat, Bunny had started both engines and was ready to taxi. The police had woken to the situation and ran in front of the aircraft; one man was making frantic signs with his arms. Bunny moved the aircraft forward, while I waved a hearty goodbye. The police moved out of the way. I kept on waving from the cockpit side-window. As we turned off the parking apron onto the taxiway, I saw behind that the police had received a good blast of dust from our propellers and were rubbing their eyes and setting their pugris straight. We got to the runway, and without more ado, lined up and took off. It was four o'clock in the afternoon. We set course for Karachi. Kirti and I went back to count the passengers and make out bogus manifests for the Karachi authorities.

The confusion in the cabin was total: we discovered that we had forty-seven souls crammed into the aircraft's twenty-eight seats. I could not put forty names, with seven babies, on the manifest, nor could I be sure that the aircraft would not be inspected by some zealous official at Karachi where we had to refuel. I made out a list in quintuplicate, of twenty-five names, comprising all the males, some females, and a smattering of babies. The balance was mostly grandmothers, young children and the remaining babies. These last we sat on the floor between the seats. We then placed boxes and bedrolls on the seats so that the people on the floor were not visible. The idea was to disembark twenty-five souls at Karachi and leave the rest in the aircraft. Any snooping policemen would find the aircraft apparently empty, except for luggage.

Karachi was in chaos. There were Muslim refugees coming in, Hindus departing and the usual crowd of sightseers and marauding police. Fortunately the sun had now set. We were met by Mr Gokaldas, a Muslim who had previously been in our Delhi office, until his insistence on wearing his red fez at all times had led to him being beaten by Indian patriots in Connaught Circus. The next day he had applied for transfer to our office at Karachi Airport. Still wearing his fez, Mr Gokaldas shepherded the twenty-five passengers to the waiting room. The rest of our load, whom we had succeeded in terrifying into silence, lay like corpses under the baggage as the aircraft was refuelled. No-one came to look inside. We had a four-and-a-half hour flight in front of us. There was no cloud, only a full sky of stars. We were worn out so 'George', the automatic pilot, took over. The passenger cabin lights were out, the passengers had made themselves as comfortable as possible and all forty-seven of them appeared to be fast asleep. Fifty pairs of eyes were closed as Dakota VT-AXD, flown by 'George', droned its way across the Rajasthan desert.

Bunny and I came to life as the glare of Delhi's lights was seen against the night sky, some eighty miles away. We landed at Willingdon just before midnight. Our family was now in their new home.

We flew to many other places in the Punjab to pick up refugees. We never knew how many passengers were waiting for us, and so we brought back everybody we could cram into the aircraft along with their tin trunks and bedrolls. The strips we landed at had been built during the war, and now were without control authorities, or petrol; just a crowd of refugees being harassed by the police digging around in their wretched luggage, looking for gold ornaments, money or anything else that took their fancy. There were always arguments at the airfields. People of one party would try and get a place in somebody else's aeroplane; money would come out and be exchanged for seats. Some crews sold extra seats and pocketed the money. Families did likewise by selling seats to people who could not afford a whole aeroplane. No one ever offered us money to do anything. Only once did we ever get anything from our refugees. On another trip from Quetta we brought back a Sikh family. At night between Karachi and Delhi the Sardarji came up to the cockpit and offered us a fruitcake, baked by his wife. It was very good. We finished it and went back to sleep.

Our evening entertainment if we were not too exhausted was to visit Sundari 'The Beautiful One'. She was a Punjabi gana-walli from Lahore. She and her mother had fled to Delhi, accompanied by male relatives who made up her orchestra of tabla, shahnai, harmonium and sarangi.

Inside the Ajmeeri Gate, on the south-west side of Old Delhi, was a long two-storeyed barrack block. At night all was dark. The shops on the ground floor were boarded up and secured by heavy chains and large padlocks, and the windows were shuttered. From the floors above two narrow stone stairways descended, and from each, as from ancient gramophone horns, came faintly, the high-pitched rhythmical quavering of girls singing. Inside this block was the seventh heaven of paradisiacal delights. The first floor was a warren for five-rupee prostitutes, each guarded by her family or pimp, and each having a string charpoi covered by a soiled quilt. On the second floor were small rooms on both sides of a long passage for the singers.

A visitor looked into the rooms, chose the most beautiful girl or the one with the sweetest voice, entered and sat on the floor by the wall. Opposite him was the 'gadi', a mattress, on which sat the musicians and at one corner the girl's mother, who had been a gana-walli in her day.

Sundari was very beautiful, more mature than most singers, and had very fair skin. She was well-rounded, full of composure and contentment, dressed simply in choli and a pastel-coloured sari. She wore the usual dangling gold ear-rings, gold necklace, and a thin gold bracelet through her right nostril. She accompanied her singing with graceful and fluid arm movements and her hands formed the traditional mudras that emphasised the songs' meaning. She had a large repertoire, from classical gazzals to modern Indian film songs. Her attraction for us was her unattainability, her dignity and charm.

In that small room, devoid of furniture, and beneath a low-powered naked bulb, Sundari was the centre of adoration. Her beauty was enhanced by contrast with her orchestra of four pan-chewing, unshaven and scrawny men, dressed in grubby pyjamas and long black sherwani coats with the buttons undone. They blew, tapped, squeezed and sawed with unflagging gusto.

Sundari had cause to remember us. The audience would ask her to sing their favourite songs. As she sang she would come to each devotee and sing to him. The custom was to show one's pleasure by holding up a folded ten- or hundred-rupee note, or place the note over one's heart, and so entice the singer to come nearer and take the money. Her audience were mostly well-to-do business men. We were the exception. The others lavishly teased her with hundred-rupee notes, but she was lucky to get five rupees from any of us.

Over the next five years, whenever any of us came to Delhi he would call on Sundari. I last saw her in Bombay where she had spread her 'gadi' in a similar warren, euphemistically called Congress House.

At the end of January 1948, we flew our Dakota back to Bombay for a rest period.

1a: Little ayah, Lindsay & Murray, Bangalore, 1923.

1b: Sepoy Sahib, Bangalore, 1923.

1c: Murray & Lindsay with their father, Col Vass Anderson, 1927.

2a: Anderson 'Ma' & Anderson 'Mi', St Ronans.

2b: Author in Sunday Best, Cheltenham College, 1935.

2c: Cadet Drury fainting at Passing Out Parade, 'The Shop', 1939.

3a: 2nd Lieut MCB Anderson, 8th Bn RTR, 1939.

3b: Mark One Infantry Tank.

4a: End of course at Old Sarum, March 1941.
Back row: Bowes, Charles-Jones, Penman, Seggie, Anderson.
Front row: Wilson, Larsen, Mould, Higson, Bailey, Thomas.

4b: Author, Mount Farm, 1941, landed after 6th sortie.

5a: F/Lt Nebbie Wheeler, DFC, RAF Benson, 1941.

5b: F/O Sydney Dowse, RAF Benson, 1941.

5c: F/Lt Per Hysing-Dahl, DFC & bar. RAF Benson, 1941.

6a: F/Lt Leslie Whitaker, RAF Benson, 1942.

6b: F/Lt Bob Large, DFC.

7b: F/Lt Prince Emanuel Galitzine, Coleby Grange, 1945.

7a: F/O Jimmy Muir, 1944.

7c: Author, DFC & bar. 1945.

8a: White 'dicer' Spitfire, used by PRU for low-level photographs from below cloud.

8b: Standard pick-up Lysander used by 'A' Flight 161 Squadron.

8c: Mustang with drop tanks.

9a: Major C Sleigh, RE, ('Uncle-Father'),
& Estelle Bell Sleigh ('Mum').

9b: Lieut. A V Anderson ('Sandy'.
Died at sea, July 25, 1958).

10: 2nd from left, R/O Merchant, 3rd Capt Prince Emanuel Galitzine, 4th F/O Agniholtri. Air Services of India.

11a: R/O Kirtikar, 1948. Cockpit sketch by author.

11b: Kirti & author. Tea at Jammu, 1948.

11c: Capt Kapur, 1948. Cockpit sketch by author.

12a: R/O Trelokekar & author by Brahmaputra, 1951.

12b: Incident at Machuka, 1952.

12c: Dillip Mitra, author, R/O Menon, F/O Sen, Capt Singh, returned from Machuka.

12d: A flower of the Abor Hills, 1952.

13a: Capt Budziokowski ('Budji'), chief pilot of Himalayan Aviation.

13b: Capt & Mrs Frank Czekalski, Capt 'Ziggy' Zigernierski, Grand Hotel, Calcutta, 1952.

14a: Joe & Doreen Koszarek, early 1950s, Bombay.

14b: Joe Koszarek, Peter Baldwin on wall. Co-founders of Indamer.

14c: Capt Johnny Brenand, Manager of Indamer, Calcutta.

15a: 2nd left, author, 3rd Joe Koszarek, with Indamer staff, Juhu, 1964.

15b: Capt 'Bull' Bulsara, en route Kabul.

16a: Author, 1955.

16b: F/O Jimmy Bottliwallah, Capt Ivan Reardon, R/O Teddy Grubert, Bahrain, 1954.

17a: 2nd left, Prince Emanuel Galitzine, 3rd Inga Lissanevitch, 4th Boris Lissanevitch, front, Nicholas Lissanevitch. Arriving in Kathmandu.

17b: Author, Capt Jai Singh, R/O Shome. Pokara, 1956.

The temple at Pashupatinath

18: Temple at Pashupatinath, Kathmandu.

19a: Self portrait by author, 1953.

19b: Abor girls by author, 1953.

PART 2

CHAPTER 13

Assam Airlift

THE next area of chaos which had been building up from the first days of Partition was in the eastern areas of India. The northernmost point of the newly formed East Pakistan was just south of Siliguri. The gap between Siliguri and the Sikkim border, about 40 miles, was the only land passage between Bengal and the Indian state of Assam, the Kasi Hills, Manipur, and the Naga and Lushai Hills, the last two bordering Burma.

The formation of East Pakistan virtually cut off access to and from the tea- garden areas of north-east India from Calcutta, their main port for export. Railways and roads no longer served the areas they were made for. The great Brahmaputra entered East Pakistan just west of the Kasi Hills, so river and canal traffic were denied unhindered access to Calcutta.

The airlift started in earnest in early 1949 when tea-chests had to be flown from Assam, the Douars and Tripura for export from Calcutta. The vital goods for the bazaars - medicines, building materials, machinery, cloth, food and passengers had to be flown from Calcutta. In the gap between Siliguri and Sikkim was Bagdogra, an airfield with refuelling facilities. Dakotas could refuel there and load up with tea-chests from the Douars gardens. From the entrance to Assam valley to the tea-gardens around Tinsukia, at the east end of the valley, was a round trip of 600 miles. These difficulties were to bring about many subterfuges, to enable the Dakotas to carry the maximum load to and from places so far from Calcutta.

In 1949 a massive airlift into the Assam valley by the private freight Dakotas had started. Flying over Pakistan was only permitted to the Indian airlines, operating scheduled passenger flights to Assam and Tripura. This obstructive regulation was enforced by the Indian aviation authorities. The charter companies were forced to overcome this regulation by flying over Pakistan and sending false position reports and faking the times of take-off and landing from outlying fields. In theory the route to Assam was north to Bagdogra keeping over Indian territory then flying east with Bhutan on your port side, into the Assam valley. In practice you flew straight to the Assam valley, cutting the corner while sending position reports as though you were flying via Bagdogra. Companies operating with one or two Dakotas were Indamer Company and Air Services of India, both from Bombay, and Jamair, Kalinga Airlines, Darbanga and Himalayan Airlines of Calcutta. These companies had one or two Dakotas permanently at Dum Dum, which amounted to ten or twelve Dakotas each operating twice daily on the Assam Airlift. Many tea-gardens in the Douars area and those in the Assam valley made their own landing fields by spreading cinders from the tea-drying ovens on their surfaces, making them usable during the monsoon season. Old wartime concrete runways, such as Hasimara, Misimara, Tezpur, Gauhati, Jorhat, Mohanberi, Chabua, Sookerating and those in Tripura at Imphal, Silchar and Kumbigram, once more came into use.

The monsoon did not appreciably hinder operations into the Assam Valley. Solid rain with a cloud base of 400 feet made it necessary to fly below the cloud, getting your windscreen wipers working flat out and 'pressing on regardless'. There were radio beacons at a few airfields, but the valley is narrow, and the hills to the north and south, and static from storm clouds, made it unwise to attempt let-down procedures through solid cloud. It was always wisest to get below, down to ground level if necessary, and fly visually in monsoon conditions. Once out of the valley you were over the flat plains of Bengal with its rivers, all the way to Dum Dum.

The usual programme was two flights to Bagdogra a day making a twelve-hour duty, with landing time, time for lunch, and transport to and from Calcutta. Three Bagdogras a day meant sixteen hours' duty, too long to carry on for more than two days consecutively.

I remember four accidents during the early 1949 period of the airlift. On an early morning take-off from Dum Dum, before sunrise, a Dakota got airborne from runway 180, turned right and crashed. It was discovered that the pilot had taken off without engaging his artificial horizon instrument. As he turned to head north, he put on too much bank and crashed in the circuit of the airport. On another occasion Capt George Pretzel took off from Dum Dum in early dawn. The control tower saw smoke coming from an engine and informed him by radio that his starboard engine was on fire. George feathered the starboard propeller and crashed. It was the port engine that was on fire. By feathering the starboard he was left with no power, or time. The heavily loaded Dakota crashed into the palm trees and rice fields and burst into flames, killing the crew.

Again, one early morning I took off for a flight due north to an old wartime airstrip, Hasimara. I was carrying a load of bazaar supplies, and was to return with tea-chests from Duars tea-gardens. Another Dakota, of the Indamer company, took off five minutes behind me, also for Hasimara. I landed. There were two lorries loaded with tea-chests waiting. I was unloaded and reloaded but the Dakota following me did not arrive. I took off for Dum Dum. The Indamer Dakota never arrived. Later a search party was sent to Hasimara. This airstrip was only a few miles south of the densely forested Bhutan foot-hills. The searchers eventually saw the burnt-out remains of a Dakota across a valley embedded in jungle on the ridge of a hill that could not be reached. It was surmised that the crew may have been asleep while the Dakota, flying on autopilot, over-flew Hasimara and so crashed. Another possibility was that a corroded hot-air duct bringing warm air to the cockpit, and which was heated by a surrounding exhaust jacket might have allowed exhaust fumes into the cockpit and asphyxiated Capt Stitson, Capt Bearcroft and Radio Officer Chakravatty.

Another Indamer Dakota went missing in late 1950, after the great Assam earthquake. It was carrying freight for tea-gardens and the bazaars of north-east Assam. It never arrived at its destination. The crew were Capt Waltham, F/O Rao and an unknown radio officer. Shortly after its disappearance I landed at Mohanbari, where I met Capt Ivan Reardon who had flown an Indamer D18 twin Lockheed from Bombay to carry out a search over the forest. While I was talking to him on the tarmac there was a sudden short tremor. Ivan continued his search for two days, but from the start it was impossible to find anything beneath a thick carpet of virgin forest at the north end of the valley. The area was in any case uninhabited, only visited by a few hunting Nagas and tigers.

Flying nine and ten hours a day on these charter flights called for a bull-headed attitude from the crews. The pre-monsoon cumulo-nimbus north-westers of Bengal had to be flown through regardless of their severity. The luxury of a diversion to fly around a gigantic cunimb had to be discarded if the aircraft was to get back on time, in order to do another trip to Bagdogra or Cooch Bihar. You could not tell how severe the turbulence was until you were in a north-wester. The crash of one of the early Comets occurred when it flew into a cunimb on track from Dum Dum to Delhi in 1950. The Dakotas loaded with 7,500 lbs of tea-chests heading for Dum Dum, or outward bound with freight for Assam, ploughed their way through anything that lay in their path.

Each pilot developed his own technique. We ran into the worst of the north-westers around the heat of midday. As I approached abeam English Bazaar at 10,000 feet after leaving

Bagdogra, I could see ahead of me a line of large cunimbs running south-east to the north-west, vast white heaps of cloud ascending up to 30,000 feet. Bigger than any mountain on earth, and topped by dazzling white cloud against a clear, blue sky, its shape continuously changing. Its base 500 feet from the ground, and coloured a dark grey-blue, an opaque sheet of pouring rain lashed the ground as it moved over the earth's surface.

On such occasions I would send Radio Officer Manubhai Desai and my co-pilot, Shenoy, back into the cabin to check that the ropes were over the tea-chests, so that in severe turbulence they would not bounce to the roof and then come crashing down onto the floor. They reported back that all were tied down. We all fastened our lap straps to save us from being thrown up to the cockpit roof and bashing our heads. Manubhai sent a last message to Calcutta control giving a false position, and ETA at Dum Dum. We were supposed to be over Indian territory further to the west, but were in fact on direct track to Dum Dum, which put us over East Pakistan and coming up to the Ganges. Manubhai wound in his trailing aerial, and switched off his radio. This was a precaution against a strike by lightning on the aerial, which would blow up the radio set.

Although we were in broad daylight I could see horrible flashes of pale lightning within the cunimb. They were like a line of Man-of-War, white sails billowing above, from their dark hulls flashed the irregular staccato of their guns. I throttled back to 110 mph and increased the revs. By decreasing speed, the up-and-down draughts put less strain on the aircraft's structure. The idea was to keep the aircraft horizontal, that is, in the normal flying position. I had put on cockpit lights and the pitot head heaters. We had said our prayers. The rest was up to me.

We were already in shadow as a huge anvil-shaped cloud spread out 25,000 feet above us. The aircraft entered the cloud with a slight bump. All was dark grey around us; then it got darker. Nothing happened. Perhaps I had struck a calm patch. I watched the artificial horizon keeping the little aeroplane level with the horizon bar. My speed was 120 mph, engine temperature was fine. Suddenly there was a frightful loud roar, coming from over the whole aircraft. The windscreen was being hammered by a million ice pellets. It got darker outside and the aircraft started to bounce around. We were in a violent hailstorm. From now on everything happened at once. I no longer bothered to look out of the windscreen, but kept my eyes on the instruments in front of me. A violent bank of 60 degrees to starboard I corrected. The nose came up and the airspeed fell off to 90 mph. I righted the horizon, the speed built up to 160. I corrected, watching the horizon bar all the time, struggling to keep the aircraft in a horizontal position.

The vertical climb indicator shot off the clock. I saw the altimeter needle winding in a matter of seconds to 8,000 feet, 10,000 feet, 11,000 feet. The air speed indicator fluctuated from 100 mph to 180 mph. I yelled at Shenoy:

"Carburettor heat! Oil shutters! Wheels down!"

I had to increase engine power to maintain 120 mph airspeed, and so increase an otherwise falling engine temperature. The roar of the hailstones gave way to a more muffled sound. We were flying through driving sleet. It was dark, with flashes of opaque lightning hidden in the cloud. We began a steady climb in an updraught. Then another crashing roar of hailstones started, drowning out the roar of the engine. It was now dark blue outside. I felt that we had passed through the centre, and now in the southern half of the cunimb I detected a change of colour to a light grey. The sound of the rain on the aircraft skin got softer. Suddenly we were in sunlight, blue sky above, below was the patina of green paddy fields. Away to the south I could see a dark grey blotch of Krishnagar, then Kalyan, and the French enclave of Chandernagore on the west bank of the Hooghly. How beautiful everything was. Somewhere below was the battlefield of Plassey, fought two hundred years before, and the cause of me being where I was.

I slumped back in my seat. "Wheels up, Shenoy old boy!"

I switched off the cockpit lights, undid my lap strap, and put in 'George', the auto pilot. I called up Dum Dum approach, 119.7, gave them our position as 75 miles north, and ETA in half-an-hour. I would visit the Casanova in the evening. Tomorrow was my day off, I hoped.

In time I got used to the cunimbs, more relaxed. I never succeeded in being anything but shit-scared before entering one. Perhaps it was written in our horoscopes that First Officer Eduljee Engineer, Radio Officer K N Trelokekar, and myself would meet our fate together. Once inside the cunimbs, these meditations vanished.

"Watch the horizon bar! Wheels down! Carb heat! Oil shutters!" Here we go again. The monsoon brought its own difficulties. It rained for days on end, from medium cloud and low stratus. The Assam valley was blanketed with cloud down to 400 feet, while rain fell steadily, flooding paddy fields, isolating villages, washing away long stretches of the connecting roads. There were four radio beacons down the length of the valley, at Gauhati, Tezpur, Jorhat, and Mohanbari. These were mostly rendered ineffective by moisture seeping into the equipment on the aircraft, and the proximity of the deflecting nearby hillsides.

We set off from Dum Dum and flew straight across Pakistan to Rupsi, at the entrance to the valley. It was essential to see the ground and fix your position, before flying up the wide, sprawling Brahmaputra. At Gauhati we landed in pools of muddy water that covered the old wartime pressed-steel runway. Further up the valley we could be down to 200 feet, with a visibility of 600 yards in rain and low cloud.

Landing at Sookerating

In the Second World War the Americans built several concrete runway airfields in the north-east of the Assam Valley, between the Brahmaputra and the Naga Hills. Now five years after the end of the year, their control towers, hangars and barracks stood forlorn wrecks, their windows broken, trees and bamboos growing through their roofs, their wide runways remaining as concrete avenues amidst the thick jungle.

In their glory days, four-engined transport aircraft, laden with military supplies, had taken off and climbed over the 'Hump', a range of 20,000-foot mountains east of the Lohit river, and flown the 500 miles to the Chinese bases at Kunming and Chungking.

Sookerating was in the tea-garden area of Tinsukia in north-east Assam. It was an uncontrolled airfield without facilities such as fire engines or aerodrome staff. At Sookerating the main hazard was cows. In the monsoon season, groups of cows stood on the runways keeping their feet out of the surrounding sodden forest. At the sound of an approaching aircraft, small boys carrying six-foot bamboo poles, were alerted. You flew over the runway intended for landing. Immediately the small boys whacked the cows' backsides with their poles, and drove them into the jungle at the runway edge. The boys stood on guard in case a cow decided to make a last second's dash onto the runway. The cows left their turds on the runway, which, diluted by the monsoon rains, made a slippery mulch, fatal to a Dakota applying its brakes too vigorously while turning back to the contractor, who was waiting with his lorry load of tea-chests for the return flight.

The unloading and reloading took its time, while in rain or sunshine the crew stood under the wing and ate samosas or potato bhajis, and drank tea provided by the contractor. Two coolies would be pumping petrol from 40-gallon drums, using a hand pump, into the main tanks, enough to get you back to Gauhati.

In the hot season the runways were clear. The cows and small boys preferred to remain in the jungle shade at the edge of the runway. The cows looked for the odd green leaf. A tiger from the Naga Hills might be looking for his lunch, and let out a grunt. Immediately a gaggle of cows would rush onto the runway. The small boys beat them back, while shouting and whacking the runway with bamboos, frightening the tiger and driving the cows back into the bush. Now was the time to take off.

It is fifty-seven years since I last took off from blessed Sook-erating. There may be no aeroplanes, but cows guarded by other small boys will be there. A tiger from the Naga Hills will still prowl the jungle seeking its lunch.

CHAPTER 14

The Supply Drop

IN the winter of 1950, Bunny Cariappa, Dillip Mitra and myself were sharing a flat in Theatre Road, Calcutta. Back from a day's flying from Dum Dum to Assam, we were having supper when there was an extraordinary noise from all around us, lasting a few seconds. It sounded like crockery being crushed. The ceiling fan and light began to sway. "Earth-quake!", Dillip exclaimed. It was over in seconds. In the north of Assam, 1,000 miles away, spasmodic minor shocks were felt for several months.

In January 1951, the External Affairs Department in New Delhi contacted Wingco Bill Burberry and requested him to undertake a supply dropping operation in the hills on the north bank of the Brahmaputra bordering the MacMahon Line. This line was a cartographic fiction negotiated between a Tibetan delegation and British India in 1914 at a conference in Simla. The Chinese regarded Tibet as within their sphere of influence and refused to recognise the line. The western end of this line starts at Eastern Bhutan, then follows the unsurveyed Eastern Himalayas to south of the 25,500-foot Namcha Barwa, then north of the Mishmi Hills to the gorge-like crevice through which the Lohit river flows from east Tibet into the northern end of the Assam valley. The Indian Airforce was heavily engaged in supplying the army in Ladakh facing the Tibetan border, and the troops on the Kashmir border with Pakistan, which accounted for us doing the dropping.

On 27th January 1951 two Air Service of India Dakotas were positioned at Jorhat in the Assam valley, a concrete runway airfield built during the war, and now the base for the army supply drop. Our captains were Tutu Amber, Bunny Cariappa, both ex-air force, and myself, with First Officers Leslie Gomes, Malhotra and Adi Kapadia, and Radio Officers Kopkhar, Eddie Amana and Trelokekar.

We were welcomed by Major Gurung of the Assam Rifles, whose outposts we were to supply, and by Mrs Kingdon Ward. Mr Kingdon Ward, a botanist, his wife and an escort of Assam Rifles had gone up the Lohit valley as far as Rima, when the earthquake occurred. They had to hide in caves beneath the treacherous overhangs to avoid the falling rocks. It took them three months to get out of the Lohit valley. Mr Kingdon Ward as a young army officer had been on a botanical expedition in the Himalayas in 1923*. After his excursion on this occasion he was recuperating at a nearby tea-garden. The morning we arrived, Tutu Amber and myself were despatched with parachute loads to drop at Wallong, the northern outpost in the Lohit valley. Mrs Kingdon Ward insisted on flying in my aircraft to see from the air the route she had travelled. As we entered the Lohit valley she stood at the open door taking photos of the earthquake damage to the hills, while sepoys clung to a rope round her middle.

The valley is a narrow gorge at Wallong, 15,000 ft below the 'Hump', over which during wartime, American transport had flown supplies from Assam to the Chinese. The dropping zone at Wallong was short, which necessitated, after a dropping run, a climb of 3,000 ft to where the valley was wide enough to do a 180 degrees turn, and head back for the next dropping run.

Landing at Ziro Camp, 7th February 1951

The earthquake, whose epicentre was in Eastern Tibet, affected the mountain tracks and waterways of the north-east of the

---

*See **No passport to Tibet**, F M Bailey, pub Rupert Hart-Davis, 1957

Assam Valley. At that time three Dakota crews, operating two aircraft of Air Services of India, Bombay, were flying on the Assam Airlift from Dum Dum airport. The mountain tracks of the Eastern Himalayas were destroyed as rocks and forest trees fell into the deep valleys and blocked the flowing waters with a series of natural dams. The Tsang Po rises in western Tibet, flows south of Lhasa, then continues 500 miles to flow round Namcha Barwa, 25,500 feet, and then changes its name to the Dihang, flows south, emerging into the Assam Valley at Pasighat, and 30 miles further south the waters become the Brahmaputra on its way down the Assam valley to the Ganges Delta and the Bay of Bengal. The Bramaputra became a stream, because the waters that fed it were held back by natural dams.

The outposts in the tribal districts of the Eastern Himalayas, manned by the Assam Rifles, were cut off. The tracks used by the porters carrying supplies to the posts had disappeared in rubble, making air dropping the only way to supply them, soon extended to cover the Naga Hills, bordering Burma. Portering, recruited from the local tribes, had never been popular. When I finally left India in 1967, the dropping was still going on from Jorhat, operated by Kalinga Airlines of Calcutta.

One of the most intriguing outposts was at Ziro Camp, in the Subansiri Frontier Tract. It was inside a ring of hills, about ten miles in diameter, resembling a shallow dish. The fields were cultivated by Akka tribesmen. The Assam Rifles' post was on the northern slope. There was a long swathe of grass about 500 yards long and 20 yards wide which was the dropping zone for supplies. Josh Reynolds, a tea planter living near Tinsukia, used to fly in the Political Officer and land his Auster on the strip.

I had done several free drops at Ziro. The altitude of the plateau was about 4,000 ft. It took 20 days' march through thick jungle for porters to reach Ziro from Lillabari in the Assam valley. The grass strip was slightly uphill from south to north. The bags of free drop left short marks on the grass where they fell. I surmised that the ground was fairly hard.

The Supply Drop

On 7th February 1951 I flew a Dakota VT-AUU from Mohanbari to free-drop food and clothing at Ziro. My crew were F/O Edulji Engineer, a Parsi, and R/O Kopkhar, both from Bombay. I decided "No more dropping. I'm going to land". If we had an accident, got bogged down, or nosed over on landing in soft earth, there would be hellish repercussions. Wing Commander Bill Burberry would have a fit. Delhi would suspend my licence. Mechanics would have to trek through the jungle to carry out repairs. Extra supplies of food would have to be dropped. We would lose the dropping contract.

There was another attraction at Ziro Camp. It had a legend. The Lushai Hills had the huge White Tiger. The upper reaches of the Brahmaputra had their giant Water Serpent. The Appartani Plateau had its Buroo. The last Buroo had been killed within the memory of an aged Akka tribesman, so we were informed by Mr Menzies the Political Officer. It was a horned and scaley animal, about the size of a buffalo, with saw-like scales along its back and its long, trailing tail. (An ankylosaurus?) Its bones were said to lie in a small swamp among the paddy fields.

I decided to land on the dropping zone. I dragged the Dak in with plenty of engine, full flap and plonked it down at the beginning of the sloping grass swathe. We stopped about 100 yards from the top end. The waiting troops, Akka males, females and children stood in silent amazement. The bags were thrown out. The troops pushed the aircraft round to face down the gentle slope. From now on, loads were picked up at Lillabari and 25 minutes later landed at Ziro.

The Akkas had been isolated for God knows how long. Where had they come from? A few days later Dillip Mitra came with us to Ziro. He invited what appeared to be a head man for a flight to Lillabari. There was a squabble among them as to who should go. Only one was to be taken. One was eventually pushed forward by his fellows. On the flight back to Lillabari for another load he insisted on standing at the cargo door which had been removed. A rope was tied round his middle and the troops had to pull him back when he got too close to the open doorway.

On the way back from Lillabari we carried a bicycle for the troops. When it was off-loaded one of the soldiers rode it a few yards to the piled bags of supplies. He got off, leaned the bike on the bags. There was a rush of three Akkas fighting and pushing to get at the cycle. One got on and fell off; another grabbed the bike but was pulled off. The bike was rescued and put under guard. The Akka who had come back with us was talking and gesticulating to his companions. Another squabble developed over who was going on the next trip.

When we got back from our next trip with our passenger who stood in the open doorway going and coming, there was a small riot around the bicycle. One Akka actually managed to stay on for two yards before he was pulled off by others. In a matter of days they had entered the twentieth century by air and bicycle.

The repercussions of our landing at Ziro had a similar effect in Shillong. Now the administrators who knew the area of the NEFA only from maps and reports could penetrate an area without the discomfort of seventeen days trudging through the jungle. A bureaucrat could visit Ziro by air, and after half-an-hour's visit became an authority on the tribal people. The life of a Political Officer was threatened with unwelcome change. Before, he lived quietly in the foothills. Now he was faced with a move to Ziro. Soon plans were made to build a road.

Later the Governor of Assam was flown to Ziro, followed by Pandit Nehru and entourage. Both were ignored by the locals who were still lining up for their attempt to ride the bicycle, now overseen by a sepoy of the Assam Rifles.

The supply drop ended on 25th February 1951. The three crews had completed 180 drops to the Assam Rifles outposts. The only casualty was F/O Malhotra, who went down with 'flu a few days before we were to leave Jorhat. We went to see him at the local hospital where he was being well attended to by several pretty Kasi nurses. He eventually turned up in Calcutta a week later.

Landing at Machuka, 24th February 1952

We were called back to Assam on 1st July 1951. The monsoon had broken in June. The natural dams formed by the rocks and trees which fell into the valleys of the Dihang and Dibang rivers had broken, and a deluge of water and branchless tree trunks was washed into the northern end of the Assam Valley. The forests to the south of the Mishmi Hills were swept away. We were needed primarily to maintain air contact between the north and south banks of the Bramaputra. The black torpedo-like trunks of trees swept into the river, making it too danger-ous for any form of river transport. The river started to erode the whole of the south bank from Dibrugarh to Gauhati.

In October 1951, Capt Ripurendra Singh (a Sikh) was seconded to the Assam Rifles. He had recently married an English girl. They set up house at Sadiya. 'Ripu', as he quickly became known, had the distinction of speaking fluent Tamil, having been to school in South India. In early December Mr Buyan, the Political Officer of the Abor Hills, stationed with his family in Pasighat, asked me to fly him up the Siyom river which rose somewhere to the north-west of Along. We flew up the Dihang and at Along turned left to follow the Syom. We were flying over uncharted country, and nearing the equally uncharted MacMahon line.

Flying at 8,000 ft over dense jungle the Syom river ended below a high white streak of a waterfall. "Beyond that is Machuka," said Mr Buyan. "We're going to establish a new outpost there." We turned back for Pasighat.

In January 1952 I lifted Ripu's detachment in six trips from Sadiya to Along. Before he left for Machuka, he said he would try to make a runway at least 500 yards long. Fifteen days later, on 20th February, Ripu signalled his arrival, and requested a supply drop. On 24th February at 0900 hours, I took off from Mohanbari (sweet name) in UT-AUU with a load of 7000 lbs of free-drop in gunny bags for Machuka. There were six drop-ping crew, and Dillip Mitra, Capt H P Singh, in charge of pack-ing, free and parachute drops, F/O Sen, my long-suffering first officer, and R/O Menon, a friend since my first days on joining Air Services of India in 1947.

I climbed up to 8,000 ft. The weather was lovely. River, villages and forests lay spread out over the mountains, bathed in morning sunshine which made the green look greener. I flew over Pasighat, then Along, turned to the left and followed the Siyom river. The valley got narrower and the river below in deep shadow, then ahead the bright white streak of a waterfall, the entrance to Machuka. What would we find? Once over the waterfall we were in a wide, flat valley, with mountains up to 15,000 ft to the north. The plateau was at 6,000 ft and treeless. Ahead I saw tents and the Indian flag fluttering. I landed from west to east, taxied a few yards and came to rest opposite Ripu's tent. We all jumped out while the ejection crew unloaded. I told Ripu we would be back in the afternoon with another load.

The airstrip was narrow, so some sepoys pushed the Dak's tail round so I could taxi back to the west end for take-off. I started up, and slowly taxied down the strip. Suddenly, but also very sedately, the Dak tilted and started a slow turn to star-board. In a flash I realised what was happening. My starboard wheel had sunk into a soft patch, and the wind was lifting my tail. I immediately switched off the ignition and closed both throttles all in one movement. I felt myself tilting forward. Before I could say 'Jack Robinson' the tail of the aircraft was in the air, and Sen and I were looking at the grass four feet away from our noses. I had never before been in such an embarrass-ing position, arse over tit, at least not in public.

Dillip, Menon and Capt H P Singh got out of the small door behind my cockpit seat, followed by the ejection crew. Sen and I sat, leaning forward and contemplating our embarrassing position. We were at least fourteen days march from Along, leaving the Company's Dakota VT-AUU in a place that was not even on the map. I took no interest. After this cock-up my flying days were over. The army radio was powered by a sepoy pedalling a cycle dynamo. Messages were sent in speech and morse to Shillong, but got no reply. He pedalled harder; still no reply. We were stuck and cut off from help.

Menon had wandered off to look at the situation which I had already decided was hopeless.

He came back.

"Andy! we'll get out! Dillip ... I'm sure! The props are'nt bent. Come and look. We'll get out. Let's go ... let's get the tail down!"

Menon's enthusiasm was infectious. F/O Sen came back.

"Come on Andy, the props look okay."

We got the sepoys to erect poles each side of the fuselage. Then tied ropes between the poles. A long rope was thrown over the tail and pulled carefully from each side. The tail came down and sank slowly onto the ground.

My spirits began to rise. We put a vertical measuring pole in front of each propeller, turned the blades, and measured their distance from the vertical pole as each blade tip came in front of it. No appreciable difference!

When making the runway the men had removed a bush and refilled the hole only with earth — no rocks or stones; then it had rained. The soft earth had not only caused the starboard undercarriage to sink, but the soft, wet earth offered no resistance to a very slowly-moving propeller — only one blade of each engine had cut into the earth.

We all pushed and pulled for an hour until we slowly filled the hole with stones and eventually pushed the wheel clear. Using his kukri a sepoy hacked off the bent pitot head from beneath the nose of AUU. AUU was pushed to the west end of the strip, and turned round. We got in, four crew and six Assam Rifles sepoys. We thanked Ripu for his hospitality and the work of his men. He must have been damned glad to get rid of us! We were now four hours overdue for our arrival back at Mohanbari. I opened up and took off. We got airborne, full power, the empty Dakota rising like a balloon. No vibration.

We arrived back at Mohanbari five hours overdue. Mr Jaganath the aerodrome officer had been in a flap, but knowing us he had delayed sending an 'overdue' message to Calcutta. But after our absence of four hours he could delay no longer, and informed Calcutta. Luckily, as it took hours or even days to set wheels in motion, nothing had yet started to happen. Mr Jaganath signalled our arrival back and things returned to normal.

This was the last time we saw Ripu. Eighteen months later I was flying for Indamer Company, based at Port Sudan, on the Nigerian Haj from Kano to Jedda and back. We heard through the grapevine of a newspaper report in the Calcutta 'Statesman', that Captain Ripurendra Singh, 4th Battalion Assam Rifles, together with an Assistant Political Officer, sepoys and porters, a total of 80 men, arrived at Achinmoria to set up a new outpost. This was the first penetration of the area, somewhere west of Machuka and north of Ziro Camp. The local tribesmen were suspicious of the Abor porters who they thought were going to be settled in their territory, protected by Ripu's detachment. During the night the Assam Rifles' camp was attacked by the local tribesmen. Ripu and most of the sepoys and porters were decapitated. The news was brought back to Along by a few of the Abors who escaped.

Landing at Tezu, 8th September 1952

At the beginning of the monsoon of 1952, Sadiya, the headquarters of the 4th Battalion of the Assam Rifles, lying some 30 miles to the south-east of Pasighat was again flooded by the rushing waters of the Dibang and the Dihang, and the town was literally washed away. The only remnant was the pressed-steel runway laid by the Americans during the war. Colonel Srinivassan of the Assam Rifles, whose men manned outposts in the Abor Hills, Mishmi Hills and the Lohit Valley, decided that the headquarters would move to Tezu,

25 miles east of Sadiya. We were fortunate. A wide, shallow, dry sandy river-bed, not far from the site of the new headquarters, made an excellent runway of about 600 yards long. I flew 30 flights carrying troops and equipment. The sepoys made living quarters for themselves and their families in next-to-no time, using only their kukris to cut and shape the plentiful bamboo.

The last load for Tezu was the families of the troops. They assembled at what was left of the Sadiya airfield; wives, grandmas and grandpas, umpteen small babies, boys and girls, tin trunks, bundles of bedding and sacks of aluminium and brass cooking vessels. We had done a drop in the early morning. There were no seats in the aircraft. The Dakota cabin was empty, with its smooth aluminium floor. I decided to take the whole lot in one go. We tied down the tin trunks and sacks to the rings on the floor, then got everybody inside and dispersed them between the tied-down boxes. This was to prevent them all sliding to the tail of the aircraft as I accelerated down the runway for take-off. I lined up on Sadiya for the last time, took off and landed on a firm, compact sandbank after a flight of ten minutes.

The Colonel and his men were waiting. As the families got out, Menon and I counted them. There were 110 souls! If we had pranged and all of us were killed — 113 dead, we would surely have got our names in the papers!

The interesting thing about Tezu airstrip was that the rain was absorbed into the sloping, sandy surface, it being 50 feet higher than Sadiya, making the ancient river bed more impacted, and so firmer.

The drop was taken over by the airforce in the middle of November. During our time in Assam, we had completed 400 drops to the Assam Rifles in the foothills of the Himalayas, in the Naga and Lushai Hills. In the eyes of Delhi, our whole operation had become too big to be carried out by civilians. The success of an independent airline was felt to constitute a reflection on the dignity of the Indian Airforce. Besides, we had to be paid for our work. Our efforts to make ourselves indispensable had been our undoing. We were far from alone in our disappointment. The Political Officers, bazaar merchants, civil passengers, educational and health authorities were worried. They expected short shrift from the military. They proved to be right. Problems of accountancy made it difficult for the military aircraft to carry civilian loads.

Soon after the IAF took over, they had their first accident in the Subansiri district, at Sagalle. The Assam Rifles post was on a hill top. The dropping zone was obscured from the east by a hill, half-a-mile from, and 500 feet above it. The start of the drop had to be made from east to west. As the aircraft got progressively lighter, it was possible to drop either way. The airforce pilot decided to start the drop from west to east. He opened up full throttle after passing the dropping zone, and had begun a left turn over the hill, when the left wing-tip caught the trees. The aircraft crashed in the bottom of the valley, killing six army ejection crew, and the radio officer and navigator, while the pilot and his first officer survived, after months in hospital.

Not long after this incident, the Indian airlines took over, and crews were sent to Assam from Delhi, Bombay and Calcutta. The airforce was once again required in Ladakh, on the Tibetan and Pakistan/Kashmir border, at the western end of the Himalayas. There were several fatal accidents which resulted in the civil aircrew objecting to military operations for which they had not been recruited, were not covered by any insurance, and had themselves paid for their training in civil aviation. The supply drop was therefore taken over by Kalinga Airlines and Indamer Co. Ltd, charter companies, who supplied aircraft and crew between them, and carried out the drop for the next fifteen years, until 1967.

These two companies were carrying out the supply drop in 1962, when the Chinese invaded India through Tawong on the Bhutan/India border, and penetrated into the Kameng Valley, and also overran the Assam Rifles post at Wallong in the Lohit

Valley. Fortunately the Chinese mysteriously withdrew from Indian soil, two months later. **

The night before Air Services left Dibrugarh, we flew our Dakota and landed on the new runway at Along, hacked out of the jungle on the southern bank of the Siyom River. Our two crews, Dillip Mitra, Captain H P Singh, Assam Rifles, and Mr Buyan, the Abor Hills Political Officer, were the guests of the Abors at Along at the farewell party.

We went to their village hut, made from bamboo, thatched with palm leaves, and with a hard earthern floor. We all crowded in, with Abor men, women, girls, boys and babies. There was soon a friendly atmosphere of warm humanity, mixed with the gentle fumes of maize beer. Our tankards were cut from thick bamboo with a wooden spike left at the bottom, so that we could stick them in the ground when not drinking. The hut was lit by hurricane lamps. A space was cleared in the middle of the floor, and the dancing started.

Bokin, the head man, was wearing his red cloak, his badge of office, and on his head a thick cane helmet resembling a Spanish morion. In his right hand his long sword pointed to the skies. He started to shuffle round with small, rhythmic steps, in time with the jingle of metal rings around the sword blade. He sang quietly in a sing-song voice an Abor epic of great days and of battles long ago. While he droned on, the rest of us talked, smoked, and drank apong. Some girls got up and formed a circle round him. They passed their arms round each other's waists, and started to dance a soft, swaying step, moving clockwise, and then back again. The dances were done in the village hut, built on stilts, so the dancing caused the communal hut to gently sway. Bokin sang the verses, and the girls came in with the chorus.

By now the room had a good fug of apong fumes, cigarette smoke, and the body heat of the dancers. The girls dragged us

---

See **War in High Himalaya; Indian Army in Crisis, 1962, Maj Gen D K Palet, Vr C, pub Hunt & Co., London into their circle. Abor youths and more girls joined in. We soon picked up the steps. Girls dropped out, and new ones took their place. Most of them barely came up to our shoulders. Now and then the girls would giggle at the peculiar antics of a visitor who lost his step. The yellow light from the hurricane lamps cast dark shadows on the matting walls. And so we danced the night away, on our last night in the Abor hills, among those whom we had served, and come to love.

The next morning we flew back to Mohanbari airfield, and said our farewells to the aerodrome officer and his staff, who had tolerated our goings-on with good grace.

Moonlight over Bihar, 22nd November 1952

VT-AUU, flown by Tutu Amber, took off for Bombay via Calcutta, with Dillip Mitra, the engineers and extra crew members. Bunny Cariappa, radio officer Menon and myself flew VT-COJ, filled with the stores and tool boxes. We were going to stop a few hours in Calcutta to collect belongings left behind two years previously. We intended to leave for Bombay around midnight, so control cleared us to land at Barrackpore, the airforce field, and some 45 minutes by taxi from Chowringhee.

We planned to reach Juhu at 0700 hours in time for breakfast. In the evening Bunny and I visited the Temple Bar in Dharamtalla Street, then Iziah's in Free School Street. Both places were filled with seamen and assorted riff-raff. We felt in our element. We met two lovely Darjeeling girls who drank Murree beer. The piano banged out, a trumpet blared and drums rata-tat-ed. The long-hut at Along was far away.

We picked up Menon from his hotel in Chittaranjan Avenue and arrived at Barrackpore control tower at midnight. The stairway was lit by an overhanging single bulb, which was shrouded by thousands of suicidal flying insects and bugs. Their carcasses fell on us as we climbed the steps. We entered the office and turned on the light. The aerodrome officer was asleep under a mosquito net. We woke him up. Bunny wrote out a Flight Plan and handed it to the pyjama-clad officer. He refused to sign it!

"Why?" we both shouted.

"Because you're drunk!"

"Who?"

"Cariappa."

"Bloody lie!" yelled Bunny.

"You're drunk and I'm not clearing the flight."

"Fuck you! I'm not drunk, am I Andy?"

"Of course not!"

Bunny was sweating. I was sweating. Menon, seeing a storm developing went downstairs to keep out of the way.

Bunny's eyes were horribly bloodshot. The veins of his forehead stood out like the cast marks of a demented fakir. He banged the table and demanded a medical examination by the station Airforce doctor. We demanded to see the Senior Aerodrome Officer.

The poor duty officer gave way before this onslaught. He telephoned, with great trepidation the officers' mess and asked to speak to the senior officer present. He waited. Someone came to the phone. The duty officer explained, deferentially, that Captains Cariappa and Anderson had put in a clearance for a flight to Bombay, and that as they were both drunk he would not give them a clearance. Captain Cariappa demanded an inspection by a doctor in the presence of a senior controller or the station Commander.

The three of us went downstairs to await His Excellency. Out of the dark a jeep arrived driven by Mr Thumbi, the Aerodrome Officer, a South Indian who knew us both from the days of the Assam airlift in 1949. We stood on the illuminated steps. Mr Thumbi got out and steadied himself by holding onto the windscreen, obviously full of 'chota pegs', and furious at being called away from the conviviality of the mess. More insects flew into the light above the door of the control tower. He ignored the complaining officer, and ordered him to clear the flight. Bunny shook his hand. Mr Thumbi got into the jeep and returned to the mess and more chota pegs. He was not a bad fellow. In the past he had never gone out of his way to harrass us.

We were airborne at 0100 hours. VT-COJ was aimed at Nagpur and Bombay. We had full tanks, a cloudless night sky, a thousand miles to go and nothing to worry about. We put in 'George', and went to sleep. Bunny slept in the captain's seat; I lay down on the cockpit floor. Menon-ji was in control. He occasionally bashed out a position report, and took a look at the compass to check we were still heading in the right direction. All was peace and quiet above Bihar in the blue-black star-filled sky. We landed at Juhu at 8 o'clock and reported to Wingco Bill Burberry, who as always was seeing off the morning schedule departures. He thanked me for my services. He knew, and I knew, that Air Services of India no longer existed. December 1952 saw the end of the private airline companies. They were now nationalised and became 'The Indian Airline Corporation'.

My British 'B' licence issued in 1947 was now superseded by 'The Airline Transport Pilot's Licence'. I decided to return to the UK and go to the Flying School at Hamble and study for the new licence, so that I could continue to do the only thing I could do.

The Wingco retired to the UK a few months later.

CHAPTER 15

The 1952 & 1953 Hajs

THE Faithful have long obeyed the Prophet's injunction that, circumstances permitting, they should once-in-a-lifetime make the pilgrimage to Mecca. They have made the journey from all the lands of Islam, on foot, by camel, and by dhow. Hajis from Nigeria could take two years on the pilgrimage. They left their families, their businesses and their lands. On the journey they were preyed upon by slave-traders, robbers and officialdom. They had to carry enough money to see them through the years of their pilgrimage. Unscrupulous captains of dhows, sailing from Karachi and Bombay, and once at sea, might demand more money from the pilgrims, and when they did not get it, stranded them on sand spits off the coast of Oman or on the beaches along the Hadhramaut coast. The pilgrims were a lucrative source of income for thousands along their way. However, with the advent of air travel, the airline companies, ticket agents and air crew made money, while the Hajis saved it and got back to their homes in two months instead of two years.

The five years of Haj operations which Indamer carried out from 1952 to 1956 were the result of a *tour de force* by Peter Baldwin and Joe Koszarek. In my view none of their subsequent charter contracts ever equalled the Haj. The first operation was flown between Aden and Jedda by two Indamer Dakotas chartered by Aden Airways during July and August of 1952. In the same year Peter Baldwin went to Afghanistan, where he entered into a contract with a Kabuli entrepreneur,

Mr Ioubi, to carry 2,000 Afghan Hajis to Jedda in the following year. Armed with an Aden Airways and Afghan contract,
Joe Koszarek persuaded Hindustan Aircraft of Bangalore to
lease eight surplus Dakotas. So for the Haj season of 1953
Indamer gathered ten aircraft, leaving two freighters flying
from Calcutta.

The year before, the Haj operation had not gone smoothly,
with the loss of one aircraft and crew. The contract was with
Aden Airways for two Dakotas to fly Hajis from Aden to
Jedda, and their return. The disaster occurred during the return half of the Haj. Captain Bill Shine, First Officer Chinoy
and Radio Officer Mohan Singh, old Indamer hands from
Calcutta, were flying an empty Dakota VT-CGB, from Aden
to Jedda to pick up a load of Adenis. It took about five hours
to fly between Aden and Jedda at night; with a quick turn-
round the aircraft could be back in Aden for breakfast. Bill
Shine had been keeping up this schedule for two days. On the
third night he took off from Aden with about 500 gallons of
petrol, enough for six-and-a-half hours. It was all very simple.
He had done the flight to Jedda a dozen times both by day and
by night. The routine was to fly south of the Yemeni mountains, to the small sandy island of Perim at the mouth of the
Red Sea, climbing to 10,000 feet, turn onto course and follow
the Arabian coast to Jedda.

This particular night was dark, with only starlight. The sea
was a blue-black cloth, the mountains of Yemen, rising to
9,000 feet a dark mass, with a slightly lighter grey strip of
sandy desert between the mountains and the sea. In the darkness there was little to see, perhaps the lights of Djibouti to the
south, the flashing lighthouse on Perim Island, and in the Red
Sea a few small clusters of bright lights from ships heading for
Aden or Suez. Bill Shine pointed the aircraft at Jedda then
aligned the cards and put in 'George'. Radio Officer Mohan
Singh had sent his '100 miles out' position report to the Aden
control. The Dakota droned on — Bill had switched off all the
cockpit lights, leaving only the small glow from the 'wheels up'

indicator. Mohan Singh snoozed at his table with his head on his arms, illuminated by the light from the dial of his radio set.

Everything was normal. There is no sweeter sound than the engine note inside an empty Dakota. Let an engine fail and you can carry on for another eight hours, and enjoy it. An hour later Mohan Singh woke up and bashed out a position report to Aden. He went back to sleep. Bill Shine and Chinoy woke up and switched on the cockpit lights. They poured themselves some tea and ate the sandwiches provided by pretty little Julie of the Aden Airways Catering. After tea and sandwiches they snoozed again. They were now about two hours from Jedda, about 300 miles, so Singh decided to try and get Jedda beacon. He leaned into the cockpit and without waking the two in front, checked the radio compass bearing. He tuned into Jedda beacon frequency on the radio compass. He could not pick up the call sign. The needle hunted from side to side and even went completely round in a vague, perplexed manner. Perhaps they were too far out to get the beacon. He retired to his seat.

Bill woke up, looked at his watch and checked the petrol gauges. He looked outside but all was black; his eyes had not yet become adjusted to the darkness. He tuned in Jedda beacon and got a vague signal and needle deflection to port. He altered course. Gradually his eyes picked up the dark- grey desert, with here and there some black patches. They were over land, over the sandy desert interspersed with black outcrops of volcanic rock. This indicated to Bill that he was south-east of Jedda and the Dakota had drifted to starboard of track. He gave some more twists to the auto-pilot so that they would head further west and so hit the Red Sea coast south of Jedda. Something was wrong but he could not think what it was. It was too dark below. Not a single light was visible. Invariably, over the desert, within a hundred miles of Jedda there were faint yellow lights from Bedouin tents and the villages on the Red Sea coast. Nowhere could he see a glimmer. He switched on the radio compass; the needle hunted to port. He switched to audio to check the beacon call sign, but got a crackling sound.

By now all three were trying to unravel the mystery of the beacon, and becoming slightly alarmed. They were still over desert. Bill corrected with more twists to port so that they would definitely hit the Red Sea south of Jedda. They switched on the VHF and called Jedda approach but got no answer. Four-and-a-half hours were up, and they should be close to Jedda whatever the winds. Mohan Singh called up Jedda on W/T and asked them if their beacon was on, but got no answer. They were alarmed. It was getting lighter outside. The desert was now a pale grey ochre. In the east the sky was lightening on the horizon to pale blue; the stars were disappearing.

The petrol was low. They had been flying for five-and-a-half hours and Bill knew they were lost and would soon have to force-land. Mohan Singh sent a W/T signal to the ground station that they were about to force-land in the desert south of Jedda, but got no reply. Before the petrol completely finished, Bill landed with 'wheels up' on a sand dune. As luck would have it, a rock smashed through the cockpit floor and broke Bill Shine's ankles.

After landing they sat in their seats and gazed through the cockpit windscreen at the sand around them. Singh and Chinoy got out and took out the passenger seats which they piled up for a bonfire to be lit when they heard an aircraft. They removed the glass mirror from the lavatory to use for flashing signals. The Dakota would glitter like silver once the hot sun came up. The sun came up and soon the skin of the aircraft was like the bottom of a scalded saucepan. They lay in the shade, in the dry, hot, still air of 130 F. There was nothing to see around them except endless sand. They remained together, hoping that someone would find them.

At two o'clock in the afternoon they finished the warm tea. They had a thermos flask of water and some stale sandwiches left. There was no sound, no wind, no aircraft; the sound of their own voices had long ceased. The recriminations, the speculations, had stopped long ago. They could only wait. The nights cooled them, but served to heighten their agony in the hot days to follow.

They were found five days later by a Nubian camel driver. Mohan Singh and Chinoy were half-a-mile away to the west; both had collapsed on a rise of sand. They were naked, burnt and dead. Captain Bill Shine was lying in the shade of the crashed Dakota, still alive but only just. The Nubian gave Bill water to drink. His dried stomach and lungs filled with water and he drowned. The other two had wandered away to the west in search of the Red Sea. For them, hope of salvation lay in the west, looking for a camel train going to Jedda. The aircraft had landed in the Sudan — south of Wadi Halfa, 400 miles west of Jedda!

Bill Shine had taken off with the expectation of 'slight northerly winds'. In fact a strong north-easterly wind blew across Arabia that night. They had been blown across the Red Sea to the Sudan Desert. That night Jedda had changed its beacon frequency. The beacon they had picked up may have been at El Adem or some other beacon away to the north on the Mediterranean coast. Every correction Bill had made to port in order to arrive at the Arabian coast of the Red Sea had taken him further inland over the Sudan. The search aircraft of the RAF from Aden and the Americans from Dahran looked for them on the wrong side of the Red Sea. The aircraft had landed twelve miles to the east of the railway from Atbara to Wadi Halfa.

They were buried at Wadi Halfa.

The 1953 Haj

On the course at Hamble I met Capt Peter Brumby of Air Service, who was getting a job in West African Airways; also Capt Renius from Calcutta was on the course, and planned to leave India and emigrate to the USA. This was the period of the coronation of Queen Elizabeth II and the conquest of Everest by Hilary and Tensing.

We sat the exams in June 1953 at Theobalds Road, central London. When I emerged from the final exam, 'Flight Planning',

I was handed a telegram from 'Albaldini' asking me if I was available to take part in the July Haj operation. I replied "Yes". I left for Bombay from Heathrow, then a shanty town of wooden buildings and Nissan huts with floors of brown linoleum. I saw a familiar face; it was Captain Frank Whittaker, last seen in the early hours in the Barackpore restaurant eating fried-egg-and-chips. He was also answering the 'Albaldini' summons. I can't remember what aircraft flew us to Bombay. It may have been a Lancaster bomber with portholes. We got to Santa Cruz airport Bombay.

'Albaldini' was the telegraphic address of Indamer Co Ltd, based at Juhu airport, Bombay. It was a charter company, operating a few Dakotas chartered by Capt Johnny Brenand of The Grand Hotel, Chowringhee, Calcutta, flying loads to and fro from North Bengal and the Assam Valley.

Indamer had been started by Peter Baldwin and Joe Koszarek, both officers in the US Army Aircraft Maintenance and Supply, stationed at Bangalore. They had remained in India after the War. Peter married Boli Cariappa, sister of Bunny Cariappa, with whom I had flown in Air Service of India in 1947 and up to the end of 1952, when all companies operating scheduled domestic routes were amalgamated into the 'Indian Airlines', the internal operating company. (The Cariappas came from Coorg, a small hill-state in the Western Ghats, and west of Mysore. The family had long connections with the Indian Army. The current C-in-C of the Indian Army was General Cariappa. Bunny himself had been in the Indian Airforce flying Spitfires during the War. He had resigned from the Airforce.)

Joe Koszarek married Doreen Boynton, whose father was also stationed in Bangalore with the British Army. Peter and Joe moved to Juhu where they built themselves bashas of palm leaves amongst the coconut trees bordering Juhu Beach. Juhu Aerodrome was a few yards from the high tide mark of the Indian Ocean. The other occupants of the airfield were the Bombay Flying Club, started by JRD Tata of Air India before the war, Air Service of India of Scindia Steamship Company, and Mistry Airways. It had two crossed runways, three large hangars and a residential area for the families of the civil aviation authority. Santa Cruz airport, built during the war some five miles east of Juhu, was the main internal and external terminal for western India.

I knew Peter and Joe from early days. In 1948 Bunny and I had been sent by Indamer to Burbank, California, to ferry a Dakota for an Indian client. We flew back via Tutumcarrie, New York, Goose Bay, Bluie West One in Greenland, Iceland and London to Bombay.

In 1953 the management of Aden Airways again approached Joe Koszarek with a plan for Indamer to supply seven Dakotas and crew to operate a Haj from Kano, Nigeria to Jedda carrying 2,000 Nigerians. Peter Baldwin had his contract with Mr Ioubi of Kabul for 1953.

Indamer negotiated with Hindustan Aviation to lease seven Dakotas. Five Dakotas were obtained from Calcutta to operate the Afghan Haj. The Afghan sector would be run by Johnny Brenand and his wife Kitty from Bahrain, which

necessitated closing down the Indamer-Assam freight operation for the best part of three months.

When Frank and I arrived in Santa Cruz we were happy to learn that we had been booked rooms in the Juhu Hotel, run by the legendary Mrs May. The next morning we reported to the Indamer office. It was a large aircraft packing-case, on the grass between the runways. Inside were Joe, Srinivass, Gladys the secretary and Raman. A motley crew of first officers and radio officers were inside and outside the packing case, waiting for any captain to choose his crew.

Frank and I were kitted out by Raman, who gave both of us a large concertina map between blue cardboard covers, of the Bombay to Lagos route, and a khaki canvas briefcase; the latter was to last me for the next fourteen years!

As I emerged from the office I was immediately accosted by F/O Gupta and his friend R/O Kanga, both unknown to me.

Without more ado I took both on. It turned out to be a fortunate decision.

A cyclone hit Bombay at four the next morning. The wind shrieked hoarsely through the tall, bending coconut trees that surrounded the flimsy tile-roofed chalets. Coconuts fell with loud 'thunks' onto the tiles. Great basso rumbles of thunder rolled in from the Arabian Sea. Beneath my damp sheet I tried to sleep and not to think about the flight to Karachi, through tall grey masses of cumulo-nimbus cloud. Suddenly there was a tremendous flash and explosion above my head. My heart leaped; a cold blast of wind and rain swept into the room. I saw a pale hole in the corner of the roof where the lightning had struck. Rain poured in on top of the almirah. Another explosion followed. I got up. Tiles from the roof littered the stone floor in the bathroom. I found that a large piece of brickwork had crashed through the lid of the thunderbox.

At six o'clock the company car arrived, and Frank and I were driven through the floods and downpour to Santa Cruz Airport. The old wartime hangars which served as passenger terminal were in chaos. Ten Indamer Dakotas were due to leave for Jedda with 280 Indian Muslims, each pilgrim being seen off by half-a-dozen relatives. Srinavas, Raman and Joe Koszarek were running around collecting the passengers, writing out manifests, and cooking up the aircraft load-sheets. The white-uniformed customs officials were digging inside the cardboard suitcases, tin boxes and bed-rolls of our Muslim passengers. The baggage was loaded onto purloined Air India trolleys manned by our mechanics.

The air crews stood in clusters of three, captain, co-pilot and radio officer, awaiting their turn for the customs. We were a motley gang of variously dressed outcasts. (No one in Indamer wore uniform.) My passengers were driven out into the rain and onto the aircraft. My crew and I followed, damp and dispirited. I had not flown a Dakota for eight months but I felt at home again. Gupta, my young Punjabi co-pilot, had only done six take-offs and landings in a Dakota, and that under supervision in order to get the type stamped on his licence. I started the engines. I opened the throttles to warm up. Both engines coughed, spluttered and stopped. We got out of the aircraft, leaving the passengers inside, and stood under the port wing sheltering from the rain. A large beefy fellow charged up. He was soaked through. I had never seen him before but knew him to be the legendary Johnny Brenand, chief pilot and manager of the Indamer contingent in Calcutta. His wet, golden hair was plastered down, the sleeves of his shirt were rolled up tightly around his large biceps. His shirt was open displaying a smooth, massive, and slightly freckled chest.

"What's up here?" he demanded, exuding determination and leadership. I decided to oppose him.

"The engine won't run," I said. "We'd better get the tanks drained."

"They've been drained."

"Well drain them again."

A mechanic opened the four fuel draincocks beneath the wings. From each cock a jaundiced stream of piss poured out. We collected the fluid in our cupped hands, smelt it, licked it, and announced it was water. During the night, rain had seeped around the filler caps into the tanks.

"I'm not going until the tanks, fuel lines and carburettors are properly drained," I said.

"They are," insisted Brenand. "Look, there's some petrol coming now."

He held out a large cupped hand in which a few drops of green 100-octane petrol floated in the water. Indamer was living up to its reputation, I thought. I refused to take off until the systems had been flushed out. We walked off through the rain and returned to the Juhu Hotel, leaving Srinivas and Raman to deal with the passengers.

The next morning I felt better. The sun was shining and I wanted to get away. We took off and headed across the Gulf of Cambay towards Kutch and Karachi. It was a route I had flown many times with Air Services. In front of me lay a flight of 4,200 miles with two inexperienced crew members, an old wartime VHF set, a radio beacon receiver, a map, a plastic navigation computer and a magnetic compass suspended by elastic bunjees in the middle of the cockpit windscreen.

I had just spent six months and a lot of money to obtain my ALTP Licence. We had learnt about Loran, Gee, VOR, Bushmills, bearing compasses and stars. Hours were spent, once again, going over the alphabetical malevolent coefficients that have to be compensated for in an aircraft's compass. This instrument, beloved by examiners, is engulfed in a jungle of horizontal and vertical soft and hard iron rods. They have a baneful influence on its behaviour. The understanding of their combined parameters is not made easier by the rods being imaginary and coloured red and blue. We waded through pages of useless legislature concerning 'Aerial work', lights shown at night by tethered balloons and towed gliders, international flight documents, crashes (who to inform), and other intricacies of the law. Once again we covered meteorology and flight planning. And now here I was, airborne from Santa Cruz, with a British licence which I did not need as I was flying an Indian registered aircraft on my Indian B-licence, issued in 1947. I wondered what I had learnt at Hamble that was going to get me to Kano.

We flew west from Karachi along the Baluchistan coast for 800 miles to Sharjah at the eastern end of the Persian Gulf. Here we refuelled and then flew 300 miles to land at Bahrain Island, twelve hours after leaving Bombay. Five hours later, after crossing 800 miles of the Arabian Desert we landed at Jedda. Our passengers set off by bus for Mecca. Joe Koszarek who had left on the last Dakota the day before was there to meet us. He told me to take off immediately for Asmara on the Eritrean Plateau. I had to fly the General Manager of Aden Airways, Mr De Graffe-Hunter and his wife, to his headquarters. We got to Asmara twenty-four hours after leaving Bombay.

The next morning we took off empty for the direct flight to El Genina on the western border of the Sudan. From here we flew 900 miles across French Equitorial Africa and arrived at four o'clock in the afternoon at Kano. I was due off at midnight with my first load of twenty-eight Nigerian Muslims, for the flight back to Jedda.

The routine of the Haj now started. How I hated those midnight take-offs from Kano. The nights were mostly cloudy, often with pouring rain from a cumulo-nimbus that sat on top of the airport. As it thundered the black night was slashed by pale orange flashes of lightning. Strong gusty winds drove low cloud and rain across the runways. We took off with full tanks, twenty-eight large Nigerians and their luggage; this made us 3,000 lbs over the take-off weight permitted by the Indian authorities, but they were 5,000 miles away in New Delhi.

I usually flew at 4,000 feet over the first 300 miles of scrub-land to Lake Chad. No lights shone anywhere; at two o'clock in the morning everybody was asleep. Even on the darkest night I could distinguish the scrubland broken by the pattern of the water and tall grass of Lake Chad. This mysterious stretch of water on the southern edge of the Sahara Desert generated its own weather. All around might be clear, but over Chad would be a towering cumulus thundering and flashing. We ploughed through these storms and emerged to the east in clear, starry skies; 600 miles of dry scrub lay between Chad and El Genina. We struggled against a 30-knot headwind, our ground speed barely more than 110-miles-an-hour. Most of the time Gupta and I slept. 'George', the auto pilot, flew the aircraft while Kanga bashed out inaccurate position reports to Khartoum. No one cared where we were, and if there were any other aircraft flying the route they were well above us. I lived in terror of an engine failure and then having to drag the Dakota back to Maidugri or Fort Lamy. Both of these air-fields closed at sunset.

Around 4 am the night was at its darkest. We could have been stationary. I peered through the windscreen for the first sign of dawn on the horizon. I would panic in lone fear lest some astronomical disaster had occurred to the sun. Dawn might never come again.

"Oh God, please let the dawn come."

The Hajis were asleep, slumped in their uncomfortable seats. At last I detected a thin faint light on the horizon. The sky got lighter, a pale mauvey-blue; the stars receded slowly until they were visible only behind the aircraft. The crimson rim of the sun slowly appeared and I watched in wonder at its steady, miraculous rising. I began to see a few earth-tracks through the thin dry jungle. The worst was over as we followed a dry river bed south of Fort Abéché. After eight hours we were at last nearing El Genina, but as usual its radio beacon was either not switched on or unserviceable.

At El Genina an agony of exasperation awaited me. El Genina was the entry port for the Sudan, where we had to refuel and at the same time submit to bureaucratic examination by the Passport Officer, the Health Officer and the Customs Officer. The travel documents of twenty-eight Hajis had to be minutely examined and health certificates scrutinised for evidence of cholera, smallpox and yellow fever inoculations. As Captain of the aircraft I was responsible. Any lacuna in documentation could mean leaving one of our passengers behind. In practice, we knew that this would be much too troublesome for the officials. They would let us through — but only after interminable arguments, appeals and supplications.

The Aerodrome Officer, master of his kingdom, occupied a superior position at the top of the control tower. In the hall below, the other three sat at wooden tables, armed with ball-point pens, ink pads and rubber stamps. How they loved those rubber stamps! The Aerodrome Officer's imprint alone would finally release the aircraft. He would bash his rubber stamp down with both hands on the journey log book, then scrupulously examine the imprint for clarity. If there was the slightest imperfection he would pound the log book again and again before at last setting us free with his signature.

The Passport Officer was enormously fat, with faded hennaed hair and drooping lower lip. Invariably his ink-pad ran dry; perhaps he used it more lavishly, or kept the lid open so that the ink evaporated into the hot, dry air of the oasis. In an agony of impatience I watched him breathe a heavy, foetid, bureaucratic expiration onto his stamp. It left a weak, barely visible impression on the page. I noticed that the cotton covering of the pad was worn through. I reached over and handed him the Health Officer's pad, but it was quickly snatched back. On my next flight I brought him a new pad from the bazaar in Port Sudan, and so earned the enmity of his colleagues.

As we circled the El Genina airfield before landing, I had seen an old lorry laden with two-dozen forty-gallon drums of petrol, hand pumps and four Sudanese coolies lurching along the kutcha road to the airport. Mr Souteriadus, the Shell agent, sat in front, wearing his topee and waving up at us with his walking stick. He was the only European in the oasis. He ran the provison store with its shelves lined with unsaleable tins of tomato purée and rolls of lavatory paper. He was an elderly shrivelled Greek, lame in one leg and benign.

During the examination of the documents his gang of coolies, using hand pumps, refuelled our Dakota. Mr Souteriadus leaned on his stick and watched, impassive. Delays there might be, but in the end we would depart. He had seen it all many times before.

While their papers were being examined, the Hajis had dispersed around the white control tower into the sparse dry grass and were crapping, abluting with the aid of their aluminium kettles, and saying their morning prayers as they bowed east towards Mecca. If things went reasonably smoothly the crew now had time to eat: fried eggs and skinless sausages, cooked in foul, rancid fat, and followed by brackish tea. Two white-robed Sudanese who prepared the food had fed RAF pilots ten years before. El Genina airfield had been scraped out of the red earth during the war, to be used by aircraft being ferried across Africa from the Atlantic coast to

Egypt. Beyond the red scars of the runways could be seen the dilapidated roofs of the old barracks, all but submerged beneath billowing waves of dry thorn-bushes. It was a dismal, familiar sight that was often repeated from West Africa to Burma.

Every aircraft left reams of papers behind; eighteen passenger manifests, eighteen nil-freight manifests, eighteen general declarations. What did they do with it all, I wondered, and I wonder still. Are all our manifests still there? Or were they taken to Khartoum, by camel perhaps, for filing and codification by the statisticians of the new Republic? If we landed at Khartoum, we would have to go through this whole routine of examination again. I preferred the long grind of 800 miles direct to Port Sudan.

Once we reached the Nile the rest of the flight held no terrors. A single-track railway, which would mean life and rescue, ran from Khartoum through Shendi, Atbara and then through more desert and mountains to Port Sudan. Sometimes the whole route was covered by a thick fog of hot, sandy haze up to 15,000 feet. Visibility was reduced to a small patch of sand directly below the aircraft. After five-o'clock in the afternoon, turbulent clouds built up over the rock crags west of the Red Sea coast. In the late evenings from Port Sudan you could see towering cumulus and flashes of lightning to the west, then our short-cut across the desert seemed worthwhile for all its terrors. These storms were horrible things to get into when you knew their lower layers were pierced by 7,000 feet pinnacles of jagged rocks. Flying direct from El Genina we could land at Port Sudan before the worst storms started.

In theory our flight ended at our base at Port Sudan. Another crew was waiting to take the Hajis across the 180 miles of sea to Jedda. This crew would then return empty by Khartoum, El Genina, and reach Kano by early afternoon the next day. In this way we kept seven Dakotas flying continuously round the circuit. It took 25 hours of flying in a period of

40 hours. On several occasions there was no relief crew, so that we had to go straight round for another trip. No one flew on the Haj as much as Captain Tarkowski, a small, ebullient Pole who looked like Trotsky. Tarko's favourite dodge was to come into Port Sudan from fifteen miles out at 500 feet, and using low engine revolutions. The crew waiting at the disused Police Barracks overlooking the airfield would not hear him as they cooled off in the small swimming pool. He would refuel and take off for Jedda and so-on round for another flight to Kano. He once managed to shanghai an aircraft for seven days before he was ambushed at Port Sudan and forcibly removed from the cockpit by the awaiting crew.

During the Haj, Jedda airport was in a continuous uproar and confusion; no airport anywhere in the world could equal its chaos. Aircraft were landing and taking off every five minutes of the day and night. From all the countries of Islam the faithful came on their pilgrimage. Many arrived swathed in the traditional white seamless robe; the poor made do with a white bath towel, and the still poorer came in their everyday clothes. The women were hidden beneath black burkas, and sweated in these walking tents. Others, less orthodox, threw back the burka from their faces and sweated just the same. The heat was stifling by day and night, and very little wind blew. The air terminal was small and totally inadequate. There was a central rotunda from which radiated corridors leading to the customs, passport and health offices, the restaurant and the air traffic control. The whole place was packed with Hajis who collected their baggage around them, spread their mats and prepared to spend the next few days in the terminal building. Scruffy Saudi soldiers strolled around spitting and shouting. They carried vicious-looking sub-machine guns. The latest-model American cars drew up at the entrance to the building and sped away with the rich Hajis. As the pilgrims arrived in their thousands, they pissed and dropped their turds onto the surrounding sand. Groups of Hajis bivouacked in the shade of the nearby buildings, waiting for buses to take them to Mecca.

Some waited for their friends coming by air; others didn't speak Arabic and were lost.

1953 was my first Haj. I did three more. Each year I noticed the same dried excrescences of spittle upon the floor. I recognised some of the flies amongst the millions that attended the Hajis. The same smell of ordure hung around the buildings; even the turds, fossilised by the heat, remained in their place. Year after year I saw the same four sweaty figures behind the restaurant counter. They wore the same long, white nightshirts and little white lace skull-caps. They handed out long bread-rolls stuffed with the customer's choice of Kraft cheese, tomato, or apricot jam. They dispensed tea, black Turkish coffee, Coke, Pepsi, Seven-up, Simalco and water. Sometimes they sold fruit. Orange peel and banana skins, apple and pear cores, peach stones and strips of melon peel added to the litter on the floor.

Somehow the Hajis were all eventually transported to Mecca. And somehow they returned to the air terminal and went through the whole process in reverse, worn out, poorer but happy. Many of them never got home. Each year two or three buses travelling at speed along the road to Mecca would plunge into wayside rocks or overturn into nullahs. Elderly Hajis died during the twelve days of ritual and prayer. Young ones disappeared into Jedda to find work. Some were sold into slavery; and a few old ones died in the aircraft on their way home. I swore each Haj was my last; yet when I did my final one in 1956 it was because our Indamer Dakotas lost the business to the newly formed airlines re-equipped with four-engined jet aircraft.

In the deserted Port Sudan Police barracks, Aden Airways had made us a temporary home, which overlooked the airstrip of sunbaked sand and stones. We were looked after by two of Aden Airway's stewards, Mario, an old soldier of the Italian army who had been taken prisoner by the British in Eritrea, and young Hugo Ugolini, a good-natured, slightly smaller version of an amiable Primo Carnero. Hugo wore little white continental shorts with turn-ups. His white shirt, with high-rolled sleeves, was left sexily open down to his navel, submerged in a flabby stomach. He was deeply involved with a girl he had seen in Port Sudan bazaar. He never spoke to her, but contented himself with dreams and fantasies as he drove past her house in the mess truck on his way to collect the bar supplies. In the mornings Hugo sat at a café table and watched the entrance to her house across the sandy, pot-holed road. The girl was chaperoned by her brothers, or a sullenly vicious pi-dog. We followed the course of Hugo's romance with sympathy.

"How's l'amore, Hugo old boy?"

"Porco Dio! What I see today! I drink macchiato, and the dog come out of the gate. It walk up and down. The son-of-a-beetch, he piss on the gate and go back. Tomorrow she come!"

"Perhaps she'll piss on the gate too, Hugo!"

"Mamma mia! You laugh! You gelosia. I wait. I drink cappuccino. What you have, Capitano?"

"Beer, Hugo. Be careful Hugo. Her brothers might be watching."

"Porca Madonna! Her brothers! I watch. Don't I know. She sees me waiting and all will be victory. I tell you now she will know."

"You're going to wear those little pants?"

"Porco Dio ... why not? Let her see me, then she'll know."

"Have a drink Hugo."

"Grazie, Capitano. I have campari."

"Be careful you don't frighten her Hugo, with that large stomach and ...."

Here one made the traditional gesture of clenched fist and erect forearm.

"Porca Madonna, you think I mad!" Hugo drew himself up and sucked in his stomach. He looked like a large, friendly gorilla.

"Watch out for the dog, Hugo."

"Grazie, Capitano. I watch and I kick the son-of-a-beetch."

Hugo's romance continued as long as we were in Port Sudan. The dog and the girl both remained inviolate.

After Indamer had flown the 2,000 Nigerians and 2,000 Afghans to Jedda, twelve aircraft loaded with crews, engineers, mechanics and traffic staff descended like locusts on the quiet town of Asmara on the Eritrean Plateau. Here we had a twelve-day holiday while the Hajis said their prayers in Mecca and Medina. One hundred Indianos and a dozen Inglesi were billeted in various establishments previously arranged by Aden Airways. A large gang stayed at the Albergo Ciao, another at the Albergo Italiano and the rest were put up in a dozen pensiones. Five of us were in the Pensione Victoria opposite the big red-brick Catholic Cathedral in the Via Haile Selassie.

Every night we set off to make the rounds of Asmara's many bars. Our penultimate goal was one of the three night clubs, the Olympia, the Alhambra or the Mogambo. Hugo's younger brother played the trumpet at the Alhambra, which also featured a small Italian waiter who sang 'Vesti la giubba' on request. The Olympia and the Alhambra were staffed by local girls; the Mogambo was exclusively staffed by whites. The girls moved in the sleazy circuit from Cyprus to Cairo, Khartoum, Mogadiscu and Asmara. Many of the dangers imagined by the parents of our young co-pilots and radio officers now became a reality. They ate forbidden foods, drank 'farrin licker', and slept with low-caste black mlench girls. It would need a torrent of 'Ganga pani' to wash away their pollutions.

The Via Haile Selassie was a pleasant, broad boulevard, lined with palm trees, shops and cafés. By mid-morning the Italians were sitting at little tables under coloured awnings. They watched each other, gossiped, intrigued, drank aperitifs, and ate diminutive mezes. The sun shone,the sky was clear blue and the air pleasantly fresh and sweet. Beautiful women — Ethiopes, Eritreans, English (Memsahibs of Aden Airways), and elegant Italianos — walked the boulevard with studied unconcern. Males stood in shop doorways or sat at the tables, dressed in tight, short jackets, narrow trousers and pointed shoes, watching. It was an elaborate ritual, far removed from the jostling, spitting, cotton-clad crowds of Bombay's Hornby Road or Calcutta's Chowringhee.

After our twelve days holiday, the Indamer locusts got into their Dakotas and flew off to Jedda. The bar girls, hostesses, shops and restaurants were sorry to see us go. Captain Dickie Richards, golden-haired, with a broad Cheshire accent, would long be remembered as the King of the Mogambo. Bob Chater had a piece of flesh bitten out of his neck; we watched it for signs of gangrene. Radio Officer Pantallu had met Marusella and vowed eternal love. Young co-pilot Vaidya had got drunk for the first time. Broken hearts were left behind in the Olympia, the Bar Lucia and in the pensiones. Viva Haile Selassie! Viva Italianos! Viva Asmara! Viva Indianos! Viva Gabriella! We promised to be back next year.

We flew our Nigerians from Jedda to Kano. We had the winds behind to help us along. The weather was better and it was pleasanter to fly an empty Dakota over the long night-grind from Kano to El Genina. Again, Captain Tarkowski captured an aircraft, but now we cared less. We were all tired and longed for the Haj to be finished. Bob Chater taxied his Dak off the El Genina taxi track. It had rained the previous night, the first time in two years, the earth was soft, and a wheel sank in the mud to above the axle. He spent the next three days playing cards and drinking whisky with the four Sudanese officials. Long after the Haj was past, the four still remembered Bob. I met them off-and-on for six years, when flying monthly Bombay to Lagos for Chellarams. We became quite friendly over the following years.

When it was all over we spent two days in the Port Sudan Police Barracks, sleeping, swimming in the small pool, eating fried eggs and tinned sausages. During our six weeks of flying on the Haj, each crew averaged 390 flying hours. Captain Tarkowski, however, held the 1953 record with 450 hours. On the last day, during an excellent lunch of chicken curry and rice cooked by our engineer, Gurucharan Singh, there was a commotion from the kitchen. Hugo lumbered in and screamed

"Fire!" Some of us charged to the rescue with beer mugs, others continued eating. The fire was in the sandy courtyard. Flames leapt from a bin. After it was put out with beer and sand we discovered all our bar chits had been burnt to ashes.

The night before we were due to leave for Bombay, Captain Johnny Pascoe, the long-suffering Chief Pilot of Aden Airways, came to stay with us. He thanked us for our work and we thanked him for leaving us alone. He had arranged with Joe Koszarek for two Daks to go to Aden and fly charter flights. I leapt at the chance and persuaded Frank Whittaker to come with me. 'Mother' Rai volunteered to remain for another month as my radio officer. The other aircraft was captained by Tommy Sadler, an ex-RAF pilot. Tommy was to remain flying in India for another eight years. A great drinker, he was dapper with a little fair military moustache, and spent most of his time flying between Calcutta and Assam. He was renowned for being a West Bengal snooker champion.

CHAPTER 16

Kurrumbling Khormaksar

WHEN we arrived in Aden in mid-September, 1953, we were lodged in the Crescent Hotel at Steamer Point. Tommy Sadler was put onto the internal flights, to the Hadramaut and into British Somaliland, while Frank, 'Mother' Rai and I were to fly building artisans from the Lebanon.

Aden in the early fifties was expanding. Beneath the jagged ring of grey rock, whose pinnacles were ribboned by the winding battlements built eighty years before by British soldiers in khaki topees, Oxford shirts and blue serge trousers, there blossomed tall blocks of flats, acres of married quarters and scurrying cars. Inside the extinct volcano crater were jam-packed the white-washed stone buildings of the bazaar, police barracks and business offices. Everything roasted in this declivity of solidified lava. On the outer slopes, where the gradient permitted, sprawled long white barracks, occupied by RAF National Service airmen. RAF Khormaksar, which lay across the sandy isthmus separating the native town of Sheik Othman from the Rock, had a long tarmac runway and was dotted with more barracks, parade grounds, hangars and a surburbia of married quarters. From Steamer Point, where the large passenger boats moored, a shiny, black tarmac road ran along the base of the rock, wound upwards through a narrow man-made gorge, and descended into the crater.

At Steamer Point on the water's edge a new quayside with warehouses was being built. Further east, squashed into a corner, was the shipyard of the Arab dhow builders. Here, amidst the commercial bustle and steel ships, the Adenis carried on their ancient craft of constructing wooden dhows from the size of a rowing boat to large ocean-going vessels. No plans were needed. Forty-foot keels were laid on the sand, hull timbers and planks were cut with adzes. In this little enclave were created the beautiful dhows that sail the Arabian seas, constructed by instinct like the nests of birds.

Beyond Khormaksar runway, the baked desert area was dotted with small, white windmills, whose slowly rotating arms turned the stones that ground the lumps of salt from the surrounding sea-water pans. This was Little Aden, where the artisans whom Frank and I would fly from Lebanon, were going to construct the living quarters for a new oil refinery.

Aden was a sun-baked Aldershot, with sandy sports-grounds, ochred military lorries, khaki shorts, beer and chips. Passenger ships stopped there every month to refuel on the voyage to and from the Far East. Hordes of passengers, hungry for Japanese cameras, transistors and tape recorders, Swiss watches, British clothing and American cigarettes, crowded the shops at Steamer Point and the Crater. The bazaar swarmed with small, wiry Yemenis, Adenis, tall, thin Somalis, topeed Indians and pale, curious ships' passengers.

Our first flight was to fly 28 artisans from Beirut. We took off in the early morning in an empty Dakota with full petrol tanks. In half-an-hour we were at 10,000 feet and flying over the Yemen capital, Sana'a, perched 9,000 feet up on the mountains. To the east lay the Hadramaut, to the west the Red Sea and Africa. We flew over the sandy patch of Kamaran Island, with its British Resident, and a single red pillar-box, then up the coast to Jedda, the Gulf of Aqaba, the Dead Sea, and the east of Mount Hermon, to land at Beirut. Frank and I were looking forward to a visit to the night clubs. As we taxied onto the Beirut air terminal, the control tower told us to report to them immediately. Frank, 'Mother' and I climbed the white marble steps of the control tower. 'Mother' was behind, and seemed to follow reluctantly. On the last landing he stopped and called up to me.

"Andy, I must tell you of radio trouble."

We stopped, turned round and looked down at 'Mother'. He stood there in his baggy grey trousers, grubby shirt and an American Army windjacket which he had bought for ten rupees in Calcutta's China Bazaar. He peered up at us through his thick-lensed horn-rimmed spectacles. They were broken at the bridge and mended with Elastoplast. He was plump, ten years older than either of us, and with curly grey hair. He lived in Calcutta with his wife and six children. He was a typical Bengali babu. He would fly for days on end without complaining. His nickname was used with affection; it suited him.

"My God, 'Mother'!" I said. "Don't tell me. You didn't make W/T contact!"

"Yes, Andy. I couldn't raise Cairo or Beirut."

"Okay, forget it. But keep quiet."

In the control tower we were given the most almighty bamboo. We had flown across Israel, Jordan and Lebanon, outside the international air corridors. The Beirut control had no news of our flight until I called up 100 miles away on the VHF. I apologised and explained that our radio had broken down. We promised never to do such a dreadful thing again. We were forgiven and dismissed. We took a Mercedes taxi to the Bristol Hotel and agreed to meet for dinner at eight o'clock.

Frank and I met at the entrance to the dining room. We were a strange sight. Frank had on a crumpled grey suit and an open-necked yellow shirt with its collar turned down over his jacket. I was wearing a creased blazer and white T-shirt. Beautiful women trod the soft carpets escorted by suave, lotioned and handsome men. We stood outside the glass swing-doors and watched the cosmopolitan scene: glittering candelabra, white-jacketed waiters and white tables set with ranks of sparkling silver. The *maître d'hôtel* ushered the diners to their places with fawning deference.

'Mother' arrived. He was dressed as before, in windcheater, baggy cotton trousers and grubby shirt. He was utterly unaware of the incongruity of his appearance in these opulent surroundings. He had never been out of India before. The western luxuries of the Great Eastern and Grand Hotels of Calcutta were above his station. He had learned to eat with a knife and fork in order to consume fried eggs and chips and chicken curry in Dum Dum Airport restaurant. After a single glance from the *maître d'* we were conducted to a table behind the foliage of a potted palm tree. 'Mother' blinked from behind his broken spectacles. He hesitated before eating a mouthful. We reassured him it was not beef, but chicken.

After half-a-dozen of these flights, Frank Whittaker decided to return to the UK and study for his ALTP licence. He had been offered a job with Aden Airways. 'Mother' also announced his desire to return to his family. He was homesick for Calcutta. In the following years I often saw him at Dum Dum. He never again left India, but flew on the freight runs to Assam with Darbunga Aviation.

I heard on the grapevine in the late 50s that he had died in a crash. His Dakota had taken off from a grass tea-garden strip west of Gauhati; they were carrying 7,500 llbs of tea-chests to Calcutta for shipment to the London tea-auctions. An hour after take-off, 'Mother' sent a message to Calcutta saying that one engine had failed, and the aircraft was making for Balurghat, the small Indian brick-surfaced airstrip near the East Pakistan border. It was May, and the hottest time of the year. Another message from 'Mother' said that the good engine was over-heating and that they were unable to maintain height. The message was never completed. The crash was found two days later in a Pakistani paddi field. All the crew were dead.

My new crew was First Officer Eapen, a Maronite Christian from Kerala, and Radio Officer Narendra, a Mysorian Brahmin. Our flight was diverted to Jerusalem Airport. We were informed by the Arab Airways handling agent that there was no return load, the Jordan and Lebanese governments had stopped the export of their artisans. We were instructed to remain in Jerusalem until further orders. The fascination of the Via Dolorosa, Christ's supposed tomb, the Mount of Olives, Bethlehem and the Dead Sea were soon exhausted. We were put up at Aden Airway's expense in the Ramallah Hotel. We played tennis and ate too much. I wrote repeatedly to Aden requesting relief from bondage. They refused to answer, and continued to pay us and our hotel bills. It was five weeks before I received orders to fly my empty Dakota to the Aden Airways headquarters in Asmara.

When we arrived in Asmara it was clear that Aden Airways did not know what to do with us. But no one would take responsibility for ordering us back to India. So once again we found ourselves marooned, drawing our pay and idle. We were not alone. Another Indamer crew was kicking its heels in Asmara, also on charter to Aden Airways, waiting to take up an assignment flying for the United Nations between Beirut and the Gaza Strip. Their Dakota had been painted white and decorated with the UN insignia; they were waiting for the contract to be ratified in New York.

The captain of this aircraft was Ivan Reardon, whom I had first met six years before when we were both flying from Juhu. He was of medium height, with wavy hair, and very handsome. When he got drunk he became friendlier, more good-natured, until he finally collapsed into happy oblivion. Among all the aircrew I knew during the next fourteen years, Ivan was the most sagacious. His co-pilot was Jimmy Batliwalla, a Parsee, tall, thin, hair *en brosse*, and a short black beard. Jimmy was one of the great die-hards of Indamer, who preferred the adventurous life to the routine existence in an Indian national airline. He was a steady drinker, but never showed the slightest deviation from his kind and pleasant nature.

We soon exhausted the fleshpots of Asmara, and so before Christmas Jimmy and I decided to make a pilgrimage to

Massawa on the Red Sea coast. This, the only port in Eritrea, was then, and probably still is in ruins. It lay eighty miles east of Asmara by the shallow blue water's edge of the Red Sea, with flat, dry scrubland to the west. The sun beat down blindingly, and the winds were hot with a sticky salt humidity. The Italians had built a small suburbia on the mainland for their officials, with a Catholic and Coptic church, a hotel, bus terminus, and a station for the small-gauge railway surrounded by a carpet of black ash and cinders. The buildings were dilapidated and almost deserted. Further inland were the crumbling barrack blocks of the long-departed British and Indian troops who had liberated Eritrea in 1944. A long wooden causeway joined the suburbia to the somnolent port on a sandy island, with its police station, customs house, bars, native quarters and broken cranes. The place had been bombed during its liberation. The docksides were still in ruins, cranes lay toppled and twisted, and a sunken ship was visible beneath the clear, sunlit water.

The British military mandate of Eritrea had ended the previous year. The Italians were leaving as the Ethiopians moved into Eritrea. Exports and imports had stopped, and Massawa slowly returned to dust. The aerial ropeway constructed by the Italians to carry goods and coal the eighty miles up to Asmara had ceased to function years ago. It stood silently, its empty buckets forlornly hanging, slowly rusting throughout its length. A bus, a train and one lorry plied daily between Asmara and Massawa. All movement was by day as 'shiftas' (bandits) armed with captured rifles operated by night.

Jimmy and I went down by bus. It took five hours. As we passed wayside deserted bars and restaurants we were gradually acclimatised to the sadness of decay. These places had once catered for holidaying Italians. Now the Eritreans wandered around in tatty khaki shorts and dirty blankets, carrying basket trays of eggs and oranges which they tried to sell to the bus passengers. They seemed mystified at the disappearance of their customers. We entered Massawa across twenty miles of dry scrub. We saw the disused ropeway terminal, the crumbling barracks, and far to the east the blue sea. Finally the bus stopped and deposited us fifty yards from the Ciao Hotel.

We picked up our bags and made for the Ciao. The hotel needed a coat of paint. It was a long bungalow standing six feet high on concrete pylons. At the back was a swimming-pool next to the clear water of Massawa bay. In its day the hotel had catered for the colonial élite; now, in 1953, it struggled heroically to keep up its standards in the face of rising costs and departing Italians. Two-and-a-half years later I visited Massawa for the last time. The Ciao was deserted. I sat alone in the dining room, a zephyr (bearing the warm stench from the port) billowed the curtains and cooled the shades of long-departed guests. At night I heard the creaking of the wooden passages. I imagined that it was the ghostly re-enactment of past assignations. But on that first evening, when the sun set, we saw and heard, from the Ciao dining-room, the island port. The causeway was lit by the long row of lights. The lighthouse flashed a full beam eastwards out to sea. We could see a tower of flashing red, blue, green and yellow lights. Blasting across the still, dark waters as though purposely beamed at the Ciao were the romantic strains of *Non dimenticare*.

There was no hurry, the night was young. After our coffee we sauntered along the pitted road and pavement from one feeble pool of light to the next. We reached the lighted causeway. It was deserted. The breeze was warm, and perfumed by the scent of rotting seaweed. It was low tide. Our spirits flagged, but we hurried along the causeway, Jimmy with his long stride slightly ahead of me. We passed down dusty, narrow, deserted lanes between tall, dark buildings. A few bars were open; inside, fat Italians in vests and underpants were sipping cognac and playing dominoes or backgammon. Deafening music came from the dark blue sky. We turned a shadowy corner and the full melody of *Domani* blared down from the top of a thin, lightless block of flats. We found a doorway over which was the word 'Paradiso'. We climbed up a narrow, concrete stairway lit by the stars, emerging onto a flat roof.

Unpainted and battered metal tables and chairs stood around the periphery. Four girls were sleeping with their heads on the tables. A barman, with a look of surprise which broke into a wide grin, saw us first. He rushed to the corner of the bar and switched off the music. The sudden silence awoke the girls. Jimmy ordered "uno cognac and uno cinzano". The girls hovered around, so we bought each a drink and one for the barman. From the roof we had a panoramic view. We located the source of the coloured lights. It was the Roma. Promising to return we hurried off.

The Roma was the haunt of the few local Italians. Its lights were subdued and the music came softly from a radiogram. The girls looked prettier. They did not act so desperately for a drink, but sat quietly waiting to be accosted. Two fat Italians were pushing two hugely pregnant girls around the dance floor. The foursome danced a quick *paso doble* with speed and élan. The two dancing girls were very beautiful; one was a pure Ethopian type, and the other with the less prominent features of an Eritrean. Both had lovely dark eyes outlined with kohl, hair swept back from smooth, rounded foreheads, small wrists and delicate hands. They wore pink bedroom slippers with white fluff around their ankles, expressions of quiet contentment, and cotton flower-pattern dresses which had been let out to accommodate their stomachs.

For me, Massawa will always be dear. It was so awful and everyone so nice. We never spent more than two nights there, it was too boring. On my last visit, in 1955, it was under attack by locusts.

A few days after Christmas I was ordered back to Aden. A week later I flew my Dakota to Bombay. Ivan and Jimmy stayed in Asmara, still waiting to take up the United Nations charter.

CHAPTER 17

The 1954 Haj

THE success of our 1953 Haj created a great demand for seats for the coming 1954 season. The Nigerian Haj committee again contacted Aden Airways, who, 'Thank heaven!' sub-contracted the Kano-Jedda sector to Skyways of London, operating four-engined Avro Yorks, each of which carried three times as many passengers as a Dakota. However, Capt Pascoe chartered two Indamer Daks to operate Aden-Jedda and Ryan-Jedda.

One morning in early July, seven Indamer Dakotas took off with Indian Hajis, to fly them to Jedda from Santa Cruz airport Bombay. My crew was F/O Mahna and R/O Abrol, both new boys. Mahna had been trained at the government Air School at Allahabad, and had just got the Dakota stamped on his licence. It was always difficult to crew our aircraft for the Haj season. After experiencing a Haj operation, a young first officer could usually get himself taken on by the nationalised Indian Airline, the internal carrier.

I was flying VT-DGT, an old Dakota work-horse. It was a clear, sunlit morning. Soon after yelling "Wheels up, flaps up," and setting climbing power and 'revs', I was aware that Mahna seemed to be in a stupefied coma, transfixed, and staring ahead. Before us lay blue sky and sea, a lovely morning.

"What's wrong, Mahna?"

He looked at me, his eyes wide open and said, "It's so big! There's so much! Nothing there!"

I caught on. "It's the sea! All the way!"

He had spent his whole young life in central India. The 'sea' he knew was a blue patch on an atlas. By the time we had flown the 1,500 miles to Bahrain, Mahna was no longer in wonder. However, there was more to come during the next two months.

Our seven Daks arrived at Jedda in the late evening. Five Dakotas departed that night back to Bahrain, and then the next day positioned at Kabul for the Afghan Haj. The seventh Dak was flown by Capt Budziokowski, chief pilot of Himalayan Airways at Calcutta. 'Budji' and I each flew empty to Aden that same night and landed at RAF Khormaksar.

The next morning Capt Pascoe 'put us in the picture'. As Budji was senior and eldest, he took the 'cushiest' route, Aden-Jedda-Aden. I was assigned to RAF Ryan, an airfield 320 miles east of Aden, on the rocky 4,000 ft plateau that lies between the coastline and the Hadramaut valley 100 miles north. The Hadramaut runs from Cape Fartak in a gentle curve to the north of the plateau, westward for 500 miles to the foothills of the 8,000 ft mountains of the Yemen, crowned by its capital city of Sana.

The Hadramaut is a dry, sandy trench some 2,000 ft deep in places, and from two to ten miles wide. It has a chain of small, thriving agricultural towns, each a local 'sheikdom'. The buildings in these towns are mud skyscrapers, six storeys high, the most spectacular of which is Shibam. Aden Airways flew a daily schedule service into the Hadramaut.

F/Lt Cook, the CO at RAF Ryan (near the sea-port of Mukallah), very kindly gave us beds, if we should need them during the coming weeks, in a Nissan hut. Our route from RAF Ryan to Jedda was 900 miles across the southern portion of the Rub al Khali, 'The Empty Quarter', consisting of sand and rock from the Arabian Sea and 750 miles to the Persian Gulf, and from the Red Sea due east for 1,200 miles, to the Arabian Sea.

Taking off from Ryan at 0800 hrs we had covered 150 miles and had reached 12,000 ft. There was no visibility in any direction. We were in a thick haze of ochre sandy particles, rising up in the hot air, heated by the sun. The aircraft was being bounced around by strong up-draughts, which increased in turbulence as the sun rose higher and higher. There was nothing to see. No navigation was possible, except to keep the Dak pointing in the right direction and maintain height. It was useless to put in the auto-pilot, as the violent up-and-down draughts were too much for the auto-pilot to compensate. We hand-flew the Dak for four-and-a-half hours. There was nothing to see on our maps, except halfway across three meandering dotted lines were shown, marked 'Philby 1934', 'Thomas 1935' and undated 'Ingram'.

During all this violent turbulence, our passengers, 28 of them, sat clutching their seat arm-rests, and being sick into paper bags. The women comforted their howling babies beneath their burkas. The men sweated and placated the elder children. The whole scene was too awful to watch. We kept the cockpit door closed and got on with the business of counteracting the violence of the turbulence.

In the event of engine trouble we could only head west, and hope to maintain height above the mountains bordering the Red Sea. Gradually the sky got bluer, the sand below lighter. Circles of rocky rings appeared, being old, extinct volcanoes. We were 200 miles from Jedda, descending, increasing our speed, and hoping for the end of the horrible ordeal. Blue sea lay ahead; we were down to 6,000 ft. The sun shone with a clear, radiant clarity, the fog of flying sand left behind. The waters of Jedda harbour were a bright, putrid green, as if of some alchemical distillation. The airport was as usual in utter turmoil. Our passengers staggered down the steps to be led away to the tumult in the arrival lounges, to await their turn with police, passports and health officials.

We had at least an hour to wait for a petrol bowser before we could head back empty to Ryan. The return flight was worse. The heat of the sun, by now at its zenith, increased the violent up-draughts. We got back to Ryan at 1900 hours, for an RAF meal and bed in the Nissan hut.

For the passengers, the least of their worries was the awful flight. It took a day to motor or bus through the gorges of the plateau to reach Ryan from the Hadramaut valley. There were no roads, just tracks of gravel and stones, and the danger from gangs waylaying unprotected travellers.

We did eight Haji flights to Jedda. The sheiks brought an entourage of servants, wives, babies, relatives and bodyguards. All were delivered to Jedda, and our mid-Haj holiday began. Budji and I flew our Daks to Asmara. Our old haunts were busy entertaining the crews from the Afghan Haj. Two days later we were both ordered to position our two Daks at Jedda. Aden Airways had obtained a contract to fly Hajis from Jedda to Medina. After a Haji had completed his devotions in Mecca, many wanted to visit Medina, 250 miles north of Jedda. The Prophet had met opposition in Mecca, so much so that his life was in danger. The people of Medina offered him sanctuary. The Prophet escaped to Medina; this event is known as the Hejira, 'the emigration'.

'A prophet is not without honour except in his own country!'

For those who had the time, money and willingness to face hardships, a visit to Medina was the finale to their Haj.

We stayed in the Kandhara Palace, the air-conditioned hotel at Jedda airport, still being built. The flying time from Jedda to Medina was one hour thirty minutes. It was a horrible flight. From early morning till late evening each of us, Budji and I, did three flights a day to Medina. The direct flight was over desolate, black and dark red, craggy, volcanic solidified oozings, extending right up to Medina airfield. From the air, the pattern of prehistoric lava outflows was clearly visible, resembling sun-baked blood, aeons old, the petrified after-birth of creation. These crags radiated a terrible heat as though still molten. The up-draughts were as violent as those in a larger cumulo-nimbus cloud. The passengers ate from their lunch boxes, lay limply in their seats, and sweated. Twenty minutes from Medina they vomitted onto the floor or into the pockets on the back of the seat in front of them.

The red-black jagged lava extended to a few hundred yards from the periphery of the stony landing field, ringed by empty oil drums. The temperature at the airfield was 48° C. The passengers disappeared into a long stone building, used as a passenger terminal, selling hot Pepsi-Cola. A party of 28 emerged to take their places among the debris in the aircraft. There was no time between landing and take-off to clean up the mess. Their luggage was thrown into the aircraft, and the passengers took their seats.

Back at Jedda the seats remained in place, while the floor was sluiced down with buckets of water, ready for the next load. Our mechanics cut open the bottom of the seat pockets, and removed the cabin carpet. Those being sick into a pocket found their vomit on their feet. After three days of this, we were sent off to take a load of Hajis back to Wadi Halfa.

The return flights of our Hadramauti passengers began. Rather than return empty from Ryan to Jedda during the hottest time of the day, I flew from Ryan to Aden, night-stopped in the Aden Airways quarters at Khormaksar, and took off early morning for Jedda. In this way we arrived at Jedda at 1100 hours, loaded our passengers, arriving at Ryad at 1700 hours; then empty to Aden and repeated the schedule the next morning. Our Haj ended at last. Budji and I flew to Jedda and picked up our Indian Hajis for Bombay. I never met F/O Mahna again.

A few days later I flew my first charter flight to Lagos in Nigeria, and Accra in the Gold Coast. This flight was an irregular charter flown for two Indian trading companies in West Africa, Chellarams and Asoomals. These traders needed to move their Indian staff and families to and from West Africa. They had done so previously up to 1947 by boat, which was slow and expensive.

The earliest flight to Nigeria that I was aware of was in 1947, shortly after I joined Air Services of India. Indamer obtained a contract to operate to Lagos and Accra, but having no aircraft, as yet, of its own, they chartered an Air Services of India Dakota flown by Capt Hank Smith and Bunny Cariappa. At two to three-month intervals, wives and children of the traders' staff were flown out to West Africa, and others returned to India.

At that early date, soon after the war, smuggling of small items on the return flights was prevalent. The customs at Santa Cruz airport were rabid ferrets when searching for smuggled goods, such as small gold bars, watches, cameras, fountain pens, whisky, (Bombay being 'dry' after Independence), and jewellery. The lavatories of incoming international flights were dredged for packages of forbidden items. The crews were searched. And so it happened that when an Indamer Dakota returned from a West African charter in 1952, flown by Capt Dunsmore, F/O Jimmy Batliwalla and R/O Pants Pantalu, the aircraft was 'rummaged' by the Santa Cruz customs. The customs officers besieged the aircraft like demented char-women. They pulled up the carpets, peered into the Elsan lavatory pan, and then unscrewed the cockpit floorboards!

Behind the Captain's seat beneath a radio rack, was a four-ply wooden floorboard. Underneath were the control cables from the cockpit. They found a fair-sized cardboard box. It was filled with small ten-tola gold bars, each about three inches by one inch. There were two bottles of whisky, watches and some Parker pens. The crew were whisked off to the customs headquarters at Ballard Pier in Bombay. Jimmy Batliwalla claimed the whisky, and Dunsmore the gold Dunsmore was freed on bail of Rs 25,000. Jimmy's whisky was taken by the customs and disappeared down their official channels. Peter Baldwin paid Dunsmore's bail.

Dunsmore lived in a large house at Juhu. It was rumoured that his wife had an almirah full of mink coats! Dunsmore and his wife flew to New Delhi, and from there absconded to the Middle East. In 1953 while I was in Port Sudan it was rumoured that he was in a Khartoum jail. The customs believed Dunsmore and Baldwin were in cahoots.

I operated the Lagos charter flight several times in 1954, and managed to reduce the round trip to seven days by cutting out the night stops. This was popular with the charter party, but not with the passengers. On our return journey I would fly the 2,700 miles from Kano to Bahrain in 24 hours, only stopping to refuel. We arrived in Bahrain at midnight. By this time the passengers, women and babies, were nearly demented with claustrophobia and cramp.

The great attraction of our flights for which the passengers were prepared to endure any discomfort, was an unlimited baggage allowance. We seldom carried more than 18 passengers, plus babies. The passengers brought in luxuries which they could not get in India, and which were sold on the black market to provide dowries for marriageable daughters. The aircraft was loaded with Grundig radios, Sony transistors, Omega 'time pieces', and tape recorders. The women brought sari-lengths of Japanese material, china sets, cutlery, and festooned themselves with gold ornaments.

The customs at the airport were mainly staffed by the Sindhis, the same community as our passengers, and many related to them. It was my duty to time our arrival at Bombay so that we were inspected by customs staff known to be friendly. Presents were bought and left in the aircraft to be collected by officers at Santa Cruz. An over-zealous officer might allow through a radio without duty when the passenger presented his passport with a 100-rupee note inside.

After the flight, I would leave by the same night's Airmail Service for Calcutta, and the delights of the Assam Valley. As a general practice crews under-logged their flying time when filling the aircraft logbook. This allowed the crews to exceed the maximum monthly permitted quota, resulting in an increase of the permitted time between engine overhauls.

The Poles

In the early mornings of 1949-50 when I was flying on the Assam Airlift from Dum Dum, I would often see Capt

Budziokowski awaiting the return of one of his Himalayan Aviation Dakotas from its night airmail flight to and from Nagpur. 'Budji' was an aristocratic Pole, tall, mature, balding and bespectacled. He was the chief pilot of Himalayan Aviation, whose captains were his compatriots.

In 1939 when Hitler invaded Poland, Budji and his fellow-students were young airforce cadets. They escaped from the Germans by fleeing to Rumania, where they were interned. They bribed a ship's captain to take them to Malta. The group consisted of the future Himalayan captains Bobinski, Tarkowski, Cekalski, Ziggernierski and Budji. Their ship was intercepted by the Royal Navy. The Poles explained that they were airforce cadets. The Navy took them to Malta and shipped them to Marseilles on board the *Franconia*. They were sent to Lyons where they were to continue their flying training. The German break-through in northern France in May 1940 caused the Poles to flee to Port Vendres in southern France. They were evacuated by the Royal Navy and taken to Algiers. Eventually they arrived in Britain after wandering in a circle through Morocco to Gibraltar, and then shipped to the UK. They completed their training and were eventually posted to the Polish squadrons of the RAF.

After the war, being 'stateless citizens', they were given 'travel documents'. They came to India prior to Independence. Himalayan Aviation was started by General Mahabir of Nepal, flying Dakotas. Himalayan pioneered the flying into Kathmandu, also it operated into Leh in northern Kashmir, for the Indian military. In 1949 Himalayan flew the Calcutta to Nagpur leg of the 'Night Airmail Service'. This operation was from Delhi, Calcutta, Madras and Bombay. A Dakota left every evening from each station with mail and passengers. The four Dakotas met at Nagpur, in central India. Passengers and mail were unloaded and reloaded onto the aircraft returning to its base, arriving at Bombay, Delhi, Calcutta and Madras in the early morning.

Most of the year the flying conditions were good. However, during the monsoon Budji took the precaution of two captains flying together. In the early morning, Budji's uniform was khaki drill, coloured cravat, gold-rimmed spectacles, fawn 'brothel creepers', and smoking a cigarette from a long holder. A picture of elegance having an early morning whisky while waiting for the return of the Himalayan Dak from Nagpur. We, a bunch of scruffy aircrew, ate the standard fried eggs and chips before taking off at 0600 hours in our Dakota freighters for Bagdogra near Darjeeling, or up the Assam Valley.

After the 1954 Haj, Budji got a job in Faridabad, near Delhi, in a factory making desert coolers. He died in Delhi of a heart attack in 1961. A fellow-Pole of Budji's, Capt Bobinski, had left India to become a shopkeeper in London. In 1964, Capt Ziggernierski was flying for Air Nepal, when he decided to leave flying and join Capt Chopra on his farm in the hills north of Delhi. He left Kathmandu in an Air Nepal Dakota, flown by Capt Timmy Dastur. The aircraft crashed into a mountain ridge at 10,000 feet in cloud near Dorpatan, an administrative outpost which had an airstrip. The news of the crash was brought by villagers. Capt Randhawa flew the Pilatus Porter of the Swiss Aid Mission and landed at Dorpatan. He took off in order to search the surrounding hillsides for the crash. He failed to return, presumably having also crashed into the forest in cloud. Years later I heard from Capt Pesi Birdi, ex-India International, that Timmy Dastur was buried in Kathmandu. Capt Birdi had been a protégé of Timmy's during the years he had been training for his flying licence.

Capt Tarkowski flew on the Indamer Hadjs of 1953 and '54, then for the Central African Aviation Medical Services, where he married Ola, a Polish doctor. Later they returned to England, where Tarko flew the Avro 748 for Skyways at Lympne Airport in Kent, and where they built a house next to the Hythe Sene Valley golf course. He died at Hythe in 2001. Capt Cekalski married the lady pianist of the Grand Hotel, Calcutta, in the 1950s. He flew for many years with the Nato Flying Unit in Germany. He later also joined Skyways at Lympne. He and his wife lived in Sellindge, near Hythe, until they retired to Norfolk.

CHAPTER 18

The 1955 Haj

CHRISTMAS 1954 in Aden was dreadful. All through the festive nights the drunken songs of lonely British soldiers and airmen (mostly young boys doing their two years of National Service) mingled with the hubbub of the Muslim bazaar. The wild, fatuous hooting of ships' sirens ushered in the New Year. In my room on the first floor of the Marine Hotel, with its thick mud-and-rock walls, its warped wooden floor and ceiling, I felt marooned, as though awaiting relief in some desert fort. I heard faint cheering from the small bars around the Crescent shopping centre. I looked back on a long vista of hotel rooms and 'Inspection' bungalows from Lagos to north-east Assam.

During the months before the 1955 Haj, news came through the grapevine of the deaths of Captain Tutu Amber and First Officer Malhotra. Both had been in the small band of Air Services of India crew in Jorhat during the first Assam supply drop in 1951. They had been killed on a nonsensical Dakota evaluation test near Delhi. In 1954, a Dakota on the Night Airmail Service from Bombay to Calcutta, had crashed at Nagpur while turning to line up with the runway. The Civil Aviation authorities thought that an engine might have failed while the aircraft was on a turn, due to low fuel content in an auxiliary tank, and decided to carry out flight trials. (This was when the Dakotas had already been flying world-wide for twenty years, and were to continue doing so for another thirty.) Tutu and Malhotra had volunteered to do the test flights. Their crash was witnessed by some peasants who reported that the aircraft was not high up and was in a low turn, when it suddenly dived into the ground and blew up. I never heard the outcome of the subsequent investigation. By tragic coincidence, Malhotra's elder brother was the senior accident investigator for the Civil Aviation authority.

For the coming Haj four Indamer Dakotas were going to be decorated with a blue line and the name 'Ariana Afghan Airlines'. Another two Indamer Dakotas, in their own red and white livery, would assist on the Haj. All aircraft would be flown and maintained by Indamer crew. I flew a Dakota from Calcutta to Delhi to collect some ground station radio equipment, a gift from the Indian Government to the Afghans. My crew were again First Officer Eapen and Radio Officer 'Pants' Pantalu. Both were old hands in the Company, with whom I had flown in Assam and Aden during the last three years. We were all anxious to set off for Kandahar, but we had not counted on the Indian customs. They discovered that the Government department which was making the gift of radio equipment had not obtained an export licence. It took ten days to regularise the paperwork for the shipment, during which we had a holiday in the Ambassador Hotel, and pretty boring it soon became. In the lavish, red plush hotel bar, with its mirrors and glass candelabra, reigned a heavy silence. The Congress Party's prohibition laws had long since denuded the bar of the convivial company it had once known. I, as a 'farriner', could drink there, but not Eapen or Pants. Instead, I ordered drinks to our room, and we consumed them in dull, conspiratorial silence.

At last we took off for Kandahar and landed on a hard gravel strip, the runway defined only by the wheelmarks of last year's Dakotas. We were met by Clary D'Silva. Clary was a Goanese who for years was general dogsbody for Indamer. There was nothing he could not get, or fix — from American visas to black market whisky. During the ensuing Haj he performed as traffic officer, issued tickets, collected money and marshalled the Hajis. He was indispensable. This year he had a stocky, fair-haired Afghan assistant who was learning the job. Clary had arranged rooms for us at the Hotel de Kandahar. It lay outside the mud wall of the old city, in an area set aside for modernisation. From its bedroom windows, across a few miles of shimmering rock, could be seen crumbling ruins on a long hill, the scene of grisly fighting between Afghans and British, seventy-five years before.

The hotel stank of dumba oil, as did the Afghan bearers. Oblivious of the stifling heat, they dressed in old tweed jackets, baggy salvar, and bound their heads in ten yards of greasy turbans. The oil was used for cooking and somehow found its way into the drinking water and the tea. It was made from the poor dumba sheep's tail, an embarrassing, swollen and fatty appendage. Flies were everywhere, and settled on the soiled bed-sheets to await patiently the next occupant. The bedheads were Victorian with brass knobs, weak springs and soft mattresses which trapped the heat. The taps in the bathrooms seldom worked, and the bidets were choked with encrusted crap. Red Afghan carpets covered all the floors. There was a large reception room whose walls were painted a bilious green and lined with heavy wooden and padded armchairs of local manufacture. From the ceiling of this hall hung two giant glass candelabra. At night a feeble light came from the only bulb. The guests and servants had removed the bulbs, replacing them with the defunct ones from the bedrooms. Clary had a room of his own piled with boxes of tinned food, insecticide bombs and toilet rolls. We quickly decided to spend as few nights in Kandahar as possible, and aimed to make our night-stops in Bahrain.

Operations started the next morning. Two thousand Afghans had been booked for Jedda. Each aircraft carried twenty-eight Hajis, which worked out at over seventy flights for the six Dakotas. It took twelve hours to get from Kandahar to Jedda, including refuelling time at Zahedan and Bahrain. To carry twenty-eight large Afghans and their baggage over 900 miles of desert and the Persian Gulf between Zahedan and Bahrain, and the desert between Bahrain and Jedda, meant that the aircraft were always two thousand pounds overweight on take-off.

Vivid in my mind, and has been ever since, is the memory of every single mile of the 1,600 that lay between Kandahar and Jedda. I never set off without a feeling of apprehension of what could happen if things went wrong on the flight. For the first three hundred and fifty miles we crossed the shimmering white sands which wandered through the grey, mottled and shallow depression of the Helmund valley. The dry river debouched into a huge, dry salt lake bordering Persia. The Americans were building a dam at its non-existent head waters not far from Kandahar city. On the Persian borders rose grey, jagged mountains reaching 5,000 feet. A valley lay beyond, through which ran the single-track railway from Quetta, which terminated at the Persian town of Zahedan. We landed on a concrete runway and were refuelled. A conscientious Sikh gentleman was the Shell agent in nearby Zahedan. As soon as he heard a Dakota's engines, he left his depot with the petrol bowzer and was waiting for us when we landed.

Between Zahedan and Bahrain lay a waste of sand, gravel, and 12,000 feet high mountains. No desert travellers ever felt more elation than we did, as from 80 miles away we saw the bright blue sea off Bunder Abbas on the Gulf of Hormuz. No villages, no roads, no tents or anything green lay between Zahedan and the Persian Gulf. No radio aids helped us to navigate. We came to recognise every mile; rocks became vital checkpoints, dry nullahs longed-for landmarks, and Sugar Loaf Hill — a desolate pimple some 6,000 feet high — became a welcome friend.

From the Persian coast to the flat, sandy island of Bahrain was 300 miles of sea. Fantastic blues, shallows of emerald green and a sea-bed of ochre sand coloured the crossing. A hot vapour of sand hung above the Qatar Peninsula, 80 miles from Bahrain. The sun at midday cast no shadows. In the autumn, clouds dulled the tints of this landscape making it unrecognisable and hostile. Great piles of grey, wet clouds lay upon the mountains of southern Persia, forcing us to hug the coastline as long as we could. Six hours after leaving Kandahar we landed at Bahrain on the long, undulating tarred runway, made sticky by the ferocious midday sun. Five hours and 800 miles across deserts of orange, grey, and glaring pans of dried salt, terminating for the last 150 miles in volcanic crags, was Jedda. Mecca lay 50 miles to the south-east, to be reached by the pilgrims in buses, taxis or on foot.

For the first few days we slipped crews in Jedda, where we stayed in the Kandara Palace, a new hotel built at the airport since the 1953 Haj. But soon its discomforts made us abandon this routine and make Bahrain the base for everyone. Half of us flew the aircraft on the Kabul, Kandahur to Bahrain sector, and the other half took the aircraft over the Bahrain-Jedda sector. Nothing but the most serious engine fault could keep us in Jedda. We might be stuck there for hours, either because the Haji load was lost, or the Customs and Emigration were up to their tricks. A burnt-out generator, unserviceable radio or instruments, or even a hefty mag drop could not stop our take-off. Only an oil leak that poured out at more than three gallons an hour could keep us on the ground.

I shall never forget the first time I found myself in a sandstorm at night, 10,000 feet and a hundred miles south of Bahrain. A red glow surrounded the aircraft; the stars and the ground were invisible. Everything glowed a dull, luminous red — our faces, the instruments, and the windscreen. We were flying through a sea of blood with nothing but our instruments and 'the seat of our pants' to tell us we were the right side up. At first I was completely mystified by the crimson glow after four hours of black night and clear stars. Then I realised that the whole atmosphere was flying sand. I was flying in a sandstorm, illuminated by the fires from the line of oil wells south of Dahran. The blood-red colour intensified as the aircraft flew over the flames of the burning waste gas from each oil well. In bright sunshine the flames were almost invisible. On clear nights, from a hundred and fifty miles away, they appeared as stars low on the horizon, but in a sandstorm they illuminated the flying dust with an enveloping red glow.

On the rocky Kandahar airstrip the Hajis camped in and around the derelict hangar. Two to three hundred were there day and night. As aircraft taxied up to the loading area they blew up clouds of sand and covered the Hajis in layers of dusty powder. Afghan police dressed in thick, rough, khaki uniforms, kept them at bay. They wore heavy jackboots and German Army-style forage caps. They used their leather belts to swipe at any Hajis who dared to come beyond the line of their patrol. Each pilgrim sat on his filthy bundle of blankets and soiled clothing, with his kettle-like water pot for his ablutions and an old one-gallon tin of dumba oil. The tins came back from Jedda filled with the sacred sands of Mecca.

The dumba oil got everywhere. The Hajis cooked with it and used it on their hair. Twenty-eight one-gallon tins of dumba oil were scattered between the cockpit baggage hold and the back of the aircraft. Once the Hajis were in the cabin we never went near them. It was impossible to train two thousand wild Afghans to use the Elsan toilet. They crapped and peed on or under the seats. At ten thousand feet flying south towards Bandar Abbas one evening, we noticed the hydraulic fluid gauge level had fallen below the minimum, a common defect with our overworked Dakotas. Eapen left his seat to top-up the reservoir tank. For the rest of the flight there was the most extraordinary smell in the cockpit. We put it down to the passengers having had an extra large meal of curried goat chops before leaving Kandahar. At Bahrain our engineers discovered that we had mistaken the oil tin, and had poured half-a-gallon of dumba oil into the hydraulic system.

The aerodrome officer at Kandahar was Captain Abdullah, a 'pukka Hurrumzada', (a first-class bastard). Being in a position of authority and enjoying displaying it, Abdullah took it out on the ignorant, harmless passengers. He would strut around the aircraft or stand imposingly under the wing in the shade. Clary and his Afghan assistant called out the names of the next load of passengers. They shuffled forward, lugging their bundles and dumba tins with them. Invariably, scuffles took place between the passengers because there is a limit to the number of combinations of names that can be made out of Aziz, Mohamed, Yusuf, Ali and Abdullah.

"Mohamed Ali Khan," the Afghan assistant shouted. Four passengers stood up and moved towards the aircraft. They were intercepted by the police, and an argument started. Clary examined each ticket number and allowed the right man through.

"Yusuf Ali Khan."

Two more Afghans moved towards the aircraft, only to be stopped; again the ticket numbers were checked and one allowed through.

"Ali Mohamed Khan."

Another scuffle, and so on. Abdullah's pleasure in demonstrating his authority and our own desire for a speedy turn-round could sometimes result in violence. On one occasion two Daks landed at about half-past-two in the afternoon. We started yelling impatiently for the petrol bowzer, which was in the process of being laboriously filled from four-gallon tins. Clary was marshalling two groups of twenty-eight passengers. We wanted to get back to Bahrain by 2100 hours. While the mechanics hastily inspected the aircraft, Abdullah pushed his way through the crowd and started to strut around. As usual he was dressed, in spite of the heat, in a natty, dark grey suit, cut in the Middle East fashion of long jacket and narrow-bottomed trousers. He wore a khaki shirt and tie, and a silver karakul cap at a modish angle. Jai Singh, Jimmy Batliwalla, Bill Antia, Kamat, Pants Pantalu and myself were standing at the tail of the aircraft watching the mêlée and goading poor Clary to get a move on.

The sun was hot. The crowd had been waiting expectantly all day. Now they knew that fifty-six of them would leave. The line of waiting Hajis was only three feet from the wing tips of the parked aircraft. Abdullah took up a position in the shade of a wing. The police walked up and down, swinging their belts and watching the crowd in case there was a concerted rush for the aircraft. Suddenly, a grey-bearded old man in soiled shirt, waistcoat and pyjama, and wearing a large, loose turban, carrying his bundle of clothing, tin of dumba fat and aluminium kettle, slipped past the soldiers and quietly crouched in the shade of a wing, a few yards from the preening Abdullah. We, by the tail of the aircraft, watched in apprehension.

Captain Abdullah was momentarily motionless in surprise. The police pretended not to notice the deliberate flouting of their authority. From the corner of his eye the Captain saw us watching him. With a start, the gallant Abdullah came to life and rushed at the old man. He turned sideways, leapt into the air and attempted to kick the old man with both feet at once. The old man dodged back. Abdullah's kick hit empty air and he nearly fell onto the gravel, but saved himself by getting one leg down first. He hopped about to keep his balance in a most undignified fashion. Meanwhile, the police took their cue and started to belabour the old man with their belt buckles as he pushed his way into the safety of the crowd. Abdullah was red with fury. His silver-grey karakul had become askew, and he no longer looked a dignified and authoritative figure. We grinned and took care not to meet his eye.

In Bahrain, Chuck Brown was our traffic officer. He was small, slight, and incredibly active for a 60-year-old. Chuck was an Anglo-Indonesian or Anglo-Burmese who had spent many years in the Far East before coming to India and settling in Bangalore. Peter Baldwin took him to Kabul in 1952. Chuck had become *persona non grata* in Afghanistan when the customs at Kabul airfield found a roll of carpets filled with Persian lambskins. Chuck was accused of attempting to smuggle karakuls. He never set foot in Afghanistan again.

When an aircraft landed from Kandahar, Chuck led the Hajis to a special, wired-off enclosure where they abluted and afterwards said their prayers. Then, after the crew had eaten and the refuelling was over, Chuck led the Hajis back to the aircraft. This routine did not always work smoothly. After sitting for six-and-a-half hours between Kandahar and Bahrain, the Hajis imagined they were at Jedda and expected to be led off to Mecca. Instead, Chuck Brown, wearing a T-shirt, a straw hat, and bouncing around like a lightweight boxer, led them back to the aircraft. They refused to get in. They had just arrived and weren't going back until they had walked round the Ka'aba. Some drew their daggers and surrounded Chuck. Unperturbed, Chuck would stand on his toes and flap his arms (flying), then point to his feet, and then to the south-west, shouting "Jedda! Jedda! Mecca! Mecca! Namas! Namas!" (prayer). He would go through the motions of praying and then start the mime again. The crew would arrive and join Chuck in the pantomime. At last some ancient Afghan who spoke a few words of Hindi or Urdu, understood. The whole lot, grumbling but docile, got back into the aircraft for the next five-hour ordeal.

Captain Bobby Grey and Jimmy Batliwalla had an unusual experience making a night landing at Jedda. The airport was in the flat desert to the east of the town, and had no surrounding protective fencing. One night they were on final approach, touched down, and started to roll along the runway. The landing lights shone about four hundred yards ahead. Suddenly, from out of the dark, two camels loped across the runway right in front of the aircraft. At about 70 mph the Dak ploughed through them. There was nothing Bobby Grey could do except keep straight and hope for the best. There were violent thuds as the aircraft tried to swing to the right, but Bobby kept it straight. After the Hajis had disembarked, Bobby and Jimmy examined the damage by torch light. They found splattered all over the starboard engine nacelle and undercarriage, a horrible and gory mess. The propeller had acted as a giant bacon slicer; broken bones, pieces of carcase had badly damaged the engine cowling, oil cooler and some of the webs of the undercarriage structure had been broken. A large, prehistoric-looking bone had embedded itself in the underside of the wing. The aircraft was stuck at Jedda for five weeks undergoing repairs by Indamer mechanics.

We flew to Asmara for our holiday during the break in the Haj. That year the locusts invaded the town. They crept into the bedrooms, night clubs, perched on our shoulders, ate all the greenery, got themselves run over by cars and then stank out the whole place. On the afternoon that we left Asmara for Jedda, several of us flew into small clouds of the locusts. They hung around the Asmara plateau in swarms, and it was thirty to forty miles before we were clear of them. In the air they appeared to fly at incredible speed, horizontally straight into the aircraft. Luckily no one hit a large swarm, otherwise there would have been a disaster. As it was, our windscreens were covered with yellow pus and squashed bodies; our oil coolers became partially clogged, as did the cylinders in the engine cowlings.

The return half of the Haj was always the worst half. It went on and on. In the second half we were short of an aircraft and had to fly extra loads to Kabul, 350 miles north of Kandahar. The Hajis were worn out after the heat and up to six weeks of hardship and crowds. I remember the time I had a dead passenger on the aircraft. I landed at Kandahar with twenty Hajis to disembark, and the remaining eight for Kabul. The Kandahar baggage was thrown out. Abdullah was hovering outside the cabin door. The police were not swinging their belts. The passengers were only too eager to get away from the aircraft. They had had enough of aviation to last them a lifetime. When I entered the cabin from the cockpit, an old Haji was fast asleep the front seat. I gave him a gentle shake. He slowly toppled sideways until his head rested against the window. I was mystified. It was Eapen, my co-pilot, who told me he was dead, but "For Christ's sake don't say anything, or else there'll be a big fuss." Captain Abdullah would have rushed around writing reports for Ministers. The health officer would have been dragged out of his house in Kandahar and driven in a horse-drawn tonga to the airfield. Lastly, the body would have been put in a box and bounced all the way to Kabul in the back of a lorry paid for by his relatives. After landing at Kabul, his friends thanked us for keeping quiet. They told the officials that he had died after leaving Kandahar.

The Haj finished. Jedda airport settled down to its normal routine until the next year.

CHAPTER 19

Karakuls

AFTER the Haj all the aircraft assembled in Kabul. Peter Baldwin had obtained a contract to airlift karakuls to Beirut; according to him this would keep us all fully occupied for the next six months.

The karakul is the pelt of the Persian lamb. Our loads were to be shipped from Beirut to New York where they would be properly tanned and made into coats for wealthy ladies. The best karakuls are from lambs prematurely delivered. The mothers are tied up and subjected to a long cacophony of drum beats. They go mad and drop their lambs, which are immediately slaughtered. In this way the tiny curls of hair are softer and curlier than if the lambs were born at their natural time. Every man of parts in Afghanistan, and beyond, wears these foetus pelts on his head. Nylon pelts were available but not fashionable.

Peter gave us a room in his bungalow at Sher-i-Nau where up to six of us slept on four beds and on the floor. It soon became bitterly cold and snowed. We kept ourselves warm with a bukhari wood stove, which discharged its fumes by a metal pipe through the roof. The house was open day and night. We helped ourselves to booze, Coca Cola and fried eggs, and enjoyed privacy of a sort behind the high wall which surrounded this Kabuli zenana.

We met in the drawing room and Peter explained his plans. Two aircraft would carry out the local internal services from

Kabul across the Hindu Kush (16,000 feet high and continuously snow-covered) into the Oxus Valley to Kunduz, Masar-i-Sherif and Maimana, with another route to Herat and Kandahar. The remaining four aircraft would fly 7,500 lbs of karakuls each trip to Beirut by way of Zahedan on the eastern border of Persia, then across the highlands to Abadan on the Euphrates, and then straight to the Lebanon. There would be no return loads from Beirut, but Peter had plans for us to circle back via Bahrain, where we would pick up loads of bacon, butter and booze which he had contracted to supply to local foreign embassies.

We quickly calculated that it would take 33 hours to do the round trip, stopping only long enough to refuel. If we left Kabul at 7 o'clock, we could be back the next day at four in the afternoon. Then we would sleep for 12 hours and set off again the next morning. In this way we could each do 33 hours' flying in two days. At this rate we would total 460 hours a month and earn so much money that after six months we could give up flying for ever!

Unfortunately this plan did not take into account the attractions of Beirut night life; and anyway after our 12 hours' sleep we couldn't keep our eyes open on the following trip. In practice we aimed at seven round trips a month, which gave us 200 hours' flying. Most of the proceeds were spent in Beirut.

My crew was First Officer S P Singh, a tall, handsome Rajput, and Radio Officer Kamath, a young Konkani from the coastal area south of Bombay. Singh and I concentrated on keeping the aircraft pointing in the right direction by twisting 'George's' knobs, while we slept alternately. Kamath sent out our position and times of arrival which he worked out for himself.

The first hazard of the flight was the early morning take-off. Kabul is 4,500 feet above sea level, and the airstrip was a worn-down grass field. Old hangars lined the south side of the field, in which were kept ancient Hawker Harts and Audaxes of the Afghan Air Force. Sixteen years before, I had got my wings on this type of aircraft at RAF Station, Hullavington. After a fall of snow the take-off run was flattened by taxiing Dakotas and driving lorries over it. At the north end was a ridge of hills to climb over in a fully-laden Dakota. An engine failure would have meant landing on the nearby army parade ground or among the goats browsing in the surrounding scrub and rocks. We flew down the Kabul-Ghazni road, climbing laboriously to 8,000 feet on our way to Zahedan, 700 miles away. None of our aircraft had de-icing equipment; this had all been removed in Calcutta to lighten the aircraft so that we could carry more freight to Assam. It was bitterly cold during the whole flight, only the sun shining through the cockpit windscreen gave a little heat. The flight across central Persia to Abadan had to be made at low level because of the strong westerly winds. Hour after hour I gazed at the rocks, occasional plains of gravel and sand intersected by the thin yellow strip of a winding road. These were the rocks and sands over which Alexander, Darius, Ghengis Khan and Tamerlane had marched. Relays of horse-men of the Golden Horde had galloped mile after mile back to the blue-domed city of Samarkand on the Oxus, bearing the tidings of the great sacking of Shiraz.

One afternoon in early November after refuelling, I took off from Abadan for the 600-mile flight to Beirut. The Met office warned me of a build-up of cumulo-nimbus over the Lebanese hills. I expected to land at six-thirty, just before nightfall. It was very cold in the clear blue sky as we climbed to 10,000 feet. Singh was wearing a black leather sheepswool-lined jacket. Kummy and I had sweaters and wind jackets. We sat with our legs wrapped in blankets, like dogged trippers braving out a foul Bank Holiday on Brighton beach. I looked out to port and saw far down in the desert the clustered tents of a border patrol. I recognised them and knew we were on track. We crossed the Kirkuk oil pipeline from Iraq to Syria. I got a groundspeed check. The winds were stronger than the Met had forecast. We would be a quarter-of-an-hour late.

Two hundred miles from Damascus we were below a thick layer of alto- stratus. The sunlight had gone and the land was in deep shadow. Gradually the cloud lowered until we were embedded in it. Particles of ice formed on the windscreen and inside the cockpit. We began to freeze. The cloud around us got darker. A hundred miles from Damascus I came down to 7,000 feet, hoping to see more clearly what lay ahead. Below all was shadowed by premature dusk, caused by thick layers of cloud. Ahead of me I could see a dark, wet, blue-grey enormous cunimb sitting right on our track. Because of the mountain ridge, 7,000 to 8,000 feet, between Damascus and the Mediter-ranean, I would have to fly through the cunimb at 10,000 feet. As I got closer I saw there was no hope of flying beneath the storm. I could see the green and white flashing light of Damas-cus aerodrome, and the yellow twinkling lights of the city as it lay spread out like a fan from the foothills. In the dark blue wetness of the huge cunimb to the west of the city I saw the opaque flashes of embedded lightning. It would take me twenty minutes to fly the 50 miles across the hills. I started to climb.

We were soon in thick, grey cloud. Damascus radio beacon came in strong, but every second a loud crackle of static from nearby lightning deflected the needle towards the flash. We were all strapped into our seats, cockpit lights, navigation lights, and pitot heaters on. Singh and I put on our dark glasses, and I turned up the cockpit lights. This would minimise the blinding glare from a near lightning flash; it also made the cockpit seem more homely. We passed over Damascus; the radio compass needle erratically oscillated from north to south. I had my eyes on the artificial horizon. I noticed white ice beginning to creep from the corners of the storm panel. Then it hit us.

Suddenly it was dark grey, then wet blue, and then I no longer cared about the colour outside. The aircraft was flung up, down, and sideways all at once, by the terrific force of air currents which toyed with us as if we were a balloon. A violent bank to port followed by a lurch to starboard, and back to port before I had time to correct. Simultaneously the Dak shot up to 12,000 feet, about which I could do nothing except keep the aircraft horizontal. Ice began to form in thick, opaque layers on the windscreen. The familiar, but always disturbing loud drumming of hailstones on the aircraft drowned out the sound of the engines. It flashed through my mind how, four years before, Johnny Brenand's windscreen had cracked and then broken, letting in a cyclone of rushing air and hail. Engine temperatures had dropped. I yelled to Singh to close the oil and carburettor shutters. I increased revs and boost and put the undercarriage down, trying to keep the airspeed around 130 mph. We were shuddering violently. We shot up to 14,000 feet in seconds. We stopped going up. I had no thought of what was happening outside, our salvation depended on watching the flight instruments, and, most of all, the artificial horizon bar.

I kept heading, as near as the violent yawings, banks and lurchings would allow, a compass course of 300 degrees. The radio compass was now useless; the needle fluctuated towards every flash and then gave up and started to whirl round like a tiny propeller. I made no attempt to lose height; we would be sucked down soon enough. I opened my side window and saw an eerie sight. The whole of my port wing appeared to be bathed in a blue glow; but worse was the thick build-up of white ice around the rim of the engine cowling and over my windscreen. I could do nothing but hope that we got clear of the storm before the ice became too heavy. "Press on!"

Kummy was standing in the gangway wedged between me and Singh. He was tuning in the useless radio compass and keeping up his morale by being as helpful as he could. Poor Singh had given up. He sat in his black leather flying jacket with his hands gripping the seat, staring ahead into an ice-covered windscreen. For all I knew, his eyes were closed behind his Ray Ban sunglasses. Then everything got worse. The rattling of the hail increased. The windscreen became completely covered, even round to the side panels. The airspeed indicator began to fluctuate wildly and then sluggishly collapsed. The pitot head had iced up. I switched on the 'alternate static switch' to keep the altimeters reading roughly correct. The up-draughts took complete control of the aircraft. The ailerons, elevators and rudder were seized as though by rough, powerful hands and waggled. I could do nothing. I was shit scared, breathing fast, and feeling cold and light in the stomach. I had no idea what we were doing. Singh sat cocooned in his black jacket. Our lives at the moment depended on keeping my head and concentrating on the artificial horizon.

"How long have we been since Damascus?" I yelled to Kummy.

"Ten minutes, Andy."

It felt like so many years. How long, Oh Christ? We dropped down to 10,000 feet. Lightning flashes lit up the windscreen as though someone was signalling to us with a powerful searchlight. I managed to open the side window a few inches to revive myself with cold air. Outside, pale black night. There was a deafening CRASH like a burst of heavy flak, and a bright red flash lit up the cockpit for a fraction of a second. Afterwards, Kummy and I swore that we felt a sudden heat at the moment of the bang. I thought we were finished.

"Hail Mary, full of Grace, the Lord is with Thee. Blessed art Thou amongst women and blessed is the fruit of Thy womb, Jesus."

"Lightning strike, Kummy! How long have we been?" I interrupted my prayer.

"Sixteen minutes," Kummy shouted back.

"Holy Mary, Mother of God, pray for us sinners now and at the hour of our Death. Amen."

More lightning all round. For all I knew, we had lost our wings and I was just hanging on to the stick in an aircraft which was falling, and with not far to fall at that. Any second now we might hit the Cedars of Lebanon, our wings fluttering down through the clouds miles behind.

I kept my side window open; perhaps I could get some idea of our speed by the rush of air.

"Tune in to Beirut beacon," I shouted above the din.

Kummy lent over and tuned the radio compass on the control panel in the middle of the roof. The needle fluctuated from side to side but pointed vaguely ahead.

Now the aircraft had started to buffet violently, with a sort of juddering at the control column. I put on more revs and boost. By now we had thick lumps of ice on the port engine nacelle, around the carburettor air intake and also (although in the dark I could not see it) along the leading edges of both wings and tailplane. I imagined we must be near the final ridge of hills east of Beirut.

"Fer-uck this! Christ get us out of this!" I prayed.

I turned to port in an attempt to break out of the turbulence. I had to come down soon, if we were not to drop out of the sky like a gigantic hailstone.

"How long now?" I yelled.

"Two or three minutes to go," answered Kummy.

Then suddenly we were out of it. One second in cloud, terrified, and with my eyes glued to the instruments, the next in clear, unbelievable calm. Through the small crack in the side window I saw the stars and the pale glow of the moon. I looked below and there, reflected off the water, were the twinkling lights of Beirut. It was the most beautiful sight I had ever seen. I forgot about instruments and ice. I could see the ground and lights. The grubby night spots, their boredom, the extortions of barmen and taxi drivers, all counted for nothing. I was filled with a great love for the place and all its inhabitants; whores, taxi drivers, businessmen, Arabs in baggy pants with hairy arms and fingers, babaghanoosh, arak, the Dugout, Eve and the Casanova; I loved them all. Beirut was the most beautiful place on earth.

Kummy called up 'Kalde Tower', and we were given a 'bamboo' for not calling earlier. Below, I recognised the lights of the Hotel St George; then I made out the lights reflected from the sea outside the Kitkat and Eve. 'Crack! Crack!' Pieces of melting ice flew off the propeller blades and struck the fuselage. Ice slid off the windscreen. The cockpit was getting warmer. I could see the lighthouse flashing and the long row of double amber lights which marked the boulevard leading to the airport.

On final approach we flew over the Plaza Hotel in the Rue Al Hamra. No doubt there was a crowd of pilots boozing in the Neptune bar nearby. God bless them all! I called "short final", and put on the landing lights. I saw the threshold markings and touched down. I got a clearance to do a 180-degree turn and taxi back to the dispersal. We collected manifests, the aircraft journey log book and our suitcases, jumped down from the main cabin door, and shut it behind us. Kummy dived under the wings to put in the undercarriage pins.

Thomas, our engineer, was waiting for us in the customs enclosure. We got cleared by a pistol-toting customs officer; I gave him a carton of Lucky Strike, for which he had been plaguing me for the last month. We got into a Mercedes taxi, and within fifteen minutes we were being welcomed by the barman, and Antonio, the tall ex-jewel-cutter receptionist at the Plaza. An hour later, Kummy and I were heading for the floor show at the Kitkat.

The next morning the three of us went to the airport to see the damage. Each propeller blade had semicircles of metal burnt out of its tip, as though a metal-eating gremlin had bitten mouthfuls of aluminium from the rotating blades. The wing tips had been split open and gaped like open ducks' bills. The splits were burnt and charred at the edges. The damage indicated where strong discharges of static electricity had sparked off into the air. There were large dents on the fuselage behind the cockpit windows where lumps of ice had been thrown from the propellers and hit the metal skin. After our inspection I decided to take off that evening for Bahrain, a direct flight of 1,000 miles, and have a few repairs done there. Thomas was busy filing smooth the burnt portions of the propeller blades. It was now that Singh delivered his bombshell.

"I'm not coming, Andy," he said.

"What! You're not coming? For Krishna's sake, why?" I cried.

"Because I'm tired and don't want to," he replied.

I was flummoxed. I'd never heard such an excuse before.

"When will you be ready to come? I'll leave tomorrow morning if you like," I continued.

"I don't know when. I want to rest."

"You don't know! What about us? Are we to sit on our arses, losing flying time and money, because you're tired? Why don't you sleep on the aircraft? Kamath and I will fly."

"No, I'm not coming. I'm staying here."

I realised Singh had reached the end, so I magnaminously changed my tune.

"Alright, Singhji, you stay behind and enjoy yourself, but Kamath and I will keep on. I'll put your name in the log book. Anytime you want to rejoin the aircraft you let me know at the Plaza, okay?"

"Yes, okay and thanks, Andy."

That evening Kummy and I took off on our own. It was a lovely clear night. The storm had passed, leaving clear, cold skies filled with bright, fresh stars and a young moon. We climbed to 9,500 feet, and flew over Mount Hebron, capped with pale blue snow from the storm. I looked to port and saw our route of the previous night, now clear and calm, with lights from the villages and from cars speeding along the Beirut to Damascus road. It was getting cold in the cockpit and I was feeling sleepy already. The cold didn't revive me; it made me want to hibernate. Kummy was at the back bashing out departure and arrival messages. The seat on my right was empty. I missed Singh and his black leather jacket.

We had half-a-dozen blankets on board. I wrapped my legs in two of them, put another over my head and shoulders, and sat there in the driving seat like an old frozen pauper on a park bench swaddled in sacking. We passed Damascus, and suddenly 'George' packed up. The worst had happened. Every time I set the cards and put in 'George', the starboard wing dropped and we started a diving turn. This was a major disaster because I knew there was little chance of getting 'George' repaired at either Bahrain or Kabul. I would have to hand-fly the aircraft from now on.

That six-hour night flight to Bahrain was hell. The cold was awful. I came down to 7,500 feet but there was no appreciable rise in temperature, so I went back to 9,500 feet. The higher we were, the stronger the winds blew us along. I was falling asleep at the controls and waking up after two or three seconds. I sat myself upright, feet and hands holding the aircraft level and on course. I closed my eyes for a half-awake snooze. I woke with the aircraft off-course and in a 60-degree port bank. I got back on track for the pumping station at Badanah and called up Kummy. I told him that I couldn't keep my eyes open and he must take over. On many of our previous flights I had got Kummy to come up from his radio seat and fly the aircraft, so now I was quite content to let him sit in Singh's seat and keep the Dak straight and level, while I got some sleep.

I lay down on the cockpit floor, with my canvas briefcase for a pillow, and covered myself with blankets. I looked up into the cockpit and saw, silhouetted against the windscreen and the starry sky, a dark, hooded apparition sitting at the controls. Kamath from the Konkan coast, a Brahmin, at present looking like a ghoul, and I from Britain, by some quirk of fate, two miles above the earth in a machine made in America, at night, above the deserts of Arabia; a moment in space and time which was unique, surrealistic and utterly absurd. What was I doing here, and why was I doing it? I went to sleep.

I woke with a start. The ghoul was still sitting up-front. The Dak droned on. I slept again for a while. I got up from the floor and climbed into my seat. I signalled thumbs-up to Kummy, who, covered in blankets, returned to his radio seat. I checked the time. I had slept for an hour, and we were coming up abeam Rafa, a small pumping-station on the oil pipe to Haifa. Three-hundred miles ahead was the pipeline station of Kaisumah, with its strong radio beacon. The flight eventually ended; the longest six hours, the coldest and dullest flight I have ever done.

For nine days Kummy and I flew the Kabul-Beirut-Kabul circuit. The first time we returned to Beirut we found no trace of Singh. It was rumoured that he had fallen in love with a girl in one of the night clubs. So while Kummy and I were cold, sleeping by turns in our Dak, flying by night over Arabia and by day over Persia, Singh was getting his end in. I had arranged to get Singh's flying pay and split it beween Kummy and myself. The company was as anxious for us to keep flying as we were to earn the extra money.

The third time round, I went to the night club opposite the St George Hotel. Antonio of the Plaza had told me that it was there that Singh had found his love. It was never one of my favourite haunts, a crummy boudoir with faded red plush curtains, filled with bored, plump and plain women, much made-up with white chalk-powder. Of all the night clubs this one alone put me in mind of Toulouse-Lautrec. Fortunately the women kept all their clothes on. After fourteen days, and in spite of the extra money, I felt the need for my co-pilot. I found Singh sitting on a high stool at the mirrored bar, still wearing his black leather jacket. He was a handsome fellow, but carried his good looks sadly. He had a woman next to him, but neither seemed alight with the flame of love; perhaps it had burnt out. I joined them. Like a parrot the woman asked for a glass of champagne. I ordered three whiskies. She drank hers morosely, and more so when she realised that I had come to claim Singh. Both Kummy and I were glad to have him back. It was his turn to hand-fly the Dak while we both slept.

Later on Singh left for India. He went back to the Rajasthan flying club where he was an instructor. A few months afterwards I heard that while flying a single-engined Beechcraft Bonanza he had flown into a sandstorm over the Rajasthan desert. He crashed and was killed.

The storm and the days afterwards were like a dream. Each of us was affected differently. Singh retired behind his handsome exterior and kept his leather jacket on. Kummy took the whole thing in his stride, or at least appeared to; he had an unwarranted and embarrassing confidence in my powers and my luck. I became madder than before. I had now got a reputation as an extreme 'press on' type and this among the keenest and most aggressive aircrew anywhere. Of course, my reputation was the result of living entirely on my nerves. I was always the first to take off from Kabul; or, if not, by taking short cuts, using an extra inch of boost, or cutting out a meal at Abadan, I might overtake the aircraft in front. It was a rivalry we all shared in order to give some meaning to our otherwise ridiculous activity. At Beirut airport I would rush like a lunatic to the customs, hurrying the crew and always be the first to get a taxi to drive us to the Plaza. Two hours later, after a cold shower, coffee and three poached eggs (I was dieting, primarily as an ascetic discipline of the karma yogi), I was in a taxi on my way to the night clubs.

There were many wild interludes in Beirut during this and the following year's karakul lift. We would meet in the Plaza Bar, boozing round the juke box, then move on to the Neptune close by. On the seaside boulevard we would divide to make the round of the Eve, the Kitkat, the Dugout, the Oxford and many other delightful places. The party went on till four or five in the morning; the keen types or those whose money had run out took off in the early morning for Bahrain.

We were seldom all in Beirut at the same time; each captain was a law unto himself and flew to his own schedule. While one aircraft took off from Kabul, two might be in Beirut and one in the direct flight of 1,300 miles from Bahrain to Kabul. One night Captain Jaipal would drink champagne out of a girl's shoe at the Eve and be off the next morning, leaving a letter to the next captain pleading for him to pay his bill. Another night 'Prof' Mondol and his crew got themselves arrested in the 'Place de Karno' and were jailed. Two crews came and went before anyone realised 'Prof' was out of the circuit. 'Bull' Bulsara was kidnapped by two fat houris who guarded the entrance to the Eve, and lived to tell the tale. In a dark alley, Bob Peck was hit on the head and had his American passport, wallet and air ticket to the United States stolen. Bunny Cariappa got drunk in the Dugout and collapsed under a table. His companions couldn't find him as they staggered out of the place at four in the morning. He was locked up in the bar and discovered at eight the next morning asleep under a table by the barman and cleaners. A girl at the Kitkat fell in love with me because I bought her two whiskies every time I went there. The next morning she would ring me up at the Plaza and accuse me of unfaithfulness, as one of her cronies had seen me with the lusciously fat belly-dancer from the Oxford.

CHAPTER 20

Mrs Berrill

EARLY in 1956 I flew a Dakota to Aden. We were again lodged in the Marina Hotel until we could begin lifting the oil-drilling equipment from Salalah, 600 miles to the east, to the drilling site some 50 miles from the coast. While we waited, Aden Airways employed us on their scheduled flights to the Hadramaut. I had taken no leave for the two-and-a-half years I had been with Indamer. I had become so used to the continual flying in the Middle East — Bombay to Accra, then to Assa — that I needed a change. I decided to try for a job in Burma, and wrote to the Union of Burma Airways.

That January I saw before me a life of endless flying, endless years of living out of a suitcase. Why shouldn't I be like others and have a wife, children, car and steady job? How was I ever going to get married if my companions were Eap, Kummy, 'Prof' Mondol and Treloke?

Then, a week later, I got a telegram from the Union of Burma Airways, offering me a job immediately! No one ever had a contract from Indamer; you flew and got paid. I telegraphed Peter Baldwin in Kabul, and Joe Koszarek in Bombay. They advised me not to go, but were prepared to release me if I insisted, and they offered to take me back for the next Haj. I flew to Asmara and got onto the Indamer Dakota on its way back to Bombay from Accra. Four days later I was in Rangoon.

My services had been accepted because a group of Australian pilots had turned bolshie. They wanted more money and less taxes. The management sacked the lot. While I was studying at Hamble in 1953 for my Airline Transport Pilot's licence, there had been a batch of Burmese pilots undergoing instruction. These chaps had returned to Burma, and in 1956 had sufficient experience to become captains. I was there only to fill a temporary shortage.

The morning after my arrival, as I walked to the office from my boarding house near the Sule Pagoda in the middle of Rangoon, I realised I had made a mistake. The city was filthy, foul and fetid. Refuse lay piled high in the side-streets, and paving stones had been uprooted exposing the drains. The business houses of the Raj were dead, with the Burmese one step behind them. The people appeared apathetic and surly. The beauty of the Burmese girls was lost on me; most of them had their faces covered in thanaka paste, made from pulverised wood, which made them look like walking ghosts, and as vacant.

I was disappointed. My hopes had been too high. I was told that things were not like 'the old days'. I was particularly nauseated by the much-vaunted Buddhist respect for life. This took the form of an obsessive insistence that all living things should be free to work out thei 'karma'. A dog run over in the road, but not dead, was respectfully left to complete its karma, and be flattened by the next lorry. A week later its squashed and dried pelt was still lying in the road like a small, worn carpet.

The animals suffered no worse than the humans as a result of this doctrine: here, the Burmese were at least consistent. White and red-band Communists roamed the countryside, slaughtering each other and occasionally machine-gunning the Rangoon-to-Prome train, killing fifty or more passengers. Road and rail traffic outside Rangoon came to a stop at night. The saffron-robed punjis were as fanatical, and asserted themselves in politics and as arbitrators of social morals. They were in no way handicapped by religion beginning and ending in the temple. Two of their enthusiasms during my stay were inveighing against the lasciviousness of 'Western dances', and other

Western innovations, and their displeasure at the thin, diaphanous blouses worn by 'modern girls'. The latter evil they actively combatted in the streets. A shaven punji, clad in saffron robes and with a begging bowl, would hook a bent pin attached to a length of cotton onto the back of a passing 'modern girl', and then pull, ripping her blouse. Thus he upheld the morals of a resurgent Burma and amused the onlookers.

Before I arrived, there had been an uprising of the Christian Karens, and this was still going on in a small way among the hills to the north of Moulmein. U Nu, an ex-schoolmaster, was Prime Minister and leader of the Anti-Fascist People's Freedom League. Its platform was one of xenophobic chauvinism, which proved a heady catalyst to the students. So my hope of flying in Burma for a pleasant change from Indamer was shattered.

Two weeks in the boarding house were enough. Through the airline office I was given the address of a Mrs Berrill, who had a lovely old teak house near the residential quarters of the American Embassy, overlooking the Inya Lake. Here, for the next three months, I was very happy. It was the nearest thing I had had to home since 1950. Mrs Berrill was Ango-Burmese. Her maiden name was Scherpel. In the days of the Raj she had married a British civil servant, who died a few years after the War. The Berrills had fled from the Japanese by trekking hundreds of miles through Burma to Kohima. They spent the war years in South India.

Her sister lived in the house, but I never saw her or even heard her. She seemed to be voluntarily exiled to the back premises, where she cooked me the most lovely hot South Indian rassam, samba, and prawn curries. I used to bring back delicacies for the household from my various flights through Burma; strawberries from Anisakan, mangoes from Magwe, dried fish from Tavoy, dourian and jackfruit from Moulmein; Burmese parasols from Bassein, and thanaka wood from Pakokku for Mrs Berrill's sister. There was a very pretty young girl, although a trifle flat-chested (prominent breasts were not considered desirable in Burma), who sold strawberries at Mandalay airport. I was amazed to discover that she was fifty years old. Her preservation was due to the daily application of thanaka.

Mrs Berrill smoked cheroots all day long; the ash sometimes dropped onto her black dress and burned holes in it. Wherever she went, when she remembered, she carried, slung round her neck by a piece of string, an empty cigarette tin as an ash can. Mrs Berrill was a bridge fiend, and in the evenings I was roped in as her partner. During the game she unslung her ash can. Its place was taken by her cards, which she contemplated while puffing at her cheroot like a female Churchill. She squinted through the smoke; a profusion of smouldering ash littered her forward slopes. Now and then a cinder would fall and cause her to slap away the burning ember.

I was soon checked out on the routes by Captain Leong, a good-looking and well-built Chinese. He ran a very efficient airline, and after the shambles of Aden Airways, Ariana and Indamer, it was a real pleasure to have all the paper work, loading and schedules provided by an efficient ground staff. Shortly before I came to Burma the airline had lost one air-craft on landing at Pakokku, luckily without loss of life or even injury. The local band of Communists had buried a land mine in the earth runway during the night. The right wheel of the Dakota ran over it as it landed. The explosion blew a large piece out of the engine nacelle and tore a hole in the side of the fuselage. Before this, UBA had only one fatal ac-cident. This was when a Dakota flew into the slopes of Mount Popa, an extinct volcanic crater rising up to 5,000 feet above the flat country between Meiktila and Lanywa. Mount Popa was infamous for its snakes and as the abode of 'Nats', evil spirits, and still very much feared. We all avoided the evil mountain by at least ten miles, even on the clearest days, in case the aircraft should be drawn to its destruction by the power of the malevolent Nats.

One of Mrs Berrill's servants, noted for his laziness and being frequently absent on his drinking and gambling sessions, kept a Nat in a matchbox. By being nice to him and commiserating on his gambling losses, I managed to prevail on him to show me the Nat. It was a dried seed, and the open members of the pod gave it a vague resemblance to a Manikin. It was bedded on a piece of cotton wool. Mount Popa had many trees which produced these pods.

Six weeks after my arrival there was a students' riot in the city. The examinations were too hard, and too many had failed. This time the police, who usually stayed in the barracks on such occasions, invaded the University. They panicked and fired their rifles over the heads of the students. Fortunately for the cause, a stray bullet killed a boy standing on a small hill overlooking the mêlée. He was promptly hailed as a martyr to police brutality. Later, the Water Festival, when crowds of happy children and their elders playfully douse each other with water, became another excuse for a display of hooliganism. Youths flung water-filled brass and earthenware pots at cars, smashing windows and wounding the occupants. There was also an official campaign of harassment against the Indians. These unfortunates were descended for the most part from South Indian traders who owned stalls in the bazaar. Everything was done to squeeze them out of Burma, and as usual it was the poor who suffered the most. Many of them had been in Burma for two or three generations.

It was partly because of Mediratta Singh, a young boy from a Sikh family, that I finally decided that Burma was not the place for me. He was a co-pilot in UBA, flying with a Burmese licence. The Government insisted that his family should apply for Burmese citizenship; if not, they would not renew their residence permit. We discussed the situation. I knew as well as he did that should he become Burmese, he would be in a minority community that would never be wholly accepted. His family had strong attachments to the Punjab and did not want to lose their Indian citizenship. I wrote to Joe Koszarek and told him that I was fed up with Burma and wished to return to Indamer. I explained Mediratta's plight, and suggested that he and I could fly together on the coming Haj. Joe, God bless him, agreed and told us to make our way to Delhi. Medi was a little delayed as he had to bring his wife and child with him. After the Haj, Medi joined Ariana Afghan Airlines and was soon flying as co-pilot on their DC 4s.

I was very sorry to say good bye to Mrs Berrill. I always meant to return to Rangoon and visit her, but soon afterwards a 'Westener' could only get a two-day visa, and shortly after that, no visa at all. In three-and-a-half months with UBA I had done 400 hours' flying.

The 1956 Haj

The 1956 Haj had changed. Indamer's days of glory were at an end. Ariana Afghan Airlines was now subsidised by American Point Four Aid. The airline was being re-equipped by DC Fours, flown by American captains training a batch of Indian pilots. Indamer's contribution had shrunk to three Dakotas, and was the last of our Haj operations. We could fly the route from Afghanistan to Jedda with our eyes closed, and often did.

During our usual break halfway through the Haj, the crews made their last visit to Asmara. Jimmy Battliwalla, and my radio officer 'Pants' Pantalu, a Brahmin from Mysore, who had long discarded the orthodoxy of his cast, made up my crew. 'Pants' was justly proud of being the best-dressed man in Indamer. He commissioned single-breasted suits in dark blue and lovat green from the Bahrain tailors. He favoured stout brogues. During our short holiday 'Pants' declared his love for Marusella, an Eritrean. She had been a cabaret hostess. 'Pants' installed himself in her house on a hill to the south of the town. Jimmy and I were invited for evening meals of hot, spicy stew. He no longer accompanied us on our visits to the night clubs; instead he roamed the deserted Via Haile Selassie arm-in-arm with Marusella. A few days before we left, he announced to us that he intended to marry her. His Brahmin background and his whole way of life was completely different from hers. She was a 'mlench', and such a union would raise furious opposition from his family and community. Jimmy and I congratulated him and said nothing. The three of us left Asmara before the plan could be effected.

My first and last pilgrimage to Asmara was to visit the scene of my thirty-fifth birthday party at the Bar Gabriella. In the evening, Jimmy and I set off to find the place. The street lights in the Eritrean quarter were not working. The doors of the Bar Gabriella were boarded up. Only a faint glow from the next doorway indicated there was life around. We made enquiries and were directed further along the street. The place was dark, lit by a small, naked flame. I asked the old woman behind the bar for Gabriella. She pointed to a small black doorway in the bare white wall. Jimmy and I ducked our heads and entered a dimly-lit, low-ceilinged room. Gabriella lay on the bed, covered by a thin, white cotton quilt, showing the outlines of her slim body. Her beautiful head was haloed by a profusion of black hair. She recognised me, and held up her thin hand. I kissed it. On the wall behind was the picture of His Imperial Majesty, the Emperor Haile Selassie, Lion of Judah, with his plump consort. Over the bed was a small, coloured picture of a turbaned Coptic saint.

"Ah! You not forget Gabriella, Capitano."

"Of course not! Why are you in bed? What's the matter, Gabriella?"

"I am sick, Signore Andy. But soon I get better. You wait for me? No? I get up soon, then you come to the bar, yes?"

"Of course we shall come. This is Capitano Jimmy, Gabriella."

"Buona notte, Jeemi. I have Inglese friend long ago, his name Jeemi."

I was enjoying all this, and feeling sentimental. For the moment I turned Gabriella into the great romance of my life. She was sick, I had come to visit her, kiss her hand in sweet remembrance, and then gallantly withdraw after words of love. I was lucky to have a supporting cast. Jimmy stood at the end of the bed like a sentinel of death, tall, thin, bearded, and with his head half-an-inch from the ceiling. I bent over the bed and kissed her smooth forehead.

"Can I get you any medicine, Gabriella?" She clutched my hand.

"Oh no, Signore Andy! I alright. I take Eritrean medicine ... very good."

"Fine, Gabriella. Get better soon. Goodbye Gabriella, I will never forget you."

"Come again, Capitano."

"Yes, of course! Many times."

I turned, letting her bird-like hand drop weakly to the bed. I left the room. Jimmy followed.

"Ciao, Jeemy."

"Ciao, Gabriella," we echoed. Outside the room I turned to Jimmy.

"Come on, let's get moving."

"OK, Andy. Let's go to the Alhambra, then the Mogambo. Who was that, Andy?"

"Oh, just an old friend. Let's go. The night is young, but not for ever. Avanti pistola!"

Kabul

The Haj ended, and I was sent with a Dakota to Kabul. We were going to fly for Ariana Afghan Airlines. I stayed in the zenana occupied by Minou Bulsara, Bunny Cariappa and Jimmy Batli-walla. The house became an open bar, from which music boomed out into the small hours. The Dave Brubeck Trio, George Shearing, and Errol Garner were much in vogue at the time, while Bunny's favourite was Caterina Valente belting out 'Granaaada' and 'Malagueña'. The endless search for distraction drove people from one venue to another. There were a number of them: the French, the German, the Indian and the International. The last had been started by Peter Baldwin. At these we stood the risk of having to pay for a round of drinks. At the various married establishments, drinks were free, and if we didn't come too late we could get a free meal. The 'Hotel Bulsara' was open twenty-four hours, with free food and drinks. The music came from an ill-used radiogram, whose fidelity varied according to the fluctuations of the current from the Kabul power station. When all of us were flying it was usual to find on our return, the doors and windows open, with the radiogram still turning, and the place perfunctorily guarded by Jimmy's friendly Alsation pup, and a hairy Afghan retainer. Three years later, in the house of our chief engineer Mr Mathews, who came from faraway Malibar, their Afghan servant murdered his wife, and decamped with fifty rupees-worth of aluminium cooking pots.

My place in the establishment was the kitchen. I stirred the curries which Bunny put on to cook, but was too busy to attend to. I opened tins of tomato juice, and made omelettes for the drinkers. I supplemented the booze by squashing quantities of cheap, seedless grapes, and squeezing the juice from large, red pomegranates. These juices were fermented in the sun, and sent to the bar. They were added to the drinks to give body, and so keep down the bar expenses. The four of us lived in close, intimate bohemianism. Our relationship had long ago developed into the acceptance of each other's foibles.

Perhaps Bunny was jealous of First Officer Amladi, who used to visit our zenana, and was so like himself. After a few drinks, Bunny became belligerent towards him. Amladi had joined Indamer ten months before, after leaving the Air Force. Bunny's dislike of Amladi was embarrassing, and it is only with hindsight that I can imagine, perhaps wrongly, a possible reason. Both were popular. Our loyalty to Bunny restrained any criticism, and our liking for Amladi made us, in fairness, keep silent. He was short, like Bunny, fair-skinned, and from a Konkani business family. As a young boy, Amladi had been a cadet on the 'Dufferin', a Navy training ship which was kept permanently anchored in Bombay harbour. After leaving, he joined the Air Force. There he had flown old wartime Liberator bombers on coastal reconnaissance. He became increasingly dissatisfied and bored with the Airforce, culminating in him, while drunk on rum, a favourite beverage of the Indian armed services, calling a Squadron Leader in the Central Vistas Officers' Mess in New Delhi, a bastard. Both Bunny and he had left the Service for the same reason, but Bunny resented Amladi's implied criticism. Amladi had little respect for established custom. He scoffed at its magic, superstitions, the caste system, and he ate beef! He mocked the politicians, and likened them to dhoti-clad 'pan-wallahs', or jumped-up 'goondas'.

Bunny was proud of his military connections, and after serving with the Royal Indian Airforce flying Spitfires at Miramshah, in the North-West Frontier, then in Hurricanes over Burma, he had resigned from the Airforce. The current C-in-C of the Indian Army was General Cariappa. Bunny's community came from the small state of Coorg, in the western ghats. Bulsara was awarded a DFC in the war, and also resigned from the Service. The three of us, Bull, Bunny and myself had joined Air Services of India at Juhu in 1947. We had flown in the same operations for the last ten years; the Kashmir and Punjab evacuations after Indian Independence, the supply drop in north-east Assam, and for the last two years, in Afghanistan. I was the godfather to Bunny's son.

The newly-joined Amladi was somewhat of an outsider. The sight of him turned Bunny into a pugnacious bloodhound. Amladi would sit at the bar, with his eyes equally red, his plump face pallid, giving back in words as good as he got. Everybody ignored them, rather than risk the impression of taking sides.

One night a few of us were gathered round the bar in the Hotel Bulsara. We were all sufficiently sozzled to be indifferent to Bunny's mixture of fermented pomegranate juice and rum. Three visitors arrived; Ziggy, one of the Polish contingent, a young German salesman from Siemens, and Amladi. We welcomed them and plied them with the 'mixture'. For once, things seemed fairly amicable between Bunny and Amladi.

They ignored each other. Jimmy and I went to bed. I shared a room near the front with Bunny. It was an all-purpose room, with a large table which Bull used for his wood carving, and under which his Alsation, Caesar, slept. Bunny and I slept on camp beds.

I fell asleep and awoke later. Bunny was not in his bed. A dim light glowed from the passageway. I heard muffled, argumentative voices from the bar. I went to sleep again. I was awoken by the sound of scuffling, heavy breathing, and subdued groans from the passage. I got up and peered round the door. Bunny and Amladi were fighting. Both were very drunk and wrestling on the floor. I looked up and saw Bull peeping round the far corner of the passage. He raised a finger to his lips and grinned. The combatents fought like figures in slow motion. Amladi got on top of Bunny, grabbed his ears, and proceeded to bang his head on the carpeted floor. Bunny let fly punches at Amladi's head, and split a cheek. Both belched — even from ten feet away I got the sweet, sickly stink of booze. Their struggles got slower and slower, until they both collapsed and lay supine, panting like exhausted dogs. Bull gave me a thumbs-up sign and waved, and went back to bed. I retired, leaving them to sleep it off in the cold November air. The next morning Bunny was sleeping soundly in his camp bed. No one made any allusion to the night's battle. From then on, Bunny and Amladi were not exactly friendly, but peace had been tacitly agreed upon.

I see the days of my twenty years with my companions in Indian aviation with almost total recall. They all make up a long chain of events, which I seem, in retrospect, to have experienced with a greater awareness than anything since. Bull and I saw two drunks fighting whom we loved, and who were killed within a few years of each other.

The routes we were flying in the Dakotas of Ariana Airways were Kabul, over the 16,000 ft Hindu Kush, into the Oxus valley, landing at Kunduz, Mazar-i-Sharif, Maimana to Herat.

I was determined not to get myself permanently stuck in Kabul. I asked Peter Baldwin if he could arrange for me to go back to India. Fortunately I was needed by Johnny Brenand, for supply dropping in the Assam hills. There was a large contingent of Indamer busy supply dropping, based at Jorhat. My crew, F/O Amladi and R/O Kumat, were as anxious as I was to get back to Bombay.

The first job Johnny Brenand sent me on was to drop 35 loads of rice, wheat and clothing in the Lushai Hills to the Assam Rifles outposts, Balpui and Lungleh. My crew was F/O Namboodri and R/O Shome. Our dropping crew were coolies from the Silchar bazaar in the Kumbigram tea-garden district. They were very enthusiastic, and sometimes piled the bags too high, so that on one occasion a bag, instead of going under the tail plane, got hung up on the leading edge of the tail plane. When this happened I stopped dropping and returned to base to remove the bag, in case another bag should get stuck on the tail plane, making the aircraft unmanageably tail-heavy. Namboodri was due for his Captaincy, so he sat in the Captain's seat and did the flying, while I took his place in the right-hand seat. After this drop was over, I flew to Jorhat and continued dropping in the forests south of the MacMahon Line.

There had been an accident at Lemikin, south of the Line, in a heavily- wooded area where the Assam Rifles had a post on top of a hill. I dropped at Lemikin, and saw the remains of a Dakota lying spread-eagled on the forest of trees. It was impossible to reach the aircraft, and it was assumed that the crew, Captain Sadarangani, F/O Chandy, and our chief Radio Officer, Thakur, and six military dropping crew, were dead. It did not appear that the aircraft had caught fire.

I met for the last time, Captain Jeff Wilkes, one of our senior dropping Captains, shortly after he joined Air India International. He was killed while flying as a supernumerary crew in an Air India Boeing 707, which crashed into Mont Blanc some time in the 1960s, while descending to land at Geneva.

One afternoon I got back to Dum Dum with tea-chests from Assam, at 1700 hours. Madhu Singh, our crew transport driver, told me that my brother was waiting for me in the office. My brother! Sandy? Lindsay? There he was, my youngest brother Sandy, tall and beefy! Twelve years younger than me. I, balding, thin, bearded, looking like a dissipated remittance man. Sandy was dressed in navy-blue blazer, white shirt and grey flannels, with a RN badge on his breast pocket. He had just landed at Dum Dum to change planes. He was flying out to join his destroyer at Hong Kong, and then to Japan. My mother had sent me a photo of him dressed in white drill, leading his ship's company, marching through the streets of Malta. I had last seen him at his twenty-first birthday party in the Camberley Heath golf club, among fellow-cadets from Dartmouth, and their girl friends, in 1953. And here he was on the tarmac at Dum Dum! His plane left within an hour. He was as I remembered him, only larger; but still a small boy at St Ronans, playing rugger, cricket, then a cadet at Dartmouth. Now he was making a career in the Senior Service, while I had chucked the army.

We sat on a packing case outside the office window, and watched the Dakotas taxi in. We talked about home, Mum, Uncle-Father, the garden, and the dogs. All was well. Then he said:

"I'm fed up with the navy! I can't stomach the type, boring and blinkered. I'm thinking of leaving."

I was astounded. My first thought was for our mother. She was very proud of him. It would be a terrible hurt to her if Sandy left the navy.

"Have you told Mum?" I asked.

"No, it's only an idea."

"For God's sake think long and hard before you do anything."

"Well, of course I don't want to hurt Mum."

Don't leave, Sandy. You must stay on."

"You didn't," he mused.

"Me! For God's sake don't take me as an example! What could you do if you left?"

"I don't know. Perhaps the Merchant Navy. I can't stand the assumed superiority, the whole privileged set-up. I suppose it has to be as it is, but I don't want any more of it. It's boring!"

"Jesus Christ! Everybody finds things boring at times," I said. "You're lucky to be bored and get paid at the same time! For Christ's sake, think what a shock it would be to Mum if you left."

His plane left in an hour. We walked along the tarmac to the battleship-grey passenger terminal. I begged him not to do anything in a hurry. He said he wouldn't. In any case he could do nothing until his ship got back to the UK. That was the last time I saw him, my beefy young brother in whom I had glimpsed the stirring of dissatisfaction. A few months later, on the 24th July 1958, he was stitched into a hammock and slipped from beneath a Union Jack into Davy Jones' Locker, off Okinawa. He had died aboard ship from a polio virus infection of the brain, caught ashore in Japan.

CHAPTER 21

UNIPBOG*

IN early 1958 I was sent by Joe Koszarek to fly the United Nations Dakota at Rawalpindi. Two years before, Aden Airways had won a contract to provide an aircraft for the United Nations observer group in Kashmir. The Captain of this aircraft was Frank Whitaker, who had joined Aden Airways after the 1953 Haj. Frank was leaving Aden Airways to emigrate to Australia. Aden Airways considered the operation to be too far from Aden. The UN agreed that Indamer could take over.

After years of intensive and varied flying it irked me to spend most of the time on the ground in Pindi. The United Nations' military staff, the civilian administrators and their families, Americans, Belgians, Dutch and a few Swedes, appeared to be a bored and demoralised bunch. They were provided with every comfort, including diplomatic immunity, but they lacked a worthwhile and meaningful occupation. They watched a 'ceasefire line' between Pakistani and Indian-held Kashmir, not a very exciting occupation for grown men. When the rival forces started shooting at one another, they put in reports of the 'violations'.

The crew of the aircraft had to be 'neutral'; ie no Hindus or Muslims. My first officer was Serapio, a young Christian Philippino, who had been flying in Calcutta with Jamair for the

---

* United Nations India-Pakistan Border Observation Group

last three years. He was a large, muscular fellow, who spent a lot of time exercising with bar bells, and whose main body-building food was pork. In Muslim Pindi there was only cow, goat or chicken meat, so he had to make up for it on our visits to New Delhi. Sway, a small, plump and inexperienced radio officer had been unearthed by Aden Airways in Amman; he was a Palestinian Christian. Senevaratna, my engineer, came from Ceylon, middle-aged, large and balding, a most un-Buddha-like Buddhist. Because he and I had so much in common, age, loss of hair, and a talkative disposition, we became friends. We read books and talked politics. Every morning in the clear, cool sunlight of a North Indian dawn, he and I jogged round the Pindi sports stadium. Later we were chased out by the Pakistani athletes training for the Olympic Games.

The four of us were housed in the Davies Hotel, a genteel Anglo-Indian establishment from the days of the Raj, with faded cotton print curtains, ancient bearers, thunder boxes and grey, dusty mosquito nets. The cantonment area of Pindi was dreary. Large Pathans dressed in grubby salvars, long flannel shirts and dirty, voluminous pugris, walked about in chappals made from lorry tyres. They were administered by feudal land-lords and army officers who had moved into the white-painted bungalows of the departed Raj. Vestiges of the Raj were every-where. There were the old clubs, shadowed caverns of dark teak, attended by ancient bearers in threadbare uniforms and faded red cumberbunds. In the gloom, large silver cups in glass cases weakly glinted; trophies for tennis, polo, golf and pig-sticking. The contestants, lean Indian Army officers in Sam Browns and spurred riding boots, were dimly visible in faded sepia photographs on the walls of corridors and the musty billiard room. The grounds were tended by antique malis, thin as rakes, who lugged large cow hides of water morning and evening to the parched rhododendron bushes. Occasionally an old, open Buick rattled up the drive. Gentlemen in tweedy mufti would alight and go inside to drink a ritual chota peg in the haunted bar. Along the sides of the roads were bridle paths, trodden long ago by the mounted sahibs and their mems. A mile from Davies Hotel were the remnants of the cantonment shopping centre, with the Garrison Theatre, a cake shop, and a bookshop with old editions of newspapers and shelves of sun-baked Penguins. There was a café which still announced that it was in bounds to BORs, and next door a general store, stocking such ancient herbal products as Woodward's gripe water, Macassar oil, and present-day imported whisky.

The Pindi cantonment had its C of E church and a Catholic church somewhat on the fringe. Both were dilapidated and each still minstered by the last of the line, two old European priests. The C of E church was hung with regimental colours, hanging limply, all hope lost of ever fluttering again amidst the skirl of pipes, the booming brass, or the high, thin, airy fife. On Sundays, small groups of Anglo-Indians, dressed in the fashion of the thirties, stood outside the church to say good morning to their priest. He, poor man, was the last of the race whose blood mingled in their veins with the blood of their Pathan ancestors. They were never wholly accepted by their own country and were, to our everlasting shame, derided by the Raj. Pindi cantonment was sad; a place to dream of past polo teams and mayhem on the North-West Frontier, where tribal chiefs and colonels fought bloody campaigns; a place far from the urbanised shambles of Karachi.

The bazaar buzzed with activity. It swarmed with large flies. Pi dogs panted in the shade beneath laden lorries. Kebab shops resounded with the hubbub of bargaining over wheat, carpets and hides. Murders of oppressive zamindari were plotted; politics heated the blood while old men dreamed of days gone by as they awaited the cry of the muezzin.

Once a week the United Nations Dakota flew from Rawalpindi to Jammu, in Indian Kashmir, and thence to New Delhi. We carried one or two officers of the observer force and many crates of empty Coca-Cola bottles. After two days in the Ambassador Hotel in Delhi, we flew back to Rawalpindi with the two officers and crates of full Coca-Cola bottles. Occasionally we landed at Srinagar, had lunch at Needu's Hotel, and continued to Delhi.

Radio Officer Sway was a ladies' man, and had been to England. Occasionally he got a letter from London. He would show us the stamp, and then pass round its contents for us to smell. The letters were perfumed and were from a girl or girls who loved him. He told us that the blood of the Crusaders flowed in his veins and that his name was common in the rural districts of southern England. He imagined that the daughter of the American UN Admin Officer in Pindi loved him. She was a teenager on holiday from the States and was staying with her parents in the Davies Hotel.

One evening we all went to the local cinema. It was a typical garrison theatre, probably built in the 1860s. In 1920 it was converted to a 'bioscope', a word still used in Indian villages. It showed Western 'fillims'. The front stalls were wooden benches and the back four rows were padded for the officers and their memsahibs. Behind us sat the teenaged daughter and two girl friends. Sway became uncontrollable, twisting, turning his face sideways and glancing painfully askance at the girls. In the dark he left us without a word and took an isolated seat behind them. After the show, Sway followed the girls like a shadow. Senevaratna and Serapio were apprehensive lest Sway's mixture of Arab and Crusader blood should overpower him, and result in an incident. We invented headlines that would appear in 'Dawn', the permanently anti-American Government rag. 'Hands off our Youth, Yanks!' — 'Uncle Sam's teen girls on Pindi Rampage' — 'Female Yank Teens pollute Muslim Youth.' At the hotel a disconsolate Sway awaited us.

"She's riding tomorrow morning at seven o'clock, Captain. Where can I get a horse?"

I advised him to get up at six, waylay the grooms and ask them to bring another horse. The next morning I was woken at half-past six by Sway knocking on my door.

"I've got a horse, Captain! She hasn't started yet. Can you lend me a shirt?"

"A shirt? Are you mad? You're wearing one, for Christ's sake!"

"Yes Captain, but I want a sports shirt."

"My God! Alright, come in." I gave Sway a royal blue cotton bush shirt.

"How's that? You can keep it if it fits you."

"Thanks Captain. It's fine."

"Tell us all about it at breakfast, and be careful now."

Off he went.

A few moments later I heard horses' hooves and snorts. From my window I saw three mounted girls, in white shirts and fawn jodhpurs, walking their horses out of the gate. Soon Sway appeared seated on a large, black horse. He wore my shirt, grey trousers too tight for him, his only pair of shoes with their thin soles and pointed toes, and the nylon socks I had bought him ten days before in New Delhi. His seat was hideous. His fat bum protruded, and wide vistas of sky showed between the saddle and his knees. At that moment I admired him. Such tenacity in the face of cruel indifference was awesome. He deserved to conquer. I forgave him his smelly socks which I had had to endure when we shared a room at the Ambassador. I forgave him his silly little moosh, his scented love letters and his vanity. The hard-hearted bitch, reared on gallons of ice cream sodas and Herschey bars. After her holiday she would return by Pan Am whisper jet to the USA and continue studying for a degree in rug knitting or bowling. I worked myself into a fury of indignation on Sway's behalf. Here she was, missing the chance of being screwed by the product of Bedouins, Saracens, Assyrians, Amalekites, Phoenicians, Israelites, Babylonians, Greeks, Romans, and of course a Crusader from the southern counties of England.

While we were in the middle of breakfast Sway joined us. He was a pitiful sight. He told us he had been unable to catch up the girls, and had suffered terribly from the bouncing up and down on his trotting horse. The girls cantered across the maidan, fleeing from the bouncing Saracen. They returned along the roadside bridle paths to the hotel at a goodly trot. Sway followed but fell further and further astern. He had been terrified to pull the reins too hard in case the horse stopped. He reached the hotel gate when suddenly a car emerged. The horse 'sidestepped' and Sway, exhausted, fell from its broad back into the dust. He paid the groom five rupees. His steed was led away. Awed by his tenacious folly, none of us uttered a word.

After four months of the UN charter, I was suddenly ordered to Bombay. Captain Tommy Sadler, the West Bengal snooker champion, was sent to replace me. He had been in Calcutta for eleven years, and was a regular visitor to the Olympia Bar in Park Street, the Embassy Bar in the Grand Hotel, and various billiard clubs. It was largely due to Kitty Brenand's care that Tommy's sporting life seldom interfered with the three o'clock early morning pick-up. In Pindi, Kitty's motherly care was missing. Here there was unlimited snooker, plenty of convivial company and not much flying. On one lunchtime stop in Srinagar the crew could not be found for the return flight to Pindi; they were located after two hours in Needu's Bar. The same thing happened after a night stop in Delhi.

Finally there was the affair of the typewriter. Among other more conventional luxuries, the Ambassador Hotel in New Delhi provided a portable typewriter in each bedroom. One morning the UN Dakota was refused take-off clearance by the Safdarjang control tower. The Hotel Manager had telephoned the tower to say that a typewriter was missing from the room of one of the crew. Would they please hold the aircraft until it had been searched? Here was a nice situation. The UN aircraft enjoyed diplomatic privileges, and it would be against protocol for the Indian customs, police, or Hotel management to come on board and search it. The UN officers took charge and searched the aircraft. They found the typewriter in Sway's suitcase. As a result of this and other incidents, the UN dispensed with the services of Indamer. The contract was taken over by an Italian Dakota. Tommy returned to Calcutta, and left for the

UK two years later. Serapio went to Kabul and joined Ariana Afghan Airlines. Senevaratna joined Air Ceylon as an engineer and later got his pilot's licence. Sway went back to the land of the Bedoo.

Bahrain, 1960-1963

I arrived at Bombay in the evening. Joe Koszarek met me at Santa Cruz Airport, and took me back to his bungalow on Juhu Beach. During the dinner of sauerkraut, pork chops and apple pie, I was 'put in the picture'. He had obtained a contract from Gulf Aviation of Bahrain for a Dakota on indefinite charter. He had also made a contract with Qatar Petroleum Company to fly their Indian and Pakistani employees on leave. Up till now they had gone by ship, but this was a slow business which wasted a lot of time going and coming back and was not always on schedule. This was to keep me busy for the next four years. My crew was F/O 'Uncle' Bannerjee from Calcutta, and R/O Trelokekar from Bombay, a friend of mine for the last fifteen years.

We flew Dakota VT-DGS to Bahrain and were immediately dispatched by Gulf Aviation to Sharjah. Our Dakota was to fly Hajis to Jedda when Gulf got the clearance from the Saudis. In the meantime we were accommodated in the small desert fort at Sharjah's hard sand airstrip. Sharjah had been one of the staging posts in pre-war days for the Imperial Airways flying boats that flew from London to Karachi. The airstrip was only five miles from the shores of the Persian Gulf. Behind the control tower was a small, white, high-walled fort, its entrance guarded by two diminutive desert Arabs, each armed with an old Lee Enfield rifle that came up to their shoulders, appearing too big for them to carry, let alone to fire. At night the airfield officer and his radio man, Bannerjee, Treloke and myself, and the two Arab guards, plus the cook and bearer were locked inside the fort.

We spent seven days in Sharjah, waiting! The Saudis refused Gulf the traffic rights in order to protect their own airline. Those seven days in Sharjah were an idyllic time. Treloke lived with his eldest brother and his wife, their son and daughter, in a small bungalow in Khar, a suburb of Bombay. One of his brothers had been killed in Burma during the war, while serving as an officer in the Indian Army. Both Treloke's parents were dead. He was about five feet nine, thin, and with straight, lustrous black hair and a drooping moustache. Sometimes he sprouted a straggly, meagre beard which gave him a marked resemblance to his fellow-Maharashtrian, Vinobhai Bhave, who, with his scheme of receiving donations of land and then giving plots to landless peasants, was emulating the saintliness of the late Gandhiji.

Treloke had no pretensions, no worldly ambitions, a quiet humour, and he tolerated me. He and I discussed the the ascetic life; its precise nature and the form that this life should take for each of us, were topics for long, rambling conversations. Failure was not failure as long as we valued the goal, and its unattainability did not discourage us, because we knew in our hearts that we were both fated to go on doing what we were doing! Treloke had been an architectural student in Bombay before joining the Scindia Steamship Company as a radio officer. He gave up the sea and joined Air Services of India three months before I joined the company in 1947.

Every morning during our exile, Bannerjee, Treloke and I would walk five miles from the fort to the seaside. We trudged north, leaving the half-a-dozen palm-leaf huts of Sharjah behind us. The sand was hot and soft, the warm, tideless waters of the Persian Gulf daintily lapped the sandy beach. We splashed through shallow pools of tepid, salt water, variously coloured a clear yellow or green. Bannerjee, Treloke and I would undress and lie for hours spreadeagled in hot brine. The sun blazed directly above us. Mostly we lay silent, but sometimes we each in turn day-dreamed aloud. We lay with our eyes shut, the sun conjuring a flow of coloured patterns across our minds. There were no trees, no bushes, no buildings in sight; only the bright sea to the west, and the flat, dry, hot desert to the east, with us lying naked in between.

Treloke planned to leave flying after three more years. By then he hoped to have saved enough money to help his brother with the upkeep of the family; then he could retire to an ashram at Hardwar or Raniket, or even to the high Himalayan shores of the bottomless and sacred waters of Lake Manasarowar. He would become a Brahmacharia and spend his days looking for his guru. To prepare himself for the life of abstinence, he had taken the first step. He had a young Parsee friend who lived on a farm in Bulsar district, about 150 miles north of Bombay. Every period of leave or few days off from flying, he went by train to the farm. There he lived the simple life of the Hindu dream. He became a vegetarian, lived in a small basha, worked on the farm, said his prayers and strove to emulate the legendary ascetics of tradition.

Bannerjee was more earthly. He had been to Canada two years previously, and met a German girl. He was in love with her and she with him. One day he would return to Canada and marry her. Perhaps he would be forced to go on flying in India, as now every country was making it harder for anyone but its own nationals to get a job. Bannerjee had hopes that after his marriage he could leave India and fly elsewhere.

My own hopes were much less concrete than the others. I hoped to go on flying for another twenty years in India, and then retire and join Treloke in his ashram. We would put on the saffron, and the two oldest surviving members of Air Services of India would trudge the earth of Bharat together. We would visit all the places we had flown to, from Kashmir in the north to Sri Lanka in the south, and from Bamian in the west to Parshram Kund in the east. We would tread the hot, soft, Indian earth, like flour, through the villages, along the tops of paddi bunds and over the jungle hills, trodden by the bare feet of countless millions. Ten thousand and one miles of Indian earth would bleach our feet. Then we would die, and our ashes would be thrown to the wind by our followers.

"Yes," Treloke said. "We must have followers so that our last rites can be performed. We will not preach, impart wisdom, or work wonders."

I agreed, and saw myself, as a travelling gora sanyassi, attracting a few urchins and half-a-dozen of the more gullible destitutes.

As we lay drugged by the burning sun and floating in shallow, warm water, we recalled the twelve wonderful years we had flown together. We knew that the private companies were doomed to a steady decline. With our outdated Dakotas, foreign charters were becoming harder to get. The work we had pioneered in India was now taken by the national airline. In another ten years, at the very most, only one or two private commercial aircraft would be operating in India. We had seen it all, done it all, and were growing older.

With still no permission, after seven days, to fly to Jedda, Gulf Aviation recalled us to Bahrain. We flew Hajis from Bahrain to Dahran, a ten-minute flight, from where they were flown to Jedda in Saudi aircraft. We flew frozen meat to the oil company on Das Island, with trips to Kuwait, Abu Dhabi (a few miles south of Sharjah, then only a sandy strip on a coastal sandbank), and to Muscat. Gulf Aviation got traffic rights to fly a fortnightly passenger service to Bombay.

In the early days we carried large quantities of gold from Bahrain to Sharjah. Each gold brick was packed in a three-ply box and unloaded at Sharjah under the armed guard of diminutive, dried-out desert Arabs. The bricks were melted down into small blocks in the port of Dubai, ten miles south of Sharjah, and then smuggled by dhow to India. In Bombay, gold fetched double its international price. The Indian rupees were smuggled out by the returning dhows.

In order to stop the smuggling and the loss of its currency, the Indian Government withdrew its mauve-coloured rupee notes from the Gulf, and replaced them with orange notes. Our Dakota was chartered to fly millions of old rupee notes direct to India and return with boxes of the new currency. Neither the change of notes nor the numerous other restrictions in India could stop gold smuggling. Within a couple of months it was as flourishing as ever. Several international airlines flying into India carried smuggled gold, mostly from Beirut and Hong Kong. A large packet of gold was found in the lavatory pan of an Air India Constellation. Some BOAC crews were searched by the Calcutta customs, and found to be wearing cotton belts stuffed with thin, gold slabs. Rather than give the Indian authorities the satisfaction of catching us with gold, we never smuggled any. Instead, we confined ourselves to other equally precious articles: transistor radios, watches, Parker pens, sewing machines, cameras, whisky, and even a motor cycle (in pieces).

At one period, our smuggling became quite farcical. A new model of small, portable Olivetti typewriter became very popular in India. Every official who could get one was one-up on his less fortunate colleagues. They were required by officials of the Bombay controller of aerodromes, by emigration inspectors, by the examiner for the pilots' radio exam, and by Joe Koszarek. We did not even hide the typewriters because the customs officer searching the aircraft was as likely to be a recipient on the next flight, if not on the present one.

One evening in the middle of 1959, the Duty Officer in the Bahrain control tower rang our flat and told us that an Ariana Airways DC4 flown by Bunny Cariappa was landing shortly. He was refuelling on his way to Jedda with a load of Afghan Hajis. We jumped into our Ford truck and headed for the airport. From behind the low wall of the terminal building we watched the blue-lettered Ariana DC4 taxi to the apron. I had not seen Bunny for two years. First Officer Sadri, a Parsee, came down the steps, followed by Bunny. They sauntered over to us, Sadri with a broad grin showed the large gap between his two front teeth. He looked like a Mexican bandit, plump, with wavy hair and a pencilled moustache. He had been a Bombay motor-cycle policeman, had worked in a Cadbury's factory in England, in Huntley and Palmer's Reading factory, and washed dishes in the Savoy. His ultimate aim was to join his uncle in London and run a chain of boarding houses. He was a genuine strongman, with huge arms, muscular thighs and a stocky, bulging torso.

As we stood talking, waiting for the Shell refuelling bowzer, from the passenger door a turbanned Afghan head popped out. More heads appeared. They shouted for steps to be wheeled up. Then, without warning, the tail of the aircraft slowly tipped towards the ground, gathered speed, and hit the tarmac with a loud metallic CLUNK. A muffled cry came from the aircraft. The onlookers burst into laughter and cheered. Sadri had fogotten to attach the tail prop. He dashed to the tailplane, got below it and attempted a two-arm press. The audience burst into encouraging shouts and clapping. Bunny and Sadri shouted and gesticulated to the passengers to get forward in the cabin. The tail rose. Sadri bowed to the cheering audience. The nose wheel crashed to the tarmac, nearly collapsing the oleo leg.

This was the last time I saw Bunny. He was killed three months later taking off in an Ariana DC4 from Beirut on a clear, moonlit night. He was carrying a load of Afghan police cadets bound for training in Germany.

On the night of the crash I was sitting in the garden of Joe's bungalow in Juhu. By coincidence, Zee Cariappa, Bunny's wife, had come up from Bangalore to visit relatives, and was having drinks with us. It was one of those clear, starry nights that make one oblivious to the blemishes of Juhu, and think of it instead, with tall palm trees, shaded bungalows and long, curved sandy beach, as the most beautiful place on earth. As we drank our smuggled foreign whisky, someone put his head over the garden wall and bellowed, above the din of Indian film music from surrounding radios, that an Ariana DC4 had crashed at Beirut. He had just heard it on the BBC overseas service.

In the early hours of the next morning before I took off for Bahrain, I learned from the Air Traffic Control that Bunny had been the captain. Shortly after getting airborne from Beirut, the aircraft had grazed the top of a low hill south of the airfield. Its engines were torn off and it burst into flames. There were no survivors. Bunny's First Officer was Mediratta Singh, the young Sikh boy I flew with in Burma. Mediratta's family had had a cloth shop in Rangoon, and because they refused to lose their Indian nationality and become Burmese, they returned to India. Mediratta got a job with Afghan Airways.

Every morning our Dakota flew the Gulf Aviation service to Doha in Qatar and then to Sharjah. In July 1960 I got a telegram from my mother telling me that my stepfather, Major C Sleigh, MC, had died. I made arrangements to return to the UK for a few days. The day before I left, I flew the Petroleum charter from Bombay, bringing with me my replacement, Captain Sidhu Singh. I had known Singh three years before, when he had been flying with me as a co-pilot in Assam. He was tall, quiet and gentle. He was also a 'shaven Sikh', a sufficiently rare bird in India to warrant this slightly derogatory name. Some secular-minded Sikhs cut their hair, shaved off their beards, discarded the pugri and the other sacred symbols. Amladi was my co-pilot, who had relieved 'Uncle' Bannerjee six months previously. Karve was the radio officer, who after the excitement of the last West African charter, decided to stay in Bahrain. Treloke had gone to supply-drop in Assam.

The morning I left for the UK by BOAC Comet, I was in a strange mood. I felt I was deserting. I saw everything with detached clarity. I was leaving, if only for a few days, my friends and the warmth of their camaraderie. We all went to the airport in our truck. We had said our goodbyes, and I had promised to be back within a week. I watched Sidhu, Amladi and Karve walk across the glaring ochre sand towards Dakota VT-DGS parked opposite the control tower. In a few minutes they would be off on the morning schedule to Sharjah. They wore grey cotton drill uniforms; Sidhu capless and without his gold epaulettes; Amladi following, wearing his Ray Ban sun glasses and carrying a couple of magazines to read on the flight; Karve with his briefcase, portly and placid bringing up the rear. They climbed the steps to the passenger door. Each turned round and waved before disappearing into the fuselage. My flight was called and I was on my way.

VT-DGS never arrived at Sharjah. Karve sent the last message to Bahrain control, giving their take-off time from Doha and ETA Sharjah. No trace was ever found of our aircraft, its crew or its twenty-four passengers. The RAF searched the 200 miles of sea between Doha and Sharjah and the desert and rocky mountains of the Muscat Peninsula for eight days. They were hampered all the time by a thick sand haze. During the next two years rumours spread. Some claimed that the aircraft had flown to Russia. Months later it was rumoured that some of the passengers had been seen in Bahrain bazaar. The last rumour was that the crew of a dhow putting into Kuria Muria Island, off the south-eastern tip of Arabia for fresh water, had met castaways who claimed to be the passengers of VT-DGS.

A few weeks after the disappearance, a Civil Aviation official arrived from London. We hastily concocted a 'Flight Manual', forged a few manifests, load sheets and flight plans. The official took our statements and the documents and left. A wrangle started between Gulf Aviation and Kalinga Airlines over whose insurance company should cover the claims. There was an attempt to put the blame on the crew and so enable the passengers' families to sue for damages on the grounds of company inefficiency. We lost popularity with Gulf passengers, although our standing with the Qatar Petroleum Company was unaffected. We struggled on in Bahrain until early 1961, and then returned to Bombay and operated from there into the Gulf.

None of us had the slightest doubt that VT-DGS had been sabotaged, and this belief was strengthened, somewhat to our amusement, by two events which occurred in Bahrain airport soon after we left. One early morning, before the day's work began, the roof of the Gulf Aviation traffic office was blown off by a bomb. No one was hurt. The bomb had been in a package consigned to Muscat, and was due off in the morning Heron service. Next, an RAF Bristol Beverley freighter was flying from Kuwait to Bahrain, when a bomb went off and blew a hole in the side of its huge, rectangular fuselage. Only the Beverley's size and the fact that the control cables, fuel tanks and engines were all well above the central box-like compartment, saved it from disintegration. Shortly after this, the anti-Imperialist agents exploded a bomb on the deck of a passenger ship, carrying Indians and Arabs to the Gulf, while it lay at anchor off Muscat.

By chance I witnessed the result of one of these exploits. Early in 1961 I was flying from Karachi to Dubai (a new civil airstrip about ten miles south of RAF Sharjah). It was a cloudy, dismal day over the eastern end of the Persian Gulf, with a strong south-westerly wind. We came over the airfield and saw ahead of us a large passenger ship lying at anchor about two miles off Dubai. The sea was dark grey and white-flecked; black smoke was pouring from the decks of the ship and blowing away horizontally in a thin, dark plume. The ship was the 'Dara'. This was perhaps the greatest achievement of the forces for peace and freedom in the Persian Gulf. A bomb had been set off in the ship's hold. About two hundred people were killed and wounded, burned or drowned. The victims were mostly Indian families, husbands, wives and children returning from leave. Except for exclamations of general horror at the magnitude of the calamity, no word of condemnation for the perpetrators or their backers appeared in the Indian newspapers.

Around this time, investigations had revealed that an agent for the Sheik of Muscat had been travelling on our Dakota

VT-DGS. The agents for the Imam had placed a landmine on board. So Sidhu Singh, the gentl 'shaven Sikh' from the Punjab; Amladi, the ex-Indian Air Force Officer from the Konkan coast, and Karve, the Maharashtrian Brahmin, became the early victims of the hazards of later air travel.

In 1963 I left India and returned to the UK, where I renewed my British pilot's licence, took some extra exams which had been introduced during my time in India, and also did a course at Cranfield and obtained an instructor's licence.

CHAPTER 22

Kathmandu

IN 1964 my old employer Joe Koszarek arrived in London. Emanuel Galitzine met Joe for lunch at the Hilton. Emanuel had just returned from a sales junket in the East, demonstrating the Avro-748 turbo-prop aircraft. His last port-of-call had been Kathmandu, where after twenty years he met Boris Lissanevich, who had been running the Royal Hotel since 1952, which was renovated by him, and had been previously the property of a deposed member of the Rana faction. The only way of getting food and tourists into Nepal was by Dakota, unless they were prepared to endure a 150-mile journey from the Terrai over an 8,000 ft mountain road to Kathmandu. The Royal Hotel made its name during the mountaineering enthusiasm before and after the conquest of Everest in 1953.

Emanuel's meeting with Joe at the Hilton resulted in Indamer Co. Bombay, becoming an agent to sell the HS-748 to Air Nepal. Joe, the manager of Indamer, had already sold a Beechcraft Queen Air to the Nepalese government for ministerial transport. He contacted me and we arranged that I should go to Nepal. The HS-748 was not unknown in India. There had been a proposal to manufacture it in Cawnpore for the Indian Airlines and India Airforce. I was game for anything that would get me back to India. Joe, Emanuel and I knew that the Nepalese were negotiating with Fokkers of Amsterdam for the purchase of twin-engined turbo-prop Friendships to replace their ageing Dakotas.

In March 1964 I set off armed with Avro-748 pamphlets, ball-point pens, a few cigarette lighters and lapel badges bearing the name Avro. On arriving at Gauchar Airport, Kathmandu from Delhi by Air Nepal Dakota, the first person I met was my old friend Captain Jai Singh, a Rajput, from the 'Assam airlift' days in 1949, and during the 1954 Afghan Haj. Jai was now Captain of the King's Flight, a unit that flew the King around, ministers on inspection, and also transported army and associated freight in Dakota 9N-RF2.

I took a taxi from the airport to the Royal Hotel. The pillars of the main entrance had fallen down, and it was as usual guarded by a Gurkha chowkidar armed with a long, sheathed kukri. The driveway was of crumbling bricks flanked by a few tall monkey-tail trees imported from Japan long ago by its Rana occupiers. Boris was not in. I was given a ground floor room at the end of the long verandah. I did not meet Boris for a week. He was just the same, plump, wearing a white sharkskin jacket. Of course he did not recognise me after our single evening encounter twenty years previously. After the 300 Club in Theatre Road, Calcutta, he became a close friend of the Maharajah of Cooch Bihar, and moved to his palace in northeast Bengal. The Maharajah held tiger-shooting forays for his foreign guests in the jungles of Cooch Bihar. All the pilots from Calcutta knew Boris. The grass airfield where the guests were landed, was overlooked from the palace. Boris also ran a distillery for the Maharajah.

From the Royal Hotel Boris organised the preparation of the food for the protracted banqueting during the celebrations of the coronation of Prince Mahendra in 1955. Table linen, food, plates and dishes were taken across in handcarts to the Royal Palace from the Royal Hotel.

The pilots told me that they, and the management, thought the HS-748 was the wrong shape! Everything had to be raised seven feet off the ground before you could get anything inside the fuselage, while the Friendship, its fuselage much nearer the ground, only needed a soap box to step into the cabin. They both had the same engines, same speed, and carried the same load. The soap box won the day. Besides this, all the top brass of Nepalese Airlines had been sent by the Fokker Company to Holland for free dental treatment!

Nevertheless I spent the first two weeks trying to meet Ministers, their secretaries and the Nepalese Council for Development. These attempts took place in the Singha Durbar, a huge dilapidated building the size of Buckingham Palace. It had once been painted white. Each floor was surrounded by a wooden verandah. It was said to contain a thousand rooms, which had housed the concubines of the Rana Dynasty. The hierarchy of the Ranas was complicated, made more so, for me, a 'farriner', by the repetition of a limited choice of their names. General Sir Sushil Shamsheer Jung Bahadur Rana, appeared to be a basic six-word formula which, re-arranged, encompassed all Ranas of distinction.

One morning amidst the dark corridors of the Singha Durbar, I met a sympathetic and frustrated Nepali Forestry Department clerk. He explained that my quest was impossible. No private entrepreneur had succeeded in establishing a business. The first requisite for success was a large amount of money and a willingness to lose it. The second was to represent a foreign government, except the British! He was a graduate of Kathmandu University. There were no jobs, except when one was lucky enough to get into the Singha Durbar, drink tea, and pass on correspondence.

I wrote to Joe Koszarek and told him that there was 'not a hope in hell' of selling the HS-748, He replied that he was still the agent for Hawker Siddley in Nepal and we should hang on in case something materialised, while still being paid.

I was saved from the perils of idleness, after failing to make any headway among the administration, by a fortuitous minor calamity. One evening I was having a sherry in the Yak and Yeti bar on the first floor of the Royal Hotel. It was famous for its raised brick fireplace, which was topped by a conical copper chimney which went through the ceiling. In came Jai Singh. He wore brown brogues, flannels, a tweed jacket and a blue Viyella shirt with what I took to be his old school tie. He came straight to the point.

"Look, Andy! I'm in a fix. Capt Daulat Singh has absconded with Capt Hosie's daughter. They left for Calcutta this morning. I need you to fly 9N-RF2."

"Yes, of course Jai. That suits me fine."

Captain Hosie was an Australian flying in Air Nepal. 9N-RF2 was the work-horse Dakota of the Royal Flight, used mainly for carrying freight and on occasion, Gurkha troops.

"Let me have your licence and I'll get you a Nepalese one tomorrow. You'll be flying with Sessodea and Shome."

"Shome! Is he here?"

Radio Officer Shome was a character. An old hand with Indamer and Kalinga Airlines in Calcutta since 1950, he had flown for years on the Assam uplift and supply dropping in the NEFA. He was a volatile Bengali. When Shome was drunk he would spout verses from Lays of Ancient Rome, and for an encore, could give a good imitation of a Churchill wartime speech. Previously, when he was flying for Indamer in Calcutta under Capt Johnny Brenand, Kitty Brenand doled out Shome's pay in weekly dollops in the hope of preventing him from drinking it in one go, and so becoming unemployable for a week. Kitty kept Shome on short rations.

It transpired that Capt Singh had been offered a job with Air India International, which probably accounted, together with his involvement with the girl, for his precipitous departure.

So it was that I spent the next two years flying for Jai Singh. The King's Flight had a variety of aircraft given as gifts. There were two Chinese twin-engine Antonov aircraft, which were permanently grounded and stood forlornly on the Royal Flight's dispersal. There was also a twin-engine Russian Ilyushin for the King's long-distance flights. There were three Twin-Pioneer aircraft presented by Britain. They had arrived with no spare parts, and very soon two were cannibalised to keep one flying. The Pioneer was an aircraft that only Britain could have built! Joe Koszarek had sold the Royal Flight a Twin-Beech for ministerial visits to outlying airfields. There was also a helicopter for inspecting mountainous places. Jai could fly all the aircraft of the fleet.

Jai was a handsome fellow with greying hair and a small moustache. He was plump rather than fat, and of middling height. He held himself well and looked fine in worsteds and brown shoes. One of his endearing characteristics was his habit of constantly chewing a potent marsala of powdered tobacco, betel-nut and chuna (lime). He kept his supply in a small aluminium 35 mm film container. Every now and then he spat out a jet of red juice. His supply of marsala came from Calcutta. When he put on shorts and golfing brogues it was then he displayed a not too ample paunch. It was due to him that I was persuaded to join the Royal Kathmandu Golf Club, and so hack my way round the extraordinary hazards of its nine holes.

I spent many happy evenings with Jai, his wife and his fifteen-year-old daughter Gaitri, in their top-storey flat in an Army General's house opposite the American Mission Hospital, some five miles out of the town. On these occasions his wife gave instructions while Gaitri and I carried out the preparation for pork vindaloo, rice and dahl. Jai the paterfamilias sat drinking whisky and listening to the Beatles.

Jai came from a good Rajput family. He had been educated at Mill Hill School in north London. His son was at Mill Hill and came home for the holidays. Jai had started the Royal Nepalese Airlines in 1955 after returning from the Afghan Haj. I always had the utmost regard for him. During the next eighteen months I flew hard and enjoyed myself.

Capt Minou Bulsarra joined Royal Nepalese airlines a few weeks after I arrived in Kathmandu. He had previously flown for them, but had resigned in order to fly a Queen Air for the Ford Foundation in Delhi. I had known Bull since 1947 when we were both flying for Air Services of India, Bombay. During the next seventeen years we had been together in Assam,

Afghanistan and Aden. Bull was a Parsee and like many of his race, eccentric, volatile, gregarious and gifted. He could not read music, but played the clarinet, saxophone and guitar. He was one of the few people I met who could drink without showing it, except by looking like death the next morning.

In 1948 he married a very young Parsee girl and set up house at Juhu. They had one son and were divorced ten years later. He had a pathological hatred for incompetent authority, and an extreme attitude to things affecting his honour. He was an excellent pilot and one of the few that regularly got in and out of the Kathmandu valley, with its 9,000-foot surrounding hills, during the rain and clouds of the monsoon. He had a feud with the Directorate of Civil Aviation in New Delhi, and swore that he would never return to India. He kept his word except for the period with the Ford Foundation. While with the Foundation, Bull lived at Mainden's Hotel in Old Delhi. Due to his hospitality he ran up huge bills for booze. He was not flying enough and so decided to leave them and return to Nepal.

Bahadur Singh I met shortly after my arrival at the Royal Hotel. He lived there in a small room doing nothing. Bahadur had been an ADC to the Maharajah of Cooch Mihar. Like Jai, Bahadur was a Rajput. It was while in the Maharajah's service that he had fallen off an elephant and hurt his back. He became partly paralysed and spent the next five years having operations and treatment. He had known Boris in Cooch Bihar, and after his partial recovery he came to Kathmandu to help Boris in the hotel. Just after I arrived he had a hernia operation by Doctor Berry of the American Mission Hospital.

Bahadur was voluble, he spoke fluent but unique English. He represented a type of Indian which is frequently met, who talks nineteen-to-the-dozen but has no reading, education, or patience to listen to others. They suffer from an extreme naivety, and find enemies everywhere, whose malevolence is usually caused by differences of caste, community and wealth. On first meeting one of these people, the feeling is that one is in the presence of a madman. Perhaps it is their talking in a foreign language (English), but unfortunately it is not so, they talk the same way in their own language.

Bahadur Singh was a Kshatriya (warrior), and so imbued with excessive pride in their past martial heritage. He was affected without knowing it by a monumental inferiority complex. His *bêtes noires* were legion: Brahmins, Bengalis, Bunyas, and then Muslims. He hated the Congress, revered Gandhi, loathed Nehru as a Muslim-loving renegade, and like many of his countrymen looked back with longing to a mythical past when all was perfect, with truly holy sanyassis, fierce, fearless warriors, beautiful and virtuous women, and the Gods walked the earth. At the same time he despised the old ways of doing things and admired 'progress'. He was an amalgam of conflicting opinions, any one of which he could express with fervour if not with coherence, and when faced by the glaring inconsistency of his position, he lapsed into bewildered silence; but not for long.

Three months after I met him, another India-Pakistan fracas started. Bahadur would sit with his ear glued to my small transistor radio and swear at the incompetence of the Indian generals and politicians. One day he would rail against Prime Minister Shastri as another spineless Congress dhoti wallah; the next day he would eulogise Shastri as an incarnation of Gandhi. Pakistan advances drove him to fury, with accusations of perfidy against the Indian Muslim community. Nehru was to blame. Nehru had turned a blind eye to certain related Muslims in West Bengal who smuggled food into East Pakistan. The stories were fantastic, confused, but Singh sincerely believed what he told me. I was almost half-convinced. Double-dealing, hidden wealth and graft is the prerequisite of all people in power in India, and Nehru was not exempt.

By August it was realised that the monsoon in India had failed. This led to the usual outcry of over-population and birth control. Lippi's loop was to be the new saviour of India. Singh believed in universal sterilisation of men and women, and that all beggars should be corralled and allowed to die. He blamed modern medicine for the rise in population, and yet poured scorn on the Ayurvedic system, unless he was extolling the greatness of Ram Raj or some miraculous cure which had defeated the western system. Yet in spite of such a tiresome naivety we were birds of a feather and got on well together. At times I accused him of being an ignoramus and that the troubles of India were due to bigoted and chauvinistic people like himself. He would look hurt and bewildered. Had I gone too far? I was always restrained by Bahadur's innate kindness. He could be easily hurt. I might disagree with him, but I was careful never to press my opinion too strongly. I valued his company, and without it we would both have been alone.

In Kathmandu we were in limbo while the Indo-Pakistan affair went on, and the Chinese made threatening noises. In the end the whole situation was too much for Singh. He took refuge in listening to Radio Pakistan and exploding at their obvious exaggerations. He was essentially kind and good-natured and easily led in matters of honour. I liked him very much and I think he felt the same towards me.

CHAPTER 23

Rambles with Bahadur

ONE morning soon after my arrival, I was sitting in my large stone-flagged room after breakfast, and writing a pessimistic report to Bombay. There was a knock on my door.

"Come in," I called out.

"Captain, I am not causing you disturbance?"

"No Singhji. Come on in."

"Let us go walking, it is a holiday today."

"Alright Singh."

"But first I go to Indian Embassy. Do you believe in astrology? Tell me your date of birth and exact time of your appearance."

"I can't Singh. I know the date but not the time."

"What date is your janmadin?"

"Seventh of December 1919".

"Why bloody! You're younger than me. I am third of March 1919, exactly at midnight. I believe. If you want to believe, you believe. I don't make others believe, most of the bloody bastards are all balls y'know. I'm sick now. Oh G-o-d I'm down, my life is finished. I used to be on top once, shooting, enjoying good food, roaming. Now I'm down in the world. When I was up I prayed to the God, now I am down I pray to the God. It is the God's will. Come, let us go."

Outside was a dilapidated dark blue-and-red taxi. We both got in.

"I thought you said we were going for a walk, Singh."

"Yes, we are Captain, but first we go to the Indian Embassy to see my doctor. I must not take too much movement or the hole will open y'know. The intestine will drop y'know. It is very dangerous this hernia, if it drops I will have to go again for operation. Oh G-o-d. My life is down hogaya. I don't want to live more. What for to live, not like before, shooting! Good food! I am too much coward to kill myself."

"Now Singhji, don't talk like that, you must eat more, take exercise, get out into the sun and meet people."

"In the sun you say! Me! I live all my life in the sun! It is nothing. Exercise! How can I? And have intestine drop through the hole. I eat but don't feel like I was before. Then I eat rice, so much, like this before cooking." (Singh cupped his hands together.) "Chappati, subzi, mutton, chicken, dhal, dhai, sweets. I eat good food before, now all is down. Oh G-o-d! I'm down hogaya. Here is India Embassy, bloody big place with officers living here and there. The Britishers gave them this place. It is hundred years old. Now they come here, useless fellows. Eh! Driver! Right side! Right! Slow! Bus, Roko bhai! Now I go and see my doctor, Captain."

"All right Singhji. I'll wait in the shade."

Bahadur Singh waddled off to see his doctor. His head was bent forward and down, and his arms were slightly akimbo. He was wearing spotless white kurta and pyjama, with his bare feet in brown moccasin shoes. He had a handsome head of black hair going grey at the sides, a neat moustache, rather small eyes, and gave the impression of being a pleasant, harmless fellow. Soon he was back with two others, one a very dapper old man in grey flannels and blazer, the other a dhoti wallah with large black shoes and protruding ears.

"Doctor Sahib this is my friend. Captain."

"Good morning doctor," I said, getting out to open the car door for the grey-flanelled old man.

"After you doctor."

"No, no Captain! I'm not coming. Thank you."

299

Singh and I got into the back seat. The dhoti wallah with large shoes and protruding ears sat next to the driver.

"Thank you doctor," said Singh. "Goodbye. Chalo driver." We moved off.

"Who is that in front?" I whispered to Singh.

"He is my guru, Captain."

The guru looked more like a hair-cutting wallah. His hair was short and his small ears stuck out like curly fungi.

"I don't believe in all that nonsense y'know, but I take him. He will say what is to happen. I believe in astrology, but too many are useless fellows. They're all bloody bastards! What to do? My life is down hogaya. Oh G-o-d! I like the Britishers, not like the Americans, mean fellows. I tell you what happened in Cooch-Bihar. The American came to shoot with His Highness. No good shot, but plenty of money, the mean man. After shooting he said he wanted to sell his gun. Very good double-barrelled walnut gun. Very fine. I wanted a gun. His Highness asked how much. Two thousand and five hundred rupees, he said. 'Go and ask him Singh, he knows you.' I know this man and had shooting many times with him, roaming here and there.

"Those days were different Captain, now you pay six rupees a cartridge! No fun now! Oh G-o-d! I asked him to buy his gun. He said 'Two thousand five hundred rupees.' Not one pice less. He wouldn't come down, not one pice. In his bush shirt and half-pant, stingy mean bastard y'know. Not like the Britishers. I tell you. I was on the tea estate near Jalpaiguri. Who do I see there in Club House but old colonel who know my father. He said to me, 'Put in for a commission.'"

"When was this Singh?

"This was in the war. I put in application. He saw me in office. 'Hello Singh,' he said. 'Good morning Colonel Sahib,' I say. 'Right! Singh. How is your father?' 'He's fine and in good health Sir, and eating good food.' 'Right Singh, out you go.'

"That's how I got into army. No nonsense. The Britishers were real gentlemen. We nearly went to your Buckingham

Palace. The Prince came and saw the Rajputs in Jaipur. Tall, like your guards at Buckingham Palace. All over six-foot-six except officers. It took His Highness five years to raise battalion y'know. All clothing came from England. Jackets, pants, boots, all English make. Then Prince said to His Highness to send to guard Buckingham Palace. But just before, war started. No Buckingham Palace only Egypt desert. Over six-feet-six tall, all except officers. Then gold-striped pugri, then gold-threaded Kalani, standing like smart, eight-foot tall! I tell you Captain! Oh G-o-d!"

"But what about the gun, Singh?"

"Yes, I was in Club House having drinks. The colonel came ....."

"Which colonel, Singh?"

"The same colonel who knew my father and got me commission." 'Good God Singh,' he say. 'How is your father?' My father! He is more healthy than me, more young. He is 64, eating, walking 10 miles every day, enjoying. And me! Oh G-o-d! my life is down hogaya. Forty-five years old and my life is finished. It is God's will."

We arrived back at the Royal Hotel and got out of the taxi.

"See you later Captain. We will go for another walk."

"All right Singh. I'll wait."

Singh waddled into his room, followed by the purohit in a blue shirt, white dhoti, and carrying a blue plastic airline bag.

An hour later there was a knock on my door.

"Come in."

"You ready now Captain?"

"Yes. Come, let's go, a nice walk will do you good Singhji."

We started off, I in bush shirt and long trousers, with a straw hat and wearing Japanese rubber chappals; Singh still wearing his grey flannels and white shirt, both by now a little rumpled and creased. The sun was hot. We wandered down the drive. Singh held my arm and occasionally stumbled over a broken brick. We passed beneath the overhanging trees as we came up to the broken gateway and the sleeping chowkidar.

"The bloody bastard! I tell you they're all the same now!"

"Who? Singh bhai, keep your hair on!"

"That pundit, my guru. He's trying something new. I would live 96 years he said! More money, that's what he wants y'know. Not like before, now only money, everybody wants money. Oh G-o-d! how to make money? He said 96 years what good for me if I live like dog. It is karma Captain. You believe in karma Captain? I don't believe in all that, but it is my karma. Sometimes you have to believe. My operation, the one before, cost me two lakh rupees. Where from I get all that money? Ah! God is great! My father, my brothers, my sisters. I am only bachelor. When I am lonely I like to go to Buddhist temple and sit quietly four, five, or six hours in the shade."

"But Singh, you're a Hindu. Did Shankaracharia live in vain?"

"What matter, Captain? This temple, that temple. God is great. It's all the same. I take prashad and sit quietly. I do that when I am lonely y'know. Ninety six! The bloody bastard, who's he trying to play tricks to? And look at me. My life is over, After operation I can do nothing. If I had health I would do anything, going here and there, this way and that way. Without health, Captain, you can do nothing. Oh G-o-d!"

"Singh, what happened about the shotgun and the colonel?"

"What a lovely gun! Those Britishers know how to talk y'know. Colonel said 'What, Singh old fellow you doing here? How's your father?' He remember my father! 'He is enjoying good health Sir and eating good food.' 'Good Singh,' he said. 'Why you here?' 'Somebody tell me Sir, that one planter wants to sell his gun, Sir.'

"Then he took me to other drinking planters and said to one man, 'You got your gun for sale, quick now, go and get it.' And that poor bastard had to go all the way to his bungalow and bring his gun. Lovely English gun, walnut, blue barrels and box. The planter said he wanted fifteen-hundred rupees. The Colonel said, 'How much you got, Singh?' 'Here Sir,' and I bring out from bush jacket pocket all I have. Seven hundred rupees! 'Right! It's sold,' said the Colonel, and I paid only seven hundred rupees to the poor bastard! That's how the Britishers are. Gentlemen! No money, but have honour. Honouring my poor old father, 64 years old, but younger than me y'know. It's my karma.

"Captain, don't think I play tricks but let us take a rickshaw. I have pain here. Doctor said no movement."

"Alright Singh, as you say."

We were now opposite the Kathmandu post office. We climbed into a cycle rickshaw.

"How much, brother? Down to the bridge?" Singh asked the rickshaw wallah, a thin youth dressed in dirty faded blue shorts, an old army battle dress jacket and wearing a large pair of ancient army boots.

"Two rupees, Sahib."

"What! All the way down hill and two rupees. I'll give you one-and-a-half rupees. Don't try your cheeky tricks with me!"

"Alright."

We moved off slowly, both of us squashed together in the seat while the rickshaw wallah laboured, first with his weight on one pedal then the other. We gathered speed and the bell started to ring, warning the crowds of pedestrians in the narrow streets of the bazaar.

"But Singh, if you don't like it here why don't you go back to Cooch Bihar and His Highness?"

"His Highness is always roaming now, and the Palace is full of servants and other low fellows. It is too humid there. I must have dry air for my back, the doctor says. Oh G-o-d! Those Bengalis, bloody bastards. I hate those fellows."

"But Singh bhai, I've spent many years in Calcutta and I didn't find them bad."

"You Captain! You are different, mixing with business men and high-class wallahs. I tell you they are most cheeky fellows, most intreegy. I hate those people. All the time they fool you and most dirty over money. I am Kshatrya, they are useless Brahmin, Vaishya and low Sudra types. They eat fish Captain!

That foul stinky Hilsa. They eat its eyes! Oh G-o-d! I see them. Even Bengali Brahmin with his dhoti, like skirt. Like shrieking woman. Very cheeky, very intreegy. I hate those bastards."

"How do you find it here, Singh?"

"The Nepali he is a wonderful fellow. But these Newaris in Kathmandu are not so good. Also a little intreegy, but not bad. They not very good over money matters. You come to Jaipur. I say we meet at twelve o'clock. Not like that here. These fellows don't come at all. Lazy fellows. It's this crowd in the valley. The Newars and useless Ranas. They are worst type in all Nepal, not like hill fellows. Hill people are very fine fighting types! Not like this people. The Ranas are the worst. But here it is not bad. You can talk, meet them, but they're not trustworthy fellows."

We were getting to the outskirts of the town. We passed a roadside scene of buffalo heads being hacked to pieces with small axes. Bits of bloody meat lay around. Dogs nibbled here and there. Thousands of flies enjoyed themselves in the sun as they licked the bloody titbits. A crowd of women and children stood around waiting for their portions. The more fastidious flies sat upon the onlookers.

"So they eat buffalo here Singhji?"

"Yes Captain. Poor, low-down people eat buffalo. Only cow is sacred, not buffalo. The Americans eat it like anything. Only low-class eat it here. How can they eat it? I don't know! They don't eat cow meat. Only low class and Americans, not others."

"Do you eat buffalo Singh?"

"I eat any meat if I have it. I don't eat cow, not because of religion. I don't believe in that rubbish. I eat any meat."

"But Singh, surely you don't eat cow?"

"I don't know if I have eaten cow. I don't know. I don't believe in all the cleansing puja. I don't eat cow because nobody give it to me. Same I don't take fish, no I don't take fish. Not because of religion. I just don't take fish. Nobody give me cow so I don't eat cow. Eh brother! Slowly! Not so fast. Eh! Stop here. Buy some sweets."

The rickshaw wallah stopped opposite a sweet shop, on our left was a pan and cigarette wallah. We blocked the narrow muddy passageway. A trickle of dirty water wended its way down a small drain in the passageway. Children squatted by the walls with their little shirts tucked up and shat yellow messes. Pi-dogs sniffed, some ate. The pan wallah had a dirty gunny sack over his doorway as a screen. On our left was the sweet shop with its earth floor and low entrance. Barfi, perra, ladoo, brown sausage-like gulab jahms swam in sticky liquid, some on cracked plates, others in tarnished brass dishes, and all inside ricketty glass cases. The cases were open at the back to allow the flies inside. Singh gave the rickshaw wallah one rupee four annas.

"Buy some perra bhai. One rupee. Bring two gulab jham, one for me, one for sahib," Singh commanded.

"We have gulab jahm Captain. Very good here."

"Alright Singh. Thank you."

Singh leaned out of the rickshaw.

"Eh, pan wallah. English Capstan cigarettes?"

"Yes Sahib."

"Give me four."

"What, Sahib! Only four and you sitting with a white Sahib. Take a packet!"

"What is this? You cheeky man. Come on, four Capstan."

The perra arrived, done up in a small parcel of dried leaves and bound with cotton thread. The rickshaw wallah handed Singh and me a small thin earthenware cup, red, and beautifully made. Inside were two dark brown sausages soaked in syrup. I took a bite of mine. It was delicious, a small, baked pudding of flour and sugar covered with a sweet syrup.

The pan wallah got up from his cross-legged position and came over with four cigarettes in a Capstan packet in his outstretched right hand. Singh examined the packet and inspected the writing on the cigarettes.

"Eh bhai! These are Pakistan Capstan. No good. Give me Hindustan Capstan. You got Hindustan?"

The pan wallah had no Hindustan Capstan, so the transaction was off, and Singh got back his four annas.

"Chalo driver. Don't go fast down this hill. You get no more money for reaching early. Horrible things those Pakistan Capstans, Captain. Same name, same company, but Hindustan ones are too good."

We continued down the lane. Ahead I could see a wide dried-up river and the lane crossing by a long bridge. Singh had also brought a newspaper package. It looked as though it was a wrapped bottle. He unwrapped the paper and I saw a bundled handkerchief. He untied the handkerchief to disclose some crushed yellow marigolds: to this lot he added the perras in their dried leaves, and then wrapped them all up in the newspaper. This was his prashad, or offering to the Gods.

"Before at his Highness I ate good food, good clothes and running this way and that way, shooting. I have an hour free and I take my gun for shooting. What food! It was the God's wish. When I was up I prayed to the God, now I am down I pray to the God. It is my karma. Oh G-o-d! Eh bhai! Slowly! You won't get more money. Why should we kill the cow? It is not religion that I don't eat cow meat. Cow is for us from the Gods. We use its milk, urine, dung and whatnot. It is for us. What for forty-three crores of peoples? If we kill the cows how can we live? Forty three crores peoples kill the cows and finish in one day. All the cows dead, where can come from milk, urine, dung, this and that? That is why the cow is holy animal for us."

The rickshaw stopped by the bridge and we got out. Singh paid him off. We walked down to the dry river bed. There was a large peepal tree and under its branches was a small, dirty little temple, a square affair with an earthern seat each side of its low entrance. As we came up to it I saw sleeping on one seat, and laid on a filthy rag, a small girl-child about the same age as my two-year-old daughter. She lay on her back, her little dress pulled up over her chest, flies on her eyes, on her snotty nostrils, on her mouth and settling on her little female crack, as she lay with her thin bony legs outstretched. She was my daughter, but I had no power so I passed her by. From the small entrance leading into the presence of the deity came out two pyjama-clad Nepalis. One held the head of a black cock in his left hand, and the body in the crook of his right arm. They walked over to the nearby corner of the seat where two other crouching Nepalis were hacking away.

"Dirty filthy place," said Singh. "They're going to cut the cock. I don't believe in that business. It is low-class people who do that. I hate those low-class fellows. They give our religion a bad name to the foreigners. I don't hate really. God is the creator. We must love them. We hate Bengalis and such-like and we hate God. That is not right. We love God and love his makings. Come, let us cross here. What a dirty filthy place!"

We had arrived at the river's edge, the bank was built up of stone steps. The river was now a parched, sandy waste. Next to the stone steps were a few inches of discoloured water. People were abluting their hands, feet, faces and various brass vessels. These were the supplicants at the nearby temple.

"Singhji, does this river ever get full of water?"

"Yes Captain. In monsoon time it gets full of water all the way across. You see that bridge, it will fall down next monsoon. It will drown all these bloody bastards. Americans, Indians and foreigners give aid, but no one builds a good bridge to go to the Kali temple. It is too far from the palace! I tell you, foreign aid is swindling aid."

The river was about one hundred yards wide and down-stream was an ancient brick bridge. I saw that each pylon was corroded away for about six feet above the sandy river bed. We started to cross the parched waste.

"Where are we going Singh?"

"There Captain! It is Kali temple. Kali is very powerful. We Rajputs worship shakti."

"But Singh, I thought Kali was a Bengali deity."

"Bengali! I hate those bloody bastards. So cheeky, so intreegy. Kali, Durga, Parvati, all the same. Our side it's Durga, this side Kali, that side (here he waved his hand vaguely over his head.) Parvati. It is shakti. Power! In Calcutta they have Kali puja in October and mix it with Durga. Durga and Kali are the same and so is Parvati. Shiva loved Kali, then he loved Parvati or Durga, it's all the same. Parvati has one-thousand-and-one names. It's the shakti we worship. We Rajputs worship power. Come Captain, I go and do puja, and you enjoy here in the shade."

"Thanks Singhji. I will wait on the verandah. Do a good puja, it may help to change your karma."

"I don't believe in all that, Captain. God is great! I go now."

We stepped over another near-stagnant stream and climbed up the stone steps to the Kali temple. Singh was conspicuous in his white shirt and grey trousers. There was a low verandah in front of the temple with a wooden roof. Singh left his shoes outside a small door, unwrapped his offerings throwing the newspaper on the stone flags, and entered the inner sanctum, bending down as he did so to pass through the low doorway. I remained outside to watch the scene. On each side of the temple doorway sat two old women selling the usual wares: cigarettes, beedees, pan leaves, betelnut, small clay lamps, josh sticks, twisted string wicks, and cigarette tins of variously coloured powders. Vermilion was the most common colour, and was used for making the tika on the forehead after the ceremony.

There was a small crowd of worshippers squeezing in and out of the doorway. A bell clanged. I looked through a side door and saw a square temple in the middle of a stone court-yard. Around the carved wooden eaves of the inner temple, stuck up with nails, were photographs of various odd-looking men, some with glasses, others with bald heads, and one looked like the King in his field marshal's uniform, and wearing his black-rimmed spectacles. These were pictures of pundits and important persons who had visited the temple, and included a film star. The floor inside and outside was covered with the debris of dead flowers, bits of sweets, spittle and pieces of paper, all of which were attracting the attention of the temple flies.

A small boy about three feet high with only a dirty shirt on, and that around his stomach, began to bang the bell hanging outside the temple. He was playing. Then an old man came out and went down the stone steps to the stagnant water. He performed his religious ablutions with his right hand. Flick, flick, water into each eye. Flick, flick, some liquid into his mouth. Flick, flick, water on his old bald head. Then with both hands cupped he splashed water three times in front of him. He then took up water in his cupped hand and carried it up the steps, and drenched a large, shiny stone Shiva lingam while he whispered a mantra.

Singh emerged from the temple door backwards with his head bowed down to miss the lintel. He shook the crumbs from his handkerchief and put it in his kurta pocket. He put on his brown shoes. I went over to him. He was talking to one of the women.

"Capstan cigarettes? You've got Hindustan Capstan, not Pakistan? Right, give me four."

He turned to me. "Here Captain, put these in your bush-shirt pocket. Come, let us walk along the bank and cross by that rotten bridge."

We started off, climbing slowly along the river bank.

"You see those stone steps? There are two-hundred and fifty-seven of them leading to Shwayambhunath, and I cannot climb them to say prayer to God. Before when I had health it was different, now I am like this, older than my father. Oh G-o-d! Two hundred and fifty-seven steps! We will go by car another day Captain. It is easier."

"Who lives in these mud huts by the river bank Singhji?"

"Those are very old dharamsalas Captain. Used in good days. Any fellow could come and stay there. Before, all sorts of sadhus and holy men came and went. Then purohits lived there, dirty fellows. They brought all sorts of bad things to religion like girls, this and that. Come, let us sit under the peepal tree. It gives coolest shade in all the world. Lord Buddha sat under peepal tree. Come, you sit on this murti. I sit like Buddha."

I looked at a very old smooth stone statue. A god's head and shoulders above the earth, perhaps Shiva.

"What! Sit on Shiva, Singhji?"

"It doesn't matter Captain."

"What about the Nepalis? They might get angry seeing a mlench sitting on Shiva's head."

"Oh well, you sit over here and I will sit there."

We sat opposite each other. Singh looked around, his shoulders bowed. There were steps going down to the river bed and a long flight of stone steps leading to another temple. People passed us. Some gave us a glance. Children mounted the steps to the temple carrying dishes of flowers.

"We have peepal tree over our side too, very cooling. Now it is June. How jolly it is in Mussoorie. My father, brothers, sisters and their families and all the children go to Mussoorie for hot season. We have a big house, one hundred rooms, gardens, orchards, mangoes, lychees, pears, plums, all sorts of fruits. We get seven or eight thousand rupees yearly from contractors for the fruits. Very peaceful life, nobody there after May. All the children go to school. My mother was very happy there, we all had happy times."

"Why don't you go back there Singh? I'm sure you would be happier."

"It is my karma Captain. I came here and got operation, my hernia. What to do? Mussoorie is very quiet. Same climate as here, resting place in hot season during Britishers' time. Come, let us have a cigarette before we move on again."

We smoked in silence.

A little girl came slowly down the long flight of steps, one at a time. Her smooth hair was in a long plait, she wore a little red cotton choli and long blue cotton skirt. Her feet were bare. She carried a brass dish with the remnants of her offering. As she got closer I saw she was quite pretty, but her face was heavily pock-marked. She had been visited by Kalimata. She passed by in silence and went her way.

"Bloody bastard!!" Singh broke his silent rumination. "Ninety-six year he say I live! He wants more money. He's trying some new tricks."

"Let's move on Singh."

"Yes we must go. Slowly."

We started to cross the stone bridge. It was crooked, with tufts of grass growing from the walls. In the middle of the dry river bed about a hundred yards downstream was a pile of refuse. There were banana leaves, dead flowers, soiled paper, broken wooden boxes, tins and other indiscriminate refuse. Around this stood two cows munching moodily, two pi-dogs gnawed bones and growled, and two small boys poked the refuse with sticks.

"What for they born Captain? Are they no better than pi-dogs?"

"It is their karma Singhji."

"That is all balls. I tell you truth, it is rubbish."

"Then what to do Singh?"

"It is all foreign aid programmes. Americans, Russian, Indian, Chinese. The rich get richer and the poor poorer. It is the rich man who gets the aid. Look at this bloody bridge. No decent bridge to go to temple! I tell you truth Captain. My father said 'Bahadur, always tell the truth,' and I tell you, I always tell the truth. The Gods won't help if you tell lie. Foreign aid is rubbish. It goes into the drain, or a few factories for poor people to work. Who gave foreign aid to western countries? I tell you true, nobody. They made their own aid. No foreign aid down this bloody road."

We had crossed the bridge and started up the hill we had come down by rickshaw.

"This is dhobi thana Captain. Don't look in tanks, the water is filthy. Look how white the shirts and pants are. This is special caste that do this work. Things are better now. Before chickens were one rupee, now they're twelve rupees."

"How's that better Singh?"

"Better for poor people, they get more money now. Look, here is buffalo chopping place. Dirty filthy place!"

We were now approaching a crossroads on the outskirts of the town. In the middle of the crossroads was a dilapidated corrugated iron-roofed, circular bandstand. It had escaped my notice as we came past in the rickshaw. A web of electric wires converged on it from the surrounding buildings. The wires continued under the roof to the mid-point and produced a single pendulous fruit in the form of a dusty electric light bulb. The bandstand was deformed and dirty. Women and children and dogs sat or lay beneath its shade waiting their turn to collect portions of the dismembered buffalo heads.

"Why is the bandstand here Singh?"

"That is from old happy days Captain. Some no-good Rana built it for the band to play in, on puja days. Those were better days, now it's radio fillum music and common stuff. Good military band is the best, like we had in Jaipur Guards."

A rickshaw passed us with a young American boy in it. He had his rucksack between his feet, and was dressed in a none-too-clean shirt and khaki trousers.

"Look at that Captain. Did you see that filthy person?"

"Who, Singh?"

"That American in the rickshaw."

"You mean the Peace Corps wallah?"

"Yes I tell you truth, this American aid is all balls, driving around in jeeps, here and there. Dirty stinky fellows."

"Not all, surely Singh."

"Those Peace Corps wallahs are the worstest. Girls and men sleeping with common dirty people. In Jaipur I took some to see my friend. I opened the door of his room. He said, 'Please go outside, you are all smelly.' So I sit them on verandah and get bearer to bring soft drinks. My friend call me and said, 'Who are these smelly persons Singh?' 'They are from most civilised county in all the world. From USA,' I told him. He said 'We are poor but we take bath daily, why do they have to smell?' Dirty, filthy fellows. I tell you Captain, absolutely stinky! I have seen girls in leather trousers, here in Kathmandu. They travel all round the world in same trousers. You go into hills and you will find Americans walking around, dirty shirts, dirty half-pant. Who are they? They're not tourists! Or Peace Corps. They're Intelligence! That's what they are. They don't bath! You see here Peace Corps on bicycles, dirty shirt, dirty pant, without shaving. And Captain I tell you truth — their feet are dirty!"

"Their feet, Singh?"

"Yes! You look next time. They have dirty feet. Why can't they wash? Most civilised country in all the world. Absolutely filthy smelly. I tell you one night a dirty long-haired beard-wallah came in a small low-type Citroen, all bent and dirty. He walked up the steps. 'Have you taken food?' I said. 'No.' 'Why not?' I say. 'I have no money,' he said. So I called bearer and tell him to bring double supper for me. I tell him please don't sit in my room you are too smelly.' "

"Where was this Singh?"

"At the Royal Hotel, last year. Then I said you take bath and I give you clean kurta and pyjama, but he said no. He wouldn't take bath. Dirty, stinky fellow. I got durrie from the stores and he went and slept in his low-type Citroen. I fed him for eighteen days! He slept in his car and read books. He never took one bath. I asked him, 'Why you come to Nepal with no money?' He said he was learning yoga and brought out his notebook. He had many good addresses of rishis. I know some too, so I know he is not fooling. 'Why did you come here?' I said. 'I decided to go and see a rishi near Lucknow', he said, 'so I set off but my car broke down and I had a lot of trouble. When I got there rishi said 'I knew you were coming today, here take food. You must be hungry after your troubles. You stay today and go tomorrow.' The rishi brought out all sorts of fruits, mangos, lychees, bananas, pears. 'Here, take mango', he said. Then the rishi told him to come to Nepal as only in Nepal could he sell his dirty filthy Citroen."

"The rishi told him to come to Nepal to sell his car? That's not very spiritual, Singh."

"The rishi told him truth. You can't sell old car like that in India. Too much duty. I helped him sell it. He got five thousand four hundred rupees NC. The rishi told him to go to Nepal and he would meet someone to feed him. 'That's me,' I said, 'Yes Mr Singh', he said. 'But I never asked you, did I? You asked me, and I told you the truth.' True enough, but he never took bath for eighteen days. Later the bearded wallah, dirty filthy fellow, stinky like anything, went to UP, but he never wrote me.

"I tell you, the Peace Corps fellows are good for country. They go back to USA and get into foreign service. Their minds are not puffed up like big sahibs. They know how poor people live, and very useful for country in diplomatic post. Then some of the roaming Americans write books and make money, but they don't take bath. Think how many crores of rupees is needed to keep these Peace Corps fellows. They roam around in dirty shirt and half-pant and no bath. Even poor people take bath."

We were now back at the hotel and walking up the drive.

"Well, here we are Singhji. We had a nice walk."

"Oh G-o-d! Home!"

"Now have a nice rest Singh."

We mounted the deserted front verandah. No one was in sight.

"Yes Captain. I'll take bath and have food. You coming for chicken curry?"

"No thanks Singhji. I'll take my sun bath."

"BEARER" shouted Singh.

There was no answer and no one appeared.

"Bloody bastards," Singh continued. "They're sleeping around like pi dogs. BEARER! Mera chabi lao!"

"Don't shout Singhji, you'll only annoy Mrs Scott. Look, here's your key on the door nail."

"Thank you Captain. That Lakshman is a lazy fellow but not a bad boy. I take bath now."

Singh entered his room and I returned to mine to wash my feet.

CHAPTER 24

Tantric Tigers

IN the early days of our friendship Bahadur Singh and myself were both victims of Nepalese bureaucracy. My difficulties I have described. Bahadur Singh was being paid by a Lucknow business man to see to the setting-up of a factory to manufacture electrical fixtures at Hetauda, a small town on the south side of the mountains from Kathmandu. The factory was not yet built. Singh was immersed in the procurement of materials for its construction. His main concern was a permit to import 10 tons of corrugated iron sheeting from India. Permits were issued by the State Trading Corporation situated in an old Rana's palace near the Royal Hotel.

The first long walk that we had taken together had been a little too much for Singh after his hernia operation. He had long since ceased to do anything in the Royal Hotel. Boris would never have turned him out. Boris was also pursuing a scheme to breed pigs in a valley south of the mountains at Sathapur, about eighty miles from Kathmandu. Boris had told Singh that he would be sent to the site to look after the land and superintend the construction of abattoirs, feeding pens, store-houses and refrigeration rooms. The scheme, like most of Boris's ventures, had vast possibilities. Singh was naturally interested in any venture which would give him occupation and provide security. He preferred the pig scheme as he owed much to Boris, but on the other hand he had been given money and employed by the Lucknow industrialist before Boris had approached him. Bahadur trusted Boris to keep his word more than he did his own countryman. We discussed the problem endlessly, and came to no conclusion.

During the ensuing months he asked my advice on another three schemes. One was the dealership in Rajasthan for the products of a distillery being set up at Bhairewa. The second was to start a business to produce wooden boxes for the bottles of booze. In this he was helped by a Muslim contractor, and the two of them spent hours in amicable discussion and plans. The last scheme was to approach the Nepalese government to extract lime from huge deposits in inaccessible hills for the use in the Russian sugar mill in the Terai. All these possibilities ran concurrently and necessitated long hours of discussion and reports to me of his visits with various persons of power.

I remember one very painful episode in the Yak and Yeti bar of the Royal Hotel. Singh and I were sitting round the hearth fire in the middle of the bar, with its conical brass chimney, an innovation of Boris's and famous in Kathmandu drinking circles and beyond. Singh was sipping his brandy. In came Jai Singh. We hailed him. He sat down next to Bahadur. Bahadur was always deferential towards Jai.

"How's the distilling going Bahadur?" asked Jai.

"It's opening next month Jai."

"Next month! That's quick work. You want to look out for that Kumar."

Kumar was the Indian entrepreneur who had interested Palace circles in putting up the money for the distillery.

"I tell you Jai, it's a great scheme. I'll make lakhs if I get the agency for Rajasthan."

"You'll never get any agency for anywhere. You're nuts if you think Kumar will give you anything. You bet your life he's got it all lined up for his own friends."

"He told me he wants a local man in Rajasthan. All I need is fifty thousand rupees to buy the initial stock."

"Fifty thousand! Where are you going to get that from?"

"Well, I thought you might put up some money. It can't fail."

"Me! By Christ you've got some nerve. What about the piss they're making? Why should I put up any money?"

"It's real scotch! They've got a Scottish man from UK who is showing them how to mix the whisky. They've got barrels of concentrated scotch coming from UK to give it the real taste. I've seen the labels and the bottles. It'll be better than Black Knight or Diplomat. It's going to be more expensive too. Then they're making rum for the Gurkha troops, and brandy."

"Balls Bahadur. You'll never get a look-in in Rajasthan. There'll be real big money wallahs who'll pay big bucksheesh to get the agency. How can you waste your time on such nonsense."

"You say nonsense. I say balls to you. Kumar promise me agency if I raise money. We can make one rupee a bottle easily."

"One rupee a bottle! You're nuts. Is that all Kumar will give you? Who pays for the local taxes, state liquor licence, godown storage, transportation ? You'll be lucky if you get one naiya paisa."

"You think I a fool."

"You're damn right I do. You get Kumar to give you his proposal in writing, then I'll think about it."

Bahadur Singh was embarrassed because this exchange took place in front of me. I had told him very much the same thing as Jai, but less bluntly. If anybody was less business-like than Singh it was I, and he had quickly and loudly demolished my objections. Bahadur never forgot the row with Jai. The next day they were as pally as ever, but months later Bahadur told me how he had been insulted by Jai, and could not forget how a good scheme had been ridiculed. Jai was less patient than I was with Bahadur, probably because he had had longer to put up with him, and got sick of his scatterbrained schemes.

I owe a debt of gratitude to Bahadur. On those days when I was not flying we went for long walks all over Kathmandu. Sometimes we went by cycle rickshaws. Sometimes we had to go up a hill which was too much for the wretched rickshaw wallah. At such times I would get out and push the rickshaw from behind, while Singh sat in the seat, and the rickshaw wallah pushed at his pedals. Singh would call out, "Push harder Captain!" Then as we reached level ground the two pushers remounted, and Singh would nudge me in the ribs grinning sideways at me, but wisely making no comment.

Later, as Singh's hernia healed, we hired bicycles and so went further afield. It was on these long rambles that I learnt most of Singh's life story, from the time he was commissioned into the Indian Army until the present. At first I found it difficult to keep track of his long, disjointed tale. I was frightened that my interruptions might cause him to dry up. I need have had no fears. He was constantly distracted with the result that his story could skip ten or twenty years. A distracting sight would bring him to the immediate present or a few days previous; a face in the crowd would start another reminiscence. He could break off a tale while he chewed a pan, and then start off on one uncompleted from a few days before. I therefore began to adopt a firm tone with Singh. I kept him rigidly to the point, with dates, places and names. As a raconteur he improved, but the strain had an effect when he would burst into impatient swearing. "Why bloody! I tell you Captain, they're all stinky fellows." "What for he say that to me? The bloody bastard!" And "Oh G-o-d! I'm down hogaya," were some of his favourites. The last became less frequent as his health improved.

Singh had a few intimates. He would disappear for lunch or dinner and then on his return tell me his adventures, usually gastronomic, and about people he had met. One crony was a fat little good-natured Bengali, called Mr Gupta. He was a resident agent for a world newspaper network. His main task appeared to be interviewing and photographing celebrated tourists or mountaineers, and occasional reports on the political goings-on among the embassies. Mr Gupta chewed pan continuously, which gave him pale brown lips and small globules of red-brown dried saliva in the corners of his mouth. According to Singh, Mr Gupta slept all the time unless actually kept awake by talking or pursuing his trade.

One day Singh took me to see Mr Kaul, a professor friend of his. He lived on the first floor of a ramshackle brick house outside the town and opposite the Agricultural Department. We went by bus. He was asleep in an adjoining bedroom behind beaded curtains. We entered his house unannounced. Singh and I sat down in wooden armchairs around a table piled with loose papers, Film Weekly, Motherland (one of the local rags), an empty Char Mini cigarette packet.

Professor Kaul entered in his pyjamas, tall, slim, unshaven, peering through his spectacles intensely and with a blanket around his thin shoulders. My presence, a white sahib, the first he had met for a long time, and certainly the first to enter his house, had an immediate effect on him. He smiled, sat down, offered me a cigarette from an empty packet, called out for orange squash to be brought in, and then turned to greet Singh with great affability. I decided to bring the situation back to normal and get Professor Kaul off his best behaviour. At such moments I had a prescribed set of mannerisms which were usually adequate to rid me of my sahibdom and end with most people's hair coming down.

A woman came in with drinks. I smiled at her, did namaskar and took an orange squash. I crossed my legs and started to shake my outstretched foot in the Indian fashion. I helped myself to one of Singh's Capstans, and offered one to the professor. He refused. I lit Singh's cigarette and my own. I put my cigarette between the bottom joints of my third and little finger, clenched my hand, and placed my fist against my mouth and sucked smoke and air into my lungs. This was the usual way of smoking a cigarette among Punjabis, Sindhis and Mussulmen, so that the tobacco did not touch one's lips. The clenched fist formed a primitive hookah, allowing a lot of air to go in with the smoke. I flicked my fingers and so let fall some ash upon the concrete floor. I took a sip of orange pani.

During these antics Kaul and Singh had been talking. My performance had not been unnoticed. I remained silent and looked around the room. Luckily I had my leather chappals on, so I took them off and as I shook my leg I waggled my toes. Kaul turned to me and asked me what nationality I was. This I always took as a compliment to my performance. I said I was from the UK. He raised an eyebrow. I told him how pleased I was to meet him and that Singh had already told me of his historical researches into Nepalese history. He insisted on showing me photo slides sent from the British Museum, of manuscripts relating to the distant past of Nepal. I asked him about the Gurkha attacks on Ranjit Singh's empire at the end of the eighteenth century. We talked while Singh sipped his orange drink and looked around the ill-kept room. The professor was well away.

I knew that Singh was as anxious to go as I was. Singh asked the professor for a glass of water. The professor shouted for water and the woman came in with three glasses. We each took one and gulped them down in the usual manner. Singh and I stood up. The professor blinked and took the hint. I left the preliminary farewells to Singh. The professor invited us both to lunch, but without specifying a day. We accepted. Thus politeness had been shown without any danger of us actually coming. I had one last dig by saying that I was a vegetarian. I looked stonily at Singh, signalling him to keep his mouth shut, which he did. The professor assured me that he seldom took meat, which I could well believe as in Kathmandu goat and chicken were very expensive. We parted with namaskar and handshakes and descended the stone flight of stairs outside the building.

With Mr Gupta and his Muslim contractor friend we usually ate chicken kabaabs, chips with tomato sauce, and drank beer in the Park Restaurant. For a month during the Indo-Pakistan war the Park was without beer of any kind, Indian or foreign, so we were forced to drink tinned Guiness, of which the Park had a stock. The Park was fashionable, being the only western-type restaurant in Kathmandu. During this month students with their girls sat at tables eating ice cream and drinking Guiness.

I accompanied Singh to marriage feasts. My presence helped Singh to extricate himself after an hour or so, and also increased his local standing. On these occasions we dressed as was fitting, Singh in his double-breasted dark blue blazer and grey flannels, and myself in a dark grey ill-fitting flannel suit which I had bought hastily in London before leaving for Bombay, from Moss Bros. Without exception the approaches to the residences were by narrow, muddy paths and then through boggy gardens. The houses were narrow, crooked, with small rooms, narrow dark stairways, filled with youths fashionably dressed, and crowds of ill-clad children. At such times I was a vegetarian, it being easier to eat vegetable preparations than negotiate bones or chew the meat of some goat I may have seen being dismembered that morning.

We sat around the walls with a large table in the middle laden with rice, pilau, chicken, mutton and vegetable curries, kabaabs, dhai vada, chiura, chena and sweets. Small cups of sweet tea were served, also beer, whisky, brandy, rum and orange juice for the ladies. On one occasion Father Moran appeared, all gregarious bonhomie as befitted a priest in the midst of a happy, indifferent bunch of perpetual pagans. The talk was in Nepali, Hindi, English and Punjabi. Singh and I enjoyed these parties provided nothing hindered our departure. We arrived, paid our respects, ate the food, drank, paid our respects and left within the hour.

One day Singh came into my room, unannounced, and sat down. He remained silent and picked up the previous day's Calcutta Statesman. I continued lying on my bed and reading. I decided to remain silent too, and let Singh speak first. I was reading Avalon's (Sir Frances Woodruffe) book on the Tantric mysteries lent me by Jai Singh. I half suspected that Singh wanted something unusual. Singh broke the silence.

"Captain, have you got any money?"

"What … what's that Singhji?"

"Have you got some money?"

"Yes. How much do you want?"

"It's for Irish Sweepstake Captain. Every year I buy tickets, but now I must pay in foreign exchange. Can you lend me five pounds sterling — I'll pay you in NC."

"Nepalese currency is no good to me, Singh."

"Why not! You can buy your air ticket to UK with NC. I'll fix it with the Air India manager."

"Well, OK Singh. We'll go halves. If any ticket wins we share the prize."

"OK. Very good. When can I have the money?"

"Now."

On our walks we discussed all the things we could do with our winnings. As a western materialist I advised Singh to bank his winnings in England, or Switzerland, anywhere except bring the money to India. At six per-cent interest I reckoned Singh would have an income of sixty-thousand rupees a year.

"Why bloody hell, that's better than His Highness!"

We discussed Singh's possible emigration to England, where he had some friends. Singh decided on a world tour. We made out an itinerary. We had difficulty in spending his yearly allowance. Finally Singh decided that he would buy himself a bungalow with rice fields, sugar cane, fruit trees, and a Land Rover. He was going to give the rest of the money to charity. It took us two weeks to finalise his plans. I suggested that he should visit the temple and do puja. Bahadur thought I was teasing him, but I put on my most serious face and continued to advise this course.

Jai Singh had also been consulted during our two weeks of deliberations. Between us, Bahadur Singh was persuaded to do what he had wanted to do all along. Jai was ambivalent in religious matters. He was orthodox but at the same time had great fun, which we shared together, in pulling the legs of his co-religionists, especially in the matter of performing rituals, the spiritual content of which they had no knowledge. Jai had a firm faith and like many Catholics was on terms of intimacy with his God. He made fun of flummery and superstition.

Jai was a true Rajput, a believer in Shakti, the principle of energy and power as represented by Parvati, the consort of Shiva, who in his turn represented the 'Will'. The primeval duality from which substance was created is found in the entities of Puruksha and Prakriti, of which Shiva and Parvati are manifestations. In Tantric yoga and Tibetan Lamaism these two principles are reproduced a thousand times as each God, Will, dances in copulation with his Shakti, energy. In Hinduism each person worships his God in the manner befitting his spiritual state. Thus the truly unattached and spiritual man or woman can worship directly the principles of Puruksha and Prakriti; and so-on down the ladder, or even horizontally, since none are inferior to any, being the same supreme principle in different forms.

In Jai's bedroom his wife had set aside a decorated shrine with pictures of Shiva and Parvati, spiritually entwined. At certain times of the day his wife performed puja.

One morning I came out of my room for breakfast and found Bahadur Singh sorrowfully slumped, wrapped in a blanket, and huddled in one of those boat-like cane-backed chairs with long wooden arm-rests associated with gymkhana clubs, colonels, and chota pegs. He was unshaven and had his eyes closed. He had not been too well recently but his condition surprised me as it indicated a relapse.

"Good morning Singh old boy, what's wrong?"

"Oh G-o-d! My life is down hogaya Captain. I've seen the American mission doctor and the Indian Bombay doctor. I have hoves or some such nonsense. It is burning round my stomach, large bumps with pimple and giving forth water. Doctor Berry is giving injections. I take injection and ointment".

"How many medicines are you taking, Singhji?"

"Well, I'm taking Doctor Berry's injections and the Indian Embassy medicine. He is best doctor in Kathmandu. And I'm taking Tantric. I don't believe in Tantric but I said 'Come on, if it works it works.' So I took Tantric."

"It sounds as though you must have a hell of a mess inside your stomach, Singh. I hope you know what you're doing."

"Here. Look here, Captain."

Singh pulled up his kurta and pulled down the cord of his pyjamas to display his navel and a fat pale stomach. I saw the large bumps 'giving forth water'. The whole area around his middle was covered with a congealed mess of various colours.

"They're not hoves, Singhji. You've got hives. What's that?" I asked, pointing to his navel.

"Tantric."

Tantric was two beautiful little heraldic tigers painted in white and red, and outlined in black. Their heads, one on each side, faced the declivity of Singh's navel. Some of the pigment was beginning to flake off as from an ancient fresco in a humid cavern.

"That's Tantric, Captain. Very powerful. I musn't take bath. The other one didn't work. Let us see! I don't believe in this rubbish, but the pundit came one night and put them on my stomach."

"Where did you get him, Singh?"

"The Indian Embassy doctor sent him, Captain."

"Well, I hope all these mixtures work. You should take more exercise and stop worrying. That will make you better."

"Stop worrying? How can I? Yesterday I went to the procurement officer. Four hours I sat there. The bloody bastard told me to come back today. How many times I take drinks with the bastard! Six times I have gone to his stinky office. He promise ten tons of C1 sheets for Hetauda factory but now he makes trouble. He wants bucksheesh, that's what he's up to. I tell him I have no money, all I want is procurement permit."

In spite of what must have been a very painful condition Singh still managed to waddle around.

I did not see Singh for four days. I took 9N-RF2 to Pokhara and flew freight and troop shuttles up and down to Bhairewa.

For me, a transient visitor of a few days amidst the past and future centuries of the Himalayas, Pokhara represented unfulfilled hopes below the divine gaze of the twin peaks of Annapurna and Daulagiri, standing 26,000 feet above the green foothills. The village was on the slopes on the west side of the valley. The grass airstrip had been made by levelling paddy fields and was about 1,500 yards long. Five miles south of the strip were the foothills rising 4,000 feet above the valley, while to the north five miles away rose the foothills culminating in the glorious snow-clad Himalayas. In the Pokhara valley squalid poverty was everywhere. Men, women and children carried huge loads on their backs, supported by a rope band around their foreheads. Females were the more common beasts of burden. It was an incongruous sight to see a tall European mountain climber, after months in the hills, arriving ruddy, bearded and carrying his rucksack followed by half a dozen barefoot dwarf-like females laden with his tin trunks and camping equipment.

The villagers' wants were few: cloth, food, salt and kerosene contented them. Their gods comforted them, and the religious festivals provided a welcome holiday in their hard lives. Pokhara lay 130 miles by mountain track to the west of Kathmandu, and about 80 miles north of Bhairewa on the Indian border. Apart from walking, the only means of communication was the air service. The valley was 20 miles long by about 8 miles wide, and lay 4,000 feet above sea level.

From the air, like the Kathmandu valley, it had the aspect of a Shangrila, which however was quickly dispersed on landing. Two miles to the south of the airstrip was a lake formed by the damming up of a stream and the catchment area for a small hydroelectric scheme. This was supposed to bring electricity to Pokhara. From the dam small concrete canals had been made leading to the waterfall which awaited the installation of the turbines. These turbines were in dilapidated wooden crates on Bhairewa airfield where they had lain in wind, sun and rain for two years. Their weight and size were too much for a Dakota.

They awaited the completion of a road from Bhairewa to Pokhara which was marked out on its way through the mountains by an earth track. Indian contractors were blasting the hillsides 20 miles from Bhairewa and it was estimated that another five years might see the road completed. On the airstrip stood a complete and rusting steamroller. It had been transported in portions by Dakota years before and stood as a monument to the road building scheme.

Because of Pokhara's scenic splendours it had been chosen for development as a tourist centre. To this end a government tourist officer and his wife lived in one room of the inspection bungalow. This was a five-room oblong bungalow overlooking the airstrip, standing on the west side and on a slight rise. It had no running water, the single WC could not flush, lighting came from hurricane lamps, and it was made of lightweight aluminium sheets. This place was called the 'Sun and Snow Hotel'. The tourist officer wandered around like the ancient mariner ready to buttonhole any sympathetic tourist and pour out the story of his abandonment, and the great schemes he had sumbitted to Kathmandu for the improved comfort of visitors.

I spent many nights in the Sun and Snow shivering under cotton quilts and kept awake by the reverberation of its walls. The wind, the rain, the comings and goings of a few, caused the Sun and Snow to rattle along its length. A whisper could be heard by all the occupants. If anyone brought a local girl to his bed the performance kept the whole hotel awake. Dogs growled and fought over the kitchen refuse. When the time came for the girl to leave there was the sound of her frightened whispers, whispers of encouragement and growls as she negotiated the hungry pi dogs on her return to the village. Sleep was impossible until 3 am. At 5 am, my crew and I were out of bed and getting ready for the dawn take-off to Bhairewa and our 12 hours of shuttling, carrying anything from Gurkha troops to 40-gallon drums of petrol. The King had built a country palace by the side of the lake. It was called Ratna Mandir, after his Queen. Across the lake was a much smaller stone farmhouse, built for Prince Basundra. Everything except blocks of stone had been brought to Pokhara by Dakota to build these houses. For most of the time they remained empty patrolled by a few chowkidars and flunkeys of the royal household. Capt Daulat Singh, my predecessor, had managed to get inside Ratna Mandir. The entrance hall was decorated with a frieze of the snow-capped Himalayas, coloured like gaudy ice-cream cones, the lower valleys were a rich emerald green and the whole glorious panorama was moulded from concrete by artisans who had lost all vestige of the taste for which their ancestors were justly renowned.

On many of our flights from Bhairewa to Pokhara we brought 7,500 lbs of milo and cotton-seed oil. These supplies were for one of the most miserable communities of foreigners in Nepal, the Tibetan refugees. At the south end of the Pokhara strip was a camp of bamboo matting, gunny bags, and a few tents housing the families. They were distinguishable from the locals by their costumes, and by their physical appearance. They wore long felt coats made from yaks' wool (black or dark ruddy-brown), knee-high Tibetan felt boots, and wore their black hair in two plaits and wound round their heads. All were dirty, unwashed for countless days. Their clothing was in rags and their boots worn out. On the hottest days they still wore their felt robes, like sahibs of yesteryears, keeping up the traditions of their distant land. As a concession to the heat some of the men slipped their robes off their shoulders and let them hang, suspended by a rope tied round their waists. They were much taller, better built and more imperious than the small people of Nepal. Their food came from various charitable organisations and they were looked after by two or three Europeans of which the most memorable was a buxom good-looking Scots girl dressed in the same rags as themselves. She came to meet our aircraft and organised parties of men and women who staggered off to their camp carrying a bag of milo on their backs. They kept their dignity in adversity by the time-honoured method of sticking together and bearing their difficulties with stoicism.

A few miles to the east of the airstrip was a mound of trees. At night from the verandah of the Sun and Snow a dim light could be seen coming from this mound. Here among the trees was a small leper colony also administered by a Scotswoman, elderly and dedicated to her work. For me Pokhara was a place of lost causes, a place of ambition thwarted, as though the divine gods above wished to show the pointlessness of man's efforts and the lesson of accepting one's karma. Another scheme which collapsed was the sheep project sponsored by the New Zealand government. A young New Zealander with his wife and four-year-old daughter had lived for two years in a bungalow ten miles from the village amidst the flat and river-crossed bed of the valley. The sheep died. The grass was inadequate and the more nutritious varieties that had been imported refused to grow. The locals could not afford to fence off large tracts of land and so deny the area to their goats and cows. In August the New Zealand family left.

CHAPTER 25

A Visit to Pashupatinath

BACK in the Royal Hotel after one of my stays in Pokhara, Singh suggested after breakfast that we go to the Pashupatinath temple. I was glad of another ramble with Singh. He had partially recovered from his 'hoves' as he persisted in calling his affliction.

"We go by bus to temple. It is only twenty minutes from the Park Restaurant. It is Shiva temple. Very old and famous. Come, Captain, let's go."

We set off down the drive. I was interested in Singh's Tantric tigers which may have been the cause of his partial recovery.

"Singhji, tell me more about about your Tantric sadhu and his power."

"You met him before, Captain. You remember he came with us in the taxi from Indian Embassy."

"What! that dhoti wallah with a blue shirt and protruding ears?"

"Yes! He's a bloody bastard. He told me I live 96 years. Swindling swine. Tantric is very powerful Shakti. Shakti! Power! We Rajputs worship power. It didn't work on my stomach. The man was no good. It takes twenty years to become a good Tantric sadhu y'know. Y'know about Tantric? I tell you. It is special sort of knowledge. It takes long time to get the power. The Tantric believe in three things, wine, women and meat. They drink and get stinky drunk, eat meat with blood on it and have a hundred women without pleasure. I see, Captain,

329

women go mad after these buggers. They must have twenty years of learning the secret knowledge. Then they use their power only for good. I see with my own eyes, a bad Tantric in the bazaar near those filthy temples opposite Bhairab murti. This dirty fellow with long hair and red shirt. People didn't believe him. He turned to a pi dog next to him and said powerful mantra and the dog dropped down dead. That's Tantric. Shakti! Only good sadhu the best. Look! Here is the bus. Get in the back. We will be near door. These dirty fellows smell like Peace Corps."

As the bus lurched down the road towards the aerodrome, before turning off to the left for Pashupatinath, Singh was being questioned by an old man who sat next to him. I stood in the aisle wedged between locals, and holding onto the hand rail. The old man asked Singh where I came from, then how long I had been in Kathmandu and what I was doing. He asked Singh where my wife was. We turned off down a kutcha road of mud and potholes. The roadside was piled with earth on which were laid large cast-iron water pipes. These pipes were to be seen all over Kathmandu and were part of an Indian Aid scheme for drains or fresh water supply. We arrived at the last bus stop where a crowd of people were waiting to return to the Park Restaurant.

"Come, Captain, get out. We're here."

We wandered down a concrete road, through a park of ancient trees. The last 200 yards of the concrete road were flanked by houses with shops on the ground floors selling bangles, cigarettes, cloth and other bazaar stuff. At the end I could see the tall porch with a gate leading into the temple.

"This is very busy temple, Captain. It is the temple of the God of Nepal, Lord Shiva. There is Gujeshwari temple over that hill for women. It is built on top of Parvati's yoni...."

"For Christ's sake Singh, what are you talking about?"

"I tell you true! My father said 'Bahadur'...."

"Forget what your father said Singhji. Get on with it."

"Lord Shiva was carrying the dead body of his Shakti to find proper place for burning and he took so long that pieces fell off.

A hand there, a foot here, and her yoni fell off by that hill. They built a temple on top of it. We go next week. They have very big puja there, Captain. The King comes, that's why there is pukka concrete road."

We arrived outside the gate. A Gurkha policeman with a cane sat on a stool under the arch. His duty was to stop the mlench from entering the sacred temple.

"I won't be long," said Singh. "You can look in through the gates and see everything. I'll buy some flowers and perra. You don't mind waiting here, Captain?"

"Of course not, Singhji. Here's a rupee to buy some prashad. I want to help buy the prashad. After all, you will say prayers for both of us and if I offer prashad through you the God may let us win the sweepstake."

"Yes, very good, Captain. We buy two rupees' prashad, and I say prayers for both of us."

I sat down on a verandah step by the side of the road and near the entrance gate. Next to me was a very old shrunken woman, bent low and with a shaven head, dressed in a thin faded saffron robe. She looked at me with rheumy eyes and held out a shaking bony claw. I gave her half an anna. I saw Singh, after removing his shoes, enter the gate with our offering.

I looked around and observed the scene. Clustered around the entrance squatted women and old men with their trays of pan leaves, betel nut, beedees, cigarettes, twists of string wicks, agarbatti and tins of coloured powders. Young and old were going in and out of the entrance, all dressed in their finery. The young girls wore cholis and sarees and most were heavily made up after the fashion of Bombay fillim stars. The men wore black jackets, churidhar pyjamas and large black shoes. The young bloods wore white shirts and tight pants and sharp pointed shoes. All left their footwear by the temple gate.

Singh came out with a vermilion smudge on his forehead and a yellow flower behind his left ear. His first act after putting on his shoes was to buy a pan and two Indian Capstan cigarettes. He saw me and waddled over.

"I do puja Captain. Here, take your flower. I give you tika."

I placed a wilted and sorrowful yellow flower behind my left ear while Singh bent down and helped himself to a pinch of vermilion powder from the nearest vendor's tray. He marked my forehead.

"Look! Captain. Come here! Look through the gate. There! You see that man standing up under that small roof? You see? Well, he is very famous sadhu. He has shakti. He came to Kathmandu eleven years ago and stood by that tree. He stayed there standing night and day. He sometimes leans against the tree. He never speaks. Night and day he stands. Each and every hour he stands! At first they put police to watch him in case he was fooling. Then King said he could stay. Now he has small roof over his head. Eleven years! He has got powers! Come, let us cross over the river and look at temple from other side."

We turned away, wandered slowly back a few yards and turned off down a narrow muddy lane. A number of small tanks lined the sides of the lane, each with stone carvings of the gods, about six to eight inches tall, around it. The little figures were beautifully carved and worn smooth by the wind and rain. In the middle of each tank, some dry, others with half an inch of muddy water, stood a stone Shiva lingam emerging from stone lotus petals. The lingams and stone statues were a common sight all over Kathmandu; their beauty is the reality beyond maya. They are so lovely and in such numbers that one becomes unaware of them, until caught in a moment of vacancy one looks and sees them again as if for the first time. Around them is the squalor and poverty of Kathmandu. The devotion, discipline and love which brought their beauty into being has gone for ever. The time of the gods on earth has passed, and only their statues remain behind. Nowhere in Kathmandu did I ever find any appreciation of their worth. They were occasionally objects of devotion whose true significance had long been forgotten. Tawdry imitations and copies abounded in the shops catering for tourists.

Singh and I came to another lane leading down to the stone bridge which crossed a small river below the temple, the sacred river Bagmati, which joins the sacred River Ganges one hundred and fifty miles away.

"Here is burning ghat, Captain. We cross over this small bridge and sit on those stone steps. We can see the temple from there. Go and look at the dirty murti in that little temple, Captain. The tourists love them."

I went over to a small temple in the middle of a stone court-yard to one side of the bridge. Around the eaves of the temple roof were crudely carved wooden figures of mortals opposed to the sublime gods further up. The mortals, in groups of two, three or four, enacted every conceivable sexual practice making a scene of orgy which few of the onlookers would ever be likely to enjoy or imagine.

We crossed the stone bridge over the Bagmati, a small nearly dry stream. I noticed that the bridge was supported on a modern addition of two large steel 'I' beams. Upstream in front of the temple were a few pools in which naked children played. On the bank opposite the temple were terraces of large stone steps, about thirty yards long, and ascending thirty feet up the slope. Above these the hill continued, overgrown with bushes and tall trees. We climbed up the steps and sat down with our backs to a line of small shrines each heavily carved. Looking inside their small doorways I could see the inevitable stone lingam. These shrines were small temples erected by the families of dead Ranas.

The temple wall across the stream was level with our eyes. We could see its gold roof and coloured carvings while a great crowd of heads moved in the temple courtyard. From a portico in the temple wall a steep flight of stone steps descended to the stone flags along the bank of the Bagmati. Three stone plat-forms projected into the bed of the stream.

"You see the platforms, Captain? They are for burning the bodies. The royal family and other sahibs get disposed of there. That one at the bottom of the steps is for His Majesty. All the kings get burnt on that platform. Before, there used to be plenty of water but now the new irrigation canal has made all the water go the wrong way. No one cares for the temple now. It is modern civilization to have the canal."

We sat in silence and watched the small boys bathe and splash. Then three large shaven-headed Brahmin priests came down the stone steps from the temple. Each had a shendi — a small tail of knotted hair from the crown of his shaven head. They were laughing and joking loudly. They wore dhotis and gunji frocks. Each carried a ball of mud in one hand with a clean dhoti over his arm. They came lurching, reeling and shoving one another.

"What's going on Singhji?"

"Some nonsense. It is time to take bath before food. You watch them. That one there is big and fat. They all eat good food, rice, ghee, and sweets. They're doing puja for some dead Rana with that mud. The ashes are mixed with mud. They get paid for a whole year to do it. They work the mud balls away in the water. Some nonsense."

The three Brahmins took off their vests, displaying pale, pasty torsos and their sacred threads. They chased away the small boys by splashing and throwing sand at them and then all three sat down in the largest pool. The water came up to their navels. The balls of mud began to dissolve in the water, colouring the whole pool with an ochre cloud. With their free hands they splashed each other and laughed.

"Look at that big bastard! Look at his Rolex watch! It must have cost rupees eight hundred and be waterproof. Look at him sitting there like a big ape and smoking that cigarette. I tell you true, Captain, they're scoundrels. What a face that fat one's got. Those other two are older but behaving like lafarts. You see how he flicked his cigarette into the water. He's no good. Fancy taking baths with that Rolex on so that everybody can see it. Now they're getting out. I hate those bastards. Food is calling them. I tell you true that the fat one is no good. They go after women in the temple and fuck them. I tell you true Captain. You watch them!"

The three wet Brahmins got out with diaphanous clinging dhotis, showing their white lungotis beneath. The pool they left was the colour of light mud. They began the ritual of changing their dhotis for dry ones and putting on their vests. The big ugly one started to climb the steps taking them two at a time with bandy legs and reeling from side to side. As he got half-way up he passed an aged woman who slowly and apparently painfully mounted the steps. She looked as though she suffered from a pelvic complaint.

"Look! Look! He's watching the woman, Captain! The dirty bastard. I tell you these unclean fellows. Look! He's looking at her!"

I was completely taken aback by what followed, much to Bahadar Singh's delight.

"Did you see that, Captain?" Singh was clutching my arm. "He put his big fat dirty tongue out at her. He probably fucks that woman. What a foul fellow."

The big ugly Brahmin had got above the woman who took no notice of him. He had turned round and stuck out his large tongue at her. The tongue looked long enough to touch his third eye, elongated no doubt by kekari mudra. He glanced at his companions lower down. They laughed and scampered past, indifferent to the woman, and disappeared through the temple door. She continued to climb slowly and painfully.

"They're pigs, I tell you. Not like before," said Singh, gratified by the incident as bearing out all the unflattering things he had told me about today's pundits and sanyassis.

Further up the stream emerged from between steep banks, with trees meeting overhead. By the water's edge were small caves with old wooden doors.

"Who lives in those caves, Singh?" I asked.

"Those are old homes for sadhus and powerful rishis. They are the dharamsalas. Sort of free rooms for visiting Yogis. No-one comes now. The King gave ten lakhs a few years ago to repair the temple roof. The roof is solid gold y'know. It is very old temple. Underneath is the real temple built by

335

Shankaracharya. He came to Nepal from South India to stop Buddhism. It was getting too powerful in India. He was the greatest rishi and a great Raj Yogi. He built the first temple. But it's all dead now. No water for people to take bath. Purohits fucking girls, wearing Rolex watches and smoking cigarettes. I tell you true, Captain, it's no good now. Before, people got sick, they came to temple. Now they go to some foreign-trained doctor. They go to cinema. They wear fancy clothes. It's all balls. What is life? It is to be happy. Now they want transistor radio, motorcar, terylene pant and shirt, nylon saree and lipish-stick. I tell you, I know sons who pimp for their sisters. Good family girls! I tell you if they can't go to cinema they pimp for their mothers."

"Why Singh?"

"To get money for cinema. Then they want to got to bar, or eating place like Kwality or Gaylords. They want to buy motor car to go to races, to sit in the Grand Hotel because others do. It is being modern. Why! Half these bastards have only one pant and one nylon shirt. They buy any old cheap watch, gold colour, and roam here and there with 555 tin with Char Mina cigarettes inside. Now latest fashion is for dark glasses like French fillim star. When I was ADC for His Highness Cooch Behar I see in Calcutta boys pimping for their sisters so they can all go to Metro dressed like modern. But they look like prosti-tute. If girl does that for pleasure I don't mind. That's not sin. I must have woman, it is good for health. Some women want man so that they can go to sleep. That's alright too. But I hate those girls that go for money. I tell you, Captain, it's all modern civilisation. Alright in America, England, France, Germany, that is different. But here they want to show off how modern. I tell you true, Captain, all is fashion, fashion."

"Come Singhji, let's go back slowly."

"Oh Lord, my hernia is paining. I'm down hogaya! My life is finished. I have body pain all over. I'm older than my poor father."

"Now don't talk like that, Singh. It's bad for you."

"I tell you it's fashion, fashion. All modern! No religion. Foul fellows fucking...."

"Singh, stop it! You're working yourself up. It's bad for your hoves. Let's have silence for a few minutes, okay?"

"Yes, you're right, Captain. Silence is best. My poor father he often say 'Bahadur, silence is golden.' I tell you Captain, he...."

"Singhji! Silence! Now!"

We recrossed the bridge.

As we walked slowly, Singhji clutching my elbow to support his flagging spirits and to some extent his pain-racked body, a small boy of about eight years old, clad in rags, hobbled across our path on two crutches. His left leg dangled paralysed and thin as a bird's.

"Well, Singh bai," I said, "you can't blame modern civilisation for that. They've been crawling around and saying their prayers at the temple for three thousand years."

"It's his karma, Captain."

"Karma! Balls! I have a western medicine curative dose in my pocket, shall I give it to him or leave him to his prayers? Tell me, Singh."

"Give it to him, Captain. You are his karma."

We went on up the kutcha lane towards the bus stop. On each side were trees and grass.

"Lovely here in the hot season, y'know. This is picnic place for people who come for puja."

Tell me, Singhji, how did you hurt your back?" I asked.

"I fell off an eleephant, Captain."

"Fell off an eleephant! How, for Krishna's sake? Go on, give me the details and stick to the point".

"His Highness of Cooch Behar was shooting in the jungles north of Rupsi. You know the place, Captain. You've seen the jungles from the air. It was in there. We had famous fillim star John Huston and some American woman who killed her husband. Very famous. I was standing on the howdah and the driver didn't warn me. He started the eleephant. I toppled sideways and fell on to next eleephant. I was like a bridge and my back bent so." Singh bent his outstretched fingers backwards. "My feet on this one and my arms on the other. My back was bending. Afterwards I was stiff but alright. Then later my legs hurt and then I was paralysed all over. I went to Calcutta Lakeview Hospital. H.H. was very good. I had specialist and operations and in bed here and there for four years. I never went back to H.H. I lost many friends and two lakhs of rupees. Before, I was handsome, playing tennis, cricket, shooting, playing gin rummy with Her Highness and now and then having woman for health's sake. I went to Bombay doctors, mission hospital at Velur, everywhere. I suffered many body pains, Captain."

"Yes, I'm sure it must have been terrible for you, Singhji, but now you are better."

"It is my karma".

"How did you come here?"

"I know Boris who was making foreign liquor in His Highness's factory. Then after I got better, Boris ask me to come and help in Royal Hotel. It good climate for my back in Kathmandu. Then I hurt my back again, bouncing up and down in Land Rover, when Marco Polo come to Kathmandu."

"Marco Polo! What's that Singh? Do try and tell things clearly. I can't follow. It sounds like nonsense."

"No nonsense, Captain. True, Marco Polo French fillim company come to Royal Hotel."

"When?"

"1960 or '61. I forget now."

"Tell me about it."

"Not now, Captain. We all go mad and lose lots of money."

"Not you, surely."

"Yes, I lose five hundred rupees and hurt my back on the bloody roads. Look, here comes the bus. Push in front of those stinky fellows. I come behind you."

CHAPTER 26

At the Royal

IT was in September, after the monsoon, when I got to know Federenko, another White Russian, who helped Boris and ran the bar and kitchen. I had seen him behind the bar checking up on the stocks and in the evenings wandering off to his bungalow in the adjoining compound. Singh had suggested to Federenko that I might be able to help him. In this he was mistaken. I occasionally flew 9N-RF2 to Calcutta to bring back baths, basins, air conditioners, crockery and furniture for the new wing of the King's palace. Bahadur suggested to Federenko that I might be able to fly up his new 500 cc BSA motorcycle, which was in the Calcutta docks awaiting transport. This brought Federenko, Bahadur and myself together in long discussions during which we heard of the many difficulties besetting the BSA.

After many months the crated motorcycle arrived by boat. Federenko was worried and excited, like a father expecting the birth of his first child. He had prepared one of the Royal Hotel pigsties as a home for his offspring, and during the day was usually to be found sitting sadly inside or moving a box here, a cupboard there. Each night he locked the door with a large brass padlock, leaving an empty crib while his BSA languished in the Calcutta docks or in the customs shed. It was a difficult period for all of us; we could offer few words of encouragement, knowing as we did the vicissitudes of the Indian customs authorities. It was consigned to Kathmandu and therefore technically in transit and so not liable to Indian customs duty. However, there were complications. The shipping agent in Calcutta who handled all goods for Nepal was hopeful. He had sent Federenko a large form to be filled in and which necessitated paying a bond to the Indian customs. The bond would eventually be paid back when the motor cycle crossed the Nepalese frontier. This was assuming that it came by rail to Raxaul on the border. The Indo-Pakistan war was just over but the Indian Railways had not yet recovered from the increased chaos which the conflict had caused. Bahadur's idea was that if I flew the motor cycle from Dum Dum Airport it would miss the formalities at Raxaul. However, I could not oblige. Every flight from Dum Dum was superintended by the Nepalese consular officials in Calcutta and I could not smuggle a large crate through the customs and onto an aircraft loaded with His Majesty's imports.

I went to see Bull, who as usual was co-operative and optimistic. Federenko sent off telegrams to the agent, and arrangements were made to send the motor cycle by a Royal Nepalese Dakota. The day it was due to arrive, Federenko was up at five o'clock and went off to the airport in the Hotel Land Rover. Bull, who was flying the aircraft to Dum Dum, had a very worried and insistent Federenko on his hands. By good fortune, due to the recent hostilities and Chinese threats, the tourist traffic had declined so that the aircraft coming back from Calcutta was nearly empty. Federenko's BSA was loaded as well as a number of oozing wooden boxes marked 'Pork' but containing beef for various foreign residents in Kathmandu. This subterfuge was condoned by the Nepalese customs, as no cow meat, by royal decree, could be eaten in Kathmandu.

One evening Federenko asked me mysteriously to accompany him. We made our way to the old pigsties lining the garden wall. One housed the old gardener and his tools while the other was for the BSA. Federenko unlocked the large padlock. He opened the door and displayed his brand new BSA in pieces and wrapped up in brown paper lying on straw in a wooden crate. It was a great moment. It took Federenko a week of slow loving care and consultation with the handbook to assemble his bike.

Federenko had a touching faith in the superiority of British workmanship. He discovered much to his chagrin that a special spanner used for assembling the front forks was missing, as well as having been sent the wrong spare driving sprocket. Correspondence ensued, but with no result. Three months later I went to England for Christmas leave. I returned to Kathmandu with twenty pounds' weight of spare parts, enough to last Federenko for fifty years. I did this mainly to restore Federenko's faith in the thoroughness of British industry. He had received his crash helmet two months before the BSA arrived. One morning, after breakfast, he took his helmet, dressed himself up in a black leather jacket and plastic string gloves and sat astride his palpitating BSA He set off for the bazaar and his daily shopping. His appearance in Kathmandu bazaar created a sensation. He told us that he had received three offers for immediate purchase of his bike and his outfit.

In the evenings as Bahadur Singh and I sat drinking our coffee in the dim lights of the dining room, Federenko would come over and join us. At first he talked of nothing but his rides on the BSA The amount of tarmac road in Kathmandu was very limited. Apart from the overcrowded, twisting and pot-holed lengths of the town, there was the 100-mile Indian-built national highway from Kathmandu to the plains of the Terai. For about 15 miles from Kathmandu the road was fairly straight and flat, then it wound its way up the 8,000-foot hillside and eventually descended to the plains. The road was busy with large overloaded lorries driven by daring Sardarjis. Anybody knowing the manoeuvres of Calcutta taxis, or the horrors of the grand trunk road from Calcutta to Delhi, will have some idea of the dangers Federenko had to face. The large ten-ton lorries which brought supplies from the plains were wholly owned and driven by Sikhs. This community had great skill in maintaining lorries without spare parts and in driving their overloaded and ramshackle vehicles.

Federenko was very excited the first time he reached 90 mph We feared for his safety. But as the novelty of his BSA wore off, our topics of conversation during coffee became general. I pumped Federenko. He had been a young cadet, in the same military academy as Boris, when the Russian Revolution started. Both had escaped via the trans-Siberian railway to Vladivostock about the same time as Admiral Kolchuk ended up under the ice at Ulan Bator. The young Federenko arrived in Shanghai. He became a musician, and formed his own band. He played in the night clubs of Shanghai, Manila, Hong Kong and Bangkok. He arrived in India just before the Japanese entered the war. He played in the Imperial Hotel in Delhi, the Grand in Calcutta, and in Lucknow. He had also been a professional photographer. He was very sympathetic, a philosopher, and without the gregarious Slavic temperament. His life as a musician had made him an observer. He had come with Boris to Kathmandu to supply the music, and as things gradually came about he became involved with the cuisine. The Nepalese cooks were trained by him and produced the best table in the east, for which the Royal Hotel was famous.

When King Mahendra had required banquets for his coronation, weddings and ambassadorial functions, it was the Royal Hotel which provided the food, everything being prepared under Federenko's supervision. Bread, cakes, bacon, ham and sausages were still made at the Hotel and also sold to outsiders. Bahadur Singh had played his part in these royal feasts. While I was at the Royal Hotel there was one occasion that gave me some idea of how things must have been in those days. Two weeks before the great day, Bahadur was despatched by Boris in the RNAC Dakota service to Benares. Here he contacted 'contractors' for the supply of 200 assorted birds, guinea fowl, chickens, ducks, turkeys and water hens. I had always thought of Benares, or rather Varanasi, its name of Vedic times which was changed after Independence, as a place for silks, sadhus and burning ghats. Bahadur assembled his birds, after much haggling and threats to cancel the orders, and loaded them onto two trucks which motored to Raxaul where they were transhipped from Indian to Nepalese lorries.

Bahadur came back by air from Simra to Kathmandu, leaving the lorries to follow. They arrived but not without casualties. Birds had died, and some had been pilfered, but the numbers ordered allowed for the wastage on the journey. The survivors were put into cages at the back of the Royal Hotel. I think the occasion was the visit of the French Ambassador from New Delhi who was coming to pay his respects. The French did not have an embassy in Kathmandu, but it was rumoured that they were about to establish one. Fortunately for the few residents in the hotel, the visit was postponed indefinitely, and so they ate the birds. When six weeks later the French ambassador came, his party put up at the Royal Hotel. The day before the party at the Palace was spent in digging out and cleaning silver dishes, tableware, table cloths and other paraphernalia. All the stuff was put into large baskets or tied up in sheets and taken by hand-cart to the Royal Palace a few hundred yards away.

Due to the paternal attitude of Boris towards the staff there had been no dismissals as the fortunes of the Royal Hotel declined. Half a dozen of us were waited on by twenty bearers, most of whom stood around in white jackets, pants, and little Nepali caps giggling and whispering, or at times the whole lot would mysteriously disappear to the kitchen. At one end of the dining room was the kitchen passage hidden by a heavily carved wooden screen, one panel of which depicted darkly the copulatory embrace of Shiva and his Shakti while another had a dragon twisted three and a half times, representing the erotic mysteries of Kundalini Yoga. Singh would get up at times and go to the kitchen. There would be shouting and then silence; Singh would emerge followed by a sheepish young bearer bringing us our chicken à la King in a china bowl. The bearers went on strike while I was there. Before I left many of them had gone to posts in the other hotels which opened at that time.

Because the Royal Hotel produced much of its own food, Boris had kept pigs which were sometimes allowed into the garden. Boris also had a small dasha on the hillside overlooking Kathmandu with a fine view of Swayanbunath temple. Here he kept more pigs and had a small swimming pool. Unfortunately I never visited the place. The last miles had to be done on foot. Because of the declining fortunes of the Royal Hotel, Boris had decided to start a pig farm with attendant slaughterhouse, sausage machines and cold storage. The products of the farm were to be consumed by various embassies, the Chinese and Russian being the most demanding. Boris also envisaged the export of pork in cold storage lorries to Calcutta. The Russians were also interested in sausages for their workers who were coming to build a portion of the east-west highway in the plains of the Terai.

At first the scheme was centred on the dasha and languished for lack of funds, but the situation was saved by a tourist. Ingrid Bergman, the film star, came to Kathmandu. She stayed at the Royal Hotel. This was about a year before my time, when the Royal was already declining. She was fêted, and went to Boris's dasha. The upshot was that she agreed to put up some money for the pig scheme. Boris had been saved again. He went to Europe to purchase equipment. A site was chosen 80 miles south-west of Kathmandu near Satharpur. Bahadur Singh was to be resident factotum during its early stages with a promise of a small bungalow to follow.

Singh had doubts. He felt that Boris was getting himself into a dangerous situation. Boris would be at the mercy of knowledgeable and unscrupulous locals, especially as he would be dependent on them for puchasing land, labour, food and permits. Also, the road to Hetauda from Sathapur was bad, floods were frequent and the humid heat of the valley during the hot season was not suitable for pigs. All Singh's misgivings may have been valid but, as I pointed out, why should he care, unless he dreaded the jungles of Sathapur, for Boris would stand to lose little. The scheme could be made to drag on for years. Certainly, everybody from Boris downwards stood to benefit even if nothing came of it eventually. I remembered something I had read about George Sanders, the film actor, investing in a giant pig scheme in England or Scotland in which thousands and thousands of pounds were lost; at least someone had benefitted so why should not Boris and all the locals be better off whatever happened.

There comes a time for all of us when things slow down, opportunities become less frequent and ambitions less extravagant. Boris had decided to make Kathmandu his home with occasional sorties to Europe to meet his friends. It had taken him almost fifty years to make a semicircular journey on the periphery of his native country. Perhaps at moments he felt close to his motherland, or ready to make a dash across Tibet to Mongolia and then once more down that railway he had travelled as a boy. Did he at moments, when he sang sad Russian songs at a party in his appartments atop the Royal Hotel, imagine that a cataclysmic collapse of a regime would allow him to return home from his Odyssey? If so, then Kathmandu was geographically nearer to the dust of his little father than many other places.

Kathmandu was not a bad place to pass one's days. Everybody knew everybody else, there was always something happening — a visiting celebrity, a mountaineering team, and recently the thrill and excitement of being engulfed by a large neighbour. Unfortunately, the outside world gets bored with its playgrounds, bureaucrats kill the golden goose, and international alarms frighten all but the most intrepid tourist. A new type of tourist had appeared in the gutters of Kathmandu. These were the European disciples of non-attachment, would-be sanyassis of which the continent had full knowledge but had grown sceptical. They stayed in the cheapest hostelries, smoked bhang, drank rose, pineapple or banana whisky and gathered in the Tibetan restaurant. They spent no money and did nothing to create a suitable atmosphere to attract tourists. It was all very picturesque and delightfully horrifying to see the wretched poverty of the Nepalese, one expected as much, but quite another thing to see one's own compatriots slumming around in scruffy abandon. In the days of the British Raj, erring members who let the side down had been shipped quickly back to the UK. It was mystifying to the locals, who had as their goal a land of plenty based on bourgeois rectitude and scientific wonders, to see people from the cultures they wished to copy behaving voluntarily in the manner they wished so ardently to discard. It was an anachronism which their simple minds could not understand. The well-dressed young person in the Kathmandu of 1966 got inspiration from the Teddy boys of ten years ago. Of hippydom they had had enough and were struggling to leave it behind.

The building next to the Royal Hotel was the American Embassy. It had glass doors, a stars and stripes standing in the entrance hall with an attendant marine on guard, and behind a desk with a sign indicating 'Enquiries', a pretty Nepalese receptionist. Across the road was a large bungalow in which half-a-dozen marines lived surrounded by the luxuries from the PX. (Equivalent of the NAAFI.)

I once got inside the bungalow late at night when all other drinking places were shut. A number of young fellows from dispossessed Rana families were drinking Budweiser beer and neglecting to pop their one-rupee payment for the drinks through a slit in the bar counter. A radiogram played the latest while young marines stood host. On a mound about four miles from the town was a large walled-in Rana palace used by the American Aid Mission. Numerous jeeps painted green and with a heraldic device of two beefy white hands clasped upon a targe striped, came and went continuously, driven by Nepalese in grey 'Dicky' shirt and pants. The whole caboodle impressed one with its purposefulness and air of plenty. The Nepalese working in the offices and driving the cars had never had it so good whatever result the mission might have on the rest of

Nepal. From the US Embassy a jeep service ran every hour on the hour to the Aid mission. Outside the mission gates was a small helicopter pad with two helicopters, while a few miles away on a neighbouring hillside a small airstrip had been built for their turboprop Pilatus Portus.

This picture of lavishness and bustle was further augmented by a US reading room in the main bazaar, and by a house up the road from the Royal Hotel and beyond the Indian Embassy, for the boys and girls of the US Peace Corps. Just opposite the King's Palace was the terminal to the aerial ropeway. The ropeway connected the rail head at Hetauda with Kathmandu and was supposed to bring up supplies, although I never saw it working. It was dead and the sheds crumbling, reminding me of a similar defunct ropeway I had seen years before between Massawa and Asmara in Eritrea.

The mere presence of the Americans did much to bring employment and wealth to those Nepalese connected with their activities. The other embassies attempted in varying degrees to emulate the Americans. The most successful but far behind were the Russians, with the Indian Embassy and its Aid mission coming a poor third, then the Chinese, and lastly the British Embassy, which did nothing, as befitted Britain's diminished position. The British Embassy had a new building, with a bungalow complex for work and a single-storeyed mansion for the ambassador. Everything was painted white with asphalt drive-in, a Gurkha on guard and a lawn with surrounding flower beds. The old British Embassy, established by treaty a hundred years before, had been given to the Indian government. The locals regarded the British Embassy with respect, partly because its inmates kept themselves to themselves and were therefore attributed with Machiavellian influence in high places. In fact the British Embassy was respectable, had little influence and was mainly concerned with paying Gurkhas serving in the British army and retired Gurkhas, who were Nepal's largest earners of foreign exchange, and in maintaining the status quo of the Gurkha Brigade.

Artists

Kathmandu had its artists. Guja and Boris's second wife, Inger, represented for me the modern school, while there was a large indigenous population busy producing copies of ancient statues and forging Tibetan Tankas. There was another foreign element of Tibetan refugees who made coarse Tibetan coats and rugs with highly-coloured dragon designs. All three schools were very much dependent on the tourists.

I met Guja as a result of a fight he had late at night with Bahadur Singh. The next morning at breakfast time Bahadur Singh was furious at the way he had been treated by Guja. He had been kept up late at night in order to help his friend, but Guja had turned on Bahadur and called him a 'bloody bastard' several times. Guja had refused to leave the Yak and Yeti bar although the two Nepalese barmen had gone, the bar had been locked up by Federenko and the fire beneath the conical brass chimney had died. Guja had demanded that Singh go to Federenko's room and get the keys to the bar. Singh refused knowing it to be useless. Then Singh had helped Guja down the cold marble stairs. Guja wanted to go to Singh's room and drink some brandy which earlier on Singh had unwisely mentioned. Guja drank all the brandy and swore at Singh for not having more. Guja said he was going to my room to wake me up on the off-chance that I, as a monied foreigner, might have a stock of booze.

Singh fought with Guja on the stone verandah running the length of the ground floor. Guja again called Singh a 'bloody bastard' and a 'toothless Rajput lion'. Guja was unable to ride off on his bicycle so he threw it into the fish pond opposite the main entrance. I listened to Singh's tale, made incoherent by his indignation, with much sympathy because I felt he had gone out of his way, at two o'clock in the morning, to protect me.

Later Guja told me how he hated the statue in the middle of the goldfish pond. The old Rana, probably at the same time as he imported the Japanese giant fir trees, had installed a Victorian bronze piece in the middle of the pond. It showed a naked woman with her hands upon the heads of two naked little children of indeterminate sex as they sat at her feet. Each child held a fish in its hands. Once upon a time water had sprayed from the fishes' mouths sprinkling the little group with sparkling droplets. One arm of the woman was now missing, leaving an unattached hand on a child's curly crown. Every morning Federenko and Thomas, an old Indian factotum, fed the goldfish with breadcrumbs.

Guja was a middle-aged Maharastrian, slim, good-looking and volatile. He painted excellent pictures of pagodas and Kathmandu scenery. All his pictures sold well to the tourists. He also had fun with impressionistic blotches of monks, and fields in their seasonal colours. He lived in a room in a very old house on the way to the airport. It was difficult to get to his home during the rains because of the mud.

Shortly after his midnight fracas with Bahadur Singh he appeared again in the Yak and Yeti and announced that he was having an exhibition of his paintings the following week. This was timed to coincide with an influx of tourists. The exhibition was to be held in the Royal Hotel ballroom. I met Inger at this time; she had returned from one of her trips to Europe. Inger, Guja, Bahadur and myself were busy for three days putting up Guja's pictures on the walls and on specially made bamboo screens.

The ballroom was on the first floor at the head of the marble stairs. It had a marble floor. Its walls were hung with large six-foot tall pictures in heavy carved golden frames dulled by age. Illustrious generals of the Ranas' families stood sentinel around the walls. Most were dressed in the uniform of the British Raj with lal-kurta navy blue overalls with red stripes, spurred Wellingtons and draped with gold cords at their shoulders. They stood in martial poses, some resting an arm on a pile of books on top of an Ionic column. The backgrounds were heavy dark red drapes with an occasional window looking out into a garden. One portrait was very fine. A silver-haired noble gentleman stood in cream trousers with a silver stripe. Across his creamy chest hung a dark red silken ribbon. A mauve cloak covered his shoulders and upon it was the large resplendent silver star of the Order of the Bath. The hilt of his sword showed at his side.

Against Boris's orders we removed some of the ancient portraits to make way for Guja's paintings. While Bahadur and I were lowering the cream-coloured gentleman in his mauve cloak, Bahadur put his thumb through the side of the picture. It was then that we discovered that the portraits were painted photographs executed by Mr Chakravatty of Calcutta. The cream-and-mauve general had already had a tear in the background drapes which had been skilfully mended with cellotape. We drove nails into the walls and hung up Guja's pictures. But it took us a lot of time and serious thought to arrange the pictures, accompanied by hoots of laughter. Inger was not showing on this occasion.

For the seven days of the exhibition Guja sat from morning till evening in the ballroom. Sometimes he escorted an American tourist around his paintings. Singh and I went at four o'clock to have tea with Guja. We discussed his day's sales and how much he stood to make. He sold nearly all his paintings. As a result of this exhibition a lady secretary of the US Aid Social Club approached Guja with a commission to paint a large mural. It had to show representatives of all the nations of the world dressed in their traditional costumes and united in convivial drinking of their national booze. In spite of the difficulty of his assignment Guja perservered for several months. I never saw the finished mural although we had several previews of sketches. Guja existed wholly on the proceeds of his paintings and because of this he caused us considerable worry. After a sale he became very generous and insisted on buying everybody drinks. Instead of Char Mina cigarettes he took to Kents or Winston, which Federenko sold in the Yak and Yeti. His money never lasted more than a month or two.

The Missionary

Towards the end of the year there appeared at breakfast at the Royal Hotel a character who became the most mysterious and extraordinary I was to see in Kathmandu. Neither Bahadur or myself ever spoke a word to her. We beheld her only at meal-times. Her statuesque, fair and imperious beauty caused a sensation. Bahadur Singh was particularly awed and subsequently mystified by her actions. Bahadur's long stay at the Royal Hotel had convinced him that any female travelling alone was out for one thing only. But in this case he was mistaken. It soon became known that Ruth was a missionary from the Jehovah's Witnesses who had come to convert the Nepalese to her brand of Christianity. She decided to direct her attack at the royal household, the earthly guardians of Lord Shiva. The audacity and magnitude of her ambition left us all bewildered. Such an undertaking, by her very sincerity, outstripped the farcical and we waited for news of her efforts with impatience.

Her first targets were various princes, brothers or half-brothers of the King. She dined at their homes, returning by royal vehicle in the early hours of the morning in her evening dress. Prince Basundra, the King's second brother, was one of her early victims. Prince Basundra was about thirty-five. When he appeared at the Yak and Yeti he sat silently accompanied by his long-standing companion, Barbara, an American with a large Alsatian which she exercised on the Kathmandu golf course wearing blue jeans.

When the missionary arrived in Kathmandu Barbara was away in Europe. Bahadur assumed that the missionary's real object was to oust Barbara from the Prince's affections, and her early morning returns to the hotel lent weight to this hypothesis. The King had given Prince Basundra various government portfolios but because of his disinterestedness or his incapacity for mundane administrative problems he had been set free and now spent his time, as much as Kathmandu and his infrequent visits to Europe allowed, as a playboy. His wife, the Princess, had a head for business and had started the Annapurna Hotel across the road from the Royal and in competition with her husband's interests.

The finance for the missionary's journey and stay in Kathmandu had been left to the Jehovah's Witnesses in the will of an elderly lady who died in Los Angeles. She had specified that the money was only to be used for the purpose of bringing the truth to Nepal. On second thoughts the missionary may have been a Seventh Day Adventist, but difference of doctrine would be quite incomprehensible to King Mahendra, Queen Ratna and their attendant court.

The missionary dwarfed all of us in the Royal Hotel except Federenko. She dressed stylishly in black. She chose to convert from the top rather than exhort the masses in the bazaar. In this she was undoubtedly right as she had none of the spiritual intensity or the adopted poverty of a female sanyassi, and besides, she did not speak the lingo.

I learnt from Mrs Scott, Boris's mother-in-law, who looked after various dogs and ponies that wandered around the garden, as well as her small antique shop where she sold Tibetan tankas, statues, prayer wheels and other relics, of the progress the missionary was making. She came occasionally to chat with Mrs Scott, both sitting in the small shop amidst the artifacts of paganism.

It soon became apparent to me that the missionary had the most vague and ill-informed idea of the Hindu religion or of the particular form practised in Nepal. She started therefore under an enormous handicap against the like of which the early fathers of the church could have made no headway. They at least were thoroughly conversant with the paganism of their time and so could argue, exhort and reason with their opponents, and were willing also in the last resort to suffer martyrdom. The missionary, I am sure, would have been glad to be a martyr, but martyrdom without being able to expound one's cause intelligibly and sow the seeds of doubt in the minds of would-be converts is useless. The missionary put her trust in God and expounded His word from the Good Book, quoting chapter and verse to a sozzled and silent Prince Basundra while the party ate chicken curry, popadom and drank whisky, the missionary drinking perhaps gin-and-orange.

I heard just before I left on Christmas leave that Prince Basundra was getting fed up with listening to the words of prophecy and damnation. If any religion has 'books', none can have more than Hinduism. The royal family were the heads of state and religion, and Nepal prided itself on being the only Hindu state in the world, India having forgone this distinction when she chose to be a secular state. If the missionary had succeeded, her achievement would have put the conversion of Constantine in the shade.

But who am I to say that she has not succeeded when God works in such mysterious ways and his mills grind so slowly? There already existed in Kathmandu the ubiquitous Catholic priest, Fr. Moran, and a convent school. Fr. Moran contented himself with administering the sacraments to the faithful and providing education for the children of the well-to-do. Before I left I heard that the missionary's visa might not be extended and that she would have to leave after the expiry of two months. When I returned from the UK in January 1966 I was surprised to find her still at the Royal Hotel and that Barbara had returned from her holiday.

Tourists and mountaineers come from all over the world in moderate numbers to see the sights of Nepal. Because of the difficulty of getting about and the short duration of their stay, few tourists can see more than the Kathmandu bazaar, temple carvings, and the surrounding mountains. The scenic splendours of Nepal have been frequently photographed and published in glossy albums. I was fortunate in being able to fly the length of Nepal frequently, and so see the glory of the mountainous abode of the gods in all their splendour, from early dawn to late evening, and at times to gaze spellbound at the majesty of Annapurna and Daulagiri by moonlight. The whole magnificant range, from Kanchunjunga in the east, Everest, Annapurna, Daulagiri and beyond to the west, stood as huge snow-covered sentinels ever-present and all-seeing above the mortal activities below them. On clear days as I approached at 10,000 feet in 9N-RF2 from Benares, Patna or from the west from Lucknow, their silent white, gold, and pale-blue splendour riveted the attention, like a stage backcloth lowered from the heavens.

This effect was enhanced by a haze which rose from the valleys like a veil of Maya separating the reality of Brahma from human desires. Well might the ancients have believed the Gods dwelt in the awe-inspiring pinnacles. If the gods live anywhere it is surely here. As western low-pressure systems originating half-way across the globe, crossed Nepal from west to east with their attendant vast clouds of rain and snow blanketing not only the Gods but also the lower hills and valleys, flying in such conditions brought its problems, and forced one to become familiar with winding rivers and the terraced mountain slopes. At such times one flew above the valleys with white foam-streaked rivers far below; on each side were the hills hidden in cloud or veiled by sheets of sleet or rain. Only a day or even hours before, the hills had been bathed in sunlight, green, friendly, and dotted with small villages whose inhabitants had terraced their slopes with small fields, some no wider than an arm's length. On the two-hundred-mile flight from Kathmandu to Mustang in the west, I never ceased to marvel at the contoured terracing, the work of centuries, like lovingly fabricated jewellery. High inaccessible places were covered by forests that remained perpetually green.

The Kathmandu valley had its beauty throughout the changing seasons, but for me it was spoilt by the knowledge of the shambles awaiting me as I neared the airport. Fortunately the administrative chaos, self-important politicians, and the assumed superiority of the urbanites did not penetrate far into the hills. Official visits were seldom, decrees died from lack of perseverance and their impracticality. Kathmandu is the capital of Nepal; its writ extended mainly to the accessible lowlands of the Terai bordering India. Officialdom left the dwellers in the heights alone. In Kathmandu's ramshackle streets I saw Bhotias from the hills, who came to the metropolis to see its wonders, standing at the corners, being cheated in the bazaar and making their purchases as yokels do the world over. The Bhotias were dirtier, if possible, than the most miserable in Kathmandu. But they were robust, carrying loads of wood and tins of kerosene on their backs, supported by a headband. They came in family clusters, children and elderly all loaded, walking from great distances on bare, gnarled flat feet. They carried on a large smuggling trade with the Chinese in Tibet, by selling tins of Indian kerosene and Indian medical supplies. The hair of males and females was plaited and coiled round their heads. They wore black jackets and skirts of yak wool. They worshipped remote gods, ugly or beautiful representations of the psyche, associated with Lamaic Buddhism.

The foreign Embassies acted as fountain-heads for largesse, all of it politically motivated. The Swiss contribution was on a much lower scale than the larger nations, but it was practical. They established a milk bottling factory in Kathmandu, and also half-a-dozen centres in the remote hills where they taught the art of cheese making from the milk of goats and yaks.

The Israelis had a large construction company which was busy building a new runway at the airport suitable to take a Fokker Friendship turbo-prop aircraft which the Royal Nepalese Airline were about to purchase. Just before I left, the Israelis sent army parachute instructors, and 9N-RF2 was modified for such use, as well as carrying on its less spectacular duties. The British had recently presented the three Scottish Aviation Twin Pioneers. The aircraft arrived in June, and their first public function was to drop flowers on the city maidan during the King's birthday celebrations.

They carried about 3,000 lbs of freight or fourteen soldiers. They were for the Nepalese Army and to form eventually an Army Air Corps. The whole idea was so nebulous that few of us thought anything would come of it. K B Singh and I flew.the Pioneers. It was irksome to fly the length of Nepal with four-teen soldiers at 110 mph when a Dakota could carry twice the load and quicker. There were few fields that the Dakota could not get into. Besides this there was no overhaul base for the Pioneers closer than Singapore.

Mr Clarke from Scottish Aviation came with the aircraft, but had brought no spare parts. He put up in the recently opened Annapurna after enduring the Royal Hotel for two nights. The Royal Flight engineers and mechanics maintained the aircraft. There were no Nepali military pilots or mechanics. There was some talk of forcing Nepali pilots from the local airline into an embryo airforce. There was a constant reminder of their possible fate in the shape of those Antonovs built and presented by the Chinese to Nepal some years previously. These aircraft stood forlornly with sagging fabric and unserviceable engines in one corner of the Royal Flight dispersal. The Chinese were more successful in penetrating the bazaar with excellent ball pens, cheap silks, cotton prints and gents' suiting material, and a shoe factory near Kathmandu. They had also completed the alignment of a fantastic road from Tibet through Namche Bazaar at the foot of Everest, to Kathmandu, and were rumoured to be starting the alignment of a road from Kathmandu to Pokhara.

The Russians, not to be outdone, had completed a small hydro-electric scheme to the east of Kathmandu which was looked upon as a great boon, when the wires should be connected up, to augment the old diesel generators which supplied an erratic and feeble current. The coming of electricity to Kathmandu was received with mixed feelings. Two or three years previously the city had a curfew from six at night to six in the morning, thus encouraging family life and the maintenance of traditions. The electric light caused the lifting of the curfew, with the consequent roaming around, social activity, cinema-going, and parading of the young. This was considered a bad thing and as weakening old customs.

The Russians had supplied the King with an Ilyushin 14, which went away for four months every two years for inspection at Tashkent. They also contributed two large helicopters, and but for the presence of Russian engineers who came frequently to the airport to look after them, would have gone the way of the Chinese Antonovs. The Russians had also built a sugar factory in the Terrai, but it was well known to be a shambles. They were also involved in building a portion of the East West highway in the Terai, but the scheme had not at that time started.

The Indians also had their schemes; their main contribution was constructing a dam at various headwaters near the Indian border, and in building various lengths of roads. I had frequent evidence of their road building between Bhairewa and Pokhara. The road was about 100 miles long as it wound its way through the mountains. The northern-most portion of 70 miles had been dug out of the mountain sides by village labour, while Indian contractors were blasting a road between the plains and the first obstacle at Tansing. Flying over the gorge one could see tiny dots of coolies, compressors and tents, all clinging to the rock face. At frequent intervals during the day clouds of dust rose in the air and the forest below was scarred by falling boulders as they blasted their way across the vertical cliff face. The efforts of everyone seemed to come to nothing, leaving rusting machinery, plans postponed, schedules long abandoned, and when something worked it ran down like a clockwork toy whose key had been lost or spring broken.

The Dakotas of the RNAS also suffered from the general malaise, especially during the Indo-Pakistan war when spare engines and propellers from Bangalore were not available. They were cannibalised, the victims standing on the tarmac without a propeller, or in some cases missing both engines, as their companions carried on flying. For those that got airborne was the constant stark reminder of their fate should anything in its innards pack up.

There was one machine, because it was new, that worked without the handicaps of no spare parts or qualified staff. This was the delightful small-gauged steam-engine and two coaches in the amusement park. The Indian aid mission had provided it. It ran round a small track with a bridge, a tunnel, a few signals, a siding with engine shed and a real little station which sold two-anna tickets. It even whistled when it approached the station. Bahadur Singh and I never failed to have our ride whenever we went to the amusement park during our evening rambles. The park was opened while still half complete for the Nepal International Fair. It was partially walled-in and the entrance gates were decorated with gaudy paintings of Gods on canvas erected on tall bamboo arches.

A month after the opening it rained and caused a partial collapse of the wall while the coolies were struggling to complete it. The Chinese and Russians had splendid stalls, advertising their help to Nepal. They displayed printed cloth, shoes, pens, tinned food, jam, simple engineering machinery, and farmers' hand- tools. Other stalls sold soft drinks, ice cream, crockery, samozas, and gramophone records. There were games of chance, with flickering lights, crowds and shouting megaphones. The electric lights were brilliant and the whole place drowned in blaring fillim music, each stall competing with song for the attention of its neighbour's audience.

The opening was a great success. Crowds milled around with excited bewilderment. There was an Indian circus, with performers in white cotton tights and bloomers. High-born ladies, including a pathetically fat Princess, stood behind the gambling stalls, wearing rich sarees. 'Dam-occracy', after an initial setback some years previously, must be seen to be working. The sacred political catchword, of which no criticism was tolerated, was 'Panchayat Raj'. This was an ideology lifted from India, where local interests were under the control of local elders. Its concept was not new, being a throwback to the legendary 'Ram Raj', two or three thousand years ago. It only perpetuated the universal shambles and left everything much as it had been before, but it necessitated a Minister, Panchayat conferences, committees, a policy, and distribution of 'Development Funds'. Thus 'Panchayat' and 'Development' married the idealised past with modernism in the hope that their union would bring forth 'Progress'.

CHAPTER 27

Durga Puja

IT was in the early autumn of 1966 that Joe Koszarek wrote to Jai informing him that I would have to return to Bombay in three months time. Joe explained that he intended to start a crop spraying unit and to this end he had purchased two Piper Pawnees, and recruited Capt Sequira from the Bombay Flying Club at Juhu airfield. I was to be the other pilot for this venture. Jai, of course, agreed but pointed out that I could only go after he had recruited another Dakota captain.

The important festival of Durga Puja was approaching. In Nepal this festival is performed with enthusiasm. It celebrates the victory of the fierce many-armed goddess Durga, who, sitting on a ferocious tiger and brandishing a different weapon in each of her ten arms, had slaughtered the evil Buffalo, Mahishashur. Elsewhere the god Rama slaughters the evil demon Ravana from Sri Lanka! In Bengal the fierce black goddess Kali is venerated at this period.

It was not feasible for the Royal Flight to slaughter a buffalo at its Puja festivities — too large and too expensive. Goats were substituted. On the day of the festival Jai picked Bahadur and myself up at the Royal Hotel. Bahadur was dressed in blue blazer and grey flannels, I wore my grey flannel pinstripes from Moss Bros, and Jai was in tweeds and brown brogues. We chugged our way in Jai's Austin A40, on three cylinders, to the airfield. The office and stores of the Royal Flight were at one end of a concrete dispersal, on which were lined up the Royal

Aircraft. The first aircraft was the Russian Ilyushin used by His Majesty for foreign visits, then Dakota 9N-RF2, next the Beechcraft Kingair, then two Chinese-built Antonov planes, next the French Alouette helicopter for transporting dignitaries to mountainous districts, and lastly the three Twin Pioneers. By now only one of these was flyable because two had been cannibalised to keep one airborne. They were all lined up and awaiting their turn in the ceremony.

On our arrival at the flight hut we were met by my first officer and radio officer, Sessodia and PK Shorne, the two engineers, Mr Mizra, Mr Devi, and the good-looking, tall Burma Shell refuelling officer, and a group of mechanics. Everybody did namaskar to Jai. Jai inspected the aligned aircraft, noting that each had its small black goat before it, tied to a log of wood. One of the mechanics was a purohit by caste so could officiate at the ceremony and recite the sacred mantras. In front of each aircraft a small mandala picked out with coloured powders had been drawn.

Jai called for silence. We assembled on one side of the tarmac. The Royal Ilyushin was first. The purohit approached the goat, caught it by its ears, whispered the sacred words and sprinkled it with water. The goat shivered. One mechanic held its rear legs and another its head, stretching its neck. Thapa, the senior mechanic, raised the kukri and struck down with a 'thunk', neatly severing the willing victim's head. Everybody cheered. The mechanic holding the goat's rear legs dashed round the Ilyushin, leaving a trail of blood. The purohit drained some of the blood into a small brass dish and anointed the propellers and fuselage while reciting the sacred mantras.

The next aircraft was 9N-RF2. Jai offered me the honour of the decapitation. I refused on the grounds that I was a 'mlench', not a Nepali whose festival this was. The second ceremony went off satisfactorily. There was a hitch at the Twin Pioneers. The purohit whispered the sacred words and splashed the victim, but it refused to shiver or shake off the holy water. Things hung fire until Thapa took a pail of water and poured it over the victim. It attempted to dance round, irritated by the deluge, but was firmly held by its head and rear legs and quickly dispatched, amid cheers from the audience.

It was all over. The little corpses lay in front of the aircraft, blood encircled each machine, and each engine and propeller had been daubed. Jai led the way to the flight hut where saucers of chiura, samozas, cashew nuts, a flagon of rice wine and bottles of Sinalco awaited us. The Burma Shell agent danced a few steps with Thapa, as we clapped. Jai made a speech, thanking all present for the previous year's good work. Beedees and cigarettes were lighted up. The sacrificial carcasses were allotted to the mechanics to provide a mutton curry for the next two weeks; Jai made a speech, put a tikka of coloured powder on my forehead and announced that I was leaving early the following year. Jai drove myself, Bahadur and the Shell agent back to the Royal Hotel where we adjourned to the Yak and Yeti bar.

In most parts of India there is no blood-letting at this Puja. In Bengal it is 'Kali Puja'. In other parts it is called 'Dashera'. This is the occasion when artisans ask for a blessing on the tools of their trade, and mark their implements with a vermilion tikka.

Last Flight to Calcutta

Before I left Kathmandu I did my last flight to Calcutta. Jai Singh, Shome and I took off for Dum Dum at six o'clock in the Royal Dakota 9N-RF2. By the time we were over Gaya it was a brilliant clear moonlit night, with a fairyland of twinkling lights 8,000 feet below. The moon shimmered on the still, shallow waters of lakes and sluggish rivers. Large, dark patches of jungle divided the lights of one tiny village from another. I knew it was the last flight I should ever do over Bengal. Over Asansol, 100 miles from Calcutta, we saw the pale orange glow from the filthiest, and yet most vigorously alive city in the world. It gleamed like a poisonous phosphorescent growth; a fungus sucking its strength from the surrounding vegetation.

That night Jai and I made a pilgrimage to Iziah's bar. It was eight years since either of us had been to Iziah's. Everything was the same except that the place was now air-conditioned. Dolores, fat and hideous, was sitting with a group of shippies at the bar and drinking Bangalore beer. She had been long past her prime nine years before, when she had haunted the Bristol Hotel in Chowringhee. She was partially encased in a tight, spangled, mauve dress; her hair was the colour of piss; she flashed a row of rotten teeth. Still, she was the only woman there worth talking to because she had a modicum of brains and a sense of humour. Jai told me that she had a grown-up daughter who was or wasn't following in her mother's footsteps. I can't remember which. When Iziah's closed, Jai and I left for the five minutes' walk to the Grand Hotel. A taxi slowly passed and Dolores' head appeared out of its rear window.

"You want a lift boys?"

The next morning we were woken by the bearer with our tea and 'The Statesman'. I started on Dolores.

"Jai, what did you think of Dolores last night?" I asked him.

"Andy, not now. It's too early. Besides, I don't want to think about Dolores."

"Why?"

"Because she depresses me."

"Why?"

"Because she makes me feel old. Do you realise how the time has passed? I wonder if the girls in Massawa are still the same."

"But Jai, don't you think it was pathetic when she called to us from the taxi? Perhaps she was lonely. She must be long past picking up boy friends. We should have accepted her offer."

"You're nuts! She probably called to us because she felt sorry for us! Two old dead-beats leaving Iziah's without poon."

I read the paper. There was a small column about Hedy Lamarr. When Jai came back from the bathroom I asked him if he'd read about Hedy.

"You mean the bit about shoplifting?"

"Yes. Don't you think it's rather awful? Remember, she was once the most beautiful woman in the world. And now she's reduced to shoplifting, and gets caught too! She made millions and now she's being sued or is suing somebody."

"They're all the most beautiful woman in the world at some time to someone," said Jai.

"Even Dolores must have been once," I replied.

"God! Impossible!" exclaimed Jai.

"She has a daughter so she must have woken a spark in someone."

"Not necessarily."

"Hedy's a sort of Hollywood Dolores. I wonder which of them is better off."

"For Christ's sake Andy, crap up about Dolores. If you're so struck on her you can pick her up this evening."

"I'm not struck with her. I feel sorry for her and Hedy."

After lunch, still in my sentimental mood, I went to Suite 102 of the Grand Hotel, on the chance that I might meet Johnny and Kitty Brenand. I knocked. There was no answer. A passing bearer recognised me and told me that Captain Sahib had moved to Suite 302. I was lucky to find Johnny at home. I had last seen him in 1958 before going to Rawalpindi. We'd had a bloody row. I had no idea what it was about but I remembered parting, vowing never to speak to him again. Then he had been big, beefy and blond and in the prime of opulence, smoking cigars and playing golf.

Now, Johnny Brenand's gold hair was tinged with grey. He was thinner and had grown a full beard. He reminded me of Gabby Hayes, the old gaffer of many a cowboy film. We sat on a cane sofa upon red cushions; the floor was red-tiled and covered with a red Afghan carpet. On the walls were hung his old Javanese wooden busts, and on a small bar made of split bamboos stood tall Japanese dolls in kimonos. To my surprise, Johnny at once apologised for the row we had eight years before. We got onto the subject of God and the soul. There had been rumours for some time that Johnny Brenand had got religion and now he was giving me the proof. He believed 'God is love'; all Gods are the same; all we had to do to be happy, and to make the world a better place, was to love each other. I believe he was attending a Catholic guru in the small French enclave of Chandernagore, a few miles north of Calcutta and on the Hoogli. He exuded calm, like a long-suffering schoolmaster determined to maintain sweet reason under extreme provocation. He had become another victim of the all-pervading 'Brahma Gas'. In place of the Airline Manager, browbeating me into carrying a 2,000 lb overload to Rupsi, he was now a convert to the spiritual life.

As I left the Grand Hotel after my encounter with Johnny Brenand I came face to face with Bannerjee. It was eight years since we had lain in the saltwater pools on Sharjah's beach while we waited for Gulf Aviation to get permission for our Dakota to carry pilgrims from Sharjah to Jedda. He had married his German girlfriend, they had a son and lived in a top-floor flat in South Calcutta. He flew a Dakota for Jamair from Dum Dum to Assam six days a week. He still had plans to emigrate to Canada. As for Treloke, my radio officer of those days, he and I were never going to walk the soft earth of India as wandering sanyassis. He was killed in 1965 with Captain Namboodri and F/O Arab while returning from a dropping sortie to Machuka, the scene of my embarassment in 1952. They were dropping bundles of blankets and clothing for an Assam Rifles outpost. One bundle of blankets hit the leading edge of the tail plane and burst open, causing the contents to be draped over the port elevator. It became difficult to maintain the Dakota in level flight, as Nambo flew back the 100 miles to Jorhat. Treloke sent a message that it was becoming progressively more difficult to maintain level flight. The aircraft was swooping up and down and losing height. They had passed the foothills on the north bank of the Brahmaputra. The aircraft, still losing height, plunged out of control into the thick forest. I don't know if it was ever found.

A visit to Bodhnath
It was after the Christmas of 1966 that Bahadur and I made a pilgrimage to Bodhnath. This was a tall, white, pointed pim-

ple, lying about three miles to the north of Gauchar airport. The stupa was ringed by a wide circle of rickety two-storeyed houses. In one of them lived 'Chini Lama'. He combined the office of spiritual head of the local Tibetan Buddhists and that of a wily entrepreneur selling religious bric-a-brac to tourists.

We sauntered to Bodhnath through the paddy fields. It was late afternoon, with high, grey cloud and a warm humidity which rose from the wet fields. I knew I was soon to leave Nepal. There was only one story (which he had alluded to several months before) I had not heard from Bahadur.

"Tell me, Singh bai, about Marco Polo," I said.

"No! No! I can't tell you. It's private story about Boris. He won't forgive me if I tell about his cock-up."

"Oh come on, Bahadur! I'll not tell a single soul. You've told me lots of things. I'm going away soon, Singhji. Come on, tell me. Please."

"Well, Marco Polo was a big cock-up. French fillim company came to Kathmandu and stayed in the Royal Hotel. Boris entertained and fed the Productor ..."

"Productor!" I interrupted. "You mean Conductor ... no ... Director or Producer. You've got me muddled now, for Christ's sake."

"Conductor, Producer, all the same Captain. Let me go on with story if you want to hear."

"Go on, Singhji, go on."

"Well, Boris fed Productor and artists, free. They live like maharajas on Boris's food and booze. They not pay one rupee. All Kathmandu went mad. Greatest excitement since King's coronation. Boris became great leader and organising man. Without him they could do nothing. I went to Assam in Land Rover and hurt my back again, over the bumps."

"Wait, wait, for Krishna's sake, what's going on? When was this? What year?"

"It was some time around 1961," said Singh. "Company was French, and they wanted a fillim adventure of Marco Polo.

They came to the Royal Hotel like locusts. No money but promises of lots coming. Laughing, drinking and music."

"Was this before Ingrid Bergman or after?"

"Before, of course. What matter? Do you want to hear story, or ask silly questions?"

"What did Boris do?" I placated.

"He got all stitchers, and carpenters, and mistris in Kathmandu busy. They made wooden swords, shields with knobs on, spears, felt boots, lama hats and Pushkin coats. He got designs from artists and paid everybody from his pocket. They drank and ate food, and every night there were Russian songs and playing guitar in Boris's flat."

"What happened to your back?"

"It was all because of bloody Marco Polo that my backbone got stuck like first time. Before, I was cured, but Boris sent me off in Land Rover to Assam, Dooars, Hetauda and to place of battle near Ramsingh. I drove Land Rover over bad roads and my back got bounced up and down and got bad again."

"What were you doing, driving around?"

"Why, I was looking for eleephants, horses, ponies, food!"

"Elephants?" I queried.

"Yes, eleephants. You can't have battle without eleephants and food. Boris told French Producer that he would get everything. It was difficult to get eleephants. I got five from Shah-n-Shah in Terai forest holding. Ponies were easy. I bought bags of grain for horses and for feeding Gurkha troops."

"Gurkha troops?"

"Yes, troops. Boris got British Embassy to send chitty to all retired Gurkha soldiers living in hills and villages. They were to come to Ramsingh on special day for filming battles of Marco Polo. They were going to wear felt boots and things, and have battle. They built wooden fort, too."

"Christ! What happened?"

"Big cock-up. French fillim man told Boris they were going to Paris for conference, and coming back with money, actors, cameras in month's time. Boris had paid for everything. I show you all the stuff in Royal Hotel. It is locked up in downstairs room like shameful thing. Mrs Scott wears old pair of Marco Polo felt boots. She sell you a pair for ten rupees. Then they say goodbye and all go. Never come back!"

"Never come back?" I echoed.

"No, never. Not one bastard show his face again. Boris lose twenty-five lakhs."

"Impossible!" I exclaimed.

"I tell true! Twenty-five bloody lakhs! All Royal Hotel's profits! Boris has court case in Paris to get money back."

"He'll get nothing from Paris," I prophesised.

"He has court case for four years."

"It's fantastic."

"Boris, British Embassy sahib and me were nearly killed by Gurkhas."

"Killed? How? Why?"

"Hundreds of Gurkhas came down with chits from British Embassy and arrived at Ramsingh. They wanted pay, food. No pay, no food, no French fillim company. They surrounded Boris, other sahib and me. They took out kukris and threaten to give us the chop if no pay or food. Everything gone, just five eleephants, ponies, horses and grain. I had bad back from bouncing all over North India for Boris. It was very serious situation. King was very angry, so British Embassy and Boris pay troops, gave them some rice and said sorry. Gurkhas walked back to villages. All finished."

"My God, how awful. Let's hope Boris's pig farm isn't another Marco Polo."

Bodhnath lay ahead as we came to the shallow, fast-flowing waters of the Bagmati. It was not wide — about 30 feet. The opposite bank was shaded by trees, behind which the Temple of Guheshwari stood, dark and decrepit, 'visited by women supplicating for issue'. Singhji announced that he could not cross as he had no intention of taking off his brown shoes, or of rolling up his grey flannels. We could cross further up.

"Come on Singhba — I'll carry you across. I want to see Guheshwari and Pashupatinath for the last time."

"Carry me Captain? You, a sahib! What if someone observes?"

"I'm your friend Bahadurj — I'm no sahib to you, am I? Besides there's only a few women around."

"Okay Captain."

Singh held my chappals and I waded in, carrying him piggyback into the sacred head waters of the Bagmati, which later flows into the Holy Ganges.

On our return journey I was tempted by demons to drop Singh into the sacred waters, but we reached the other side, two idiot pilgrims tramping the path of Lord Shiva and his dead Shakti.

Magic

It was Bahadur Singh and not the missionary who nearly effected my conversion.

I came out of my room on my way to breakfast. As usual I went round to Singh's room. I knocked on his door. There was no answer. I banged again and turned the door handle. It opened. I entered the warm, snug bedroom. The curtains were drawn before the windows. Bahadur was enveloped beneath the blankets and a cotton quilt.

"Bahadur Singhji! Ai Bahadur bhai! Get upji baiji! Utauji!"

Grunts and groans came from the blankets. Singh's touselled head of greying hair emerged. He peered at me with small, sleepy eyes.

"Good morning Captain," he croaked. "I'm very tired. I had late night."

"A late night Singhji? Why? You're not turning to booze are you?"

"Oh no!"

"Well, why are you so tired?"

"I have great secret for you Captain! I have told nobody. I am waiting for you."

"What is it?"

"I can't tell you now. I get up and take food. Then I show you. I awake all night with my secret."

"Not one of your girl friends I suppose?"

"Oh no! This is religious. I show you later."

"Okay Singh. Do you want breakfast, it's getting late?"

"You wait for me. I'll be quick. Those lazy bearers won't give me any breakfast if you don't come. The bastards!"

Singh got out of bed, wearing a crumpled white kurta and pyjama. I drew the curtains and opened the window. Outside was the early morning mist of a December day in Kathmandu. The day would be pleasantly sunny when the mist cleared. Singh disappeared into the bathroom. I picked up the previous day's 'Statesman' and read the eulogies of praise for the 'Spirit of Tashkent'.

"Arrchk - Arrchk - Arrchk - oik - oik - Arroughk."

Singh was at his toilet. He had just sung the Song of India during the clearing of one of his 'nadis', namely the mouth and throat. He had a thin strip of plastic with which he cleaned his tongue and then poked it down his gullet for the final crescendo.

"Singhjee", I bawled above the din. "For Krishna's sake hurry up!"

"Coming Captain."

I returned to the Statesman. I heard the water from the tap filling the aluminium lota. Singh was on the last stage of his ritual toilet. (A week later Singh was chased out of his room by Mrs Scott in order to make room for a sudden bonanza of tourists. He moved in with me and we cohabited for the next three months until I left Kathmandu).

Singh came out. He dressed himself in grey flannels and blazer, brushed his hair and then rubbed a little Johnson and Johnson talcum powder over his face, and said:

"Right Captain, I am ready. Let us go for food".

We walked down the grey stone verandah and then mounted a cold, deserted marble staircase. Portraits of generals in lal kurta, gold braid and sprouting Kitchener moustaches looked down upon us as we came to the first floor dining room.

After breakfast Singh and I went to his room. It was cooler and Lakshman, our mutual servant, had tidied up and opened the windows.

"Shut the door Captain. This is secret. I don't want any other fellows coming in. Look now I show you Tantric magic."

"Magic! Singh, you must be nuts."

"No, no! Really Captain. True. I show you. All night I was awake doing Tantric magic. I tell you true!"

"Who showed it to you?"

"Yesterday I went to see Professor Kaul. I met Tantric sadhu at his house."

"Tantric sadhu!" I exclaimed. "Not that chap with the large ears who drew those tigers on your stomach!"

"No, no! Not that bloody bastard."

"Well, who?"

"You don't know him. We had some whisky and then the sadhu, he show us magic."

"Did the sadhu have whisky?"

"Of course. He is very good man."

"What was he wearing?"

"What! Why you ask me all this fool questions?"

"I want to know, Singh! Tell me what the Tantric sadhu was wearing."

"He was wearing nice grey suit coat and churi dhar pyjama."

"Did he have a wrist watch?"

"Of course! I don't know! I didn't look specially."

"Well, he doesn't sound like a sadhu to me; drinking whisky, wearing a suit, watch."

"I tell you he was Tantric sadhu. He is Professor Kaul's friend. You think you know everything, like a tourist."

"What was his name?"

"Why you want his name? Bloody hell! You won't see my secret!"

"Come on Singhji, don't blow your top. I want to get the background before I see the great secret, What was his name?"

"He was a bloody Shestra! Now shut up or I won't talk."

"Alright, go on."

"He is a modern sadhu, very powerful."

"Alright, alright. Go on for Lord Krishna's sake. What happened?"

"I show you."

Singh picked up a match box from which he took a used matchstick and a small strip of cotton cloth about four inches long and half-an-inch wide. Then he took out a small dried rudraka, a seed used for making the string of beads for a sanyassi rosary.

"Now watch Captain. I fold the strip in half and put matchstick between and up here in the fold. Now I roll the strip round the match."

Singh rolled up the strip with the matchstick between, and placed it on the seed. We waited. Then Singh picked it up and unwound the strip.

"Look! Captain! It worked! Look, there!"

Sure enough the match was no longer between the folded cotton strip.

"See! How it get outside?"

I was amazed, but sceptical.

"Try again Singhji."

Singh folded the strip in half and placed the match in the fold and then rolled the strip around the match. He put it on the seed. We waited.

"Why are we waiting Singh?"

"It is for the power of the sacred seed to work. You do it this time Captain."

"Me Singhji? But I'm a mlench, unclean."

"Don't worry about that, it is the power of the seed."

I tried, but with no success. I rolled the match up again and put it on the seed. This time Singh unwound the strip and the match was out of the fold. We tried it by not putting the match between the fold, and when we unrolled the match it was between the fold.

"Not every time Captain. About five times in ten. I tried all night and it works only some of the times."

I was amazed and sceptical, but less so.

"It's Tantric magic power Captain. I tell you it's magic."

I was almost convinced, but knowing Singh I was reluctant to share his enthusiasm. There must be a trick, but I was sure Singh was the victim as much as I.

"Look Singhji, why don't you say some prayers. We might be able to make it come out of the fold more often. Go on, say some prayers."

Singh looked at me from his small, slightly slanting eyes. He didn't say so, but he was wondering if I was teasing him. I was and I wasn't. I also had hopes that it was genuine. Perhaps like Alastair Crowley I had had to come to Nepal to see my first material manifestation of the spiritual world. I was prepared to be a believer. The fact that Singh, a good-natured simpleton, should be the medium of my conversion, seemed to me to be entirely in keeping with the mysterious ways in which God dispenses his grace.

"I tell you Captain, it is Tantric magic. Look, the match cannot come out of the fold by itself. It is magic!"

"You're right Singhji," said I, casting western scepticism to the winds. I felt a communion with Bahadur Singh. It was the feyness of my Celtic blood in tune with the blood of the Rajputs.

We unrolled the matchstick many times. I became more and more credulous, and was busy reworking my whole cosmology while Singh sat.

"Singhji, this is terrific," I said. "We must keep it secret. Does Jai Singh know about this?"

"Oh no! I tell you now. We must do it some more times to test the power. It's the seed y'know. Special holy seed of Sanyassi."

"Look Singhji, now don't get angry, but I have a suggestion. Let us try it by not putting it on a seed. Let's rest it on this cigarette stub and see what happens."

We did so, and lo and behold it worked!

"Why rest it on anything?" I said. "Roll it up and leave it on the table."

Singh did so. We waited, unrolled the strip. Lo and behold the matchstick was out of the fold.

Singh was still as firmly convinced of the Tantric magic as at the beginning. But for me a small worm of doubt began to wiggle in my mind. Now I had to extricate myself from my previous enthusiasm without Singh being aware of my *volte face*. I had to regain my position as the western rationalist amused by and tolerant of the superstitions of the natives.

At one stage, for a few minutes, I had been completely won over. I had been even more eager than Singh to acclaim it as Tantric magic. After all, Singh was a believer from generations back while I was the seeker anxious to be converted.

"Look Singh," I said. "Let me go and get Federenko. If it is a trick I'm sure he will be able to see it."

"Okay Captain, go and get him."

I left the room in search of Federenko. We had been two hours performing the magic rites. I found him in the pigsty cleaning his BSA.

"How is it going Federenko?" I asked.

"Very nicely Andy, but I can't find the fuses."

"What about under the seat next to the battery?" I suggested.

"I've looked but no sign. The handbook only shows a diagram of the circuit."

"Federenko, have you got a moment to spare? Bahadur and I want you to come to his room. He's got hold of a trick which he believes is Tantric magic. We've been at it for two hours."

"Okay, I've finished here and in the kitchen."

In Singh's room Federenko took the matchstick and strip of cloth and for five minutes quietly rolled and unrolled the matchstick. He then announced that it was a trick, not magic, and that he could do it every time. He showed us that it depended on which way you unrolled the strip. Singh blinked at me and Federenko. I felt sorry for him, and relieved that I had managed to extricate myself before the denouement.

"Why! The bloody bastard. He fool me! I spent all night on this trick. I tell you true they're all worthless fellows. Stinky bugger!"

I left Kathmandu in March 1966. The Royal Nepalese Airline had received its first Fokker F27, and the pilots were doing their flying training at Gauchar airport. Joe's new venture in Bombay was a crop-spraying unit of two Piper Pawnees. I was supposed to train the pilots and myself, get the aircraft and engineering section into shape, and be ready to take to the field for three months by the end of May.

On the morning that I left Kathmandu, I divided my nylon shirts, cotton trousers and bush shirts between Lakshman and the hotel reception clerk. I gave my small transistor radio to Bahadur. He drove me in the hotel's Land Rover to the airport to catch the service to Delhi. The departure hall was crowded. Ruth was there, but not travelling. She was with another healthy, blonde and massive woman in a print frock. The Bengali Shell agent was drunk. A small group of Nepali pilots were giggling loudly and making ribald remarks about Ruth. She was either enjoying their badinage, or was cocooned in joyful purity.

The flight was called. Bahadur accompanied me out to the tarmac. We clasped each other in farewell. He was dressed in white shirt and striped tie, grey flannels and navy blue blazer, the picture of a sahib. I wondered for the hundredth time what he had seen in me, the antithesis of all the 'Britishers' he had ever met. I promised to write. As I turned to climb the steps into the old Dakota, he plucked my arm.

"Goodbye Captain, come to Rajasthan one day. I give you good chicken curry. Here, take the present, you like these."

Bahadur pushed a packet of ten Indian Capstan into my hand. I didn't have time to thank him. We had been good friends.

Epilogue

ON my return from India in 1967 I joined Autair at Luton, flying the HS-748.

After a year living in London and motoring between Hampstead and Luton, I joined Skyways of London, who operated the HS-748 from Lympne airport near Hythe, where I met again Capts Tarkowski and Cekalski. I bought a house in Hythe.

It was some time in 1970 that I heard of Jai Singh's death at Gauchar airport, Kathmandu. Jai was piloting a Royal Flight helicopter, and lifting a piece of equipment to be installed on the periphery of the airfield. As the load left the ground it developed a swing which made the helicopter uncontrollable. The helicopter and load crashed to the ground and Jai was killed.

Later that year Captain Minou Bulsara, the instrument rating examiner for the Nepal Airline, was checking out the crew flying the morning flight in a Fokker Friendship, from Kathmandu to Palam airport, New Delhi. There was a shallow fog when they arrived, and Bull went to the cockpit to observe the crew's instrument landing. He stood in the cockpit between the Captain's and First Officer's seats. The seat belt sign for the passengers was on, and the crew were strapped in. The pilot misjudged the touch-down and bumped the nose wheel heavily onto the runway. Bull was thrown between the crew's seats over the throttle pedestal and onto the instrument panel. He died later of his injuries.

In 1973 Skyways was bought by Dan Air. I operated out of Gatwick, Newcastle and Aberdeen. From the latter we flew oil workers to the Shetlands from where they were flown by helicopter to the oil rigs in the North Sea.

In 1979 I was 60 years old, and had reached Dan Air's obligatory retirement age. I applied to Skyways Air Freight, operating a Dakota from Lydd airport, a dozen miles from Hythe, and was taken on. Captain Cekalski was also flying the Dakota. After one year the company went bust. Thus my flying days started with Flt Lt Wisikiersky's good advice to a new pilot in 'B' Flight No 1 PRU, and ended flying with Capt Cekalski of my India days. I retired after 40 years piloting, and 22,000 logged flying hours. It was enough.

A few years later I was surprised to hear that Bob Large of the Lysander Flight, 161 Squadron, was also living in Hythe, close to Capt Tarkowski!

Glossary

agarbatti	Perfumed, slow-burning joss sticks.
apong	Rice wine made by Abor tribe.
barfi	Sweet made from curd.
basha	Village hut.
beedees	Thin, dried rolled-leaf cigarettes.
bhai	Brother
chalo	"Let's go." (Polite form: "Chaliye, Sahibji").
chena	Mostly chopped betel nuts rolled in a leaf.
chewra	Pieces of betel nuts, chewed and spat out as a blood-red juice.
choli	Women's bodice, worn with a sari
chota pegs	Small measure of liquor.
chowkidar	Domestic watchman. Gurkha chowkidhar carries his kukri. (qv)
churidar	Creased, narrow cotton trousers, worn by Muslim women.
crore	Ten million. (A hundred lakhs.)
dhai vada	Rice cake in curd.
dharamsalas	Places of rest and repose. Hostel accommodation.
dhobi wallah	Laundry man.
dhoti	Long, cotton cloth, worn by men round waist and between legs. Hindu dhoti wallahs, 'old fashioned'.
down hogaya	Miserable, unwell.
Durga Puja	Devotional celebrations to Goddess Durga, i.e. Kali.
durrie	Bedspread.
gana walli	Woman singer.

ghat	Shallow river location, for loading and unloading boats, for bathing and washing.
goonda	A trouble-maker.
gora sanyassi	'Gora', slang for white man. 'Sanyassi', Hindu holy man.
gulab jahm	Muslim sweet made from wheat and syrup.
gunji	'Gunji frock', cotton vest.
gunny	Coarse woven hemp, used for sacks.
haj	Yearly Muslim pilgrimage to Mecca, near Jedda, Arabia.
humie	Humid.
jenamdin	Birthday.
Ka'aba	The black rock at Mecca perambulated by the Faithful during the haj.
Kali	Goddess, black with protruding red tongue, appertaining to Bengal.
kekara mudra	Yogic posture of protruding tongue to touch 'the third eye' (in centre of forehead).
kukri	Curved knife of Gurkhas of Nepal.
kurta	Shirt, coat.
kutcha	Raw, uncooked.
ladoo	Soft, ball-shaped sweet.
lafarts	No-good 'wallahs', rowdies.
lal kurta	Red coat.
maidan	Grassy park.
Maya	Veil that separates us from the Gods.
milo	Wheat and rice flour for making chappattis.
mlench	Non-believer, unclean. (Sanskrit.)
mul-mul	Thin cotton material.
murthi	Idol, statue.
namaskar	Salutation, hands together as in prayer.
naya paisa	New money.
nullah	Rivulet, canal, or ditch.
paddi bunds	Earth walls separating rice fields.
pan-wallah	Seller of betel nuts, beedees, chewra.
perra	Sweet similar to marzipan.

pongo	Army officer.
prakriti	Vulgar.
prashad	Flowers, sweets, as gifts to temple.
pugri	Turban.
puja	Religious celebration.
punjis	Burmese monks.
purohit	Religious teacher.
rishi, sadhu	Holy man (Hindu).
shalwar	Punjabi tapered trousers.
Shestra	Nepalese caste name.
subsi	Vegetables.
tankas	Devotional flags.
thana	Jail.
tika	Caste mark on forehead.

Lightning Source UK Ltd.
Milton Keynes UK
UKOW02f0728060516

273677UK00001B/43/P